DIRTY
LITTLE
SECRETS

DIRTY LITTLE SECRETS

Military Information You're Not Supposed to Know

JAMES F. DUNNIGAN
ALBERT A. NOFI

WILLIAM MORROW AND COMPANY, INC.

New York

Recognizing the importance of preserving what has been written, it is the policy of William Morrow and Company, Inc., and its imprints and affiliates to have the books it publishes printed on acid-free paper, and we exert our best efforts to that end.

Library of Congress Cataloging-in-Publication Data

Dunnigan, James F.
Dirty little secrets : military information you're not supposed to
know / James F. Dunnigan and Albert A. Nofi.
p.   cm.
ISBN 0-688-08948-8
1. Military art and science.   2. Armed Forces.   3. Munitions.
I. Nofi, Albert A.   II. Title.
U102.D834   1990
355—dc20   90-39362
                                                      CIP

Printed in the United States of America

3 4 5 6 7 8 9 10

BOOK DESIGN BY KATHRYN PARISE

In fervent hope that Titivillius
has not led us astray too often

PREFACE

There are nearly 900 items in this book. Most of them are indeed "dirty little secrets" of the military variety. The murk that surrounds military affairs makes many of these items "secret" from the general population; this is not necessarily deliberate. A lot of these "dirty little secrets" are also a mystery to some defense experts, military professionals, and political leaders. The murk is largely created by the difficulty uniformed and civilian observers alike have in sorting out what is really going on in military affairs. We all tend toward a love/hate relationship with military affairs. Most people are quite unenthusiastic about military solutions to problems, and thus averse to a close examination of war and what goes into it. But ignorance in this area is not bliss. It simply allows all manner of foolish, inept, misguided, and outright criminal activities to be carried out in the name of National Defense. Each year, thousands of books are published on military affairs. Most are ignored, and fewer still are read closely. It's a dense subject that tends to produce equally dense prose. Our approach is different. We have broken the military mysteries into manageable bits. Some of the items herein are indeed dense, but none are so long as to be daunting. We have condensed decades of experience in military affairs into a collection of items that will provide something useful for just about any concerned citizen.

We do not pretend to know everything there is to know about the military. There is too much that can be known, and it is a field that is in constant flux. Military policy and technology can change almost daily, and sometimes even the simplest things can be complicated. As elementary a matter as how many men and women wear Uncle Sam's uniform is by no means easy to determine. The actual number under arms can vary by many thousands from day to day, what with retirements, discharges, and enlistments all happening at different rates. To get around this problem, the Defense Department usually refers to "average annual strength" or "year-end strength," which are about as precise as one could wish to get, roughly 2.1 million. However, these figures omit National Guard and reserve personnel on temporary active duty, about 70,000 people. Now try to fit in the 30,000 or so in the Coast Guard. Then consider how difficult it gets when trying to figure out how many the Russians have.

Although the authors have been collecting military "dirty little secrets" for years, there are many that even we have not heard about. And we are certainly capable of making a mistake. As a result, readers are encouraged to let us know where we've been off the mark, and to send in any "dirty little secrets" that they may wish to share with us for use in future editions of this book.

And, finally, there are the enormous changes that have taken place in the Warsaw Pact nations, and Russia in particular, since 1989. Many items herein refer to the nearly half century of U.S.-Russian military confrontation, and this confrontation may be gone. The Cold War arms race mentality is fading, but in practice the troops and weapons remain. Until Russia settles down into whatever its future form will be, the possibility of some sort of military encounter between the armed forces of the "East" and "West" remains. Even if Russia and America become the peaceful neighbors they have traditionally been, many of the 80 million troops maintained by other nations will still go on doing all that this book describes. Even after a reduction in forces, little will change in Russia nor in the United States, save for the scale of the "dirty little secrets."

A NOTE ON SOURCES

All of the information came from open sources. That is, none of it is classified (state secret) data. Well, as far as we know, none of it is secret. While much of it came from published sources, a lot came from people in the business. In an effort to protect our informants, and save a lot of space, we have not listed the sources for each item. This gives any of our many human sources a running head start from their local security officer in the event a bit of classified information was unwittingly passed on to us. Note also that most of these items drew from multiple sources, so citations could be a bit lengthy. If you must have sources for some items, contact the authors and we'll provide them. Each of us has listed phone numbers.

ACKNOWLEDGMENTS

SPECIAL THANKS TO:

Austin Bay, Jay Blucher, John Boardman, Dan Bolger, Richard L. DiNardo, Steve Cole, Walt Grant, Sterling Hart, Mark Herman, Ken Hoffman, Doug MacCaskill, Mike Macedonia, Ray Macedonia, Steve Patrick, Alan Rehm, Jim Simon, Vladimir Sobichevsky and the staff of the Defense Language Institute, Mercedes Almodovar, William Cruz, David C. Isby, Steve Zaloga, Dennis Casey, Sherry Arden, Daniel David, Petro Sodol, Margaret Moore and the other fine folks at the New York Public Library, Thomas J. Wisker, Bernard Dombrowski, Joan Marlow, John Boardman, Joe Ward, Jennifer Williams, Susan Leon, William Roberts, Shelby Stanton, and Trumbull Higgins, not to mention Keith Palter, Tyrone Bomba, and the staff of *Strategy & Tactics* magazine, and Mary S. Nofi and Marilyn J. Spencer for putting up with one of us.

CONTENTS

CONTENTS ☆ 14

PART ONE

Ground Forces

Worldwide, ground forces employ the vast majority of troops. Navies and air forces are increasingly loaded down with gadgets, while the foot soldier is still, well, a foot soldier. Even the poorest countries can afford ground troops. While most of the world's armed forces contain a lot of infantry, there are also a sizable majority serving in tanks or operating artillery and other heavy weapons, and some countries have a lot of troops operating antiaircraft and electronic warfare equipment. But keep in mind that no war is over until the infantry of one side occupies the territory of the other. This is one of the few constants in warfare over the centuries. This chapter digs into some of the strange aspects of contemporary ground combat and weapons technology.

But Who Can Tell Without a Battle?

"It is not the big armies that win battles, it is the good ones." —Maurice de Saxe, eighteenth-century marshal-general of France and noted rake

Get a Horse!

In this day of mechanized warfare, with tanks that can move at better than 60 km per hour, the daily combat rates of advance are not that impressive. The fastest sustained daily advance rate by an army is still that of the Mongol horse archers 700 years ago, who regularly maintained over 20 km a day for extended periods. Rarely has a twentieth-century mechanized army managed a sustained rate of 20 km a day. In fact, one of the fastest-moving armies in this century was the 1950 Chinese Army in Korea. It did better than 10 km per day on foot for several weeks. In World War II, the German Blitzkrieg, at its best, sustained only 5 km a day in Russia (1941), 10 km a day in France (1940), and 17 km a day in North Africa (1941). The Arab-Israeli wars of 1956 and 1967 did scarcely better, and contemporary exercises show advance rates of under 10 km a day.

The critical factor here is sustained rate of advance (the rate at which the entire army moves forward), regardless of what individual units may do, since they may greatly exceed the average. Horses can live on grass for a while and troops can live off the land up to a point. Mechanized armies must generally stick to the roads and need an enormous fuel and maintenance system to keep moving and dragging all their baggage along. This slows them down, even though most vehicles can zip along at sustained rates of over 50 km an hour, and individual units may average 100 km in 24 hours.

"It Does Not Compute . . ."

In late 1988, Russia announced a series of troop reductions, including substantial withdrawals from Eastern Europe. The numbers announced did not, however, square with information about Russian forces generally accepted in the West. For example, it was said that 5,000 tanks, six armored divisions, and 50,000 troops would be removed from Eastern Europe. According to commonly accepted Western data, Russia has only about 9,000 tanks in Eastern Europe. The same data holds that six armored divisions equals over 60,000 troops and about 2,000 tanks. This doesn't necessarily mean that the Russians aren't telling the whole story or that Western analysts have been way off the mark for many years. An equally likely explanation may be found in the Russian reference to "reorganization of units in a defensive posture." Changing the organization of divisions to include a smaller number of tanks would be in line with a more defensive posture. A third of Russia's 50,000-plus tanks are forty-year-old models that don't stand much of a chance in combat against more modern models. By early 1989, Russia had announced new organizations for their combat divisions that included sharply reduced numbers of armored vehicles.

MBT

MBT is military shorthand for "main battle tank." While just abut any fighting vehicle with a track is called a "tank" by careless observers, tanks are specifically armored track-laying combat vehicles equipped with a rotating turret in which there is a fairly heavy-caliber cannon, nowadays something in excess of 100 mm. Within the tank family, however, there are both "light tanks" and "MBTs." An MBT is an enormous vehicle weighing more than thirty tons, mostly because of all the armor it carries. Light tanks, although they frequently tote artillery as heavy as that of an MBT, are much less well armored, which does give them a bit more speed, though even MBTs can reach 60 kph on roads. Because light tanks are supposed to be used for reconnaissance and in theaters where they are unlikely to encounter MBTs, their lack of protection is not necessarily a significant handicap, as their higher speed and greater agility are supposed to substitute for some of that missing armor. They are particularly useful in the Third World, where it is unlikely that any of their heavier cousins will show up. But one never can tell when one may come rumbling along, so most nations want at least a few MBTs on hand. Despite reactive armor and other protective goodies, there are no MBTs with armor that will stop most antitank weapons. The advantage MBTs hold is that they often have a superior anti-tank weapon in their large-caliber gun. The gun can fire quickly and with more accuracy than the more common antitank guided missiles. While the MBT no longer reigns supreme as it did thirty or forty years ago, it is still at the top of the antitank food chain.

Hot Flashes!

Russian-built tanks are not air-conditioned, and thus become extremely hot in any kind of warm weather. In consequence, the Russians hold their maneuvers during the spring and fall, in part to spare the troops considerable discomfort. However, most of Russia's wars have been fought in the summer. And the biggest customers for Russian tanks are various Arabs, South Asians, Africans, and Latin Americans, who ought to know something about heat.

During the several Arab-Israeli wars, many Arab tanks were put out of action not by mechanical failure or battle damage, but merely by heat exhaustion of the crew. So common was the problem that some Arab leaders were convinced Israel had a secret weapon that inflicted physical weakness on enemy troops. In contrast, many Western tanks have air-conditioning, or at least better air circulation inside the vehicle.

How Tanks Resemble Aircraft

It is no longer the case that aircraft are far more complex and expensive than tanks. For example, there are several varieties of armor available for a tank's protection, including old-fashioned steel armor, composite armor, and explosive reactive armor. Additional ways to protect tanks include camouflage methods, which make it difficult for enemy weapon systems to find tanks. What they can't see, they can't shoot at. Tanks rarely get into a shootout with other tanks in the open. Most of the time tanks stand still, hidden in a forest or other cover. They move under cover of smoke, darkness, or bad weather. The enemy requires radar or heat sensing to detect tanks under these conditions. The heat angle, using a variety of sensors, is the most popular, as it can be used from the ground, from the air, and even from satellites. Radar can be made less reliable with radar-absorbing paints, but heat remains a ready way to spot a tank. There are several solutions. The primary source of heat is the engine, and particularly the exhausts. Filters and cold-air blowers can decrease the temperature of exhaust heat enough so that it doesn't produce an obvious armored-vehicle signature. This will defeat missiles that home in on heat. Camouflage nets that keep the heat in are also very effective in defeating air and satellite reconnaissance. The effectiveness of heat-detection devices is somewhat exaggerated, as there are often natural heat differences in the landscape of over 50 degrees. "Heat images" are made more useful with computers powerful enough to sort out all the clues. Currently, only Western nations equip some of their tanks with "thermal-imaging systems" (at over $70,000 per vehicle). Tanks on the move can be attacked from the air or by artillery using submunitions that also employ heat or radar sensors.

Like ships and aircraft, tanks can use countermeasures. Chaff and flares can be fired from the same equipment now used to eject smoke grenades. A useful sensor can detect laser light. Lasers are used by other tanks for range finding as well as by some weapons to home in on. There are already systems in development that detect laser light and then shoot a powerful laser beam back at the source in an attempt to destroy its optical components. This can be carried one step further: The same system could be used to aim the tank's gun automatically to retaliate promptly when the enemy fire is not fatal. While all of these devices can be lifesavers, they would be expensive and would make the tanks even more complex than they already are. To go all the way, sensors could even be added to detect radar warning and other ECM (electronic countermeasures) now found on aircraft. Since tanks cost about as much as many attack helicopters and the simpler fighter-bombers, the expense would be justified.

You could even emulate aircraft further by having some tanks act as "Wild Weasel" sensor and countermeasures vehicle (see page 163) and load these down with all the ECM and other sensors and gadgets. While some of the above might seem ludicrous, tanks have been equipped with smoke-grenade ejectors for some decades now. Many of the warning devices for radar and lasers are neither large, expensive, nor heavy. They would not change the appearance or cost of tanks much and could provide significant additional capability, just as in aircraft.

Dummy tanks, another deception measure, have been in use for many decades. The latest versions, some of them inflatable, even mimic the heat signature of a real tank. Some tanks actually carry a dummy tank with them. It's a complex and costly business, running a tank. Ironically, there has never been a tendency to have only officers commanding tanks. Most tanks are commanded by a sergeant. Currently tanks cost as much as some aircraft that require an officer pilot, or top-of-the-line jet fighters only twenty years ago.

The 6th Guards Shuffle of 1979

In 1979, amid great fanfare, Russia announced that it was unilaterally removing one of the ten tank divisions it had in East Germany. Later it was discovered that all was not as it appeared to be. While the 6th Guards Tank Division had been moved out of East Germany, many of its men and equipment remained in East Europe. Apparently, the division flag, records, and some of its personnel and equipment were transferred to western Russia, where a new division seems to have been formed. However, most of the troops and equipment were distributed to other units in East Germany. The tanks, of recent manufacture, went to Russian divisions in Czechoslovakia.

It's All in the Bullet.

The major infantry small arms in the world are the Russian AK-47 and the U.S. M-16. Several other nations make their own versions of these. There are several different bullets available for each weapon type. The bullets differ more than the weapons themselves. The AK-47 and M-16, for example, have ammunition made for them by several nations. Many of these rounds are identical except for crucial, minor differences in bullet design that create significant differences in wound effect and lethality. Most M-16 5.56-mm rounds do more damage than the Russian 7.62-mm rounds from the AK-47 or 5.45-mm rounds from the more recent M-16 clone, the AK-74. Non-Russian AK-47 rounds tend to do more damage than Russian-made rounds, although there is considerable variation among the many manufacturers of AK-47 ammunition. While the M-16 and AK-74 are considered equivalent weapons, such is not the case. The M-16 rounds tend to break up at shorter ranges (under 200 meters) and cause nastier wounds. The wounds caused by the AK-47 are similar to those made by pistol rounds. Thus, despite its fearsome reputation, the AK-47 is basically an automatic pistol. It's still dangerous, but hardly a superweapon. However, nearly all assault-gun rounds will break up if they hit someone at under 10 meters' range, which is a common range in combat. Beyond 10 meters, the AK-47 round generally stays intact while, given its high speed, at under 100 meters, the M-16 round virtually explodes inside a person. A similar effect is found in the West German version of the larger, full-size, 7.62-mm round used for machine guns. This larger round flattens out inside the body, and half the bullet breaks up into fragments. Oddly enough, the U.S. version of this round, designed differently, does not break up, and thus causes less damage.

Another design anomaly occurs in the latest M-16 round, the SS-109. This was supposed to be a "more humane" round that just went in and out of a person without leaving too much of a mess behind. When tests were eventually conducted on dead animals, it turned out that this round was far more deadly than the older one. Moreover, if the new round is fired from one of the early model M-16s (one in twelve-inch twist barrel) instead of the newer ones (one in seven-inch twist), the lesser spin generated by the older gun's barrel causes the longer SS-109 round to hit its target sideways and do even more damage. All of this is somewhat academic if you are hit by several of these bullets, particularly if one gets you in the head. However, in the past, it has been discovered after considerable combat that some rifles were substantially less harmful than others.

Earlier in this century, Japan, Italy, and some other nations used 6.5-mm rifles for a time. Eventually, they learned that the 6.5-mm round was much less likely to cause damage than the more common 7.62-mm one used by most other armies. The 6.5-mm weapon was lighter and easier for the troops to handle. But lethality counted more than convenience; by 1945 few armies used the 6.5-mm round anymore.

A similar contemporary example is that of the flechette. Flechettes are basically fat needles with fins on their rear, that have been used for over twenty years in artillery rounds for close-in defense. They were thought to be quite deadly, because enemy corpses found in the vicinity were torn apart by bent flechettes. Further study found that the flechettes were bent by the force of the explosive in the shell that propelled them. Were flechettes to be used in small arms, as is now proposed, they would have much less wounding potential than conventional bullets. A final problem with all this misinformation about weapons effects is that battlefield surgeons are left to find out the hard way just what kinds of wounds they will encounter. Most of the wounds are from fragments, either from shells or bullets that broke up after hitting the victim. Surgeons rarely see wounds like this in peacetime. This "learn as you go" approach is hard on the surgeons, not to mention the patients.

Darth Vader in the Trenches

Science fiction usually portrays future infantry weapons as compact gadgets that bear little resemblance to the traditional rifle. In the late 1980s, reality finally caught up with fiction. The Belgian weapons firm FN, long a manufacturer of infantry weapons, designed a radically different automatic weapon. Although designed to replace pistols, carbines, submachine guns, and other short-range weapons, the P90 could easily be the principal weapon of the infantry in conjunction with longer range light machine guns. The P90 weighs 8.1 pounds when loaded with fifty 5.7-mm rounds; an M-16 weighs the same with only twenty rounds, an AK-47 weighs 8.8 pounds with thirty rounds. The P90 is a little under sixteen inches long and less than seven inches high, with a barrel only nine inches long. Although designed for ranges under 150 meters, it has only one third the recoil of standard 5.56-mm rounds and greater penetrating and stopping power. The ammunition weighs about the same as M-16 rounds, with 100 rounds running less than four pounds. Effective rate of fire is about 100 rounds a minute, in short bursts. The ammunition is stored sideways in a clear plastic magazine on top of the weapon, so that remaining ammo can be easily checked. This feature alone is invaluable in combat. A spring in the magazine forces the rounds down and around into the firing position. Empty cartridge cases are ejected downward, allowing the weapon to be used easily by both right- and left-handed troops. While the P90 may not be the definitive infantry weapon of the future, it shows the shape of things to come.

Lock and Load

"Lock and Load" is a normal pre-combat, or danger-imminent, procedure, in which you place a magazine of live ammunition in a weapon and load a round into the chamber.

Battlefield Luxuries

"There is nothing so pleasing as to be shot at by one's enemy without result."—Sir Winston L. S. Churchill, World War II British leader and combat veteran

Chinese Copy Cats

When China and Russia broke relations in the early sixties, China was cut off from its main source of modern weapons. As a result, China reverse-engineered the Russian weapons on hand and produced credible Chinese versions. But for fifteen years, China was cut off from any source of foreign modern weapons designs, and the Cultural Revolution stopped most domestic R&D. China was able to purchase examples of some modern Russian equipment from Middle Eastern nations in the 1970s, and developed additional clones of Russian equipment, such as the BMP APC. From 1980 on, China gained increasing access to Western military technology. Western firms soon learned to be careful not to let Chinese engineers spend too much time with their equipment, as the Chinese were quick to reverse-engineer and appropriate whatever technology they could get their hands on. Western technology, however, was more difficult to clone than the simpler Russian stuff. And Western governments made unpleasant noises in response to the Chinese technology theft. So the Chinese began to enter into joint ventures with Western firms, the idea being that by merging high-tech Western equipment and inexpensive Chinese manufacturing, low-cost weapons could be produced for Chinese needs and export to Third World nations.

The Model-T of Rifles

Some years ago, it was estimated that there were more than 40 million AK-47 assault rifles in the world. Russia still manufactures a small number, having introduced the 5.45-mm AK-74 to replace the 7.62-mm AK-47. Other nations, like China, still manufacture large quantities of the AK-47. The AK-47 was derived from a German weapon introduced toward the end of World War II, the SG-44. The key element of both weapons is their use of a less powerful 7.62-mm rifle round. This "short" 7.62 had the wounding power of a pistol round, but much longer effective range. The standard AK-47 weighs about nine pounds, with bayonet and thirty-round magazine. There are several variations, including a lighter paratroop version with a folding stock. Like the SG-44, the AK-47 is rugged, cheap, and effective, with automatic or single-shot fire. It has proved a robust and valuable weapon in combat.

Rock and Roll

Not a musical term, in military parlance "rock and roll" means to "open up" with all weapons and generate as much firepower as possible. It also implies a continuous stream of automatic-weapons fire, not one round per pull of the trigger.

Battle Ready, but Not Child Proof

The principal British battle tank during the late fifties and early sixties was the Centurion, a sturdy vehicle that still soldiers on in some poorer armies. A strange fate once befell one of these behemoths. One day in the early sixties, a British tank regiment was having open house. There was lots of equipment on display, including several Centurions. One tank was open for inspection, and visitors were permitted to climb down into it and have a look around. This, of course, proved particularly popular with the children, who clambered all over the thing. Needless to say, the show went off well and was an enormous success. But then an inspection revealed that the little ones had inflicted considerable damage on various interior parts of the tank, including the breech mechanism, though no one was ever able to figure out how they had managed it.

Good Old Robots

All the talk of robotic weapons makes people think that these items are recent innovations. Not so. The Germans used radio-controlled torpedo boats in World War I and remote-controlled tanks, aircraft, and missiles in World War II. Development continued after the war, resulting in such items as ICBMs, cruise missiles, and "smart" torpedoes, mines, and bombs. Many senior commanders, however, are reluctant to put too much effort into developing these robotic warriors. Bureaucratic inertia is probably an important reason for this lack of enthusiasm, coupled with some legitimate skepticism on the part of senior officers. But it may also have something to do with the fact that these tin soldiers don't salute, march past you on parade, or line up trembling before you in fear of a court-martial if they screw up.

The T-55 Forever

Of the nearly 160,000 tanks in use today, over a third are the forty-year-old Russian T-55 and its clones. Including the Chinese T-59, nearly 60,000 of the T-55s have been produced. Production of this, basically a World War II–era tank, began in the late 1940s. The Russians stopped making them in 1979, but China still produces the T-59. While armor and firepower were inferior to many Western and German World War II models, the T-55's main virtues were speed, simplicity, low profile, and price, which enabled it to be produced in quantity. In combat it acquired a reputation for quickly going up in flames, as fuel was stored right behind the frontal armor. Nevertheless, nearly all of Russia's 100-plus low-readiness "cadre" divisions are equipped with T-55s. Most of Russia's East European allies still use it extensively. It's a favorite among Third World nations looking for a cheap, easy-to-use tank capable of awing unruly mobs of unhappy citizens. Most T-55s remain in use because replacements are too expensive. Until recently, few T-55s were upgraded. The Israelis captured hundreds during the 1967 and 1973 wars and added more powerful guns, fire control, and other systems. East European nations have been rebuilding theirs, concentrating on new engines and fire control. The Chinese are collaborating with Western firms to upgrade their T-59s. Even the Russians are now upgrading theirs with additional armor, better fire control, and new ammunition. Expect to see T-55s operating well into the next century.

Business Must Be Good

At the end of World War II, only three nations, Russia, Britain, and the United States, were in the business of producing tanks. Since then, most industrialized powers have gotten into the act, including France, Sweden, Switzerland, West Germany, Italy, Austria, Japan, Israel, and Spain, plus Poland and Czechoslovakia, as well as several Third World countries, including India, South Korea, South Africa, Argentina, and Brazil, who are soon to be joined by Egypt, Pakistan, Taiwan, and possibly Saudi Arabia. Thus, since 1945 the number of countries in the tank business has increased by over 600 percent.

Better Living Through Chemistry

U.S. Army expenditures on offensive and defensive chemical warfare capabilities over the decade beginning in 1986 will run to an estimated $15–$25 billion, unless there's a treaty to further restrict chemical weapons. This is highly possible, as the major powers are beginning to become nervous about the chemical-warfare capabilities of some of the Third World nations: The CIA estimates that about twenty nations already have such weapons.

TOW Triumphant

One of the few ATGM (Antitank Guided Missile) systems that has been in combat and performed well under many different conditions is the U.S. TOW system. A testament to the faith troops have in it is the number in use. There are currently some 25,000 TOW launchers in use worldwide. About 70 percent are with U.S. forces. Over a quarter-million missiles have been produced in the last twenty years.

Park

Park is a traditional military term for the totality of an army's heavy equipment of a particular type, as the "artillery park" or the "tank park," rare in American usage, and widely heard in some foreign armies.

The VW of Tanks

One of the most widely sold tanks is the Russian T-54/55 series. It's also one of the easiest to operate and maintain. First built in the

1950s, it is the most commonly used tank in the world, and is still built by the Chinese in a version they call the T-59. As of the beginning of 1990s, the inventories of the forty-nine nations that own this tank (whether bought or captured) are (Chinese version following the /):

Afghanistan	540	Laos	30
Albania	15/15	Libya	1,800
Algeria	300	Mali	25
Angola	300	Mongolia	640
Bangladesh	30/90	Morocco	7
Benin	4	Mozambique	150
Bulgaria	1,800	Nicaragua	190
Central African Republic	4	Nigeria	80
Chad	30	North Yemen	540
China	0/11,000	Pakistan	50/1,000
Congo	35/14	Poland	3,200
Cuba	420	Romania	1,300
Czechoslovakia	3,100	Russia	21,000
East Germany	2,300	Somalia Republic	70
Egypt	900	South Africa	10
Equatorial Guinea	8	South Yemen	460
Ethiopia	500	Sudan	130/10
Finland	65	Syria	1,400
Guinea-Bissau	30	Tanzania	12/22
Guinea	26	Togo	2
Hungary	1,490	Uganda	6
India	950	Vietnam	1,500
Iran	100/260	Yugoslavia	930
Iraq	700/1,200	Zimbabwe	15/35
Israel	440		

Throw a Track.

Throwing a track is one of the most common disorders to which tanks and related vehicles are subject, when the track comes off the wheels. This happens because of poor maintenance, or poor driving over broken terrain. The crew can put it back on, but this can take an hour or more.

The Reluctant Dragon

To be counted among the world's less-well-conceived antitank guided missiles is the U.S. Army's Dragon. Its short range (1,000 meters) and slow speed (nine seconds flight time at max range) makes it easy to counter with a few sprays of machine-gun fire. The Dragon gunner must maintain a very steady view of the target in order to achieve a hit, and bullets whizzing around his head do little to facilitate the needed concentration.

The guidance system has had numerous problems, though most have now been solved. The weapon weighs thirty-two to forty pounds, depending on the sight used. It requires a bipod to aim and fire, and its warhead cannot penetrate the frontal armor of most modern tanks. The Swiss Army is developing an improved model of the Dragon, but the U.S. Army has given up and begun looking for a replacement. This did not discourage the Russians, who produced their own version (the AT-7) in the late 1970s. Meanwhile, U.S. troops still have large quantities of the Dragon system.

Tank Mutations

Since World War II, most major tank models have remained in service continually from their introduction. The older models would gradually become increasingly ineffective against more recent designs were it not for upgrade programs.

The best example of this is the Russian T-55. Well over 60,000 T-55s were built, about half of which were exported. The design dates to the late 1940s, a direct result of Russian experience with their successful T-34 of World War II fame. The T-55 is the first upgrade of the T-54, done in the 1950s to correct several of the initial model's design flaws. A second major upgrade was performed by Israel on the hundreds of T-55s captured during the 1967 and 1973 wars. This included a new gun, the NATO 105-mm weapon, as well as new radios, fire-control gear, and a fire-suppression system.

In the 1980s, Israel began installing a Western-designed engine. All of these changes more than doubled the T-55s effectiveness, even though it had the same armor and cramped internal layout.

Other nations, such as India, Egypt, and Pakistan, have followed the Israeli approach. Russia and Warsaw Pact nations have also upgraded their T-55s, but only to the extent of new fire-control systems, better ammunition, and new engines. Many nations are also adding reactive armor. The net result is a tank that can have a fighting chance against modern ones and an edge against unmodified tanks of earlier generations. A similar program has considerably enhanced the usefulness of the U.S. M-60 tank, which was better to begin with, and remains competitive with even the most recent models as a result of the upgrade.

Runner

A tank more or less in proper working order is known as a "runner." American units also tend to use the term "up" (for operational) or "down" (for inoperable). The term "tits up" is also used to indicate a vehicle that is down, or not a runner. The word "runner" is also used to designate a soldier who literally "runs" messages around a battle area. He does this on foot, often at great personal risk. It was in this capacity that Adolf Hitler won the Iron Cross in World War I.

Still Active After All These Years

During the Vietnam War, TV viewers became used to seeing the boxy, U.S. M-113 APC—armored personnel carrier—trundling across the rice paddies. It was a relatively new vehicle then, and 75,000 were eventually built. Most are still in use with dozens of armies, including the U.S. Army. In addition to use as an APC, the M-113 is frequently converted to an armored command post and a heavy-weapons carrier.

The Green Machine

Among its fans and foes, the U.S. Army is frequently known as "the Green Machine." This comes from the green uniforms, and green paint on weapons and equipment. Green for equipment came in during the last century. Green uniforms replaced blue early in this century, although blue remains the color of the army's full-dress uniform. Actually, the green used to be "olive drab," and is now "army green," but most often camouflage is worn. But somehow the "Olive Drab Machine" or the "Army Green Machine" or the "Camouflage Machine" doesn't have the same martial ring to it.

Son of Jeep

Each HUMMV, or "Hummer," the replacement for the WW II–era Jeep, costs the U.S. Army $20,000 to $35,000, depending on options. The Hummer is a little larger than the Jeep and generally sturdier, more mobile, more agile, and has more varied uses. Whereas the Jeep was essentially a four-seat convertible, a Hummer is more like a multi-seat pickup truck. The air pressure in the Hummer's tires can be varied to suit the terrain and climate, making it considerably more agile than any comparable vehicle. In addition, the Hummer has been designed so it can be used in a variety of roles, there being five basic models and fifteen different configurations; light truck, ambulance, command car, communications vehicle, ammo wagon, and lots more, greatly simplifying spare parts procurement, maintenance, and driver training. Because the Hummer carries more than a Jeep, it can fill more roles while still serving as a lightweight vehicle. So pleased is the army with the 25,000 Hummers it already has, that it has revised its procurement plans and intends to acquire about 5,000 more than originally planned, up to about 60,000.

Reacting to Reactive Armor

In 1987 it was revealed that many Russian tanks in Eastern Europe were equipped with a copy of Israeli-developed reactive armor. The add-on armor is actually blocks of high-speed explosive that nullify shaped-charge warheads used in Antitank Guided Missiles (ATGMs). The impact of an incoming round causes the explosive blocks to detonate, neutralizing the armor-piercing jet of super-hot gas from the warhead.

Counters to this take two forms. The easiest is to add a long, thin tube to the front of the ATGM warheads containing a small explosive charge that will detonate the reactive armor prematurely, thus allowing the ATGM's shaped-charge warhead to explode successfully and penetrate the tank's armor. The tricky part of this approach is the split-second timing. Reactive armor has not been thoroughly tested or used in actual combat, except briefly by the Israelis.

The second approach is more expensive. This involves replacing the shaped-charge warhead with one or two top-attack warheads. A top-attack system must have the missile-guidance control system modified so that the warhead detonates over the tank, penetrating the thinner top armor. But reactive armor may be there, too, thus defeating even this approach. This flaw is overcome by using a shaped charge that forms a metal jet instead of simply superheated gas. This has problems, as the metal jet takes longer to form and must explode farther away from the tank. The guidance-system requirements also become a bit more complex with the metal-jet approach. Whatever the solution to reactive armor, there is now an atmosphere of uncertainty about tank vulnerability that will only be resolved if these various devices are actually used in combat.

Out of Retirement

Among British Army reservists reactivated for the Falklands War in 1982 was a WW II mobile field-bakery unit nicknamed "Lizzie," recalled from the Museum of Army Transport.

The Pot Calling the Kettle . . .

During the 1970s, the Swedes did a considerable amount of research on the lethality of military ammunition. They concluded that the U.S./NATO 5.56-mm M-16 round was "inhumane" because it broke into small fragments when it hit a person. Eventually, it was pointed out that the larger Swedish 7.62-mm round did the same thing, only to a greater extent.

No Modernization Necessary

The bicycle currently in use in the Swiss Army is the same model introduced in 1905.

Need a Russian Tank?

They can be had, for a price, from A F Budge Ltd, Retford, Nottinghamshire, England. They also carry a large line of Russian Armored Personnel Carriers. Be warned, however, that all are pre-owned, and some have a little damage, the original owners not always having been inclined to give them up willingly.

Ground-Based Radar

Since the 1960s, ground radars have been an increasing part of the infantry commander's arsenal. Although radar broadcasts a signal that can be detected and jammed or shot at, it still can provide invaluable intelligence. And radar detectors are just another item moving infantry don't want to carry. Radar is particularly useful on a fluid battlefield containing large areas where you have no troops and you want to make sure the enemy has none, either. In particular, you are watching out for fast-moving armored units. Tanks and APCs are large objects and relatively easy to spot on a radar. For example, a typical infantry radar can spot armored vehicles at a distance of 30–40 km, a group of soldiers moving on foot at 20–25 km, and individual troops at 15–20 km. This doesn't work very well if there are woods or other obstacles to slink around in, but there are always open areas needing surveillance.

Israel has a long-range system that can spot trucks and tanks at 100 km, but this is only useful from heights overlooking flat terrain. Closed-in areas can be covered with acoustic sensors, little microphones that broadcast back what they hear. A computer with a library of sounds can analyze the signals and tell the operator what is probably out there. The latest U.S. ground radar has a special feature that allows it to detect troops in dense foliage up to 300 meters away. This is more practical, as setting up sensors in the bush is not always possible. Manpack systems weigh under 100 pounds, broken up into three or more components. Batteries are good for a few hours or more. These radars add a lot to infantry security, especially when you consider that for over fifty years infantry have been accustomed to setting up positions tied together with radio and telephone-wire communications. It's getting harder and harder to sneak up on the grunts.

First-Quality Cheap Tanks

In their drive to out-do each other in performance, the major tank producers have created tanks that, at $2.5 to $6.0 million each, are too expensive for most Third World armies. These less affluent nations have been forced to buy secondhand vehicles that are much less capable, very expensive to maintain because many of their components are worn, and, at upward of $1 million apiece, only relatively cheap. Several innovative solutions to procuring inexpensive MBTs are being tried by Third World powers, the first being the addition of current Western components to secondhand, and cheap, Russian tank chassis.

The Chinese have taken this one step further. For over twenty years, the Chinese have built their own version of the 1950s Russian T-55 design. The Chinese vehicle, the T-59, is now to be built with a combination of Western components in cooperation with the U.S. Textron company. This "East/West" hybrid (the "Jaguar") will weigh forty tons. The U.S. company will supply the engine, possibly built under license in China, as well as the running gear, fire-control systems, and a British-designed 105-mm gun. At $1 million, the Jaguar will be less than half the cost of new Western or Russian tanks.

Tank Etiquette

When tanks prepare for action, they "button up," closing and sealing all hatches.

Fancy Protection for Light Armored Vehicles

For over a decade, exotic armor and other devices have been developed to increase the protection for tanks. Little has been done for light armored vehicles, particularly personnel carriers. At the same time, weapons capable of making a hash of light armored vehicles and their crews have increased. Automatic 20–30-mm cannon have proliferated, and these are particularly lethal against light armor. Finally, in the late 1980s, a composite armor was developed in Italy for light vehicles that previously had to make do with aluminum for their armor. The lightweight composite armor stops most projectiles under 20 mm and provides much better protection against larger (20-plus mm) cannon rounds. In addition, light vehicles are making greater use of Kevlar curtains to further reduce the effects of fragments that do penetrate light armor. The grunts are not nearly as safe as tank crews, but every little bit helps.

Eurostyle ATGM

Although the U.S.-made TOW ATGM (Antitank Guided Missile) dominates the market for long range (3,000-plus meters) systems, a European group of NATO nations has produced the best-seller for medium-range systems. Nearly 250,000 MILAN ATGM have been sold. Each weighs thirty-two pounds and has a range of 2,000 meters. Eight thousand seventy-three-pound launchers have been sold, as well as 4,000 thermal sights that enable users to fire at night and through fog and smoke. A new warhead was produced in 1989 to defeat reactive armor.

Electromagnetic Antitank Weapons

The U.S. Army is presently testing an electromagnetic "rail gun" to study its potential value as an antitank weapon. The experimental weapon uses two electrified parallel copper rails. When a round is placed on the rails, a copper band around its base completes a circuit that propels the round at enormous speed, with velocities running up to 14,200 feet per second, nearly five times that achieved by an M-16 round. At such speeds even plastic projectiles can pierce tank armor. The army believes it has a good idea here, but it concedes that it needs possibly as much as ten years of work before the device is practical. Considering that the experimental antitank rail gun is twenty feet long, weighs twelve tons, and requires an enormous electrical supply, the estimate may be a bit optimistic.

Diesel Versus Turbine

Modern tank designers have two choices for tank engines, diesel or gas turbine. The diesel is cheaper to buy but more expensive to operate, even though it uses less fuel. Diesels are getting more expensive as power needs increase, since the engines must become more complex and, predictably, less reliable. Although the gas turbine consumes more fuel, this is a problem that can be accommodated in several ways. For example, the turbine engine is lighter and smaller than the diesel, so additional fuel can be carried to match the diesel in the weight and range department. Although the turbine uses more fuel when idling than the diesel, it can be equipped with a smaller APU (auxiliary power unit, just like jet aircraft that also use gas-turbine engines). Because turbines come up to speed quickly, use of an APU would not degrade system performance. Turbines are easier to start in cold weather, although their air filters clog up more quickly in dusty or sandy conditions. Turbines are quieter than diesels and, coupled with the U.S. M-1's quieter tracks and road wheels, create a tank that can literally sneak up on battlefield opponents. On the negative side, infantry have found that taking shelter behind a turbine-powered tank is quite uncomfortable because of the greater volume of hot air thrown off by the "jet" engine, which is what a turbine is. Despite the advantages of turbines, diesel tanks will be around for another twenty or thirty years because turbine cost is justifiable for only the highest-performance vehicles.

Details, Details

For nearly a hundred years, artillerymen have taken into account things like temperature and wind and occasionally the rotation of the earth while aiming and firing their guns. Tanks, until recently, were unable to gather such information and benefit from the added accuracy it supplied. Now, wind and temperature sensors, mounted on the turret, continually update the fire-control system so that when a round is fired it will be as accurate as possible, and more accurate than those fired by an enemy not using such devices. The Israelis are installing these sensors on their latest tanks.

And They're a Bitch to Keep Running.

The United States Army currently owns about 34,000 armored vehicles in sixteen different basic models. Nearly all of these are track-laying (as in bulldozers), armored, and full of gadgets. These vehicles require hundreds of manhours of maintenance each year, as well as thousands of dollars' worth of spare parts. The most modern tanks require more maintenance than World War II fighter aircraft.

And Change the Oil, Too.

Given normal usage, the average tank wears out three road wheels per year. The U.S. M-1, however, has much sturdier road wheels (nearly twice the useful life, because of better materials and engineering), one of its many minor advantages.

A Short History of Reactive Armor

Reactive armor is not armor, but blocks of explosive placed over a tank's armor. When struck by a shaped-charge (HEAT) or solid shot (APDS) antitank round, the explosive reacts quickly and detonates outward, toward the incoming round. This reduces the penetrating power of the HEAT round by 50–70 percent, and the APDS round by 25–35 percent. First developed by a German firm in the 1970s, the initial production version was made by an Israeli company and used on Israeli tanks during the early 1980s. The Syrians captured some from a wrecked Israeli tank, the Russians got hold of it, and this helped them with their existing reactive-armor program. The Russians soon produced a workable version. By 1985 they began equipping their tanks with it. This caused some military experts to panic. However, while Spain purchased reactive armor from Israel, France, Germany, and the U.S. Army evaluated it and decided not to use it because their tanks were already well-enough protected. The U.S. Army also noted that reactive armor was not "cost-effective" and was dangerous to use in the presence of friendly infantry. Not only would friendly troops be at risk when reactive armor exploded, but the tank's own fire-control and communications equipment could be damaged by the explosions. While the reactive armor might save the tank from destruction, it could make it temporarily unable to use its primary weapons. There has not been much unclassified information on the actual effectiveness of reactive armor, but the above indicates that reactive armor is not a panacea and brings with it certain problems. Naturally, it is expensive. It also adds a ton or more of weight. The Spanish adopted it because they are using older, thin-skinned tanks. The Israelis use it because they also have a lot of older, thin-skinned tanks. They also place a higher value on protecting their well-trained crews. The Russians probably want it because of quality-control problems with their version of British-developed composite armor. Also, Russia has been seeking a defense against NATO portable antitank weapons, which are becoming more effective and more numerous, threatening Russia's enormous investment in tanks with increasing vulnerability. Reactive armor, despite its drawbacks, is seen as a means of keeping the Russian tanks viable on the modern battlefield.

"Splish, Splash . . ."

The United States Army is planning to replace the equipment in its 1,200-plus field laundries. The new equipment, which uses Freon, a chlorofluorocarbon, instead of water, will not only permit clothing to be laundered in extremely cold and extremely hot weather, but will also be able to neutralize some chemical and biological contaminants. There has been no comment on how this program will be affected by the 1987 Montreal Convention, which calls for a drastic reduction in chlorofluorocarbon production by 1992 in an effort to preserve the ozone layer, or the Environmental Protection Agency's call for a total ban on such chemicals.

Surprise!

"Nothing concentrates the military mind so much as the discovery that you have walked into an ambush."—Thomas Packenham, British historian

Now, All We Need Is a Cherry Tree.

The West German Army is experimenting with a motorized "cherry picker" mounting for MILAN and HOT antitank missiles. The idea is that the vehicle could hide behind various convenient obstacles, exposing only the business end of the cherry picker, on which are mounted a half-dozen of the rockets. This would greatly improve the chances of getting off a shot before being detected by the enemy, thus increasing the chances of a hit, and, incidentally, of surviving to fight another time. The United States has had a similar system for over a decade.

"Boots-Boots-Boots!"

The standard U.S. Army combat boot is sufficiently durable to survive eight years of peacetime use, but only six months of war. The chief reason for this is the inability to properly dry out boots under field conditions. In addition, boots endure a lot more fire, firepower, and accidents in combat.

Heavy Metal

Going into the 1990s, the U.S. Army is paying about $4 million each for its main battle tanks, the M-1 "Abrams." The M-2 "Bradley" APCs (armored personnel carriers) cost about $81 million each. For this reason, these APCs are now called IFVs (infantry fighting vehicles).

The Artillery Gap

Much is made of Russian advantage in terms of weapons quantity in Central Europe. One of the numbers is for artillery. The Russians have 11,000 guns to NATO's 3,000. What is ignored about these numbers is the importance of ammunition and the opportunities to fire it. Russian gunners would have three problems if they ever confronted NATO forces. First, they must fire quickly, as, according to their own doctrine, they could expect highly accurate retaliatory ("counterbattery") fire from American, West German, and, to a lesser degree, British artillery within minutes of opening up. This is due to computer-driven counterbattery radars and highly efficient communications among the artillery units of these particular NATO powers. The second problem is the amount of fire needed to have any useful effect on NATO targets. According to the Russians' calculations, they must put 100 to 2,000 tons of shells on a NATO armored unit to disorganize and damage it. The variation in necessary tonnage reflects the many ways the NATO unit is deployed. It takes only about 100 tons of ammo to damage a NATO unit if it is bunched up for a hasty attack. If the same unit is dispersed for mobile defense, 2,000 tons are needed. There are several degrees in between. A Russian artillery battalion can fire three or four tons of shells a minute. They could get off ten to twenty tons before they were likely to get any return fire from NATO artillery. If the battle were chaotic, as is often the case, NATO artillery might not be ready to fire back. The Russians' solution is to have a lot of guns, which gives them two advantages. They could use four or five battalions to deliver the needed fire, and then move the guns before NATO counterbattery fire arrived. Or they could move the guns to within sight of the target and deliver direct fire. This would be dangerous, as the target could then fire back. But much Russian artillery is now armored and self-propelled, so it could take some punishment without getting wiped out. Direct fire is four to five times more efficient than the normal indirect ("can't see the target") fire. So you would save a lot of ammo. This brings up another Russian problem: ammunition supply.

A Russian division carries with it about 5,000 tons. Another 5,000–10,000 is available from rear-area supply units. If the defender is prepared and direct fire is not possible, you have a big problem. There are too many targets and not enough ammo to go around. Moreover, the fast-moving self-propelled guns require more cargo vehicles to chase after them with ammunition. Keeping track of where the guns and ammo vehicles are becomes a real puzzle at times. One partial solution to the ammunition-supply problem is the use of improved conventional munitions (ICM). These shells contain either dozens or hundreds of smaller bomblets. They are more expensive to make and require higher levels of technical ability, or else you have a lot of expensive duds. Russia is making some ICMs, but still relies largely on old-fashioned high-explosive shell. Last, most Russian artillery is still towed. Only the fifty or so active divisions in East Europe and on the Chinese border, plus some units in Western Russia, have self-propelled guns. The towed stuff is at even greater risk to efficient counterbattery fire. Note that the Russians traditionally take guns to shells, while Western armies take shells to guns. To do it the Russian way, there must be an opportunity to build large ammo dumps without enemy interference. This doctrine has important implications for operational flexibility, logistical planning, and traffic control. The Russian artillery advantage is not all it appears to be.

Gun Bunny

Artillery crewmen who manhandle the ammunition are generally known as "gun bunnies," (or "ammo humpers"), which is less correctly used to refer to all artillerymen, who are more correctly "cannon cockers" or "red legs," though infantrymen—"grunts"—have been known to refer to them as "the Gang that Couldn't Shoot Straight," because "friendly fire" isn't always friendly.

Least Squares Linear Regression

Since 1940 the lethality of tanks as measured by the armor-piercing ability of their guns has increased by about 450 percent, while their protection as measured in thickness of armor adjusted for angle and quality has risen only about 340 percent. In effect, whereas in 1940 there were a number of main battle tanks—German Panzer IVc, French Char B—that mounted guns too weak to pierce their own heaviest armor, no modern tank is proof against its own weapon. This is one reason why tank designers are making their vehicles more nimble and equipping them with more sensors and defensive items like smoke grenade launchers.

Tanks, but No Tanks

In the decade ending in 1987, Russia and other Warsaw Pact powers outproduced the United States and other NATO powers by 2.6 to 1 in tanks and by 2.5 to 1 in other armored fighting vehicles (AFV). In this period, Russia produced some 25,300 tanks and 46,000 other AFV, and its allies produced another 4,800 tanks and 7,600 other AFV, while the United States turned out 7,600 tanks and 10,800 other AFV, and the other NATO powers some 4,000 tanks and 9,300 AFV.

Toy Tanks

The U.S. Army has recently developed a new decoy version of the M-1 Abrams tank. Costing only $3,300 and weighing about fifty pounds, disassembled the dummy tank itself is about the size of a duffel bag, while its portable generator is about the size of a twelve-inch television. Nevertheless, when erected, which can be accomplished by two men in a few minutes, the decoy not only looks like a real M-1, but also simulates its heat signature, to fool infrared detectors. What's more, it can take several hits and still stay standing, giving the enemy the illusion that they missed, or that there are more of your tanks around than they thought. Field exercises under realistic conditions have shown that units can be held up for over an hour dealing with a few of these dummy tanks. Because they appear to be real tanks from a distance, the detecting unit must stop and destroy them as if they were real tanks. This can take over an hour, which is an expensive chunk of time on a fast-moving battlefield. The dummy tanks are particularly valuable if you are outnumbered and have to withdraw. Leaving a few of the "dummies" behind will slow down the enemy and allow you to get away in one piece.

The Tank Gap

The quantity and quality of tanks available for combat are a benchmark of ground combat power. Warsaw Pact (WP) tank forces in Central Europe are considered superior to their potential NATO adversary, but this depends on how the tanks are counted. In peacetime, NATO has 12,000 tanks in Central Europe, of which 6,700 are manned by regular troops. The rest are with reserve units. WP has 18,000 tanks in the area, of which 10,000 are manned. Depending on how the battle went, it would take one to three weeks to get the reserve tanks manned and into combat. Thus, at any given moment WP has a 1.5:1 advantage in quantity.

After a mobilization, the ratio stays the same. Or does it? Over two thirds of the NATO tanks are state-of-the-art M-1s, Leopard IIs, and M-60a3s. Less than half of the WP tanks are roughly equivalent T-72, T-64, or T-80 models.

The biggest discrepancies are in the crews. NATO training methods stress that the crews must spend a lot of time in the vehicles and in the field while firing hundreds of live rounds each year. In contrast, Russian crews fire ten rounds a year, and the little time they spend in a tank is not in one they will go to war with but rather an older model used exclusively for training. While NATO crews enthusiastically compete for international tank-gunnery championships, the Russian military press complains about the inability of crews to keep their tanks from running into walls. Worse for Russian tank crews, their vehicles are less likely to protect them from injury, either in accidents or combat. Western tanks have superior fire-control systems, often containing a thermal-imaging system that allows firing in spite of darkness or smoke. Russian tanks are also deficient in mobility and engine reliability. Their adoption of three-man crews and an autoloader further increased system complexity and reduced the number of crew available for maintenance. Russian tanks are also more dangerous and fatiguing to work in, particularly with the autoloader. So cramped are their tanks that they must carry much of their fuel externally, which makes them vulnerable to ignition by enemy fire. The final complication is that the Russians are likely to be doing the attacking. Combat experience has shown that one defending tank is worth two or three attackers. Somehow, the tank gap doesn't appear to be there.

Jungle Bashing

"Jungle bashing" (or "jungle busting," or "breaking bush") is the art of driving a tank through forest or thick brush.

Airborne Armor

Many nations have airborne troops, but only Russian airborne troops insist that nearly all their operations include air-delivered armored vehicles. Their principal airborne armored vehicle is the BMD, a seven-ton APC with less than an inch of armor. A nine-ton variant carries a 160-mm mortar. A Russian airborne division of 6,500 men has over 400 armored vehicles. The Russians can go with this much heavy metal because most potential targets on which their paratroopers are likely to drop are in nations adjacent to Russia or its allies. As the Russian border is studded with military airfields, the Russians can use their short-range transports and heavy-life helicopters. The United States, in contrast, expects to lift troops from American bases and carry them thousands of miles to the battlefield. The Russians would obviously have an advantage with their light armored vehicles. Their airborne forces are expected to support the main Russian ground forces, which comprise masses of armored vehicles. U.S. airborne forces are intended for rapid intervention where speed, and not firepower, is critical.

"My Friends All Drive Porsches. . . ."

Including obsolescent and obsolete runners, there are about 160,000 main battle tanks in the world. The largest tank parks are:

Russia	54,000	Poland	3,950
U.S.	16,000	Israel	3,850
China	11,000	Turkey	3,600
West Germany	4,950	India	3,700
Iraq	4,500	Czechoslovakia	3,400
Syria	4,000		

In addition to those mentioned, the other Warsaw Pact powers also have substantial tank parks:

Bulgaria	2,550
East Germany	3,000
Romania	1,900
Hungary	1,300

Aside from the United States, West Germany, and Turkey, the tank parks of the other NATO powers are relatively modest:

Italy	1,740	Belgium	334
Greece	1,360	Denmark	210
France	1,340	Norway	120
Britain	1,200	Canada	114
Spain	840	Portugal	66

Luxembourg and Iceland have none. In addition to Iraq, Syria, and Israel, all of the Middle Eastern powers have substantial numbers of MBTs:

Libya	3,000 (some estimates put it higher)
Egypt	2,400
Iran	1,000
Jordan	975

While India easily holds supremacy in the South Asian tank race, Pakistan makes a fair showing with 1,600. The tank parks of all the East Asian powers together barely begin to approach that of China: North Korea, 3,000, Vietnam, 1,750, South Korea, 1,700, Japan, 1,200, and Taiwan, 300. Aside from countries that have no tanks whatsoever, the smallest tank park is that of Togo, which for some reason owns two non-air-conditioned T-55s.

Raw numbers, however, are not the only way to measure the size of a nation's tank force. Adjusting the figures for population helps suggest who are the most heavily armed folks. On this basis, there are approximately thirty tanks per million people in the world. The top ten powers are:

Israel	836 tanks per million people	Bulgaria	282
Libya	702 (if not more)	Iraq	255
Syria	327	Czechoslovakia	217
Jordan	321	South Yemen	189
Mongolia	310	Russia	188

These figures rather clearly reveal the intensity of the Middle Eastern arms race, where only Egypt, at 44 per million, is not among the top ten. Note that none of the NATO powers make the top ten. Figures for them are: Greece, 130, West Germany, 82, the United

States, 67, Turkey, 65, the Netherlands, 62, Denmark, 41, Belgium, 34, Italy, 30, Norway, 29, France, 24, Britain, 21, Spain, 21, Portugal, 6, and Canada, 5, plus Luxembourg and Iceland, which have none. Even the weakest Warsaw Pact powers do better than virtually all of the NATO powers: East Germany, 176, Hungary, 123, Poland, 102, and Romania, 82. In South Asia, Pakistan, at 15, surpasses India, 5. This basis of calculation also alters the Far Eastern situation, with North Korea leading at 137 per million, South Korea, 33, Vietnam, 26, Taiwan, 15, Japan, 10, and China, 8.

People Who Know

"The best tank terrain is that without antitank weapons."—Russian military doctrine

The Russian Disarmament Advantage

Russia's unilateral move to cut its armed forces in the late 1980s was prompted more by economic and demographic problems than anything else. NATO may be forced to respond in kind because of public pressure or simply to reap similar economic gains. However, because of the unique organization of Russia's armed forces, disarmament takes away less of its strength than similar cuts in Western forces. Russian armed forces are organized in a cadre system. That is, most divisions have only part of their personnel strength (not enough to man all equipment), although all have a full complement of equipment. Currently only about a quarter of the 200 divisions are at full strength, while the remainder have from 10 to 50 percent of their troops.

Since the 1950s, Russia has discarded practically no major weapons. In particular, over a third of Russia's tanks are of 1950s vintage. To accommodate these weapons, the number of tanks per division was increased. But these older tanks require more maintenance to keep them functional, leaving less time for everything else. By cutting manpower and retiring older tanks, Russia will actually make more time available for training, since the troops won't have to spend as much time keeping the old clunkers functional. About a third of the tank strength will be scrapped, although the number of antitank and antiaircraft missiles will be more than doubled. The number of divisions won't have to be cut, just the average portion of full-strength personnel. More divisions will have only 10–20 percent of their manpower, instead of 30–50 percent. As in the past, these units will be filled out by former conscripts in the event of a major war.

Types of Armies

There are about 165 armies in the world. However, most of them are not real armies. As determined by their primary role, there are essentially four types of armies: ceremonial armies, political armies, police armies, and real armies. For recently independent countries, having an army is like having a flag, a symbol of sovereignty, and besides, it looks good when paraded on official occasions. In addition, in many developing countries the army represents a sort of political party, regularly staging coups, in some cases with different units even espousing differing political lines. This is nothing new: The ancient Greek and Roman empires fell because the professional soldiers eventually spent too much time fighting with each other over who would run the show. Then, too, many armies are essentially police armies; their primary purpose is to keep internal order, frequently by means of massacre and other forms of terrorism against their own populations. Real armies, although they have ceremonial, political, and police functions, are those that devote most of their time and energy to getting ready for war with an external foe. No more than a third of the armies in the world are real armies.

To some extent, the type of army a country has reflects its needs. But needs can change, and ceremonial, political, and police armies usually don't do too well when confronted by a proper army. Consider some recent instances. In Sri Lanka, the army, a largely ceremonial force, virtually disintegrated when confronted by the Tamil insurgency, and quickly developed a penchant for massacre rather than battle, which only exacerbated the situation. Similarly, the Libyan Army, which exists primarily as a police force and ceremonial body, has proved itself incompetent against four opponents—Chadians, Egyptians, Tunisians, and Tanzanians—in a series of clashes going back more than a decade. And the Argentine Army, primarily a political and police force, found that the British Army and the Royal

Marines were not quite what they were expecting, after several years of "counterinsurgency" warfare in which some 12,000 people died, mostly unarmed and including numerous women and children. Of course, under pressure, the character of an army can change. But this is difficult, painful, and expensive. In 1948 the Arab armies were largely ceremonial forces with some police experience, which did them little good against Israel, with thousands of World War II veterans in its ranks. Defeat tended to politicize most of the Arab armies—in the fifties it was said that there were three political parties in Syria, "the I Army Corps, the II Army Corps, and the III Army Corps"—which led to further defeats in 1956 and 1967. It was only then that the principal Arab armies began to become real armies, whereupon their tactical performance improved markedly. There is, incidentally, a fifth type of army, which may be termed the commercial, of which there is only one example, the Fijian Army, which, while a well-trained and efficient force, has as its primary purpose the acquisition of foreign exchange for that island nation by means of remittances from its battalions on international peacekeeping duties in the Middle East.

Dial-a-Battle

Vehicle simulators, primarily for aircraft, have been used for over fifty years. These have become much more sophisticated, with many aircraft simulators so realistic that pilots using them often forget they are not in actual aircraft, as evidenced by the sweat pouring off their faces and the nervous timber of their voices as they participate in the simulated combat. Current combat-aircraft simulators also allow more than one fighter to operate together against realistic opponents. The major problem with these simulators is that they are expensive, often more expensive than the aircraft they simulate. In the late seventies, the U.S. Army realized that what it needed more than realistic simulators of vehicles was a realistic system for training the units that used the vehicles. By using the then-new inexpensive microprocessors to create less realistic simulators, the army could afford simulators for entire units. Another recent innovation, inexpensive local area networks (LANs), could link all these simulators together, and using satellite links allowed groups of LAN-linked simulators to train with each other. By the late eighties, the system was working. The graphics were crude, and the equipment in the simulator was not exactly what would be found in a tank. But the crews didn't seem to mind. They demonstrated the same fear and stress pilots have long expressed in highly accurate aircraft simulators. The system, SIMNET, uses microcomputers to hold an electronic map of the battle area and keep track of individual vehicle status (damage, fuel, ammunition, etc.). It is a marked move away from sophisticated technology at any cost. Each tank, APC, or artillery simulator costs only $250,000. A helicopter version costs $350,000. The only thing lacking is a simulator for infantry, which is forthcoming, although not without difficulty and probably much greater expense. This type of simulator recognizes how important it is to train vehicle crews and the units they must operate with. This pays enormous dividends in combat.

And No Soldiers, Either

"One must not judge everyone in the world by his qualities as a soldier: otherwise we should have no civilization."—Erwin Rommel, World War II German general, "the Desert Fox"

Bore-Sight a Weapon.

"Bore-sight" means to align the fire-control system with the cannon, usually on tanks or aircraft. In use, the weapons get out of alignment with the fire-control system, so they have to be adjusted from time to time. Bore-sighting involves actually looking down the bore of the gun barrel to reference points and adjusting the fire-control system accordingly.

"Who's Wagging Whom?"

In modern armies the proportion of the troops who actually engage in combat has been declining steadily in favor of those who perform logistical, administrative, and other support services. Some notion of the extent of this trend may be gained by examining the "teeth-to-tail" ratio in the U.S. Army in this century.

Period	Year	Combatants	Noncombatants
WW I	1914	87%	13%
	1918	66	34
WW II	1939	88	12
	1945	57	43
Korea	1950	67	33
	1953	60	40
Vietnam	1964	75	25
	1972	53	47
Present	1990	50	50

Interestingly, the ratio of combat to noncombat troops at the beginning of a war is always higher than that at the end. Some of this change is due to the misuse of the seemingly limitless supply of manpower made possible by lavish wartime draft calls—"Let's use some of these guys to paint the rocks around headquarters"—but much of the increase in support personnel is a reflection of the changing character of war. Modern weapons consume ammunition at a prodigious rate, and massive logistical and maintenance arrangements are necessary to keep the combat troops in action. The technical and administrative skills necessary to do this can be improvised far more readily than can combat skills, particularly given that in peacetime armies tend to be far smaller than in war, so in peacetime armies usually have more combat-trained personnel. In wartime, while the expansion of the administrative and logistical base of the army may result in an apparent statistical absurdity, with almost as many men behind the front as on it, in fact, the guys on the firing line cannot survive without the enormous numbers passing the ammunition and other tools. However, given the relative immunity from danger of the rear-area personnel, this can create a serious morale problem, as was the case in Vietnam, where only about 20 percent of the troops in the theater of operations were actually engaged in direct contact with the enemy.

Russian Elite Troops

The policy of selecting your best troops for use in separate "elite" units has a long history. This has one major drawback, in that you have potential NCOs and exceptional soldiers withheld from the majority of units. This significantly lowers the quality of the deprived units. It is often discovered that the benefits gained from having the more effective elite units do not compensate for the lowered quality of the majority of units. Despite this, during the 1970s the Russians began to expand their elite parachute and commando forces. By the mid-eighties, they had a quarter-million such troops, primarily in the army. This paid off in Afghanistan, where Regular Army units proved ineffective in combat. However, the generally low caliber of NCOs in the Russian Army is only made worse by allowing the better troops to volunteer for the elite units. The Russians insist that they do not cull each year's conscripts for the elite forces. But in practice the paratroopers tend to be ethnic Russians, and the training washes out those who haven't got "the right stuff." In the event of a major war, the leadership shortage at the troop level in the majority of Russian units could prove disastrous, as it has in the past. The Russians feel they have no choice in this matter, as they need at least a few units they can depend on for reliable combat duty in peacetime.

"Quantity Has a Quality All Its Own."

As a preliminary to negotiations on reducing conventional forces in Europe, NATO released its estimates for NATO and Warsaw Pact (WP) forces. They show:

Category	NATO	Warsaw Pact
Troops	2,200,000	3,100,000
Combat Aircraft	3,997	8,250
Tanks	16,424	51,500
Helicopters	2,419	3,700
APCs	4,143	22,400
Other Armored Vehicles	35,351	71,000
Artillery (100 + mm)	13,857	43,400
Antitank Weapons	18,240	44,200
Air-Defense Weapons	10,109	24,400
Self-propelled Assault Bridges	454	2,550

Satellite photos make it fairly easy to get an accurate count, but the mention of disparity in quantity between NATO and WP raises an uncomfortable subject: quality. Combat experience with NATO (frequently U.S.) and WP (mainly Russian) weapons in the past has shown the NATO stuff performing much more effectively. The Russians acknowledge some technological edge to the West, but frequently mention the relative lack of skill among Third World users of Russian weapons. Yet combat experience in this century has shown that Russian troops are not quite up to the same standard as Western soldiers, at least not on a man-for-man basis and especially not in the opening stages of a war. So agreement on any force reductions in Europe requires that the quality factor be dealt with. This leads to some embarrassing questions as to just how good, or bad, WP weapons and troops are. To get a lot of WP forces withdrawn, NATO must make the case that the WP stuff is very good. To keep a lot of their forces, WP negotiators must push the "we are ineffective" angle. Each side will have to profess to being worse than it thinks it is in order to retain more of its forces.

Let the Market Decide.

It is generally recognized, even in Communist countries, that a free market is the most efficient way of determining the true value of an item. Consider tanks. There are a lot of U.S. M-48 and Russian T-55 models on the market, both products of 1950s technology. With great consistency, prospective buyers are willing to pay as much as 50 percent more for a reconditioned M-48 than for a late-model T-55, and still more for a "basic" 1960s vintage U.S. M-60a3, in contrast to Russian T-72s, of roughly the same vintage. Considering the relative performance of these vehicles in past battles, this price differential appears to accurately reflect the combat value of each tank.

Got a Lite?

One lesson the United States thought it learned from Vietnam was the need for division-sized forces that could be readily deployed to remote trouble spots. It was quickly realized that a U.S. Mechanized

Infantry Division required 1,500 C-141 sorties and nearly two weeks to reach the Middle East. After many studies, it was determined that with a new type of division only 500 sorties and one week would do the trick. Thus was the new Light Infantry Division created. Troop strength was reduced to 10,500, largely by eliminating a lot of support troops and heavy weapons. Dropping tracked vehicles like APCs and tanks eliminated not only crews but also a lot of mechanics and supply personnel, plus an enormous amount of airlift. By 1985 there was talk of making most U.S. divisions "Lite" by the end of the century.

Then reality hit. The U.S. Light Infantry Division (LID) was a throwback to World War I. The infantry got where they wanted to go by walking. Yet most potential Third World opponents used vehicle-borne infantry. The enemy troops might only be running around in buses and pickup trucks, but they would be moving a lot faster than U.S. LIDs. It was a ticklish situation, as the addition of more vehicles would make movement of the LID by air more difficult. The LID has not yet been in combat, so no one is sure just how badly things might turn out. Meanwhile, the three LIDs are drifting toward limbo and have attracted the attention of the budget cutters, who observe that their elimination would save some $9.5 billion over five years.

An Army in a Taxicab?

At the beginning of 1989, the smallest proper army in the world was that of the Gambia, which consisted of just forty-nine officers and men. Organized into a single company, the little army is equipped with eight Ferret scout cars, recoilless-rifles, and small arms, and is supplemented by 400 paramilitary police troops, with whom they form a battalion. The distinction of having the second-smallest army in the world is shared by Dominica and Grenada. Both West Indian countries have armies of about eighty men each.

Refugees and Military Operations

In 1914, when Germany invaded Belgium and then swept into northern France, several million people fled their homes to head south seeking safety, greatly impeding the advance, and then the retreat, of the French, British, and Belgian armies. In 1940, when the Germans came again, over 2 million Dutch and Belgian civilians fled before them, followed shortly by about 8 million French civilians, so that within the first five days of war over 10 million refugees were on the road, once more greatly hindering the movements of the Allied armies, while hardly slowing up the advance of the enemy, who ruthlessly swept them aside with bombers and machine-gun fire, a feat that the Germans would duplicate in Russia the following year, though the crowds were smaller, as many Russians at first thought the Germans had come to rescue them from the Communists. In late 1944 and early 1945, as Russian troops began to overrun East Prussia, Silesia, and Pomerania, about 13 million German civilians took to the road, fleeing westward, once again impeding the operations of defending forces, while over 2 million perished as a result of the enemy's onslaught. About half of the population of West Germany—which is not very wide—resides within sixty kilometers of East Germany and Czechoslovakia. Within a day or two of a Russian invasion of Western Europe, 20–30 million refugees could easily be on the roads westward. The problems that such a stream of humanity would create for NATO armies are unimaginable.

Precious Resource

"Strategy is the art of making use of time and space. I am less concerned about the latter than the former. Space we can recover, lost time never."—Napoleon Bonaparte, French soldier

What Am I Bid for this Fine T-62?

One day, while on maneuvers in Czechoslovakia, a Russian tank crew got lost. Wandering around, they soon came upon a country inn. Having no money for drinks, they cleverly sold their tank to the innkeeper for as much booze as they could drink and carry. They were eventually caught, while sleeping it off. The tank was recovered, hidden behind the inn, before it could be cut up for scrap and parts.

Down for the Count

Although no one talks much about it, in 1953 the U.S. Army "took a dive," the 45th Infantry Division of the Arizona National Guard hitting the mat during the filming of the motion picture *The War of the Worlds*. More recently, the New York City 42nd Infantry Division played a similar role against supernatural forces in the film *Ghostbusters*. All this may explain why the army is so eager to obtain high-tech weapons. After all, what would we do if some alien stormtroopers from outer space *did* land armed with death rays?

But That's a Secret.

About fifteen years ago, a major New York-based war-game publisher was preparing a design that would simulate tactical armored combat between NATO and Warsaw Pact forces in Central Europe. Research into the characteristics of the tanks, armored personnel carriers, and antitank weapons of the two sides proved difficult in a rather surprising way. Various official publications of the U.S. Army provided extensive information on the most up-to-date Russian equipment, but were rather sparing of data on a number of new American items, with little asterisks scattered about various tables to indicate confidential information. Unfortunately, though things like ground pressure, horsepower-weight ratio, and armor basis may seem rather esoteric, the missing data was, in many cases, of particular importance to the integrity of the design of the game. The problem appeared to be insoluble until one staff member by chance wandered into the Four Continents Bookstore on Fifth Avenue, a Russian-operated outlet for Soviet bloc publications in English. Lo, there in the history and military section was a manual on tank warfare that contained a good deal of information about even the most recent Western equipment, information that would subsequently prove to be reliable. However, true to the patterns of Cold War warfare, the book was rather sparing of data on a number of contemporary Russian designs, with a liberal sprinkling of asterisks on all the tables to indicate confidential information.

"I Beg Your Pardon!"

At British Army maneuvers in July of 1987, a battalion of 600 heavily armed territorials—national guardsmen, in U.S. parlance—managed to get itself lost during night exercises. They were supposed to move into a nearby village, which was expecting them, and "occupy" it. They strayed out of the maneuver area with the result that they occupied the wrong village at about dawn, causing some of the startled residents to think that the Big One had begun.

War in Peacetime

Except for a brief period in 1968, the British Army has been continuously in action somewhere in the world since 1940.

Tons of Pain

During World War II, each enemy casualty required from one to five tons of bombs and shells. Modern soldiers are better-protected by body armor and more plentiful armored vehicles. Current bombs and shells, however, are made more lethal, using either hundreds of bomblets per bomb or shell ("cluster weapons") or greater accuracy ("smart weapons"). It is difficult to determine just how much tonnage is required per casualty today, because these new weapons have not seen heavy use. However, it probably still requires a ton or more of munitions per casualty. The big losers are those troops without modern protective devices who encounter an enemy with modern bombs and shells.

Reconnaissance by Fire

Shooting at an area to see if anyone responds is known as "reconnaissance by fire." A variant, "reconnaissance by grenades," involves chucking grenades at an area to see what happens. This is a standard practice during house-to-house fighting. It saves your troops a lot of grief, but can be tough on civilians who happen to be cowering nearby.

Just Being Neighborly

Since, out of deference to the sensibilities of the Soviet Union and its Warsaw Pact allies, the Austrian Army prefers not to conduct its autumn maneuvers in the vicinity of the Czechoslovakian or Hungarian frontiers, these annual exercises are usually conducted in the interior of the country, or over near the Italian and West German frontiers. Neither NATO nation appears to object to the proceedings.

General Fumblefingers

The U.S. Army does a great deal of war-gaming using computerized models to enable field officers to gain some familiarity with the conduct of war under relatively realistic conditions. These games frequently involve senior officers directing simulations of operations on ground over which they would have to fight in the event of an actual war. Needless to note, one area that is a continuing favorite for such war games is the Central Front in Germany. Now, by an accident of inter-Allied politics during World War II, the American occupation zone in Germany remains the present deployment area for the bulk of U.S. forces assigned to defend the Central Front, specifically Bavaria. By an accident of geography, this happens to be the area of Germany that is most favorable to the defense. As a result, the strongest army in NATO has the most favorable terrain, while some of the weaker allies, such as the Belgians and the Netherlanders, have sectors that are highly unfavorable. Nevertheless, American officers assigned to play the Russian role in the war games almost inevitably make their principal offensive efforts against the American sector, perhaps subconsciously hoping to see how well the home team can do. And similarly, officers assigned to the NATO side almost invariably assume that the principal Russian thrust will come, of course, in the American sector. But there are always a few spoilsports, and so, from time to time, a clever fellow assigned to play the Russians decides to hit the Belgians or the Dutch or even the British. The result, more often than not, is a sobering lesson in the efficacy of war plans that are predicated on the assumption that the enemy will do what we expect of him. And more than one officer has stepped away from the gaming table older but wiser.

Who's On First?

"Battles are very confusing."—John Keegan, British military historian

Call Out the Reserves!

Not only have Americans contributed considerable amounts of anti-aircraft missiles, small arms, communications equipment, and medical supplies to support the Afghan guerrillas in their war against the Kabul government, but nearly 700 mules as well, which marks the second time in recent years that equines have been used in a so-called mechanized war. The first was when the British drafted some of the local horseflesh during the Falklands conflict when their motor transport proved inadequate.

"The Names Have Been Changed to Protect the Innocent."

By hoary tradition, the opposing sides in war games, whether played on a board with cardstock counters or in the open with live bodies, are designated as the "blues" and the "reds." An equally antique custom assigns the designation "blue" to the side representing the defending "good guys" and "red" to that representing the attacking "enemy." However, on NATO maneuvers in Germany, this 150-year-old tradition is regularly discarded, at least in part. Thus, while the "good guys" are still called the "Blue Army," those playing the "enemy" are termed the "Orange Army." This is done out of deference to the sensibilities of the Soviet Army, the real "Red Army," just across the inter-German border, which provides the raison d'être for the maneuvers in the first place. Nevertheless, though the name may be "orange," the colors used on the maps still show the enemy as "the Reds." Most of the European neutrals follow this practice as well. The U.S. Army also uses terms such as "the threat" or "the aggressor" to describe the bad guys. In Communist armies, the good guys are always red and the bad guys are blue (and other colors).

No Pictures

Personnel assigned to the Special Forces and to Special Operations units are not permitted to wear their distinctive crossed-arrows branch insignia in official photos.

U.S. Nuclear Weapons for Saudia Arabia

U.S. negotiations to sell Saudi Arabia M-1 tanks got snagged on one curious issue. The top-of-the-line U.S. ammunition for the M-1's gun uses depleted uranium. This metal is one of the heaviest known, and is very effective in punching holes through enemy tanks. It is so named because all the harmful radiation has been "depleted" from it as a by-product of manufacturing nuclear fuel. But because it's still considered a "nuclear" material, it is controlled by the U.S. Nuclear Regulatory Commission. In effect, these antitank shells are technically "nuclear weapons." Because of U.S. laws restricting the export of nuclear weapons, problems arose in selling the shells to the Saudis. Although these shells have not been used in combat yet, they have been tested against various types of armor. Rumors persist that when they penetrate armor and come under enormous stress, they do produce brief but high bursts of radiation. This seems to be because a chunk of depleted uranium will absorb most of the radiation it produces through normal decay, which it cannot do once shattered. However, it is unlikely that the resulting "pulse" of radiation will cause injury or illness, particularly given the damage produced by the explosive effect and shell fragments.

Better Living Through Motorization

One beneficial side effect of the elimination of horses from armies is that troops are no longer susceptible to mange, glanders, or any of a number of other equine diseases that can infect people.

Old Paintski

It wasn't until the early 1960s that Russia completely eliminated horse-drawn transport in its army. In 1950, half the transport vehicles in the army were still horse-drawn. The United States had eliminated horse-drawn transport nearly twenty years earlier.

Motor Stables

The common term for performing maintenance on vehicles is "motor stables," derived from the term for taking care of horses in the old army.

Cousin Germain

There are two 82nd Airborne Divisions in the world. The better-known one is the U.S. 82nd Airborne, descended from a division raised in 1917, which was converted to an airborne formation in 1941. It distinguished itself in World War II, and remains a major element in the U.S. strategic reserve. The other is the Nigerian 82nd Airborne Division, descended from the British 82nd African Division raised in 1943, which distinguished itself in Burma during World War II. Later reactivated for service during the Nigerian Civil War (1969–72), the division presently constitutes the elite element of the Nigerian Army, with airborne, amphibious, and special-warfare capabilities.

Up Close and Personal

In this century, and particularly since 1940, the average range of engagement for infantry troops has been under 50 meters, while for tanks it's remained under 500 meters. Oddly enough, the infantry has made remarkable progress in creating more effective short-range weapons, while the tank designers have spent prodigious sums to create guns that are more accurate at longer ranges.

"Boots-Boots-Boots—Movin' Up an' Down Again!"

Over the last ten years, the British Army has issued three different types of boots to its troops, and is currently working on yet a fourth design, which it promises will be "radically different."

Road Space

Imagine a typical Russian tank army, normally consisting of three or four armored divisions and one or two motor rifle divisions plus supporting artillery, antiaircraft, engineer, helicopter, and organic service units, with some 65,000 to 75,000 men, 1,600 to 1,700 tanks, and 1,000 to 1,200 other armored fighting vehicles, plus nearly 200 helicopters and aircraft, 700 pieces of artillery, and 400 rocket launchers. If such an army were to march westward from Berlin along a single road (a matter about which NATO would presumably raise an objection) its head would reach Aachen on the Rhine River at about the time its tail was leaving Berlin, a distance of about 300 miles as the crow flies, but considerably more given what Napoleon called the "minor sinuosities of roads." With normal attachments of separate combat units, specialist troops, and logistical formations, the head of the column would be halfway between Brussels and the North Sea before the tail cleared Berlin, another 150 miles.

"The Right Way, the Wrong Way, and the . . ."

The army way is usually described as "SOP," which is short for "standard operating procedure," the way the army wishes things to be done. SOPs, while frequently the butt of jokes and the hobgoblin of little minds, are actually an invaluable element of military life. The object of training is to establish the norms of behavior under various conditions so that when orders are received, they will be executed in the spirit in which they were intended. This greatly eases communications and command by reducing the amount of detail that orders must include. It is thus not for nothing that on military staffs, training, which seeks to develop SOPs as the norms of behavior, is entrusted to the same officers who would be responsible for planning operations in the event of war. SOPs are written for the lowest common denominator; thus, they indicate the education level of a military organization and are a prime reason behind the military's consistent interest in well-educated soldiers. Russian SOPs are much simpler than those found in Western armed forces, which should tell you something about what the respective armed forces expect from their troops.

T/O&E

T/O&E is military shorthand for "Table of Organization and Equipment," the official statement of the number of men and equipment considered proper for a particular type of formation, and the way in which the formation is organized. The listings are meticulously detailed, down to the number of clerks, pistols, Hummers, and so forth. Large T/O&E units, such as divisions, are built up through the grouping of smaller T/O&E units, such as battalions, which are in turn formed from still smaller T/O&E units, companies. Higher formations, such as corps and armies, are not usually T/O&E, although made up of T/O&E formations. Creating a T/O&E is a fine art, as demands for complexity and completeness must be balanced with the need for flexibility and agility, as well as available resources. Manpower considerations are always difficult, as one man more or less at the company level can translate into thousands of men armywide. The uniformity and historical consistency provided by the T/O&Es is the foundation of all military intelligence. T/O&Es tend to evolve slowly and reflect accompanying changes in doctrine and training.

Mobile Warfare

Counting everything from tanks to trailers, and from howitzers to Hummers, a U.S. armored division has 5,989 vehicles, or about one for every three men.

Divisions

The basic money of account in ground warfare is the division, a force of 5,000 to 20,000 troops, combining infantry, artillery, armor, and support elements under one command and capable of sustaining independent operations for a relatively extended period. Junior partner to the division is the brigade or regiment, also usually a combination of elements, three of which generally go to make up a division. Counting only troops actually organized into divisions and brigades, at the middle of 1989 there were about 1,050 divisions on active duty in the world, roughly one for every 4.8 million people. These figures rise to about 1,350, or one for every 3.8 million people, if organized reserve forces are included. Counting such reserve forces, the ten countries with the greatest number of divisions are:

Nation	Divisions
Russia	210
China	200
Vietnam	60
North Korea	50
U.S.	41
India	41
Turkey	40
Ethiopia	31
Iran	30
South Korea	27

The raw number of divisions that a power can mobilize on short notice is not necessarily the only way to evaluate its military strength. If one considers how many divisions a nation fields on the basis of its population, an entirely different picture emerges, as can be seen in the top ten powers in terms of millions of people per division upon mobilization:

Nation	Mil/Div
Israel	0.3 (16)
Switzerland	0.4 (18)
North Korea	0.4 (50)
North Yemen	0.4 (13)
Uruguay	0.5 (6)
Paraguay	0.5 (9)

Nation	Mil/Div
Albania	0.5 (6)
Cuba	0.6 (18)
Bolivia	0.6 (12)
Finland	0.6 (8)

Note that none of the NATO or Warsaw Pact powers have made this list, though three of the rather heavily armed European neutrals have. Of course, only about half of the armies indicated here are equipped and trained as proper combat armies. The million population per division figures for the Warsaw Pact powers are:

Bulgaria	1.0 (9)
Czechoslovakia	1.1 (14)
Russia	1.3 (210)
Hungary	1.8 (6)
Poland	2.0 (18)
East Germany	2.8 (6)
Romania	2.9 (8)

The comparable figures for the NATO powers are:

Greece	0.7 (15)	West Germany	3.3 (18)
Turkey	1.4 (40)	The Netherlands	4.5 (3.3)
Portugal	1.7 (6)	Belgium	4.9 (2)
Norway	2.1 (2)	U.S.	6.0 (41)
Spain	2.5 (16)	Italy	7.2 (8)
Denmark	2.5 (2)	Britain	9.4 (6)
France	2.8 (20)	Canada	12.7 (2)

Luxembourg and Iceland have no divisions.

As can be seen, neither superpower does as well as some of its allies. In fact, the European neutrals do better on average than either power bloc. Aside from Switzerland, Albania, and Finland, noted above, figures for the principal neutrals are:

Sweden	0.9 (9)
Austria	0.9 (8)
Yugoslavia	1.0 (24)

We'll Do It with Mirrors

Claiming to base their estimate on their experiences in World War II, the Russians long maintained that in any future conventional war their armies will be able to advance about seventy kilometers a day. However, their best sustainable advances in World War II were of about 50 km a day, and those occurred in late 1944 and early 1945, at a time when the Red Army had more than three years of hard-won combat experience under its belt, and were made against greatly inferior German forces lacking air support. In the event of a war in Central Europe, the Russians would find their advance impeded not merely by NATO air and ground forces (which by their own estimate are virtually equal to theirs in numbers), but also by their own lack of experience under fire, a failing that would probably tell more heavily against them than against their opponents, who would have the same problem (it is always easier to defend than attack). The net result could as easily be a stalemate or a reverse as an expected three-day advance to the Rhine.

Paperwork

"The concentration of troops can be done fast and easy, on paper."—Radomir Putnik, Serbian field marshal, 1912–17

Development and the Future of War

Although even relatively large-scale maps continue to show cities as little points, most cities in the industrialized world sprawl languidly far beyond their formal boundaries if one considers their suburbs, which are in many cases quite densely built up. The urbanized belt that extends virtually without interruption from the northern suburbs of Boston to the southern fringes of Washington is being rapidly duplicated in Germany (in the Rhineland, the Ruhr, and other areas), across northern and western Italy, throughout Belgium and the Netherlands, across vast areas of France, and in much of South Korea and Japan. Such conurbations are increasingly taking on military importance, for they represent significant obstacles to rapid advances by armored forces. It would be virtually impossible to move an army through such an area in the face of even relatively light opposition, and their increasing sprawl may make it equally difficult to find a way around them, even given the existence of superhighways. In many other parts of the world, resort development is rapidly encroaching on militarily valuable beachfronts, creating walls of reinforced concrete structures that would greatly enhance the defense while providing significant obstacles to rapid movements off the beach. Landings of the sort that characterized much of World War II in Europe from the Western standpoint—Sicily, Salerno, Normandy, Provence—difficult as they were in 1943 and 1944, might well be impossible today in the face of equal resistance. Note also that West Germans show an uncommon fondness for reinforced concrete in their civilian commercial buildings.

High Tech, Low Labor

The experimental 9th High-Tech Division, a highly agile formation designed for ease in airportability with a high combat potential in a "fluid" environment, proved so popular in the early eighties, what with its "dune buggies" and other unorthodox equipment, that there was talk of raising several such divisions for use in odd sandy parts of the globe. But then some wiser heads took a closer look. As it turned out, the 9th could put only 648 men into foxholes, roughly 4.5 percent of its strength, in contrast to the 82nd Airborne Division, which has a foxhole strength of over 5,000 men, roughly 33 percent of its total manpower. The High-Tech required too many men to man and maintain the equipment. As a result, soon afterward the 9th High-Tech Division was reorganized as the 9th Motorized Division, and later became the 9th Mechanized Division, with a foxhole strength of about 5,000. While much heavier and less agile than under its old T/O&E, the 9th now has a considerably better chance in a sustained slug-out.

Water Obstacles

It's not easy invading, or defending, Western Europe. One of the more troublesome items is water, in the form of rivers, streams, and canals. When moving east or west through Western Europe, you will encounter a minor water obstacle, on average, every 5–10 km. Many of these can be forded, but some require a self-propelled bridge. Every 30–60 km you find an obstacle at least 100 meters wide. These require some more serious bridge-building. Every 100–150 km you come up against a major river (1,000 or more meters wide). There are many bridges, but with a war going on, the ones you want to use may be destroyed or may simply not exist at the place you must cross.

There's Accuracy, and There's Accuracy.

Modern artillery can hurl 90-pound shells over 20 km with considerable accuracy. But not absolute accuracy. The troops calling for the fire have to take into account unavoidable accuracy problems caused by wind, humidity, air density, temperature, and minute differences in the propellant charges for each shell. For example, a 155-mm shell fired at a range of 15 km will normally be off by at least 2–3 meters right or left and 60–70 meters long or short of the aiming point, assuming the gunners aimed at the right location in the first place. As the range increases, so does the probable error. At maximum range of about 24 km, the right-left error will be 10–15 meters and the long/short error will by 90–110 meters. This is why you hear of troops being hit by "short rounds" from their own artillery. It's often unavoidable because the battlefield is not a neat and orderly place, and troops often find themselves too close to the enemy when they must call for artillery fire. In a situation like that, the troops at the front have to weigh the chances of getting hit by their own artillery fire versus what damage the nearby enemy forces can do to them. War is hell for a large number of reasons.

The High Cost of Being Next

When it was revealed in 1988 that Russia had equipped thousands of its tanks with reactive armor to defeat Western ATGMs, there was much interest in how these missiles would be upgraded and how quickly. As it turned out, Western ATGMs were being steadily upgraded over the years, and there was no big problem in stepping up the process to deal with the latest Russian move.

The next generation of Western ATGMs are another matter: These are expected to be substantially improved. The chief U.S. candidate for the ATGM of the nineties is the FOG-M (Fiber Optic Guided Missile). These are expected to cost $125,000 per missile for the first 16,000. Range is expected to be about eight kilometers, with a larger warhead and increased accuracy and lethality. Weighing at least 100 pounds each, they would only be fired from vehicles. While FOG-M would cost over ten times as much as current ATGMs, such as TOW, it would have several advantages. First, the operator and launcher would be less vulnerable to counterattack. FOG-M is fired straight up, then it levels off and heads for the target. Next, the FOG-M would be more accurate. A fiber optic data link would carry information from the sensors in the warhead to the operator's TV-like screen. The sensors, when perfected, could penetrate smoke, fog, and darkness. And the FOG-M could carry a more powerful warhead, which would make enhanced enemy armor less effective.

FOG-M would probably not completely replace lighter ATGM, but would assume much of the workload now assigned to systems like TOW. (All this assumes, of course, that the FOG-M works.)

Standardization in the Russian Army

It's much overrated. In practice, the Russians have two major problems. One, they actually have in service a larger number of models of the same equipment types than any other army. For example, first-line tank divisions can have four models of tanks (T-62, T-64, T-72, T-80) as well as significant variations in equipment for each model. Their second error is that they allow regiments, or even battalions, to have more than one type of tank. This needlessly complicates training, logistics, and maintenance. These problems extend to many other weapons and equipment types. They get away with it most of the time because they rarely use their weapons in peacetime. When they do stage maneuvers, it is almost always in carefully organized exercises whose primary purpose is to look good, not to give the equipment a realistic workout. This fact is often overlooked by Western analysts.

Space Problem

Space is increasingly on the minds of defense planners, the terrestrial, not the outer, kind. The growing capabilities of modern weaponry and the fluidity of contemporary tactics are creating problems in providing adequate training at existing military bases. A World War II fighter required about five square miles of maneuvering room, while its modern counterpart needs about forty square miles, and fighter aircraft currently on the drawing boards will probably require double that space. Similarly, a World War II–vintage U.S. Army mechanized infantry battalion, with about 1,000 troops, needed about six square miles to perform its exercises, while its modern counterpart, which has fewer men, needs about 125 square miles. Now, consider the real estate needs of a full division, with fifteen combat battalions, which must train together in peace so that they can fight together in war.

Meanwhile, the maximum range of even conventional artillery has doubled or tripled since World War II, while that of missile artillery now reaches into the hundreds and thousands of miles. And new types of munitions, such as "smart" bombs and robotic weapons, will also make extensive demands on maneuvering grounds. The enormous areas involved pretty much preclude realistic training for most powers, particularly those in Europe and the smaller Middle Eastern states: Israel is so small that the hottest jets are already almost incapable of turning within national airspace when operating at high speed. As a result, several armed forces have attempted to secure training space in other nations. Belgian Air Force pilots will soon join the West German and British airmen who have long trained at U.S. air bases such as Sheppard in Texas, Nellis in Nevada, and Williams in Arizona, and at Canadian ranges at Goose Bay, Labrador, all in remote desert or wilderness areas. The Italian ranges at Deccimomanu, in Sardinia, are regularly used by several NATO air forces and Switzerland, which probably constitutes a violation of that country's historic neutrality policy. Two other European neutrals, Austria and Sweden, may be working on some sort of cooperation in this regard.

On the ground, Britain and several other friendly countries have become involved in training at places such as Fort Irwin, with its thousand square miles, as well as at Fort Ord, both in California, and at Canadian bases in Manitoba and Alberta. But this is only a short-term solution, for these places cannot handle the demands of both domestic and NATO ground training. Moreover, problems are developing in the United States and Canada. Environmental concerns have limited certain kinds of training, such as marine amphibious exercises. Perhaps more serious, however, is the effect of increasing suburbanization. Many posts formerly isolated in the wilderness are now within sight or sound of extensive suburbs. Formerly isolated Norton Air Force Base, long an important training installation in the desert sixty miles east of Los Angeles, is now being approached by that city's suburbs. Because it is enmeshed in Los Angeles's air-traffic congestion, the base is to be closed. Fort Belvoir, formerly nestled in a wooded part of northern Virginia, a thirty-minute drive from the Pentagon, is now so hemmed in by Washington's suburbs that it is no longer suited for the army's engineering school, which is moving to a less congested area in Missouri. The problem, which is expected to get worse, is currently under study.

Lost in the Clouds

Over ten years in development, the U.S. Hellfire missile finally came into use during the late eighties, with over 30,000 ordered. Basically an air-launched, "fire and forget" antitank missile with an 8-km range, it finds its target by homing on laser light reflected off an enemy vehicle. This enables the firing helicopter to avoid exposing itself to the enemy. The laser is provided by ground troops or another aircraft, often a helicopter. Unfortunately, lasers are degraded by fog, mist, and smoke. Moreover, it is easy to spot where the laser beam is coming from and shoot at it. Without the reflected laser light to home on, the Hellfire is lost. This can be a serious problem as the most likely area of use, Central Europe, is an area frequently covered with fog, and Russian armored vehicles carry lots of smoke. Another problem is that the onboard computer is not fast enough to handle launches at more than 600 km per hour. This makes it difficult to launch from fixed-wing aircraft.

Not unmindful of these deficiencies, the defense contractors are devising expensive improvements. These include new seekers that do not require someone else to keep a laser beam on the target. Either an infrared (heat) sensor or millimeter wave-radar seeker are the most likely candidates. Infrared is cheaper, but is also degraded by smoke and fog. A faster onboard computer will allow launch from fast moving fixed-wing aircraft. The new computer will also allow Hellfire to dive on armored vehicles, thus avoiding reactive armor. Air launch from fixed-wing aircraft will also increase Hellfire range 25–30 percent. A more efficient rocket motor will increase basic range from eight to eleven kilometers. Different warheads are being developed. Meanwhile, Hellfire is being repackaged for firing from land vehicles and ships. Given the Western track record with high-tech weapons, the Hellfire will probably continue to develop into a reliable and effective weapon. In effect, Hellfire will truly become a robotic, "fire and forget" antitank weapon. Reality is catching up with science fiction as more of these "fire and forget" weapons reach the troops.

Immobile Mobile Artillery

Experience to date with self-propelled artillery shows that these gun vehicles rarely move more than 20–30 km a day. Even the most mobile forms of warfare do little to increase this distance. While in theory the guns can move several hundred kilometers a day, problems with finding targets and coordinating operations with the movement of other units, both friend and foe, greatly reduces the distance the guns can actually move. There is also a major problem with ammunition supply, as the convoys of trucks or armored carriers holding ammo supplies must make frequent contact with the guns.

Kaserne

Kaserne (German for "barracks") is also U.S. Army slang for barracks, due to occupation duties since World War II. The term is not widely used outside Germany. For example, in Korea the barracks are commonly called "the compound."

A Weighty Problem

A properly outfitted medieval knight was less burdened by his armor than a modern infantryman is by his full set of equipment. After all, though a knight's armor might occasionally weigh as much as 100 pounds, it was rather evenly distributed over his body, and he had a horse to help carry the load, while an infantry's burden rests disproportionately between his shoulders, and he has only his two legs to help carry it. In this century, the weight of an infantryman's equipment and arms has consistently been excessive. About eighty pounds has been rather common, a hundred pounds not unusual. The Russian "norm" for paratroopers is eighty-eight pounds. In extraordinary cases, the load could run much higher, so that some American troops went into Grenada and Panama with 120 pounds, and in the Falklands British troops "yomped" as much as 140 pounds. Armies have been aware of the problem for almost as long as it has existed. Studies by the U.S. Army suggest that no soldier should carry more than about 30 percent of his body weight—say, forty-eight pounds—into combat, nor more than about 45 percent—seventy-five pounds—in other circumstances. Yet efforts to lighten the load have proven only moderately successful, and run counter to the trend toward more gadgets and specialized equipment needed to meet the changing character of the battlefield: In effect, any savings gained by using lighter equipment of one sort is canceled by the need to add yet another doodad.

Consider the rifleman's basic load:

Clothing, Boots, Personal Items	21.1 pounds
M-16, Loaded and with 6 Spare Magazines	16.3
Grenades, 2	2.0
Helmet and Flak Jacket	11.6
Sleeping Bag and Accessories	10.0
NBC Protective Gear	8.5
Entrenching Tool	2.5
Rations for One Day	3.0

The total comes to seventy-five pounds, but includes only the most basic equipment, with just 210 rounds of ammunition. Now, think about the effect on overall weight caused by the need for additional ammunition, rations, and such commonly issued items as night-vision goggles (1.9 pounds), portable radios (2.9 pounds), LAW anti-titank rounds (4.7 pounds), and, soon, handheld satellite-navigation receiving sets (secret). Then think about special cold-weather gear. Nor is the rifleman's burden the worst. A grenadier's is about 8.9 pounds heavier (grenade launcher and grenades in lieu of M-16). A man toting a SAW—"squad automatic weapon," formerly known as a light machine gun—carries 14.5 pounds more, and a mortarman something like 40 pounds more. The troops, of course, are very aware of the problem, and in combat tend to shed equipment rapidly if not closely watched and well-disciplined. Usually, the first things thrown away are those they consider least useful. But it's all likely to be useful, depending upon the situation. The root of the problem is that the infantryman should not carry too much equipment, but everything he has to carry will be desperately needed in some circumstance.

Pass the Ammunition.

The average U.S. infantryman fires 6,000 rounds of rifle ammunition per year in training. This is several times the amount used annually by Russian Army infantry. Generally, the more ammo a soldier fires in practice, the better he is at firing for real.

Top

"Top" or "top sergeant" is the nickname for the first sergeant, the senior NCO in a company, who actually runs most administrative aspects of the unit. Going into the 1990s, aside from senior officers, the only combat-experienced leaders in the army will be these senior NCOs. The first sergeant is usually referred to as "the top," at least by officers and senior NCOs. Awestruck troops often revert to "Yes, sir!" This is a no-no, as only officers are to be called "sir." The forty-plus-year-old first sergeant reports to the company commander, an officer in his twenties. In combat, the first sergeant often ends up running the company, especially if the officer in command is killed or wounded. Many armies call their senior NCO "sergeant major." In American usage, the sergeant major is the senior NCO assigned to each unit all the way up to the most senior NCO, who is "The Sergeant Major of the Army." Air forces and navies have similar ranks, with "petty officer" replacing "sergeant" in the navy.

A Warm and Cozy Feeling

Or hot and claustrophobic, depending on how you look at it. These are the feelings of troops equipped for chemical warfare. To protect against all chemical agents means putting on an airtight suit and gas-mask breathing apparatus, using filters, not bottled air. The suit gets hot fast even in temperate climates. The mask restricts vision, speaking, hearing, eating, drinking, and recognition of one's fellow sufferers. Bowel movements and urination become difficult, and even potentially fatal, unless a chemical-proof latrine is available. Getting wounded has almost certainly fatal consequences. The worst part of all this is that troops will have to suit up even when there is only a threat of chemical weapons being used. Finding out when there are chemical weapons in the area thus becomes a major activity. Currently, this is accomplished with small chemical detectors carried by troops, as well as more lavishly equipped recon vehicles that can scout ahead for signs of chemical contamination. During the nineties, several nations are expected to deploy lasers that can detect chemical contamination at a distance of several kilometers. Ideally, helicopters could flit around using the chemical detecting laser to find unaffected areas the ground troops can pass through. Actually, the helicopters need a little help themselves. Spending most of their time close to the ground, they are more exposed to chemical agents than the higher and faster fixed-wing aircraft.

"That's a Secret, Comrade."

Russia has had a mania for secrecy for many centuries. Since World War II, this mania has severely restricted distribution of accurate information within the Russian armed forces. This has become more obvious since *glasnost* has begun to peel aside the security classification of so many items. For example, the maps that Russian soldiers would use in wartime are not available until war actually breaks out. Many aspects of new military equipment are only revealed to a few officers, who will have to rapidly instruct operators when war breaks out. In the long term, there are more serious problems. For example, many books about World War II operations, written by senior officers who were there, were classified secret when they were written in the 1950s and 1960s. Staff officers authorized to read these books then used the data to develop current Russian military doctrine. This left little opportunity for comment or criticism of doctrine, as few other officers or citizens had access to the books. That this doctrine frequently proved ineffective indicates that some comment and criticism was warranted. These books are now being declassified. The resulting discussions, on both sides of the Iron Curtain, should prove interesting.

No Matter How You Slice It . . .

While the division is the principal maneuver element in ground combat, merely counting the number of divisions a country has is not necessarily a good indication of its combat power. Divisions vary greatly in size, due both to the different character of various types of divisions—airborne, infantry, light infantry, mechanized, armored, and so forth—and also to national organizational preferences. Thus, while a Russian airborne division only has about 6,500 men, the equivalent U.S. formation is about 16,000, which is actually larger than any Russian divisional model. Further complicating matters is the fact that most armies hold considerable combat power outside of divisions, in corps and army-level pools of artillery, tank, helicopter, and engineer units. And, of course, the front-line troops cannot function effectively without strong logistical support from the rear.

To help evaluate the importance of these elements, the "division slice" was invented. Put simply, the division slice is the total army manpower available, all the way back to the recruiting stations, divided by the number of divisions. The resulting figure actually gives a better notion of overall combat strength than does a raw comparison of numbers of divisions. Thus, assuming sixty days of mobilization, the United States would have about forty-one divisions—including marines—with a division slice of about 42,300, in contrast to Russia's 210 divisions and 32,800. The fact that the Russian divisional slice is only about 70 percent of ours is not necessarily significant, given differing notions of organization, logistical support, strategy, and tactics. Thus, Russian doctrine essentially views divisions as rounds of ammunition, to be expended as needed, while American doctrine sees them as sustainable entities. The differing numbers, are due to the fact that the U.S. unit requires more administrative and logistical infrastructure than the Russian one, as well as a reliable stream of replacements.

Among the NATO powers, the largest field-army division slice upon mobilization would be that of the Netherlands, with 3.3 divisions at 68,000 apiece, including plenty of reservists as replacements, followed by Britain, with 6 divisions, and West Germany with 18 division equivalents. Both armies have a slice of about 65,000 men, followed by Spain with 16 divisions at about 60,000, Belgium, 2 at 56,000, Italy, 8 at about 55,000, Denmark, 2 at 35,000, Greece, 15 at 32,000, Turkey, 40 at 30,000, France, 20 at 29,000, and Canada, 2 at 23,000. This leaves out Norway, with 2 divisions, which statistically would be at about 93,000 apiece, but most Norwegian troops are to be dispersed in small units due to the character of the national territory, Portugal, which would field about 6 security divisions plus a single mechanized brigade within sixty days, with a "division" slice of about 90,000, plus Luxembourg and Iceland, which have no divisions. In the Warsaw Pact, division slices are rather similar: Romania, with 8, has a division slice of about 75,000, East Germany, 10 at about 45,000, Hungary, 6 at 38,000, Poland, 18 at 34,000, and Czechoslovakia, 14 at 32,000. The European neutrals all have rather high division slices due to their large reserve pools: Austria, 8 divisions at 130,000, Sweden, 9 at 65,000, Switzerland, 18 at 32,000. While these figures include some people who contribute very little to the combat effectiveness of a frontline division, such as internal security troops, they exclude others, such as air force personnel, who have a very direct effect on the battlefield. Considering only NATO and Warsaw Pact forces, which would be in place within sixty days of an increasingly unlikely mobilization, including air forces, NATO would have about 115 divisions and a division slice of about 32,000, while the Warsaw Pact would have about 190 divisions and a division slice of about 21,000.

The Fifth-Year Drill

Most Russian combat divisions exist primarily in the form of parking lots and sheds containing idle equipment. Only 10–50 percent of the troops are present, and they travel to separate training centers to practice with well-worn versions of their own stored equipment. But every five years most of these divisions are mobilized as a test of their ability to go to war. Local reservists are called up to fill out the ranks. These troops are conscripts who were released from their two years' service in the past five years. The equipment is cranked up, and the entire division clanks off for a week of exercises. The vehicles and equipment are then returned to their storage areas, and efforts are begun to get everything ready for the next mobilization. However, as with most armies, the date of these mobilizations is usually no secret to the division's officers, so they have plenty of time to prepare. As their career prospects depend on successful execution of the mobilization, most divisions get through the process with a minimum of chaos. Such was not the case when, without much warning, divisions were mobilized in Asiatic Russia for the invasion of Afghanistan in 1979 and in western Russia for a planned 1980 invasion of Poland. These two exercises were quite a mess, with many reservists simply not showing up. Many of those who did appear were greeted by much confusion. The Russian General Staff is still contemplating the implications.

Priorities

"Maneuvers are often media events rather than full-scale war games."—Donald W. Sampcor, USMC

Russian Airborne Capabilities

Throughout the eighties, the Russians developed air-assault and airborne capabilities for all levels of operations. Infantry regiments may (rarely) send a rifle company of 100 troops up to twenty kilometers into enemy territory to seize a key objective. A division would supply Mi-24 gunship helicopters (each carrying eight troops), or Mi-8 transport helicopters (twenty-eight troops each). More normally, a division would organize a one-to-three company operation up to fifty kilometers beyond the front. A Russian Army of three to five divisions could send a battalion from 20 to 200 kilometers into enemy territory. A Russian Front—army group—of two to five armies could deploy up to four battalions, with lightweight BMD APCs, from 20 to 200 kilometers into enemy territory. Mi-6 heavy lift helicopters would carry either two BMDs or 65 troops. A front normally has 24 Mi-6 or 24 Mi-26s and 32 Mi-8s. A theater command (TVD) with several fronts has one or more airborne divisions and as many helicopters as a front as well as a few dozen transport aircraft. In practice, each airborne division has two air-transportable battalions (infantry battalions that have trained to move by helicopter) and the ability to move two or three infantry companies at one time with its own aircraft. Armies and fronts can call upon the larger transport resources of the TVD. As the Russians believe in mass, most airborne operations would be conducted by the TVD with large units. Smaller airborne units operating in support of army, front, or division goals would be closely tied in with TVD level operations, if only because they would all be sharing the same pool of TVD helicopters and fixed-wing transports.

"Oh! What a Feeling, Toy-ota!"

For nearly two decades, the impoverished Central African desert country of Chad was racked by a series of civil wars that left it easy prey to the ambitions of Muammar Qadaffi, who sought to annex an extensive mineral-rich tract of land in the northern part of the country under the terms of a treaty of dubious legality concluded during World War II between Fascist Italy and Vichy France. By the mid-1980s, Chad was virtually partitioned. Then, in late 1986, Qadaffi overplayed his hand. In a clumsy attempt to manipulate one of the contending factions, he ended up driving it into the arms of the other. The newly reunited Chadians, with French and American logistical support, were soon on the offensive. Being too poor to afford lavish equipment, the wily Chadians improvised. One expedient proved of enormous value. They mounted antitank missile launchers on Toyota trucks and went zipping off into the wilderness. The results were impressive, despite an enormous Libyan superiority in equipment, including the latest Russian tanks and other mechanized vehicles plus air superiority. Frequently operating at night, the fast-moving Toyota columns overran several Libyan base camps, almost before the defenders knew what had hit them. In encounters with Libyan armored forces, the Chadians would split up into teams of two or three Toyotas and run circles around the enemy, firing antitank missiles as they moved. The Chadian offensive lasted about five months, from December of 1986 through April of 1987. Although the Libyans succeeded in hanging on to some portions of northern Chad and even made a successful counterattack or two, the war ended with the Chadians holding most of their objectives, and trying to figure out what to do with an extraordinary amount of booty. Asked if their tactics would have worked against a first-class army, a Chadian officer replied, "No, but then we weren't fighting a first-class army, were we?"

Fast on Your Feet

"Battles are won by slaughter and maneuver. The greater the general, the more he contributes in maneuver, the less he demands in slaughter."—Winston L. S. Churchill, British Prime Minister during World War II

"How Are You Going to Keep Them Down on the Farm?"

The Swiss Army must pay Swiss farmers about $500 a year to keep mules and horses on their farms. Although the animals have long since ceased to be efficient for farm work, the Swiss Army finds them useful for reconnaissance and for moving supplies in many parts of its mountainous homeland. Because they would like to assure a reasonable supply on hand in the event of war, they pay the subsidies. Without the government payments, nearly all farmers would dispense with these animals.

"You Speak Good English for a Russian."

The 32nd Guards Motor Rifle Regiment, widely regarded as the most effective Russian combat unit in the world, is staffed by Americans.

It is the unit organized to give U.S. infantry and tank battalions a realistic workout at the U.S. Army's National Training Center (NTC) in California, where a glorified version of laser tag is played. This "Soviet" unit operates according to Russian doctrine, using largely Russian equipment. They rarely lose, mostly because they're always practicing, while their opponents are only at the NTC for a few weeks. And besides, it's fun being the bad guys, and even more fun winning most of the time. Russia has a similar training center in the Caucasus, a region of Russia resembling West Germany. There, a special Russian unit mimics U.S., British, or West German troops. They don't have the technology of the U.S. NTC, but the concept is the same.

In the Field

An army unit taking its vehicles and weapons and moving out into the country to operate as they would in combat is "in the field." Here, the troops live in tents, vehicles, or wherever they can find shelter, and everyone suffers through a miserable time until they return to the kaserne. You can't fully appreciate this experience until you've tried it. It's not like camping out, because the primary purpose of the exercise is to take your combat (or combat-support) unit wherever military requirements stipulate. It always seems to rain or snow, and many of the movements are at night. When you get where you are going, often while it's still dark, you have to park the vehicles in the bush (without lights) and set up a defensive perimeter. If you're really unfortunate, you get to pull the first two-hour watch in a perimeter foxhole while everyone else sacks out. The only positive aspect of being in the field is that the usual bothersome aspects of military discipline (standing around in formation, constant saluting, neat uniforms, etc.) are relaxed. This is known as "getting away from the flagpole." After a while you get used to it, unless someone is shooting at you. But that's another story. Related term is FTX (for *field training exercise*).

The Dark Side of Experience

During World War II, the Red Army discovered that it was very advantageous to use lots of engineers in support of crucial attacks.

For a primary effort, two or three divisions might attack on a single 10-km front. The enemy would often have this sector defended with minefields and fortifications. There might also be water obstacles (rivers, swamps) in front of or behind the enemy position. Engineers were trained to clear mines quickly and destroy fortifications. They also knew how to use special equipment to get troops and vehicles across water obstacles. The engineers would take heavy casualties, but at least they had the skills and equipment to get the job done. Without the engineers, regular troops would take far heavier losses and quite likely not advance at all. In 1942 the Russians used two or three companies (each of about 100 men) per kilometer of attack frontage. By 1944 they were using over a dozen companies of engineers per kilometer. Currently, they plan to do this again, with over a dozen companies of engineers per kilometer. Unlike the 1944 engineers, however, today's have no experience under fire and none in leading major attacks. Engineering operations are a tricky business. History has shown that it is unlikely so large a number of engineers will be able to operate effectively in such a small area during their first exposure to combat. Even during World War II, where there was plenty of opportunity to practice in combat, it took several operations before engineer units got the hang of it. Moreover, the growth in the number of engineers available was determined by how quickly troops could be trained for these tasks. Thus, commanders had time to develop their skills gradually, with ever-larger numbers of engineers operating in a small area.

Dig We Must.

"The shovel is brother to the gun."—Carl Sandburg, American poet, biographer, and Spanish-American War veteran. A soldier in combat quickly learns that digging a hole to hide in offers better protection than using his weapon.

The Advantages of Simulated Disasters

Analysis of helicopter accidents in the U.S. Army revealed that a quarter of them resulted from a pilot's losing track of the status of his aircraft. Helicopter pilots are particularly prone to this sort of thing because they spend a lot of time flying close to the ground in all sorts of weather. This kind of flying requires that the pilot concentrate on one of several functions, often to the point of missing something else that will kill him. For example, keeping the chopper level in a sudden wind might distract the pilot long enough to run into a high power line. A fix for this problem (or at least 20 percent of the time) was a fifteen-hour course in a flight simulator that allowed pilots to experience emergencies without risking a crash. This proved as useful for pilots with thousands of hours of flight time as for those right out of flight school. An added bonus was that simulator time cost only a third of what flying a real helicopter would have cost. And simulator crashes, while embarrassing, were much less lethal.

Russian Helicopter Operations in Enemy Territory

An excellent example of planning for a type of operation that has never occurred before is Russia's new doctrine on how to handle helicopter operations in support of air-assault troops attacking positions in the enemy rear area. Russia plans to lift battalion-sized units, complete with light armored vehicles, up to 300 kilometers beyond its front line. These units will require frequent resupply of fuel and ammunition as well as helicopter-gunship support. The Russians plan to establish helicopter bases, each containing fuel, munitions, and support troops, and move these bases by helicopter several times a day to avoid enemy attack. The prospects of such a technique's working are slim, but you never know.

Some Things Never Change.

Despite all sorts of technological advances, there has been virtually no change in the tactical formations that tanks use in combat since World War II.

Role Reversal

Guerrillas have been known to secure a significant proportion of their arms from their usually better-equipped opponents. However, in at least one counterinsurgency it has been the government forces who look forward to getting better weapons by capturing them from better-equipped guerrillas. Guatemala has been fighting a rebellion of its Indian population for many decades (make that centuries). The United States cut off military aid from 1977 to 1986 because of the government's use of excessive force against civilians. The government was not able to replace worn rifles, and so it became customary for government troops to equip themselves with guerrilla weapons whenever they had the opportunity.

Patrolling No Man's Land in the Bekáa

Israel attempts to keep terrorists out of its northern border area by maintaining a client state in South Lebanon. Beyond that is the Syrian-occupied Bekáa Valley, home of many terrorist groups. In order to obtain better intelligence, the Israelis organized a special long-range patrol unit composed of Israeli volunteers from the local Golani Brigade and Lebanese Christian guides from the South Lebanon border territories. This is a typical wartime practice, which just goes to show you the state of the peace in Lebanon.

Offensive Defense

Russian defensive doctrine was first developed during the 1920s by a number of generals who were later shot by Stalin. This doctrine maintains that the best way to defend the nation is to launch a massive attack at the first sign of war. The Russian armed forces have not yet been able to pull this off, but were greatly encouraged when Israel managed it in 1967. However, the Israelis fumbled their mobilization in 1973 and took a beating before they were able to carry the battle into their opponents territory. Whether this aspect of Russian military doctrine will work or not is uncertain. The Russians' offensive posture is seen by adjacent nations as unfriendly, and the USSR has shown increasing signs of a willingness to modify its sixty-year-old plans in a spirit of international friendship. Over the centuries, Russia has consistently defeated invaders by falling back and wearing them down. Then, when their opponent is deep inside hostile Russian territory, regrouped Russian forces counter-attack and drive out the invader. While this historical technique works, it does so at enormous cost in lives and matériel.

Made in Egypt, and the United States, and Russia, and France

Reflecting the vicissitudes of its recent military history, as well as a thrifty concern for the burgeoning cost of military equipment, Egypt has been remarkably innovative in combining technologies from both sides of the Iron Curtain with some homegrown devices, to come up with useful new equipment. A prime instance is the new Nile 23 armored air-defense vehicle. On an American-made M-113 armored personnel-carrier chassis, the Egyptians have mounted domestically manufactured, improved versions of the Russian ZSU-23 antiaircraft gun and the SA-7 light antiaircraft missile controlled by a French-made Thomson-CSF guidance and radar system.

Living—or Dying—with Your Mistakes

During World War II, the Russians developed a very pragmatic and effective method for insuring that weapons met the needs of the troops. Thousands of combat-experienced officers were sent to the arms factories as "military representatives." Their job was to see that the weapons were designed and built to meet the life-and-death needs of the troops. To insure this, these officers went off to battle with the first batch of a new weapon, or periodically with new batches of existing designs. In effect, you lived or died depending on how well you did your job in the factory. This system persists today. Unfortunately, there is no battlefield test to see which military representatives are doing their job and which aren't. This accounts for the numerous operational problems new and existing Russian weapons have. This is another example of good wartime systems not being able to survive in peacetime.

Hide-and-Go Tanks

Hiding a tank is difficult, but possible by seeking a "defilade" position, concealing it behind an obstacle in such a way that it can still fire. There are two varieties of defilade, "hull defilade"—"hull down" in British usage—means the hull is concealed but the turret exposed, while "turret defilade" has the turret concealed, too, with only the tank commander peeping out from cover. If a target is spotted, the driver is ordered to move the tank forward so the gun is exposed and able to fire.

Force Multiplier

Despite their heavy armor and robust construction, tanks are surprisingly fragile, and can readily be put out of action by fairly minor mishaps, such as a thrown track. As a result, most armies have made arrangements to repair tanks virtually in the midst of combat, so that they can be returned to duty as quickly as possible. Even relatively heavily damaged tanks can often be restored to some degree of use: For example, a simple procedure requiring no special tools and about three hours work can restore to limited mobility a U.S. M-1 Abrams tank that has lost its two front pairs of road wheels. All of this requires special training and sometimes expensive equipment, such as armored recovery vehicles, but the investment pays off on the battlefield, where a tank with degraded performance is certainly more valuable than no tank at all. The U.S. M-1, for example, can recover from road-wheel damage more quickly than any other tank. This can be a key advantage in combat. Israel's army has had the most experience in this regard. During the fighting on the Golan Heights on October 6–7, 1973—the opening days of the October War—about 75 percent of the tanks that the Israelis brought into action were incapacitated during the first eighteen hours of the war. However, recovery and repair services were so efficient that about 80 percent of the damaged vehicles were back in action within twenty-four hours, with some being damaged and repaired as many as five times. Thus, the Israeli investment in specialized personnel and equipment had the effect of increasing Israel's available tank strength by about 60 percent. Similar results were obtained by Russian and German "tank-recovery" teams during the massive tank battles on the Eastern front during World War II.

Field Expedient

Finding that the lack of air-conditioning in their Russian-built T-55 tanks made them extremely uncomfortable in Nicaragua's tropical climate, Sandinista tankers have fastened a small metal bracket to the armor plate by each hatch, so that when not buttoned up they can mount little electric fans to help cool off the interior of their vehicles.

Bolt out of the Blue

One of the more notable developments in land warfare during this century has been accurate long-range artillery. During World War I, most artillery could fire at targets no more than 10 km behind the front; in World War II, this increased to 15–20 km, and it is currently up to 30 km or more. The targets were usually other artillery units or anything else an army's recon and intelligence units might identify. The first few rounds would catch the enemy by surprise and inflict the most casualties, as everyone scrambled for cover. Subsequent rounds would primarily damage equipment still in the open. A new wrinkle in these "surprise" attacks is large rockets carrying submunitions. One of the more notable examples of this is the U.S. Army's new ATACMS (Army Tactical Missile System). One ATACMS is fired from the same-size container that usually holds four smaller MLRS rockets. Each missile reaches up to 150 km and delivers 1,000 antipersonnel and antimatériel submunitions. These spread over a large area and, as they attack simultaneously, give little opportunity for the enemy troops to take cover. Improved recon methods make locating rear-area enemy targets more efficient, and bring additional terror to the heretofore "safe" rear areas. This technique was first used during World War II, when Russia introduced multiple-tube rocket launchers. Although these weapons had short range, were inaccurate, and used one large high-explosive warhead per rocket, they were highly effective because they delivered a high volume of fire simultaneously.

"But It Ain't S'pposed to Be Used That Way!"

The designers of weapons sometimes don't anticipate the uses to which their creations may be put by the troops. And the troops sometimes come up with surprisingly innovative and effective uses for equipment that was supposed to serve an entirely different purpose. In 1982 British troops were embarked so hastily for the Falklands War that they neglected to leave behind their MILAN antitank missiles. As a result, they toted these into action when they landed on East Falkland Island, despite the fact that the Argentine defenders had no tanks. Since the missiles were at hand, the troops used them. In all, about 250 MILANs were fired during the campaign, proving highly effective at cracking open fortified positions. The same thing happened nearly forty years earlier, during World War II, when the first antitank rocket launchers were issued. When there were no tanks around, the troops used the weapons to good effect against entrenchments, buildings, and fortifications. The U.S. Marines currently use a special rocket launcher just for fortified positions. This is a lot cheaper than the much more expensive antitank missiles currently issued.

Monumental Folly

"Fixed fortifications are monuments to the stupidity of man."—George S. "Blood and Guts" Patton, notable World War II U.S. Army commander who made his reputation by keeping his troops moving. Patton was one of the few Allied generals the Germans respected as a field commander.

The Ups and Downs of the Russian Armed Forces

The strength of Russian armed forces has waxed and waned over the years in response to military and economic threats. The following strength figures do not include the KGB and MVD paramilitary forces, whose strength has fluctuated from several hundred thousand to half a million over the years. In 1927 the Russian active

armed forces numbered 586,000 troops. After over a dozen years
(1914–27) of world war, revolution, and civil war, most troops had
been demobilized so that the shattered economy could be repaired.
In 1937 strength was at 1.4 million as Nazi Germany made increasingly threatening noises. Just before the German invasion of Russia
in 1941, it reached 4.2 million, and by 1945 had grown to 11.3 million. Russia had been devastated once more, so most of the troops
were demobilized to assist reconstruction; by 1948 strength fell to
2.9 million, not counting a large number of paramilitary personnel
chasing down armed rebels in the Baltic states and the Ukraine.
When the "Cold War" began in earnest in 1955, strength was up
again, to 5.8 million. Khrushchev wanted to reduce defense spending
in order to build up the economy; by 1960 he had lowered strength
to 3.6 million, planning to continue reductions to 2.4 million in 1962.
But then in 1961, the Berlin Wall confrontation came along, and the
reductions were suspended. A year later there was the Cuban Missile
Crisis, and two years later Khrushchev was pensioned off. Russian
military manpower steadily increased again until 1988, when it reached
5.1 million and another reduction was announced. Mindful that the
Khrushchev reductions—and Khrushchev—were hurt by the 250,000
highly trained and compensated officers who would have been thrown
out of work, the new reductions are more modest and pay particular
attention to those officers who would be affected. Nearly 20 percent
of Russian armed forces are officers, who perform jobs taken care
of by NCOs, enlisted technicians, and civilians in Western armed
forces. Russia could probably get by with under 3 million troops.
The Russians have nuclear weapons, half a million politically reliable internal-security personnel, and a reputation for getting nasty
when their borders are violated. Khrushchev realized that economic
growth would be hampered by excessive armed forces. This proved
to be the case. If reductions are not made this time, there may not
be a next time. The jokes in Russia about "the Reds [revolutionar-
ies] coming back" have a grain of truth to them and are heard even
in the Kremlin.

"Which Way Is North . . . ?"

A study conducted by the U.S. Army some years ago concluded that,
regardless of how intelligent or well educated they were, about 25

percent of the troops involved were incapable of being taught to understand a map.

Or Something Else Will

"A first-class soldier never lets success go to his head."—Flavius Josephus, first-century Jewish historian and soldier

Land Aces

The concept of designating combat pilots "aces" if they destroy a certain number of enemy aircraft is well known. But "aces" also show up in ground combat. Experienced infantrymen know well that certain of their number are more lethal than most others. These ace infantrymen are usually more skillful and, most important, "lucky." Research has shown that "luck" is not random, but the result of opportunism and careful preparation. In other words, people tend to make their own luck. Tank crews demonstrate an "ace" phenomenon very similar to that seen in the air. What it comes down to is that less than 10 percent of your infantrymen or tank crews will inflict more than half the damage on the enemy.

Making Your Own Luck

"In the long run luck is given only to the efficient."—Helmuth von Moltke, founder of the German Imperial Army, winner of three wars, 1864–71

Gun Crews

A typical modern field-artillery gun crew consists of nine men. These include the chief of section, who is in charge of the other eight. The gunner controls the aiming and firing of the gun. The assistant gunner assists. The driver and assistant driver take care of the vehicle, the modern equivalent of holding the horses. Ammunition supply is attended to by the ammo team chief, who is assisted by four ammo handlers (or "cannoneers," better known as "gun bunnies"). This crew serves a U.S. M-109 155-mm howitzer, including an ammo vehicle. The 90-lb 155-mm shell is the largest that can be manhandled, which is one reason why this caliber has become the standard in most nations. During World War II, the standard was the 33-lb 105-mm shell; during World War I, it was the 16-lb 75-mm shell.

Weapons for War, Weapons for Peace

Nations tend to make the best of what they have when it comes to the weapons they produce and use. Russian weapons are made for wartime, where a short period of intensive use and early destruction is the norm. This limits their usefulness for intensive training in peacetime, but this is of little concern as the Russians cannot afford to maintain a lot of heavily used tanks and aircraft for peacetime training. So the troops spend a lot of time sitting in classrooms or bringing in the crops, and exercise all their gear only a few times a year. Most of the troops are conscripts who will be gone in two years, so what difference does it make? This attitude enables them to pile up enormous amounts of decades-old equipment that has seen little use. In wartime several hundred divisions could be raised, using the conscripts who had been released in the past five years. As is their custom, they would wear down any invader. Their industry cannot produce lots of equipment that can sustain heavy use for years and years. Western nations can, and do. Also, Western armies have more long-service troops who practice constantly with more complex and more robust equipment. Western industry can produce this stuff, and would resist any demands to manufacture the type of short-service-life material produced in Russia.

The Russian View of the Military Balance

Most assessments of the East-West military balance in Europe take into account only Warsaw Pact and integrated NATO forces. The Russian get a little steamed about this because of what is therefore left out. For example, France and Spain have twenty divisions available, and the Russians consider them likely opponents in another European war. Then, too, there are a couple of neutrals whom the Russians view with suspicion. Sweden and Finland, who dominate the Baltic, both have historic gripes with Russia, while Switzerland

and Austria are on the flank of an advance into Germany. There is also the matter of NATO superiority in naval forces, particularly U.S. carriers and their hundreds of long-range bombers. Moreover, though they don't often say it publicly, Russian commanders concede both that Western equipment is superior, and that they themselves have a lot of morale problems in their conscript armies. Another salient factor is the relative unreliability of Eastern European nations. Russia has had to invade its East European allies several times in the past thirty years to keep them allied. Nothing comparable to this has happened in NATO. All in all, the situation looks a bit different from the other side of the old Iron Curtain.

Tank Debate

For about fifty years, there has been an ongoing debate as to the optimal tank-platoon and company organization. The argument essentially comes down to the question of whether it is better to have three tanks or five tanks in a tank platoon. The proponents of the five-tank platoon—Germany, the United States, and most Western powers—observe that having five tanks permits greater tactical flexibility, since the platoon can be broken into two elements for fire and movement tactics, and note that the platoon can survive as a combat formation even if two vehicles are lost. Supporters of the three-tank platoon—Israel, Britain, and Russia—argue that three tanks allows greater tactical control and more rapid tactical maneuvers, since the platoon commander and his two tank commanders can be in constant visual communication under virtually any circumstances. The discussion also affects company organization. With three platoons per company—a universal constant—the five-tank model results in a company with sixteen or seventeen tanks, fifteen in the platoons, plus one or two as company headquarters, while the three-tank model gives a company of ten tanks, nine in the platoons and one for the company commander, though the Israelis dispense with this and make the company commander lead one of the platoons. Of late there has been a trend toward a four-tank platoon in several armies, including both the U.S. and elements of the Russian Army. While the debate is more than academic, since it affects tactics, logistics, leadership preparation, and overhead, neither side has

ever been able to decisively establish that its model is generally superior.

Asleep at the Wheel

The U.S. M-1 tank is a marvelous, and quite effective, combat vehicle. It does have its shortcomings. One of the least talked-about
flaws is the tendency of the drivers to fall asleep. This is due to the
design of the driver's seat, which has him in a reclining, and apparently very comfortable, position.

It's Not Just a "Battle," It's a "Meeting Engagement."

There are a number of technical terms in military usage that describe different types of battles. Of these, the meeting engagement—
sometimes called the "encounter battle"—is the most common in
modern warfare, an action in which both sides essentially run into
each other as they are moving forward, begin fighting, and feed reinforcements into the fray as these arrive.

Other types of battle are nowadays relatively rare. In a siege, one
side holes up in a defended position, such as a fortress or a city,
completely or partially surrounded by the enemy, who pounds away
at him in order to seize what he's defending, such as Yorktown or
Stalingrad.

A pitched battle occurs when, having located each other, both
sides halt, build up their forces and positions, and, in effect, have a
battle by appointment. Most of the great battles of the past, such as
Waterloo or Gettysburg, were pitched battles, though the latter was
a meeting engagement on its first day.

In an ambush, one side springs a trap on the other, a regular
feature of small-unit—squad, platoon, company—actions, but nowadays unusual on a higher level. A reconnaissance in force is an
attack undertaken solely for the purpose of securing information.
The word *combat*, which is now used to describe the experience of
battle, was formerly applied to distinct portions or phases of battles,
such as the Combat of Little Round Top, during the Battle of Gettysburg.

The Worst Are More Important Than the Best.

During World War II, copious records were kept of combat units and their performance. Some units were definitely better than others, and, as expected, units usually became more effective the longer they were in combat. One seeming oddity was that many units became more effective after their first few battles, even though their losses were not yet replaced. Research revealed that the most important losses in those first few battles were the inept troops and officers. Good people were also lost, but unit efficiency improved more because the worst troops were lost more rapidly than the best ones. Moreover, it was found that it was not efficient to send new troops in as individual replacements to units still in combat. Experienced troops were not about to trust unknown newcomers, and tended to shun them. This is one reason why rookies became casualties so quickly. It was much better to introduce replacements when the unit was behind the lines. That way the veterans could get to know the newcomers without immediate risk to life and limb.

PART TWO

Air Forces

Less than twenty years after the first aircraft flew, air forces had become major components of most armed forces. World War II saw battles involving thousands of aircraft in the air at one time. Since then, aircraft have become more effective, and much more expensive and complex, so complex that many of them have no pilots. These guided missiles have resulted in many of the more curious items in this chapter. Herein we show the many angles to this very impressive, remarkably expensive, and quite interesting branch of the armed forces.

A Gentle Reminder

"Nobody has yet found a way of bombing that can prevent foot soldiers from walking."—Walter Lippmann, American columnist, 1965

Are Airplanes the Best Antiaircraft Weapons?

Ask any aviator, and you'll quickly find out that the best defense against aircraft is other aircraft. And, indeed, it is the fighter pilot who is the most glamorous figure in modern warfare. Yet a look at aircraft losses in the principal wars since 1945 shows that the dogfight is considerably rarer than is generally believed, as can be seen in the accompanying table.

War	Cause of Loss	
	AA FIRE	AIRCRAFT
Korea (1950–53)	87%	13%
Vietnam (1964–72)	80%	20%
Arab-Israeli (1967)	90%	10%
Arab-Israeli (1973)	27%	73%
Iran-Iraq (1979–88)	95%	5%
Afghanistan (1979–89)	99%	1%
Falklands (1982)	40%	60%
Lebanon (1982)	90%	10%

These figures are approximations, including only fixed-wing aircraft destroyed in the air, and thus omit considerable numbers of aircraft destroyed on the ground by air strikes (Arab-Israeli war of 1967) or ground operations (the Falklands War). From the figures, it would seem that aircraft are far more vulnerable to surface fire—both ground and naval—than to other aircraft. However, despite the numbers, the jury is still very much out on the question. The problem is that while there has been a great deal of warfare involving aircraft since 1945, there has been relatively little air-to-air combat in those wars. In Korea, Vietnam, the Arab-Israeli war of 1967, and Lebanon, one side held, or quickly attained, virtual total command of the air, while in the Iran-Iraq war neither side had large numbers of aircraft available after the first few weeks, and in the Afghan war the only air combat was between stray Afghan and Pakistani fighters. Only in the Arab-Israeli war of 1973 and in the Falklands did circumstances permit the combatants to dispute command of the skies, thus accounting for the higher toll from air-to-air combat.

What Price Glory?

"Whatever it costs, it's worth it."—Edward Aldridge, U.S. Air Force secretary, in 1988, in response to questions on the $500-million-plus each cost of the B-2 bomber

What Makes an Ace?

As long ago as World War I, it was noted that some pilots were much better than others. These, the "aces," comprised about 5 percent of all pilots and accounted for 40 percent of enemy aircraft destroyed. It's still not entirely clear just what personal characteristics make for an ace, other than being able to shoot down five or more aircraft. It does appear that any pilot who simply survives his first half-dozen encounters with enemy aircraft develops at least a 50 percent chance of making it through the war in one piece. Not all of these people become aces, but all of them demonstrate some of the characteristics peculiar to aces. Very early on, military planners began to search for the personal characteristics unique to aces. What they discovered was not reassuring. Many of the aces were poor pilots and employed a number of different fighting techniques. Some aces even had physical disabilities that would keep them out of air forces today. After World War II, the search for what made an ace continued. By the 1960s, it was thought that it had something to do with training and being able to react more quickly than your opponent. In the 1980s, as new aircraft became ever-more complex, numerous tests were performed on highly realistic simulators. It became apparent that some pilots were simply better able to take in the situation and act accordingly. This was largely a talent: Some people can handle the pressure and confusion of combat situations better than others. While just being able to fly a high-performance aircraft produces an exceptionally capable pilot, more than flying skills are required to excel in combat. To give their pilots more of an edge in the awareness department, Western air forces are equipping their aircraft with ever-more "intelligent" instruments and displays. Still, it appears that while you can train and equip all pilots to be more efficient, a minority of them will always be better than the rest. For the moment, there are still aces who are aces simply because they have the "right stuff." There are never enough of these people, so the best you can do is try to identify them in peacetime and organize your aircraft units so the aces are in the key flying positions and the other pilots are properly prepared for their supporting roles.

Check Six

"Checking six" is the most important function in a pilot's life, when he looks over his shoulder to search the air directly behind him. Pilots refer to direction using the hours on a clock face. Straight ahead is 12. "Twelve o'clock high," means straight ahead and above.

Pilots Pumping Iron

Because of the enormous pressures from G (gravitational) forces when flying high-performance jet aircraft, pilots perform better if they are muscular. Aerobic exercise such as running is counterproductive because it lowers the heart rate and blood pressure, making blackouts during tight turns more common, as blood rushes from the brain because of the gravitational pressure. As a result, pilots are urged to pump a lot of iron and go easy on the running. The ability to withstand a few more Gs in combat can be a life-saving advantage. Working out with weights and being in shape for high-G maneuvers doesn't hurt a pilot's social life, either.

Pickle the Target.

When a pilot acquires a target with his fire-control system, he has "pickled the target." Visually, this means using a device resembling an electronic arcade game. The pilot must get an electronic "blip" over the target on his screen ("pickle" it). The next step is to fire the weapon.

The Natural Superiority of Bombers

Since the United States began its strategic missile program in 1962, $670 billion 1987-type dollars have been spent on strategic warfare. The breakdown by system was:

Bombers	32%
Land-based Missiles	19
Submarine-based Missiles	21
Defensive Measures	19
Command, Communications, and Control	9

These figures are somewhat misleading; in the 1980s, the bombers expended 49 percent of their $218 billion dollars for the entire period. The United States is the only nation with strategic nuclear forces that spends so much on bombers. Much of this can be attributed to the bomber background of many senior air-force generals and the desire to favor bombers operated by people versus missiles operated by computer. The missile crowd argues that their weapons react more quickly and are more likely to get through. This is somewhat accurate, as only a few dozen bombers would be in the air if there were a sudden nuclear attack. However, the bomber people reply that their aircraft are more flexible and can also be used for conventional-weapons delivery. Air force B-52s demonstrated this during the Vietnam War. The bomber program was also responsible for the development of cruise missiles and many advances in electronic warfare. However, it is difficult to justify the fact that bombers received more funds in the 1980s than land- and sea-based missiles ($106 billion, $38 billion, and $56 billion respectively). Note that the strategic-defense expenditures go largely for land- and satellite-based radar systems to give warning of missile attack. These expenditures were heaviest in the 1960s ($52 billion) when the systems were first designed, built, and deployed.

Trying to Find the "Right Stuff"

First the reports came out of Afghanistan about Russian pilots who were not prepared for combat, sloppy flying, and numerous airborne accidents. Then the articles appeared in the Russian military press. These were written by pilots returning from Afghanistan who complained about the ineffective flight training they had received before going off to war. It soon became clear that things were not all as they should be in the cloistered world of Russian pilot training. The problems were several. The basic one was the low efficiency

of the people running the pilot-training schools. Selection procedures let in too many candidates who simply were not capable of
being pilots. Instruction was frequently lackadaisical, and often
downright dangerous. Many candidates left out of fear or disgust.
Those pilots who did survive the process were drilled in rigid procedures and not encouraged to show any of the flair that character-
izes the most effective pilots. This was the problem pilots facing combat
in Afghanistan had to deal with.

Maintaining the quality and quantity of Russian pilots had been a
worsening problem, and in the 1980s it reached crisis proportions.
None of the many solutions applied seemed to work. Starting in 1990,
a fifty-year-old solution will be applied. In 1990 special high schools
will open for students possessing the physical and mental capacity
to become combat pilots. After four years, the graduates will already
have soloed in trainer aircraft and will be prime candidates for the
usual three-to-four year pilot-training schools. Meanwhile, a new
commander of pilot training has four years to clean out all the sloppy
procedures and lackadaisical staff in the pilots schools. Otherwise,
the first graduates of the pilot-candidate high schools will face the
same bleak future of their predecessors. Even after graduation, pilots still have to face a flying career that contains little flying. Unlike
Western air forces, where pilots spend over 200 hours a year in the
air and increasing amounts of time in realistic simulators, Russian
pilots are lucky to get 100 hours a year in the air, and Russia has
very few good simulators.

The F-16ski

The Russian MiG-29 is widely considered to be the equivalent of the
U.S. F-16 fighter. The MiG-29 was displayed at a British air show
in 1988, and Western experts were allowed to get a close look at it.
Russian test pilots put the MiG-29 through some impressive maneuvers, demonstrating what Western pilots had known about since the
MiG-15 was encountered over Korea in the 1950s: MiGs are quite
nimble aircraft in the hands of experienced pilots. Other good points
of the aircraft were the 100-km range radar and infrared-detection
system. This infrared item is combined with a laser range finder to
give its 30-mm cannon excellent accuracy. The infrared detection

system is more accurate than radar and more difficult to jam. Its range is not great, but it is more than adequate for the 1,000-meter range of the 30-mm gun. It is also used for short-range infrared homing missiles. Moreover, the fire-control system uses a helmet-mounted display so that needed weapons information is always in front of the pilot. The MiG can carry six missiles of either the infrared or radar-homing type. The emphasis they have placed on the cannon accuracy reflects the relatively low quality of Russian missiles compared to Western models. On the downside, many aspects of the MiGs construction were crude. If nothing else, this indicated lack of standardized parts. Much of the aircraft appeared custom-made. Little is known of system reliability, but the Russian norm in this area has always been much below the West's. The cockpit controls and displays were 1960s Western vintage. For a high-performance 1980s aircraft, this puts a single pilot under a lot of pressure. The helmet-mounted fire-control display helps, but there is a lot more going on in modern air combat. Other shortcomings noted were a seat inadequate for high-G maneuvers and poor rear visibility. Russian pilots' big problem is that they don't get a lot of flying time and they don't have realistic simulators to make up for this lack. After the Korean War, when MiG-15s were obtained for evaluation, Western pilots were quite impressed with the plane's maneuverability. The ineptness of Korean War MiG-15 pilots had led observers to assume that the MiG itself was a pig. It may well be that nothing has changed. If Russia begins to train its pilots as intensively as Western pilots, then there will be cause for concern.

Smart Goggles

After twenty years of development, pilots now regularly use special goggles for night flying and targeting. The night goggles intensify available light, more or less turning night into day. Future versions will be able to "see" heat sources of different intensity, thus providing vision through smoke and fog at the flip of a switch. Targeting goggles allow the pilot to "look and shoot," with weapons aiming at what the pilot is looking at. A third type, just coming into use, uses a glass sheet covering the area from forehead to mouth to display the kind of information normally found on a computer screen. The big issue now is making these devices light enough to be comfortable to wear for extended periods. These special goggles were initially developed to assist low-flying helicopter pilots, but are beginning to show up in use by fixed-wing aircraft.

Chopper Wars: The Next Generation

Vietnam was a proving ground for the helicopters the U.S. Army began to introduce in 1959. The primary chopper was the UH-1, the "Huey." These weighed four tons and carried 1.5 tons of weapons or cargo at 200 km per hour for over two hours. Eleven thousand were eventually built. In 1967 a variation of the UH-1 became the first gunship, the AH-1. Although thousands of UH-1s were wrecked or shot up in combat, the value of this "flying truck" was proved.

Twenty years later, the next generation was introduced. Replacing the UH-1 was the UH-60 (Blackhawk), weighing 9 tons and carrying 3.5 tons. It moved along at 290 km per hour for two or more hours. But the differences were far greater than that. The UH-60 could take a lot more punishment and keep going. Even when it crashed, the crew was much more likely to walk away, or at least survive. The UH-60 is a true all-weather aircraft, capable of operating effectively at night and in bad weather. Being more agile, because of a more powerful engine, the UH-60 could more easily handle low-level flying. Although moving along less than 100 feet from the ground protects the helicopter from detection and enemy fire, it has to be done at much slower speeds, normally about 50–60 km per hour. The more powerful engine of the UH-60 gives the pilot an extra margin of safety when weather, enemy fire, or an unseen obstacle is encountered. Heat-suppression devices on the engine, which deceive heat-seeking missiles, provide additional protection. Flares and electronic countermeasures are also carried. Night flying is made possible with better navigation aids and night-vision goggles. The goggles electronically brighten available light, turning night into day and making a full moon appear as bright as the sun.

The missions flown by the UH-60 are similar to those of the UH-1. The greater load-carrying capacity provides new opportunities. Fuel and ammunition for tanks and other armored vehicles can now be brought forward to keep these units moving in combat. New weapons, such as trackbuster antitank mines, can be carried in the hundreds and just dropped from the helicopter in likely areas. Unlike the UH-1, which could carry no more than ten or twelve troops, the UH-60 can cram in twenty or more in an emergency. However, despite its highly successful design, the UH-60 was not chosen by the army as the basis for its new attack helicopter, the AH-64 Apache, which is an entirely new, and extremely capable, ship specifically developed for use in combat.

V-2 Redux

While Iran and Iraq replayed portions of World War I trench warfare on their border, they moved forward to World War II in their use of liquid-fuel rockets to bombard each other's cities. This was a replay of the German bombardment of cities in 1944–45 with the V-2 ballistic missile. Between 1982 and 1988, Iran and Iraq fired 361 Russian-made Scud missiles at each other's major cities. The Scud is a direct descendant of the V-2, since it was developed with the assistance of some of the very same German technicians who built the V-2. Thirty-seven feet long, thirty-five inches in diameter, and weighing 6 tons, the Scud carries 3.7 tons of highly toxic liquid fuel and a 1-ton high-explosive warhead. It can land within 1,000 meters of its target at its maximum range of 300 km.

Between 1982 and 1985, the Iraqis fired 143 Scuds into Iran. At first Iran could not return the fire, but in 1985 the Iranians were able to obtain some Scuds from Libya, and later from Syria, North Korea, and China. They then fired them into the Iraqi capital, Baghdad. Teheran, the Iranian capital, is 500 km from Iraq, so the Iraqis were unable to return the favor. Between 1985 and 1987, the Iranians fired 40 Scuds.

The Iraqis were unsuccessful in obtaining longer-range missiles, but finally bought 300 more Scuds from Russia and used East German technicians to boost their range to 600 km. This was done first by reducing the warhead weight from 2,200 pounds to 300 pounds. Thus equipped, they launched 25 modified Scuds at Teheran in 1987 and a further 193 in 1988. Some of the 1988 attacks were made with a new Scud modification. This one cannibalized fuel tanks from another Scud missile to allow a one-ton warhead to hit Teheran. In that same year, the Iranians fired back 231 Scuds. A total of 632 Scuds were fired between 1982 and 1988, two thirds of them in 1988. The modified Iraqi Scuds would hit anywhere from 2 to 3 km from their nominal target, but when aimed at a city as large as Teheran, they would hit something. It was a seller's market for Scuds, and both nations probably paid about $1 million apiece for them. In addition, about 340 shorter range (under 100-km) rockets were fired. All told, about $1 billion was spent on this "rocket war." Over 50,000 casualties were inflicted. Missiles were considered preferable to aircraft because neither nation could afford to lose what few long-range strike aircraft they had, nor their irreplaceable pilots. Now, the Soviets are worried that all that missile technology in Iraqi and Iranian hands gives those powers the ability to hit targets in the USSR. The CIA estimates that by the year 2000, about fifteen developing countries will be producing their own ballistic missiles, with consequent effects on international relations.

The Treaty of Key West

Few people have ever heard of it, but an agreement signed at Key West, Florida, over thirty years ago ended one of the hottest wars then raging, one that pitted the army and the navy against the air force over who could fly what, where, and for which purpose. The essence of the treaty is that in exchange for a promise from the army that it would not request fixed-wing combat or long-range transport aircraft from Congress, the air force pledged itself to devote attention and resources to ground-attack missions and air-transport activities. The navy received a monopoly on maritime patrol, but conceded to the air force a monopoly over air-transport activities and heavy bombers. None of the high-contracting parties was particularly enthusiastic about the treaty, which was concluded under considerable pressure from the White House, at the time inhabited by a former five-star general. As a result, although they have generally adhered to its terms, the services have done so reluctantly. Thus, when, in the late seventies, the air force seemed disinclined to spend money on the A-10, a new ground-attack plane, Congress threatened to let the army have it, and the air force rapidly capitulated. However, in recent years the treaty has begun to fray at the edges, due partially to operational considerations and partially to advances in technology. Faced with an apparently increased threat from Russian submarine forces, the navy has agreed to permit the air force to assign older model B-52s to maritime patrol, using Harpoon antiship missiles. Meanwhile, the enormous enthusiasm with which the marine corps has embraced the Harrier and the promise held out by new developments in tilt-wing aircraft, coupled with the air force's obvious lack of interest in ground support—at present the USAF is trying to transfer its A-10s to the Air National Guard— has prompted some people in the army to consider reopening the whole question of what types of aircraft the army may own and what types of missions it may perform, which may touch off an unseemly bout of interservice rivalry such as has not been seen in nearly a generation.

The Golden Drop

The U.S. Air Force pays $6,200 each for F-16 drop tanks. Each of these tanks carries 370 gallons of fuel and is dropped (and lost) when the F-16 encounters enemy aircraft and requires maximum maneuverability and speed, both of which are decreased until the drop tank is dropped.

The Gold-Plated Hangar Queen

For nearly fifteen years, Russia has been developing its version of the U.S. B-1 bomber. The Russian version, the Tu-160 Blackjack, has repeatedly missed its expected operational date, another similarity it shares with the B-1. Twice as large as the B-1B, and 50 percent heavier, it apparently carries twelve AS-15 cruise missiles on two internal rotary launchers. Unlike the B-1B, the Tu-160 is optimized for high-speed, high-altitude operations. The Tu-160 would attempt to penetrate enemy air defense by roaring in at over 2,000 km an hour. Unless the Russians have developed some very good ECM (electronic countermeasures), they will be blown out of the sky should they come anywhere near most Western surface-to-air missiles (SAMs) or high-performance interceptors. The reasons for the Tu-160's deployment delays are becoming known. Like the B-1, the Blackjack is having persistent problems with its electronics. Even though the Blackjack electronics are not as sophisticated as the B-1's, Russia's computer technology is up to twenty years behind that of the United States. A bomber like the Blackjack is very dependent on computers to run its radars, controls, and electronic-warfare systems.

Another area in which Russia is more than a decade behind the United States is large jet engines. The Blackjack is more dependent on speed for protection than the B-1. Try as they might, the Russians have been unable to produce jet engines that are powerful, reliable, and fuel-efficient. They usually go for power, but a bomber also needs range, which requires fuel efficiency. Currently, the Blackjack engines have much less range than they need. Jury-rigged electronics and a new set of engines may give the Blackjack some limited operational availability in 1990.

Teaching an Old Tomcat New Tricks

The U.S. Navy's F-14 Tomcat fighter is nearly twenty years old. As with most aging aircraft, it is kept viable by constant upgrades to its numerous systems. Sometimes, however, vital systems are left alone too long. An example is the F-14's radar-warning receiver. As of the beginning of 1990, the F-14 is still equipped to handle only those enemy radars that existed in the early seventies. Against any of the new Russian radar equipment introduced during the last fifteen years, the F-14 would be in big trouble. Other aspects of the F-14's electronic countermeasures equipment are equally obsolete. The navy's electronic warfare R&D managers began getting heavy flak from F-14 pilots in the early eighties, to little effect.

Too Good to Replace

One of the most capable aircraft in the U.S. Navy is the A-6 Intruder all-weather bomber. Normally, the A-6 can carry eight tons of bombs over 750 km and can hit targets day or night in just about any kind of weather. The A-6 is also loaded up with tons of electronic gear and becomes the navy's Wild Weasel electronic-warfare aircraft (EA-6). Nearly 600 A-6s are in use, but many of them are over twenty years old. The first A-6 squadron entered service in

1963 and the aircraft got a good workout during the Vietnam War. In late 1988, 170 (half) of the older A-6E model were grounded because of fatigue cracks on the wings. All those heavy loads and carrier landings were taking their toll.

As good as the A-6 is, the navy wants to replace it with the A-12. However, this new aircraft will cost $100 million each, over three times as much as the current A-6. The older A-6s are being given new wings, and upgrades to their electronics and new engines will increase their cost, but hardly beyond $20 million each. Another alternative is to adapt the F-18 fighter to fly A-6 missions. This is another sad chapter in the F-18 story. Beaten out by the F-16 for the role of "lightweight fighter," as a consolation prize it became the navy replacement for the F-4. The marines were forced to accept a ground-attack version of the F-18, even though the aircraft has neither the range nor the carrying capacity to do the job as well as older aircraft. The A-6 crowd resists an attack version of the F-18 for similar reasons. Although the F-18 has a range of 1,000 km as a fighter, carrying its max load of seven tons of bombs, it would be able to go less than 600 km. In a sense, the A-6 is too capable for its own good. While likely replacements are either too expensive or inferior in performance, as of the spring of 1989 there have been no further orders for the A-6. The last A-6s will come off the production line in 1992. So the navy has only a short grace period in which to sell Congress on a replacement.

Tell That to the Grunts.

"Modern air power has made the battlefield irrelevant."—John Slessor, British military theoretician, 1954

The SAM That Took Forever

In the early 1960s, the U.S. Army began work on a new surface-to-air missile (SAM). By 1965 it was a full-blown development project called SAM-D. Its original mission was simply to provide a mobile SAM to protect army units. Aside from adding every new item of technology that appeared, in the 1970s it was decided that SAM-D ought to be able to shoot down other missiles, too. At this point, the system was growing so large that it was in danger of losing its mobility. It was also in the early 1980s and the troops were getting impatient. So, with a lot of arm-twisting, ass-kicking, and streamlining of requirements, the SAM-D finally got to the troops in 1985 as the Patriot system, over twenty years after the project began. By 1988, the capability to shoot down missiles had been added, having been dropped earlier to get the system out of the laboratory.

If At First You Don't Succeed . . .

The Russia deployment of the SS-25, a mobile ICBM, in 1985 came after twenty-five years of effort. In the 1950s, two attempts at a mobile ICBM were made, the SS-14 and SS-15. Mounted on a JS-3 heavy tank chassis, these liquid-fuel systems were unable to overcome reliability and accuracy problems and were dropped without ever being deployed. In the 1960s, they tried again, with a solid-fuel missile on a large truck, the SS-16. Range and accuracy problems again proved insurmountable, and the project was dropped, although a cut-down version of the SS-16 became the shorter range IRBM (Intermediate Range Ballistic Missile) SS-20 in the 1970s. The SS-20 became a fairly reliable system, and in the early 1980s it was used as the basis for a fourth attempt. More reliable and powerful solid-fuel rockets were developed, and most of the problems of a guidance system for mobile missiles were overcome. This worked, more or less, and became the forty-five-ton SS-25. Meanwhile, learning from all these previous mistakes, another project was begun in the late seventies to develop a new missile (SS-24) to be launched from railroad cars. Lighter, more reliable and accurate, the SS-24 is much more flexible than the roadbound SS-25 because much of Russia's territory does not have roads but is traversed by railroads. Most of the arctic areas also have terrain not suited for building conventional silos. The SS-24 went into service in 1987 in the northern part of the country.

Dirty Rockets

The Russian Scud series of rockets has been in use since the early sixties. Pictures often showed the crews servicing the missile while wearing chemical-protection gear. Many analysts assumed that the missile was primarily intended for use with chemical warheads. Not so; in fact, the latest, the D version, is primarily for delivering cluster weapons. What the crews were protecting themselves from was the missile's fuel, a combination of hydrazine and nitric acid. These are dangerous chemicals, and the Russian Army's standard chemical-defense suit gives some protection from accidents during the ninety minutes it takes to fuel the missile for action.

Attrition Aircraft

In late 1988, the British government placed an order for forty-one Tornado aircraft at a cost of $34 million dollars each. At current loss rates, this should hold them for seven or eight years. There is nothing particularly unsafe about the Tornado. For an aircraft that normally operates close to the ground in bad weather, it is one of the safest of its type. Training losses are quite normal and are particularly heavy in Central Europe, where the weather is frequently bad. But still, it's costing the RAF nearly $4 million a week just to replace training losses for Tornadoes. In 1988 NATO air forces, with a strength of 4,000 combat aircraft, lost over 120 of them in accidents. Fortunately, the rate for the thousands of noncombat aircraft is much lower, bringing the overall annual loss rate to less than 2 percent.

The Secret of Building Stealth

The most useful technical breakthrough in the B-2 Stealth-bomber project was not the aircraft itself but the technology developed to build it. Because the actual shape of the aircraft was so crucial to defeating radar detection, only computer-controlled manufacturing could build the structural components. The aircraft was designed on a computer, and the same information in the computer went straight to the manufacturing equipment. Hundreds of work sites and subcontractors were linked into the same computer system in order to avoid errors or misunderstandings. Normally, there is a lot of hand fabrication by craftsmen in building aircraft. Because of the much more precise tolerances in the B-2, this older approach would have been prohibitively expensive, if not impossible. The techniques and facilities developed for the B-2 program will make future aircraft manufacturing cheaper and more effective, even if the B-2 itself never goes into full production.

How Stealth Really Works

Radar is the biggest threat to aircraft. Stealth aircraft render radar useless, or nearly so. Radar works much like a flashlight at night. The beam bounces light off an object so that your eye can see it. Radar sends out high-frequency beams that bounce off objects. The large dish you see with radar equipment "sees" the reflected signal, and these days uses a computer to figure out where the object is. Also note that with a flashlight, the color of an object has a lot to do with whether you can see something. For example, a light-colored object will reflect more light, a dark object will absorb light and give you a much less visible "return." While a radar receiver can "see" at a longer range than the human eye, its signals are more easily scrambled. A radar signal is sent off in another direction when it hits an object at an angle. This is the primary technique of Stealth, lots of rounded surfaces. For this reason, a pickup truck gives a radar signal return of 200 (square meters). A Boeing 747 jet, with all the round surfaces typical of an aircraft, only gives a return of 100. The B-52 bomber has even more curves and has a return of 40. A cruise missile or fighter bomber has a return of 10. The B-1B bomber, designed to minimize radar return, has a return of .4. The B-2 and F-117 Stealth aircraft go a few steps further and produce a return of .01, about the same as that of a large sea gull, swan, or eagle.

The B-2 and F-117 also make extensive use of radar-absorbent materials. Just as dark objects do not reflect light, certain nonmetallic composites tend to absorb radar signals. Russian radars are being updated to handle cruise missiles and fighter-bombers. Thus, a radar that could pick up a cruise missile at 300 km would not see a B-1B until it was 140 km away, and the B-2 would not be picked up until it was 70 km off. That might not seem like much of a problem, except that the B-1B and B-2 carry sensors that tell them where the Russian radar signals are going to be weakest or nonexistent.

Yes, the B-2 can be detected, but not soon enough to scramble and direct fighters or launch missiles efficiently. Stealth is not invulnerable, but it is a needle in a haystack. Worse, Stealth bombers carry cruise missiles or short-range attack missiles. They don't even have to pass over the target to attack it. By the time you find a Stealth aircraft, your radar may have been destroyed by a radar-homing missile. More likely, the Stealth bomber, cruising along at 15 km a minute, will have left your sector without your even being sure it's gone, or that it was there in the first place.

How Stealth Is Defeated

Stealth technology does not make an aircraft "invisible," it just produces a weaker signal for the radar-receiving equipment to process. It cuts detection range of radars to about 25–30 percent of their normal capability. You can simply add more radars, or adopt a cheaper alternative like adding more radar-signal receivers. The latter method would allow the many signals scattered by the Stealth aircraft's odd shape to be reassembled by a centralized computer. It's also theoretically possible to use television signals, but the TV approach requires new receivers and powerful computers. This might work in the West, where there are a lot more TV transmitters, but Russia would have problems with the TV approach. However, even if an exact position is not determined with any radar technique, the defender can get a good idea where the Stealth aircraft is and can send interceptors to the area for a closer look. With the introduction of Stealth cruise missiles, sixteen of which can be carried by the B-2, this solution becomes more difficult. Problem is, Russia is not too strong in that kind of computer technology. Whichever solution is adopted, the bill will easily be in the tens of billions of dollars.

There are, theoretically, cheaper ways to increase Stealth detectability. Different radar frequencies that are not absorbed by the B-2's special outer skin can be used. Different radar frequencies can double the return. But first you have to figure out exactly what the B-2 is made of, build the radar, and either test it on an aircraft made of the same materials or bet the farm that your theoretical calculations are accurate. But wait, you may be able to dispense with radar. Stealth aircraft still use jet engines, which throw off a lot of heat. Infrared (heat-sensing) detectors are becoming much more common. The new Russian MiG-29 fighter uses an infrared sensor instead of radar for its cannon and short-range missiles. Satellites use infrared sensors to detect aircraft, although Western versions are considerably better than Russian ones. Infrared sensors can be placed on the ground, a lot of them, and wired to a central location to indicate the passage of a Stealth aircraft. Another visible item is the contrail of the aircraft's jet engines. A corrosive chemical can be added to the fuel to make the contrail invisible, but it can still be seen by ultraviolet detectors. The B-2 also uses some active radar, particularly for its low-altitude navigation system. However, the emissions are brief and low-powered. The principal means of navigating are with an inertial guidance system and position updates from satellites, if they still exist. The radar is used largely to keep track of altitude and upcoming obstacles.

The various U.S. Stealth aircraft projects will end up costing about $100 billion. The original estimate was $50 billion. It could easily cost the Russians that much to come up with a system that might protect against Stealth aircraft. But then, Russia could decide to dismantle much of its expensive, and increasingly ineffectual, air-defense system. The B-2 would still have a role in penetrating the air-defense systems of naval and land units. But this could also be done by the F-117. What may eventually defeat the B-2 is cost. At a likely final cost of over $500 million each, this compares very unfavorably with $32 million for each current F-15 and $18 million for each F-16 and $280 million for each B-1B. The air force also wants money for its new 1990s fighters, which are likely to cost nearly $100 million each. Cost is a formidable opponent in an era of shrinking defense budgets.

Standard Issue

During the Vietnam War, only 4 percent of U.S. fighters and fighter-bombers lost over North Vietnam were shot down in combat with enemy aircraft, and only 5 percent succumbed to surface-to-air missiles, while fully 91 percent were lost to antiaircraft gunfire directed by that old reliable, Eye-Ball, Mark I.

The Russian Air Force(s)

Although possessing nearly 12,000 combat aircraft and helicopters, the Soviet Union does not have an air force. Rather, it has four different air forces: Frontal Aviation, with over 9,000 combat air-craft, including helicopters, to support the ground forces; Air De-fense, with 1,500 aircraft to defend Russian airspace; Naval Aviation, with 1,100 aircraft to support the fleet and defend naval bases; Long-Range Aviation, with 600 long-range aircraft equipped with nuclear bombs and cruise missiles. There are a wide variety of aircraft types in service, as the Russians are slow in retiring old models.

Frontal Aviation has:

FIXED-WING FIGHTERS AND FIGHTER-BOMBERS

1,700 MiG-23	330 MiG-29
1,000 Su-17	320 Su-15
860 MiG-27	300 MiG-25
850 Su-24	300 Su-25
700 MiG-21	50 MiG-32

HELICOPTERS

1,600 Mi-8
1,200 Mi-24

Naval Aviation consists of:

240 Tu-16 bombers	70 Tu-95 long-range recon bombers
140 Tu-26 bombers	50 Il-38 recon bombers
80 Yak-38 fighters	160 Ka-25 ASW helicopters
75 Su-17 bombers	90 Ka-27 ASW helicopters
90 Be-12 recon bombers	100 Mi-14 ASW helicopters

Air Defense forces have:

FIGHTERS AND INTERCEPTORS

420 MiG-23	200 MiG-29	80 Tu-28
310 MiG-25	150 Su-27	75 Yak-28
200 Su-15	115 MiG-31	15 AWACS air-control aircraft

Long-Range Aviation consists of long-range bombers, including:

180 Tu-26	125 Tu-95
140 Tu-16	62 Mya-4
133 Tu-22	16 Tu-160 (Blackjack)

Touch Me Not.

The introduction of American-made Stinger missiles into the Afghan War in October 1986 appears to have led to an overall 500 percent increase in damage to Russian and government aircraft and a 300 percent increase in planes and helicopters shot down. More important than the damage was the effect on Russian operations. Attacking aircraft had to be much more cautious, and would frequently abort attacks if they suspected Stingers were in the area. The elite Russian air-assault troops lost some of their edge when they realized that they could not drop into, or pull out of, enemy territory with impunity.

The Missile That Would Not Die.

In 1980 the NATO nations agreed jointly to develop two new air-to-air missiles. One, the AMRAAM medium-range radar-homing missile, came along with some delays, and went into limited production by 1989. The other, the short-range ASRAAM, never got off the drawing board. A major problem with ASRAAM is the missile it is supposed to replace, the U.S. AIM-9 Sidewinder. Over thirty years old, the Sidewinder has been continually upgraded and has repeatedly proved itself in combat. Whenever the ASRAAM developers thought they had the design finished, the Sidewinder crew came out with a new version that made ASRAAM obsolete. The original design and subsequent development of the Sidewinder is a superb example of how weapons projects should be run. Sidewinder has proven so successful that nothing seems capable of replacing it, except yet another refinement of the Sidewinder itself.

Something Old, Something New, Something Borrowed, Something Blue

In 1975 the air force proposed the development of an "advanced medium-range air-to-air missile" (AMRAAM), designed to permit a single fighter to engage as many enemy aircraft simultaneously as it had missiles, each one seeking out and destroying an attacker by means of built-in radar and guidance systems. (In 1980, this became a NATO project.) More than a dozen years later, the air force admits that there are both hardware and software problems with the system. Tests have proved unsatisfactory, for whenever two missiles are fired at two targets, both appear to lock onto the nearest target, with the result that one missile scores a hit and the other misses. The air force, which terms the missile "one of our top priorities," claimed that the problem would be resolved by 1990. Despite these assurances, the Pentagon will permit only limited production of the weapon until test results improve. Meanwhile, serious doubts have been raised about the cost of the weapon. In 1986 the air force, which would eventually like to buy 24,000 AMRAAMs, predicted it would purchase 1,750 in 1989 at an average cost of $500,000 each, which was revised in early 1988 to 1,470 missiles at $561,000 apiece, and in 1988 to 1,240 at $665,000 each, and by the end of that year was set at 900 missiles for $900,000 per missile. Congress almost canceled the program in early 1986, but was assured in writing by then—Secretary of Defense Caspar Weinberger that costs would not increase, that the design would not be altered, and that the weapon's performance specifications would not be changed. The AMRAAM was conceived for use exclusively by NATO aircraft. Development was to be complete by 1986. The first production models didn't come off the assembly line until 1989. Designed to replace the 65 percent heavier U.S. Sparrow missile, over 32,000 are to be built for U.S. and NATO air forces. One of the major problems during development was that the components were not able to keep up with the design specifications. Soon after development began, dramatically more efficient electronic components appeared on the market. But as often happens in weapons-development projects, AMRAAM was stuck with 1970s technology. This resulted in a missile crammed with a lot of bulky electronics that generated a lot of internal heat. The maneuver system was also shaky because of its older technology. There was a lot of political pressure to get a missile out the door, so the initial batch will use the ten-year-old technology while those manufactured in the early nineties will use the more efficient components. In between there will have to be another extensive testing program. And you never know what will happen if some general with a wish list gets to the R&D people.

The Helpful Harrier

The USMC estimates that 200 conventional ground-attack aircraft are required to generate the same number of ground-support airstrikes as 160 Harriers—AV-8s in jarheadese—due to the latter's ability to "live" close to the front. With the mobility of a helicopter, the Harrier can drop down just about anywhere. Additional fuel and munitions can be flown in by helicopter, or brought along by truck. Most maintenance can be performed in the field.

Stinger Cost

The U.S. Army pays over $40,000 for each shoulder-fired Stinger surface-to-air missile. More than one out of every five Stingers sent to Afghanistan hit a Russian aircraft. This included Stingers lost in action before they could be fired. The kill ratio might be even higher in a major war between the superpowers. In Afghanistan, the Russians could afford to take extensive measures to avoid the Stinger. Most aircraft carried flare dispensers and would use these flares extensively. This, however, meant Russian fighters and bombers had to operate slowly and deliberately. In a high-intensity war against a modern opponent, such deliberation would be a luxury the Russians could not always afford. As Israel discovered during the 1973 war, when you must take out ground targets defended by modern antiaircraft weapons, you must accept heavy aircraft losses in order to do the job.

Tweet, Tweet!

One of the most successful aircraft designs of the post–World War II era is the Cessna T-37, a two-engine primary jet trainer with a top speed of only about 680 kph. Designed in 1953, the T-37, affectionately nicknamed the "Tweet," entered service with the air force in 1957. Over the next eight years, 1,268 T-37s were produced in several models, including a ground-attack version, the A-37, which has a much higher speed—835 kph—and somewhat different overall characteristics. Most T/A-37s are still flying. The versatile T-37 proved an attractive investment for nations wishing to stretch their defense dollars, and was procured for use by the United States and fourteen other countries, including Greece, Portugal, and Turkey among NATO powers, as well as Brazil, Chile, Colombia, and Peru in Latin America, Jordan in the Middle East, and Burma, Pakistan, and Thailand in southern Asia. The oldest T-37s have logged as much as 16,000 hours of flight time, with the average well over 12,000 hours. By 1996 all USAF T-37Bs will have completed a SLEP refit, extending their total useful life to over 30,000 hours. Regarded as a "user-friendly" aircraft, the T-37B will be the principal vehicle for jet training in USAF well into the next century.

Missiles

Missiles come in many different flavors. The major types are:

- ICBM, "intercontinental ballistic missile," an electronically aimable rocket-type missile with a global reach, 10,000 miles
- IRBM, "intermediate-range ballistic missile," a relatively short-ranged—1,000–2,000 miles—aimable rocket-type missile, essentially the category covered under the INF—intermediate nuclear forces—agreement
- SLBM, "submarine-launched ballistic missile," aimable rocket-type missiles with a range in excess of 5,000 miles
- ALCM, "air-launched cruise missile," an airplane-type missile carried within some hundreds of miles of a target by a bomber or modified airliner—no such aircraft were ever developed, however—and launched to make its own way with electronic-guidance systems
- GLCM, "ground-launched cruise missile," pronounced "Glickum"
- SLCM, "submarine-launched cruise missile," pronounced "Slickum"

- SSM, "surface-to-surface missile," narrowly defined, an artillery missile with a "tactical" reach of only a couple of hundred miles
- AAM, "air-to-air missile," an antiaircraft rocket-type missile fired from an airplane
- SAM, "surface-to-air missile," an antiaircraft missile fired from the ground or a ship: The U.S. Army once adapted the very effective Sidewinder AAM to a SAM role with excellent results.

When All Else Fails . . .

Russia has the largest antiaircraft system in the world. The primary weapons are nearly obsolete SA-3 surface-to-air missiles. Although the SA-3 radars have been upgraded somewhat, it appears that the Russians don't entirely trust them. As a backup system, they use special TV cameras that can pick up aircraft visually up to 35 km away. This allows the missile operators to guide the missiles against targets, assuming ECM do not interfere with the SA-3 guidance system. There is considerable doubt that the Russian air-defense system would be all that useful in wartime. The half-million troops that man over 1,000 SAM sites and over 2,000 interceptors are not noted for their skill or diligence. These troops and their equipment cost Russia over $25 billion dollars a year.

The Sincerest Form of Flattery

U.S.-made Stinger antiaircraft missiles have proved so devastatingly effective in Afghanistan that Russia, which secured samples for study during operations against the Mujahedin, is now manufacturing its own version, the SA-16, though the Russian-made clones are believed to have a temperamental guidance system. There is a simpler, and somewhat less effective, SA-14 model that is still deployed in large numbers.

The Not-So-Insignificant Fuze

Fuzes have long been rather simple and inexpensive components of warheads. The primary function of fuzes is to sense when the warhead has struck something and then to quickly detonate the warhead's explosive charge. During World War II, fuzes began to get very expensive, particularly with the development of the "proximity" fuze, which had a miniature internal radar that sensed when it was close to a target and then detonated the warhead. This made a near-miss a hit. Since World War II, these fuzes have become more elaborate still. Current examples of this type of fuze are found in the U.S. Army's Patriot surface-to-air missile. Each fuze for the Patriot costs $26,000.

The Incentive Theory of Missile Development

For twenty years, efforts have been under way to develop systems that can shoot down ballistic missiles before they reach their targets. Some existing air-defense systems already have that capability, to a certain extent. A notable example of this is the U.S. Patriot SAM (surface-to-air missile). Until recently, no one had a system that could do this job with a high degree of reliability. But when several Arab nations acquired ballistic missiles and the potential for equipping them with chemical warheads, Israel sat up and took notice. Israel is within range of several Arab nations' short-range ballistic missiles.

After several years of feverish development, the Barak point-defense missile was deployed in 1989. This system is deployed near a city or military base and switched on. Anything resembling an incoming warhead causes Barak to launch and go after the interloping warhead. The Barak is a small missile, eighty-five inches long and seven inches in diameter, with a wingspan of thirty-three inches. Its range is 10 km and top speed is over 1,000 meters a second. A 48-pound fragmentation warhead with a proximity fuze is used. This insures that even if the warhead is not destroyed, it will likely be deflected from its intended target. The missiles are mounted in groups of ten on an eight-wheel vehicle. A version with a built-in radar seeker is being developed.

The major drawback with Barak is that if the incoming warhead is chemical, damaging or destroying it will release the lethal chemicals anyway. Israel is a small, densely populated country. A shower of nerve gas landing anywhere near likely targets will kill or injure many people. To solve that problem, the Israelis are developing, with U.S. money, a 1,000-km-range missile system that can destroy an enemy missile soon after it takes off. This is the Arrow system. It's not expected to be in use until the mid-1990s. The United States intends to deploy it in Central Europe.

SAMs in Defense of the Motherland

Russia maintains about 9,000 surface-to-air missile launchers (SAMs) in defense of its territory. Five different missile types comprise most of these. About 100,000 missiles are available. Over half a million troops man the SAM sites or provide support. Although new generations of missiles are constantly introduced, most of the missiles are over ten years old. Keeping these missiles in shape is a very difficult task, as most of the troops maintaining them are young conscripts in for only two years' service. The electronics and mechanical components of these missiles are complex. Test equipment and spare parts are not what they should be. The missiles are often stored haphazardly, exposing some of them to the extremes of Russian climate. Readiness tests are often inadequate, or passing grades are faked. In a shooting war, many of the missiles, particularly those five or more years old, would fail to launch properly or break down on the way to their target. Against modern Western aircraft, Russian SAMs have averaged less than a 2 percent success rate. Those were export missiles, which the Russians knew were likely to be used, and they did not want to risk losing sales by shipping defective missiles. The thousands of SAMs defending Mother Russia are another story, and 2 percent hit rates may well be an optimistic figure.

I'll Have Mine with LOX.

Combat-aircraft pilots require a source of oxygen, as they spend much of their time at high altitudes where the air is too thin to maintain consciousness. American aircraft supply this oxygen from a small sphere containing highly concentrated, and explosive, liquid oxygen (LOX). The LOX is produced by machines, high-powered refrigerators, on the ground. Aircraft carriers have two of these machines. When both break down, LOX must be flown in from other ships or land bases. Some aircraft are now being provided with equipment that will extract oxygen from the atmosphere for pilot use. Oxygen is just another link in the chain of equipment that must function in order for the aircraft to be operational.

Ivan Loves SAM.

That's why Russia makes so many different surface-to-air missile (SAM) systems. Russia has a healthy respect for Western air power and some misgivings about the ability of its own air force to keep Russian ground troops from being harried from the air. In the last thirty years, the United States has developed only six new mobile SAM systems (HAWK, Improved HAWK, Redeye, Chapparal, Stinger, Patriot). The Russians have fielded eighteen SAM systems in the same period. This represents frantic efforts to develop effective technology and keep up with Western aircraft and ECM systems. The proliferation of systems also demonstrates the way Russian weapons development takes place, with a number of research institutes, design bureaus, and manufacturing plants all pushing to get their work into the field. Of the nearly 200,000 individual missiles Russia has manufactured, most are rather simple, using infrared (heat-seeking) technology. Moreover, despite all the systems produced for ground combat, they have never been able to produce enough missile systems to equip all divisions. They also don't throw away any old systems, so there are over a dozen different systems equipping the hundred or so divisions that do have SAMs. The four shoulder-fired missiles aside, all these systems use radar, and each has usually had a new radar built for it. While this creates maintenance problems, it also makes life more difficult for Western ECM, as each radar must be dealt with separately. A brief look at these systems is instructive. (Range of each system is shown in kilometers, in parenthesis).

- 1966 ZSU-23 (3 km), tracked 23-mm automatic cannon. Very successful in clear weather. Simple and effective. While not a SAM, it was this effective radar-controlled gun system that served as a test bed, and model, for future mobile SAMs.
- 1966 SA-7 (3 km), a crude copy of the U.S. Redeye SAM,

fired by one man from the shoulder. Not very effective, but not a total failure, either

- 1967 SA-6 (24 km), tracked system, very effective against aircraft lacking ECM. Principal divisional SAM. First truly mobile Russian SAM
- 1968 SA-9 (7 km), basically a heavier version of SA-7 mounted on a vehicle. Much cheaper and simpler complement for the SA-6
- 1971 SA-9B (7 km), improved version of SA-9 with better sensor
- 1972 SA-7B (4 km), improved version of SA-7. Still not a weapon you'd bet your life on
- 1974 SA-8 (15 km), complements, and sometimes replaces, the SA-6. More capable than the SA-9, but not as complex or as effective as the SA-6. Most widely used, with over 1,000 systems produced
- 1977 SA-13 (8 km), replaces SA-9B, same basic idea, a large-size infrared guided missile
- 1978 SA-10 (50 km), for defense of the homeland, but mobile enough to support ground-combat operations. First new long-range system in over a decade
- 1978 SA-14 (5 km), replacement for largely ineffective SA-7. Getting better
- 1979 SA-11 (30 km), replacement for SA-6, but no longer used at the divisional level. It's now an army-level system.
- 1980 SA-8B (15 km), upgraded SA-8
- 1986 SA-12A (80 km), another system for defending the homeland, also mobile enough to support ground forces
- 1987 SA-16 (5 km), similar to U.S. Stinger portable SAM. Very high tech for a Russian missile. Has reliability and quality-control problems. Said to be copied from captured or stolen Stingers. Russia is persistent in developing an effective portable SAM.
- 1988 SA-15 (16 km), replaces SA-8B and SA-6 for protecting the division. Better guidance system, probably still infrared heat seeker
- 1989 SA-17 (32 km), replaces the SA-11
- 1989 2S6 (4 km), tracked 30-mm gun system to replace ZSU-

23. Also carries four SA-19 (8 km) SAMs that are similar in design to the SA-13. This system replaces the ZSU-23 and SA-13 in combat regiments. New antiaircraft units will have six 2S6s, an independent radar to spot distant aircraft, and six BMPs (Standard Russian APC) each carrying a SA-16 team. Previously, the infantry companies each had SA-16s, but now these are to be centralized to better deal with the more numerous enemy helicopters expected on future battlefields.

Hey, the Damn Thing Works!

The first aircraft downed by a ship-launched surface-to-air missile under actual combat conditions was a North Vietnamese MiG, brought down by the missile cruiser USS *Long Beach* at a range of sixty-five nautical miles on May 23, 1968, nearly a decade after shipborne SAMs were introduced into service, and three years into the Vietnam War.

Hey, It Works More Than Once!

During the Vietnam War, the United States Navy brought down seven enemy aircraft using surface-to-air missiles, and, apparently, one enemy antiship missile as well.

HAWK Surface-to-Air Missiles

The U.S. Army pays $234,000 each for HAWK missiles. In use for over twenty-five years and continually upgraded, the system has proven quite effective in combat. For every two or three HAWKs fired in anger, one enemy aircraft has been brought down.

From Those Wonderful People Who Brought You the Battle of Britain

Although overshadowed by the United States, British defense technology and ingenuity remains impressive. Presently on the drawing board is the first propeller-driven frontline combat aircraft to be ordered by a major power since about 1950, and Britain's first since World War II. Known as the SABA, for "small agile battlefield aircraft," the plane is being built by British Aerospace, heir to the firm that designed the famed Hurricane and Typhoon fighters of World War II. Able to use short, improvised runways, the plane would "live" close to the front. The SABA, which has double-pusher propellers mounted on a single engine, is designed for use against helicopters and ground targets, using air-to-air missiles and automatic cannon, and has a long loiter time to permit it to stick around for extended periods. With considerable maneuverability and a speed of about 400 knots, it is hoped that the SABA will be able to survive the modern battlefield environment.

FLIRing in the Rain and Fog

The principal sensor for the primary U.S. attack helicopter, the AH-64, is the FLIR, an infrared device that looks at the heat emitted by the terrain and other vehicles. Under good conditions, this makes an excellent passive night sensor. However, in Central Europe, where the AH-64 is expected to operate, the climate is often full of clouds, rain, and fog, all of which tend to make the FLIR much less sensitive. Laser range-finding and fire-control devices are also degraded by these weather conditions. However, experienced AH-64 crews are able to overcome these FLIR-degradation problems if they have sufficient practice. This includes developing the ability to use FLIR to pick out vehicle targets lurking in built-up and forested areas and heavy vegetation. This is a tricky business that requires substantial training and practice.

Down-to-Earth

The principle difference between air-to-air missiles (AAMs) and surface-to-air missiles (SAMs) is that the SAMs usually have a longer range. This is because the SAM launchers are not nearly as mobile as the aircraft carrying AAMs. It wasn't long before someone noticed that if you needed a short-range SAM, you could simply use an AAM. Surprisingly, the United States has been alone in doing this. Up through the early 1990s, the U.S. Army's principal short-range SAM will be an Air Force Sidewinder missile mounted on a vehicle, the Chapparal. The U.S. Navy uses longer-range Sparrow AAMs where they need a lightweight, short-range shipboard SAM. The new AMRAAM long-range AAM is also being configured for ground use.

Developing the Stealth Fighter

The F-117A Stealth fighter was approved for development by President Jimmy Carter in 1978 after a year of initial development work. It was to be a "black" (ultrasupersecret) project, with all work done outside normal air-force budgeting and procurement channels. The first aircraft flew in June 1981, although a prototype crashed in 1979, an accident that the test pilot survived. Not so lucky were regular air-force pilots in July 1986 and October 1987 crashes.

The aircraft became operational in 1983, which marked the start of intense pilot training and tactical development. The odd shape of the aircraft makes it difficult for radars to get a strong signal back to their receivers. This results in, at best, a faint and flickering blip on radar screens. Radar signals bounced off aircraft are also used to obtain distance and altitude information. Because the F-117 returns such an unstable signal, radars are unsure how far away it is or what its altitude is. Moreover, the F-117 has radar-jamming and deception equipment, so even the faint radar indication of an F-117 can quickly be made to disappear or move in another direction. Heat sensors are becoming popular means of detecting aircraft, and the F-117 does not throw off as much heat as a normal aircraft. The exhaust of its two jet engines is dispersed over the rear of the aircraft, making its heat signature unreliable. Finally, to further enhance "stealth," the F-117 flies "low and slow." The F-117 is so difficult to train with because it is basically a low-level bomber that has to get a hit on the first pass. Flying at low altitude takes a lot out of a pilot, and a lot of attention must be paid to finding and attacking the target. Pilots say that the F-117 "flies better than it looks." But this is not much consolation to the pilot who must deal simultaneously with flying, bombing, electronic countermeasures, and any unforeseen emergencies. Nearly a ton of bombs is carried internally in two bays. Once a target is hit, the enemy will be alerted, and the F-117 will be in more immediate danger. The basic tactic of the F-117 is to fly alone, preferably at night and in bad weather, through heavily defended airspace to attack high-value targets like headquarters, radar sites, and so forth. Its range is less than 1,000 km, but it is small enough to be carried long distances by C-5 cargo aircraft. Rarely has an aircraft demanded so much from individual pilots as the single-seat F-117.

Cure for the Black Box Blues

The 1960s vintage F-111 aircraft was supposed to usher in a new era in all-weather, low-level flying. It did, most of the time. But there were all those unexplained crashes while flying through the muck close to the ground. Some were the result of encounters with large birds (feathery variety). Some were the result of electronics problems. It was the electronic mishaps that made pilots nervous. They like to be in control. No one likes to trust his life to a bunch of black boxes full of electronics. Then more aircraft appeared that were meant to fly close to the ground no matter what the visibility. Finally, in the early 1980s, a solution was found, and it was called ANVIS (aviators' night-vision imaging system), basically a lightweight version of the 1960s era "Starlight Scope" that could enhance any available light to make night look like day. The U.S. Army picked up on them first, using them for helicopter pilots who spent most of their time at low altitudes. It wasn't long before low-flying air-force pilots picked up on the idea. The ANVIS are not perfect. They are bulky and make it difficult to look at your instruments and the dark world outside quickly and easily. But pilots now could double-check their black boxes, and that meant a lot.

AWACS

The subject of an intense congressional debate a few years ago when the United States proposed to sell a few to Saudi Arabia, AWACS—Airborne Warning and Control System—aircraft are essentially flying air-combat command centers. Equipped with powerful radars and computers, each AWACS airplane can scan an enormous chunk of sky for hostile aircraft, and direct friendly aircraft into action as needed. The U.S. Air Force has 52 E-3A AWACS aircraft, a modified Boeing 707 with a "flying saucer" radar dome on its roof. A single E-3A can track about 1,000 enemy aircraft at once, while directing about 100 friendly ones. The navy operates about 64 of its smaller E-2s, which, though less sophisticated, have the advantage of being carrier capable. The Soviets have a small number of much less capable AWACS, and none that can operate from carriers.

Characteristics of Tactical Aircraft

Designing airplanes is at best a difficult art. When it comes to designing warplanes, the task can become extraordinary. Take the fighter. Each type of fighter has a differing set of characteristics:

Fighter Type	Thrust-Weight Ratio	Wing-Loading
Air Superiority	High	Low
Close Support	Low	Low
Ground Attack	Medium	High
Interceptors	Medium	Medium

The "thrust-weight ratio" may best be thought of in terms of horsepower per pound of aircraft: the higher the figure, the greater the acceleration. Wing-loading is the area of the wing divided by the weight of the aircraft: The lower this is, the faster the plane, but it costs in terms of ordnance and fuel capacity. Each differing set of characteristics provides for the unique requirements of each type of fighter. Thus, for the air-superiority fighter these characteristics will be speed, with fast pickup, and high agility, but low ordnance capacity, while the interceptor will have great speed, the ground-attack fighter will be able to carry lots of ordnance, and the close support fighters will be able to loiter—hang around over the battlefield—while being agile enough to escape passing air-superiority fighters, and still be able to carry lots of hardware. Each function requires a different set of design compromises. However, since budgetary constraints often necessitate giving a particular airplane as many different roles as possible, the result may frequently be an unwieldy aircraft. Thus, for every airplane which proves as versatile as the P-51 or F-4, there are many more that are as pedestrian as the F-18.

A Little Boost

Artillery usually depends more on accuracy than range. There are times, however, when you need to hit a target just a bit beyond your normal range and are willing to fire more, although less accurate, shells to obtain the hits needed. This situation gave rise to the development of the RAP (rocket-assisted projectile) in the 1960s. However, situations requiring RAP were not that common, and neither were the orders for RAP shells. Now, electronic developments have changed that. Artillery shells with guidance systems and electrically controlled fins can guide an otherwise inaccurate RAP shell right onto a small target. The U.S. Air Force has found the improvements in miniaturized guidance systems even more useful for bombs. The USAF has developed the AGM-130 rocket-boosted glide bomb. Normally, a glide bomb can glide a few kilometers and use a built-in TV or heat-seeking (imaging) system to enable the aircraft pilot to guide the warhead past air-defense systems to the target. The AGM-130 uses a rocket boost to get a range of 20–30 km. This is what "bombing" will be in the future, instead of taking the aircraft right over the target.

Spectre and the U-Boat

The United States Army has a commando force that is supported by an air-force unit equipped with special helicopters, transports, and gunships. The twelve AC-130 Spectre gunships are unique. They are the same four-engine C-130 transports-turned-gunships that ravaged the Ho Chi Minh Trail in Vietnam twenty years ago. New engines, better ECM, and in-flight refueling capability have been added. They are equipped with sensors and weapons that enable them to deliver firepower in support of small groups of friendly troops on the ground.

The Spectre operates best at night, being equipped with all-weather navigation gear and pilots who habitually practice flying at 200 feet altitude. Weapons include two 20-mm automatic cannon firing 40 rounds per second. Normally, a gun fires bursts of 200–250 rounds. Each gun has 3,000 rounds. There is a 40-mm gun that fires 100 rounds per minute; 256 rounds are carried. And there is also a 105-mm howitzer, firing 5–6 rounds per minute, with 100 rounds available, plus two 7.62-mm Vulcan-type "mini-guns." Sensors include an infrared radar (FLIR), low-light-level TV, a system for detecting vehicles by the electrical signal their ignition systems emit, and a beacon-tracking system, for ground units carrying the electronic beacons. There are also normal and infrared searchlights and a laser for designating targets for bombers equipped with laser bombs.

Countermeasures include jammers and infrared decoys. The aircraft's engines are shielded to decrease heat exhaust. Weapons are fired at altitudes from 3,000 to 15,000 feet. This keeps Spectre out of range of most small-arms fire. Just in case, there is half a ton of armor on the bottom of the aircraft. Half of the fourteen crew members fly the plane or operate the sensors while the other half take care of the weapons. The aircraft is not pressurized, because of the need to let all the fumes from the guns escape. This makes for a very uncomfortable ride at the normal low cruising altitudes. Thanks to in-flight refueling, the aircraft can spend over thirty hours in the air, traveling across an ocean, delivering fire support for several hours, and returning to base. In 1992 the new AC-130U model, called the "U-Boat," will enter service. It will have one trainable 25-mm cannon instead of two 20-mm guns plus better electronics but otherwise be similar to the existing Spectre.

My God, It *Is* Bigger!

One of the less obvious expenses of a space-shuttle program is an aircraft large enough to carry the landed shuttle, or other large rocket components, back to its launch site. The United States employs a modified Boeing 747 jumbo jet. Russia has no such aircraft. Its largest airborne load carrier is the An-124, which is structurally incapable of carrying a shuttle on its back. The Russians' solution to this problem was a new version of the An-124, the An-225, which cost them several hundred million dollars in development expenses. The An-124 can carry 150 tons; the An-225 can haul 200. Moreover, the 225 has a tail designed to provide better stability when carrying odd loads, and six engines instead of four. Although the basic structure of the An-124 is retained, the An-225 is twenty-six feet longer. The An-225 weighs 600 tons on takeoff. Work on the An-225 began in 1984, and it first flew in 1989.

Internal Cruise Missiles

The U.S. Air Force spends $1.7 million each for rotary launchers, which enable B-52 bombers to carry cruise missiles internally and launch them. These launchers operate just like a revolver. Before each missile is launched, it is rotated so that it is above the bomb-bay doors. There is a data connection between the missile and the aircraft, so that as the missile is dropped, it is commanded to start its flight sequence. This involves deploying—spreading—its wings, activating the guidance system, and starting its jet engine.

The Command of the Air

"To conquer the command of the air means victory; to be beaten in the air means defeat."—Giulio Douhet, Italian pioneer air-warfare theoretician, 1921

Air Power

There are about 43,000 fixed-wing combat aircraft in the world, including many obsolete types flown by less affluent nations. The ten largest air forces in the world are:

Russia	9,850 fixed-wing combat aircraft	France	690
U.S.	7,400	Israel	675
China	5,500	Poland	660
India	750	Britain	600
North Korea	730	West Germany	571

The figures for the NATO powers are:

U.S.	7,400	Netherlands	225
France	690	Spain	220
Britain	600	Canada	195
West Germany	571	Belgium	170
Turkey	540	Norway	100
Italy	400	Portugal	115
Greece	325	Denmark	90

Neither Luxembourg nor Iceland have any aircraft. Among the Warsaw Pact powers, the figures are:

Russia	9,850	Romania	350
Poland	660	Bulgaria	255
Czechoslovakia	450	Hungary	135
East Germany	350		

The intensity of the Middle East arms race is suggested by the fact that three of the powers listed among the top ten are from that region:

Israel	675	Syria	450
Libya	510	Egypt	450
Iraq	500	Jordan	114

The Asian arms race is one that is frequently overlooked but is also rather intense:

China	5,500	South Korea	400
India	750	Vietnam	400
North Korea	730	Pakistan	350
Taiwan	440	Japan	300

While most countries have an "air force," many of these only have a few transport aircraft. As a result, the smallest "combat" air force in the world is that of Rwanda, which has two armed aircraft. Of course, these figures can also be looked at on a population basis. There are about eight combat aircraft per million people worldwide. The ten most heavily equipped air forces in terms of aircraft per million people are:

Israel	151	South Yemen	48
Libya	119	Switzerland	42
Singapore	69	Jordan	38
Qatar	67	Syria	37
Sweden	53	Djibouti	37

None of the Warsaw Pact or NATO powers makes the top ten. The surprising development is the presence of several quite small powers on the list, as well as two of the most determinedly neutral powers, Switzerland and Sweden. For NATO the figures are:

Greece	31	Britain	11
U.S.	30	Turkey	10
Norway	23	West Germany	10
Denmark	19	Portugal	9
Belgium	17	Canada	8
Netherlands	15	Italy	7
France	12	Spain	6

Again, neither Luxembourg nor Iceland has any combat aircraft. For the Warsaw Pact powers, the figures are:

Russia	35	Poland	17
Czechoslovakia	29	Romania	15
Bulgaria	28	Hungary	13
East Germany	21		

Heat and the High Cost of Aircraft

The first all-metal aircraft, widely used during World War II, were made of aluminum. This metal was much lighter than steel, and had sufficient strength to hold the aircraft together. As jet aircraft came into wide use during the late 1940s, there arose a need for more strength and better resistance to heat. The heat problem was particularly acute in jet-engine components. Thus, in the 1950s, the use of titanium arose. Although several times more expensive than aluminum, and 60 percent heavier, it was twice as strong and could withstand twice as much heat. At first only key components were made with titanium. But as the aircraft got faster and heavier, the use of titanium escalated.

Aircraft planned for introduction during the 1990s require even more robust materials. So now we have silicon-carbide titanium (SCT), which is only 40 percent heavier than aluminum but can carry over three times as much weight and withstand over four times as much heat. SCT will be particularly needed in higher-performance engines. All this is not without cost, as SCT is over ten times more expensive than titanium. Ironically, the higher speeds are not all that useful in combat itself, and the pilots cannot physically withstand the stresses of sharp maneuvers at high speeds. High speed is crucial, however, in getting to the battle. It's the old "getting there first with the most" routine. But high speed requires much more fuel, which means you either don't use speed much or build a larger aircraft to carry more fuel. And so it goes, and the aircraft prices keep going up.

B-1, Slowly

By 1988 each of the 99 B-1B bombers had flown less than 300 hours. In 1988 the readiness rate (percentage of aircraft ready for combat) was only 36 percent, although that was an improvement over the previous year, when it was 25 percent. Most of the flight training by the 108 trained crews has not been at the normal low altitudes because of safety considerations. Problems with the electronics are estimated to cost over $200 million per aircraft to fix. By early 1989, there were only 98 B-1s left, and defects had been observed in the "swing-wing" mechanism (including puncturing fuel tanks), grounding the entire fleet. The B-1 is expected to be "mature" (eliminate most of the problems) in 1994, or thereabouts.

Strategic Bombers

The United States has 420 strategic bombers, all jet-propelled third- or fourth-generation aircraft. Russia has 160 older and slower second-generation prop-driven planes. Over 100 U.S. planes are always on alert and either already in the air or capable of getting into the air before their bases could be hit by missile warheads. Russia is still testing its fourth-generation Tu-160 (Blackjack) bomber, having built 11 examples over the past ten years for this purpose. Meanwhile, the United States has deployed 98 fourth-generation B-1 bombers and is testing the fifth-generation B-2 bomber, of which 132 are supposed eventually to be built. The United States also has over 400 carrier-based aircraft that can hit targets inside Russia. U.S. bombers are equipped with 1,700 first-generation cruise missiles. Russian bombers carry only 700 cruise missiles. The United States is planning to build 1,500 second-generation cruise missiles by 1993. In addition, U.S. bombers also have over 1,000 short-range cruise missiles (SRAM), and with a second-generation model in development. Russia has no equivalent. The United States has over 600 tanker aircraft to support its bombers and is equipping half of them with more efficient engines by 1993. Russia has 30 prop-driven tankers, but will begin to replace them with jet-propelled models by 1992.

Suicide Squadrons

The loss of a $280 million B-1 bomber as a result of a collision with a passing bird underscores the generally overlooked danger of "bird strike" to military—and civil—aviation. The air force calculates that its aircraft have unfortunate encounters with birds over five times a day, almost 2,000 times a year, with damages amounting to about $100 million, with about 1 percent of the incidents resulting in human casualties, amounting to about twenty injured, and occasionally dead, airmen a year. While large birds can cause engine failure to any jet if sucked into an air intake, for high-performance military aircraft a collision with even a small bird can be potentially disastrous, for the plane as well as the bird, given the speeds involved. Several birds can dive at speeds approaching 200 km an hour. As the bird's mass is multiplied by the relative velocities, it becomes, in effect, a solid projectile. While the air force is still studying the problem, some bird-plagued airports have taken to posting shotgun-toting security personnel along their runways.

Russian Helicopter-Pilot Training

The Russians have been training combat helicopter pilots for over twenty years. The first opportunity to use these pilots in combat came in Afghanistan. Soon pilots were returning and writing articles for Russian military journals. A year or so after this writing, articles began to appear deploring the abilities of pilots arriving in Afghanistan. Apparently, pilot training paid more attention to limiting wear and tear on the helicopters than to preparing pilots for the violent maneuvers they would have to use to survive ground fire. Eventually, the Russians had to set up pilot-training schools in Afghanistan and retrain incoming helicopter pilots. The pilot schools back in Russia had no desire to change, and gave the returning pilots a hard time when these pilots showed off their realistic combat maneuvers learned under combat conditions. Things change slowly in Russia. U.S. pilots had a similar experience in Vietnam, but changes in pilot training back home came very quickly.

Quality Versus Quantity?

In the early 1950s, the United States produced about 3,000 fighter aircraft a year, a figure that had declined to about 400 by the late 1970s, and is currently running at an average of 168 per year, although sufficient reserve capacity exists to expand production to about 450 with relatively little effort. One important reason for this decline in production runs is a marked rise in costs. In 1953 a "hot" fighter such as the F-100 cost about $2.6 million in 1990 dollars, while the F-4 of 1961 ran about $5.5 million in constant dollars, the F-5E, an "austere" fighter of 1975, ran $4.2 million, and the F-15 now costs something like $47.3 million. Of course, quality has also risen. If we give the F-100 an effectiveness rating of 100, the F-4 would rate about 220, the F-5E would rate about 190, and the F-15 about 340. The question, of course, is whether the tripling of effectiveness in the F-15 is worth the cost, about eighteen times what an F-100 ran, which forces us to have far fewer aircraft: in effect, would having eighteen less-capable aircraft such as the F-100 be militarily sounder than having one F-15?

The "Aggressor" Air Force

The United States armed forces maintain 180 combat aircraft for the sole purpose of realistically portraying likely opponents of U.S. pilots. This aggressor air force includes over twenty Russian aircraft. The remainder are various U.S. models and Israeli Kfirs, modified and flown to accurately mimic various potential opponents. The United States also has access to foreign pilots who have flown a wide range of Russian aircraft, some in combat. Russia has very few Western aircraft and no similar access to pilots with experience flying current Western aircraft.

Military-Aviation Safety Rates

Due to increased training and maintenance, the flying elements of the American armed forces are attaining their lowest accident rates in history. In 1986 the overall interservice rate of serious accidents was 2.5 per 100,000 hours flown, a "serious accident" being one in which someone is killed, an aircraft is lost, or $500,000 worth of damage occurs. The individual service rates vary considerably from the average; the army had 2.7 accidents per 100,000 hours; the air force, 1.5; and the navy and marines, 3.4. The differences may be attributed to several factors. Carrier landings and takeoffs are inherently more dangerous than operating from land bases, and, what's more, they put a considerable strain on men and machinery. This helps account for the higher navy and marine accident rate, while the army's rate is due to the extensive use of helicopters, which are more difficult to maintain and rather unstable when compared with fixed-wing aircraft. The army choppers also spend much of their time in more difficult low-level flight, a problem that affects marine air operations as well. Some idea of the progress that has been achieved in safety may be gained by noting that in 1956 the navy/marine accident rate per 100,000 hours was 3,348. By 1966 it had declined to 1,273, and by 1976 was down to 6.48.

Flying Silicon

Simulators for high-performance jet aircraft often cost as much as, or more than, the aircraft they are simulating. An example is the simulators for the new ground-attack version of the U.S. F-15 fighter. An F-15 simulator costs well over $40 million, about what the actual F-15 costs. However, the actual aircraft are flown about 400–500 hours a year at a cost of over $10,000 per hour, while the simulators are "flown" over 3,000 hours a year at a cost of only about $2,000 per hour. These simulators are expensive because they are so realistic. Tests have found that pilot training in simulators is about 80 percent as effective as training in the real thing. Moreover, you can train for emergencies in simulators that would get most trainees killed in the actual aircraft. Even though the simulators never leave the ground, the pilots take them quite seriously and often come out of them soaked in sweat and as exhausted as if they had been flying an actual aircraft. While bad flying in a simulator will not get you killed, it can cost you your flying career.

The Ancient and Honorable Chinese Air Force

The Chinese Air Force—the "People's Liberation Army Air Force"—has over 5,000 combat aircraft. The majority, however, were designed over thirty years ago. Since the Chinese lost military assistance from Russia in the early 1960s, they have produced their own versions of Russian-designed aircraft. Long unable to keep up with world progress in aircraft design, they have recently begun to make up for lost ground. But their aircraft inventory is truly disheartening. The oldest models still in service are some 200 MiG-15s (Chinese designation J-2), which first saw action in 1950 over Korea. Most of these are used for training. About 600 MiG-17s (J-4/A-5), an early 1950s design, are used primarily for ground attack. Some 2,400 MiG-19s (J-6), a mid-1950s design, are used for interception, ground attack, and reconnaissance. Some 400 Q-5s, a substantial redesign of the J-6, are used as bombers. Some 300 MiG-21s (J-7), a late 1950s design, are used as interceptors. As with the J-6/Q-5, the Chinese took the J-7 and substantially improved it as the J-8. Over 300 of these are in service and are being produced as quickly as possible. In cooperation with U.S. firms, an even more advanced version, the J-8 II, is being planned.

The long-range bomber force is extremely ancient, including a dozen Russian Tu-4s, clones of the U.S. World War II B-29. There are also 100 Tu-16s (H-6) and 500 Il-28s (H-5), both of early 1950s vintage, although manufactured by the Chinese much later. The Chinese Navy also has a land-based air force—"the People's Liberation Army Naval Air Force"—comprising 320 MiG-19s (J-6) and 100 MiG-17s (J-5), which are used as interceptors over naval bases and ships operating off the coast. Antiship bombers consist of 120 Q-5s and 140 Il-28 (H-5) torpedo bombers. China has only about 500 helicopters, most of them thirty-year-old Mi-4 models. They are beginning to build modern European models under license.

While this ancient but large collection of aircraft might appear vulnerable to a more modern air force, the Chinese position is not all that precarious. Their opponents are not present in overwhelming strength. Russian forces in the Far East are the most lethal potential foes, consisting of some 2,700 combat aircraft and helicopters. About a third of these are away from the Chinese border and would have to be brought forward. There is also the Russian-controlled Mongolian Air Force, with only 12 MiG-21s and 12 MiG-17s. Also troublesome are the Vietnamese, with some 400 older aircraft (160 MiG-21 fighters, 75 Su-22 attack, 72 MiG-17 attack, 36 MiG-23 fighters, 22 A-37 attack, 21 F-5 fighters). South Korea (36 F-16, 122 F-4, 220 F-5) and North Korea (36 MiG-29, 56 MiG-23, 180 MiG-21, 30 Su-7, 52 H-5, 40 A-5, 120 J-6, 220 J-4) pretty much cancel each other out. A particularly strong potential ally is Japan (150 F-15s and 140 F-4s). There is also Taiwan (340 F-5, 100 F-104), which is edging closer to some sort of understanding with China. China's situation in the air is not hopeless, it is merely hopeful.

The Luxembourg Air Force

Tiny Luxembourg, which has no air force, does however have eighteen E-3 AWACS combat air-control aircraft flying around with its national insignia on their wings. This is due to a quirk in international law that requires aircraft to bear a national registration number. The eighteen aircraft actually belong to NATO and were purchased jointly by twelve NATO nations. They operate out of bases in Norway, Germany, Italy, Greece, and Turkey. There are also some Luxembourgian pilots serving with the Belgians, but that's another story.

It's a Jungle Out There.

During the Vietnam War, the U.S. Army officially reported 4,643 helicopters lost in action: A further 6,000 were so severely damaged as to require extensive rebuilding. There were about 36 million helicopter sorties, so about 3 out of 10,000 flights resulted in serious damage. Lesser damage occurred more frequently. However, casualties were rare. The 10,000 damaged helicopters resulted in only

3,000 deaths and 2,300 injured. This amounted to less than one injury for each chopper lost or damaged. When you consider that the war lasted ten years and that there were always hundreds—and at times over a thousand—helicopters assigned to army aviation units, losing a dozen or so a week was not a catastrophe. Nevertheless, flying or riding in helicopters during Vietnam was still risky, or at least nerve-racking. Sundry bullet holes in the choppers did more damage to peace of mind than the helicopters, and were rarely counted as "damage."

Low and Lethal

Like the infantry, modern combat aircraft find that the safest place to be is close to the ground. This safety is relative, as the aircraft move along the treetops at speeds of 400–700 kph (100–200 meters a second). To do this sort of thing with any degree of success takes lots of practice. And even the practice is lethal. The British Air Force lost a number of Tornado fighters to training accidents through 1988 and the Dutch Air Force 17 F-16s, not to mention the air-show disaster that resulted when five Italian aircraft engaged in an aerobatic display collided over a crowd of several thousand people. Much of this low-level training takes place over West Germany, where the weather is usually terrible and the countryside is infested with power lines and nasty terrain for low-level flying in general. Disturbed by the loud noises of low-flying jets, most of the population agitates for the banning of low-level flights. The commercial airlines are also upset that large portions of West German airspace are "restricted" for the use of combat-aircraft training. If bans on low-level flying are ever enacted in West Germany, initial wartime losses of low-flying aircraft unpracticed in low-level flying would be substantial.

Airlift Problems, Soviet-Style

To lift one of the eight Russian airborne divisions, which each have some 6,500 men and about 6,000 tons of equipment, requires 1,126 sorties by the twenty-ton capacity An-12 light transport, or 639 by the forty-ton capacity Il-76, or 416 by the eighty-ton capacity An-22. Use of the gigantic 150-ton capacity An-124 or the 200-ton capacity An-224 would probably reduce the figure by half or more, though this is less certain. The trouble is that the Russian armed forces only have about 500 An-12s, 150 to 200 Il-76s, 50 An-22s, a handful of An-124s, and even fewer An-224s, for a total of no more than 800 aircraft capable of lifting combat units. The Russian do have lots of helicopters to help out, but even with these they would not have sufficient lift to move even a quarter of their airborne forces simultaneously. Of course, they could always call up hundreds of Aeroflot aircraft, but this would tip their hand in a building crisis.

Light and Lively

To airlift a complete combat-ready 16,000-man U.S. infantry division with supplies for ninety days requires 1,333 aircraft sorties, including 1,152 by C-141Bs and 181 by C-5As. An airborne division, also about 16,000 men, requires only 908 C-141B and 77 C-5A sorties, while that of a 10,000-man light division requires only 478 sorties by C-141Bs. While the movement of the light division would monopolize the air force's inventory of C-141Bs for four days, that of the infantry division would tie up all the 270 or so C-141Bs and the 125 C-5s for as many as eleven days.

Senatorial Privilege

Although the air force will not confirm the story, it has been reported that two distinguished senators with extensive flying experience during and after World War II, men more accustomed to sitting on opposite sides of the political spectrum than next to each other in a cockpit, put one of the earliest B-1 bombers through its paces on an officially "unofficial" test flight.

Everybody Wants to Get In On the Act.

Russian sources claim that in the two years after Mattias Rust landed his little airplane in Red Square, violations of Soviet airspace had risen markedly, occasionally to as many as fifty a month.

What Are We Paying For?

On October 5, 1969, a Cuban Air Force officer who had decided to defect to the United States in his MiG-17 did not come to the attention of the U.S. Air Force until he radioed for permission to land at Homestead Air Force Base in Florida, some 200 miles from his base, having successfully penetrated well over a hundred miles into U.S. airspace. This points out not severe deficiencies in U.S. air defenses, but Western dependence on intelligence. Hundreds of billions of dollars have been invested in intelligence-gathering by Western nations, particularly the United States. One of the principal uses of this intelligence system is to provide a few days' warning of hostilities. If the warning is received, the troops can be brought up to a high state of alert. In practice, military units cannot maintain a high state of readiness constantly. Russia tries to do this with its air-defense system, but it hasn't worked out very well. So while a single free-lance flyer can embarrass the armed forces, it does not prove that they're asleep on the job.

The Real Mission of the B-2

The Stealth bomber (B-2) is officially (in at least one press release) a system intended to roam Russian airspace seeking out, with the assistance of satellite sensors, mobile ICBMs. This scenario is unlikely, as the satellites would be prime targets in nuclear or conventional warfare and any threat to their mobile ICBMs would most likely trigger a nuclear exchange that would make any further B-2 missions moot. However, if a major war were fought and both sides refrained from using nuclear weapons, the B-2 would be an ideal weapon for using conventional bombs to go after key targets within Russia. Command posts, power plants, ammo dumps, military bases, satellite-support facilities, and transportation targets are among the items crucial to waging any kind of warfare. The damage would be gradual, giving the Russians time to rethink their objectives in such a major conventional war.

So Much for Secrecy

Although the air force kept its radical new B-2 Stealth bomber under very tight security for its entire period of development, when the prototype was rolled out in November of 1988, complete with a musical "Stealth Fanfare," public reaction to the multibillion-dollar supersecret project was something less than spectacular. Indeed, the actual aircraft varied little in character from predictions made in a number of aviation and defense publications, and it was very similar in appearance to both a plastic model kit that had been put on the market by an enterprising model-airplane firm and a 20,000-pound, nearly fullscale sheet metal mock-up version that had been built for $10,000 in order to help an auto manufacturer sell cars, a mock-up that the air force expressed an interest in buying.

Air Power on the Cheap

A country that stands in great need of some air power but has meager resources might consider buying a surplus executive jet. Several hundred of these come on the market each year in the United States alone, and can be had in fair order for anything from $200,000 to $1 million apiece. A minigun pod can be obtained for about $60,000 more, and a rocket pod for about $16,000. If the pod is mounted on the centerline of the aircraft, and some reinforcing is done, a fairly inexpensive counterinsurgency aircraft can be had rather quickly, and one could even fix light bomb racks to the wings. Although the plane won't last too long, since the weaponry—not to mention hostile fire—will subject its airframe to stresses for which it was not designed, it may fit the bill in a pinch.

The ICBM Accuracy Race

The first attempt at a strategic ballistic missile was the German V-2 of 1944. It had a range of 360 km and a CEP (circular error probable, the diameter centering on the target within which there was a 50 percent chance of hitting) of 6,500 meters. Capable of carrying about a ton of explosives, the V-2 would only have been decisive with a nuclear weapon. However, nuclear weapons of that era weighed over ten tons, so the V-2 hardly qualified as the first ICBM. But it was the beginning.

In 1959 the first true ICBM, the U.S. Atlas, went into service. It had a CEP of 3,300 meters. The Russians made a few false starts, but got some SS-6s into service during 1961. Each had a CEP of 3,600 meters. In 1962 the U.S. Minuteman I (CEP 2,000 meters) and Titan (1,200 meters) came into service.

In 1966 the United States fielded the Minuteman II (500 meters) and in 1970 the Minuteman III (400 meters). Russia was slower in the accuracy race. Some SS-7s (2,700 meters) appeared in 1962 and the mass-produced SS-8 (1,800 meters) in 1964. The SS-9 (900 meters) appeared in small numbers in 1966. In that same year, the SS-11-1 (1,400 meters) showed up. The SS-13-1 (1,800 meters) entered the picture in 1969.

By 1970 each side had nearly a thousand ICBMs capable of blasting each others' cities into oblivion. But the Russians noticed that U.S. missiles had continued to become more accurate than required just to hit large urban areas. It was apparent that the Americans were out to develop the ability to destroy Russian missile silos, a job that required a very small CEP. Attacking Russian silos would only be useful if Russian missiles were still in those silos, and this would be the case only if the United States attacked first.

So through the 1970s, the Russians strove to catch up, often simply replacing guidance systems in existing missiles. In 1973 the SS-11-2 (1,100 meters) showed up, as did the SS-13-2 (1,200 meters). In 1974 the SS-18-1 (500 meters) came along. In 1975 there was the SS-17-1 (500 meters) and the SS-19-1 (500 meters). In 1977 the Russians finally brought out a model that matched the American one, the SS-18-2 (400 meters), but only in small quantities. There were also a number of multiple-warhead versions of their missiles introduced, another area where the United States had a large lead. Through the 1970s, most Russian ICBMs were only accurate enough for city busting. In 1979 there were a few SS-18-3s with a CEP of 300 meters. But that same year the United States introduced the Minuteman III with a CEP of 220 meters. The MX Peacekeeper, with a CEP of 100 meters, had already been designed, but production was delayed until 1986 because of budgetary and political problems. In the late 1980s, Russia brought out the SS-24 and SS-25, but neither appears to have achieved CEPs of better than 300–400 meters. The Russian approach with these last two missiles was to make them mobile, thus rendering U.S. CEPs less critical. The Russians have had even less success with CEPs in their sea-launched ballistic missiles (SLBMs). Both sides had SLBMs through the early 1960s with CEPs of 3,600 meters. Then the United States brought out the Polaris A3 in 1964 with a 900-meter CEP.

In 1971 there came the Poseidon, with a 500-meter CEP. The Trident C4 of 1983 had a CEP of 220 meters and the Trident C5 of 1989 a 100-meter CEP. The Russians never got their SLBM CEP lower than 800–900 meters. Moreover, U.S. SLBMs carried more warheads per missile and traveled in quieter subs.

Guaranteeing the Bang for the Buck

Nuclear weapons are rather complex devices, containing precisely machined metal parts and carefully formed conventional explosives needed to trigger the nuclear material into a nuclear reaction (explosion). There are a lot of electronics included to make sure everything happens when it's supposed to. The two nuclear superpowers each have dozens of different nuclear weapons for each of their various delivery systems (missiles and bombers). To make sure that each of these nuclear weapons works, some four to ten tests of the weapon must be conducted. Since the early 1960s, most of these tests have been conducted underground to avoid polluting the atmosphere with radioactivity. Between 1945 and 1990, about 1,800 tests were conducted. More than half were American, most of the remainder Russian. France has conducted over 170 tests, while Britain and China have detonated about three dozen nuclear devices each. At least one nuclear power, Israel, is not known ever to have detonated a nuclear device, although the Israelis may have detonated very small ones underground that went undetected. The major powers do not bother to test nuclear-weapons designs once they are in inventory. The United States has performed fewer than ten nuclear tests to double-check the reliability of existing weapons. Russia may have conducted more "quality control" tests, given the Russian lackluster track record with high-tech devices. The United States has conducted so many tests because of the desire to have a wide and up-to-date variety of nuclear weapons. This has led to the production of dozens of "designer nukes"; weapons with a wide variety of exotic features. Russia has a much smaller number of more limited designs. U.S. weapons have special features for things like the amount of radiation released and variable yield (turn a dial to set the size of the explosion). These nuclear tests cost several million dollars each.

The Air War in Central America

The long-drawn-out war in Nicaragua was mostly fought in the hills and forests of that country, with an occasional exchange between ground forces and helicopters or other aircraft being operated by either the Sandinista government or the U.S.-sponsored Contras. There was, however, one genuine air battle, in late 1985. A machine-gun-armed Contra Cessna O-2A, which by some accounts formerly served with the New York National Guard, tangled briefly with a similarly equipped Sandinista Marchetti SF260 WL, one of six supplied by Libya, somewhere in the northern part of the country. Despite some superficial damage to both aircraft, the "dogfight" was inconclusive.

It Happens Everywhere

Sweden, one of the few nations that develops its own combat aircraft, also has problems with costs. Their new fighter for the 1990s, the JAS 39 "Gripen," will cost about $38 million each, nearly 40 percent over the original budget, if it ever goes into production. On its sixth test flight, it crashed. The cause was thought to be faulty computer software in one of the aircraft's many complex systems. Although these seem to have been worked out, the plane has begun to attract the attention of parliamentary budget-cutters.

Keep 'em Flying!

The U.S. armed forces own a lot of strategic missiles—ICBMs and SLBMs—and combat aircraft, plus thousands of helicopters and other aircraft. It takes a lot of men and women to keep these flying. Bearing in mind that there are about 593,000 men and women in the air force, about 582,000 in the navy, about 198,000 in the marine corps, and about 771,000 in the army, a look at these figures can be highly educational. Consider the ratio of missiles and fixed-wing combat aircraft to manpower.

Flying Combat Platforms

SERVICE	MISSILES	AIRPLANES	TOTAL	TROOPS PER PLATFORM
USAF	1,000	4,500	5,500	108
USN	640	1,600	2,200	264
USMC		600	600	330

If combat helicopters are included, the figures change somewhat.

Flying Combat Platforms

SERVICE	MISSILES	AIRCRAFT	TOTAL	TROOPS PER PLATFORM
USAF	1,000	4,500	5,500	108
USN	640	1,760	2,400	243
USMC		700	700	282
USA		4,000	4,000	193

Note that the army figures exclude helicopters, which may be armed for self-defense but are not considered "combat" helicopters. If we include these, and all other aircraft, including transport aircraft, the figures change yet again.

Flying Machines

SERVICE	MISSILES	AIRCRAFT (Combat)	AIRCRAFT (Other)	TOTAL	TROOPS PER MACHINE
USAF	1,000	4,500	3,500	8,000	74
USN	640	1,760	200	2,600	224
USMC		700	100	800	232
USA		4,000	5,200	9,200	76

The airframe-to-manpower ratio for the army is nothing short of remarkable, considering that the air force not only has a lot of things that fly without pilots, it doesn't have any tanks to operate, either.

I Dare You to Cross *This* Line!

Libya's promotion of terrorism in the seventies and eighties earned it a visit by U.S. bombers in 1986. Shaken but undeterred, Libya proceeded to build a chemical-weapons plant 80 km south of the coastal capital of Tripoli. U.S. officials began making noises about sending the bombers in before terrorists got hold of lethal chemicals. In October 1988, Libya announced that its main airport, also south of Tripoli, would be closed to commercial aviation, and henceforth any aircraft flying in low over the coast would immediately be fired on. These measures might help to prevent a conventional air strike, but the 1986 raid used heavy doses of electronic-warfare techniques to stymie Libyan air defenses. Moreover, a new raid could be conducted by the even more invisible F-117 Stealth fighter. The F-117 would have to be spotted visually, at night, and engaged with cannon, as its electronics would confound any guided missiles. Not very likely. Meanwhile, Libyan aviation authorities scramble to prepare a suitable alternative civilian airport.

Hangar Queen

An aircraft that never seems to work properly and spends most of its time in the hangar is known as a "hangar queen."

"Tout pour la France!"

Not only did the French sell Iraq surface-to-air missiles and aircraft to carry them, they also supplied the latest electronic-warfare equipment and French Air Force pilots to fly combat missions along with Iraqi pilots. Once the Iraqi pilots had enough combat experience, French pilots stopped flying in the combat zone, but continued to provide training. French technicians maintained the more sophisticated electronic equipment and worked with French scientists to modify equipment in response to operational experience. For this reason, French arms salesmen have a much easier time selling to other nations the equipment used and perfected in the skies over the Persian Gulf.

Flying Lessons

NATO intelligence units regularly monitor radio activity in East Germany. One day a Russian Air Force general flying a MiG-23 was heard carrying on a heated conversation as his aircraft attempted to land in bad weather. The MiG began to have mechanical problems, and the general began getting angry. As he came in lower, the cockpit warning system began to announce, in a taped feminine voice, that various systems were broken, and suggested alternative procedures. The general was really pissed off at this point, and as he crashed, his last words were, "Shut up, you whore, don't try and tell me how to fly an airplane."

Cost of Training

The U.S. Air Force is beginning construction of 210 C-17 heavy transports. The first one was completed in early 1990. The first squadron of twelve aircraft is to become operational in 1992. Training costs for the first three years, including simulators and other expensive items, are over half a billion dollars. Two hundred instructors will train over 5,000 pilots, engine technicians, and loadmasters a year. Note that this implies each C-17 will have more than one crew. This is common with transport, and some combat, aircraft. The machines can put in far more hours of sustained operations than their more easily fatigued human crews.

B-2 Blues

The air force hopes to buy 132 of its new B-2 Stealth bombers, at an estimated cost of between $591 million and $742 million apiece, for a total outlay of $78 billion to $98 billion dollars, which would be almost enough money to pretty much completely reequip all of the ground forces of the United States, including army and marines, active, National Guard, and reserve, some 41 division-equivalents, at an estimated cost that would approach $2 billion per division.

Aircraft Expenditures

In fiscal year 1989, the U.S. armed forces will spend about $28.4 billion on aircraft procurement, roughly 9.7 percent of the defense budget. The lion's share of the aircraft allocation will go to the air force, $16.6 billion (58.6 percent), with the navy and marines getting $9 billion (31.6 percent), and the army only $2.8 billion (10.5 percent), though about a quarter of the air force's share is devoted to ground-support aircraft, which work for the army.

Air-Combat Patterns in the Middle East

The Israeli Air Force appears to have secured a near-permanent superiority over its opponents in air-to-air combat. In the 1967 Six-Day War, Israel lost 3 aircraft in aerial combat while downing 58 of her Arab opponents, for a loss ratio of 1:19.3. Figures for the 1973 October War are still confidential, but Israel appears to have lost between 10 and 20 aircraft in air-to-air combat, as against 227 for her foes, for a loss ratio of from 1:22.7 to 1:11.4, which latter figure, if accurate, suggests considerable slippage. Nevertheless, by the 1982 Lebanon campaign, the Israelis were back in form, losing no aircraft to Syrian MiGs, while downing several dozen in return.

Shooting Down Airliners

The downing of a Korean airliner by a Russian air-defense fighter in the Far East in 1983, and of an Iranian airliner by the USS *Vincennes* in the Persian Gulf five years later, are only the most recent of a series of incidents in which civilian aircraft fell victim to air defenses. A number of other such incidents are known to have occurred: In the early 1980s, a Russian interceptor brought down an Argentine cargo plane over southern Russia; during the 1970s, Russian aircraft forced down a Korean airliner over the Kola Peninsula while Israeli aircraft shot down an Egyptian airliner over the Negev; and in the 1950s, an Israeli airliner was shot down over Bulgaria. In addition, it is believed that as many as seven Russian airliners may have fallen victim to their own air-defense forces over the last forty years, while the loss of an Italian airliner off Sardinia in the early eighties has been attributed by some to a stray NATO antiaircraft missile. It appears that many other such incidents were only narrowly averted. During the Vietnam War, British, Japanese, and other airliners traversing the South China Sea regularly caused carrier aircraft to scramble, and on at least one occasion a U.S. missile cruiser almost opened fire on an airliner. As the *Vincennes* affair shows, the growing sophistication of air defenses does not necessarily mean that such incidents will decrease. A good deal of new air-defense equipment is becoming increasingly automated, and in any case, the personnel will remain fallible. Moreover, sophisticated equipment is passing into the hands of Third World powers that may have poor standards of training and maintenance, which, when coupled with poor command, communications, and control systems, and the increasing number of civil air flights, could lead to disaster. Air Afrique flights have frequently been shadowed by suspicious Libyan fighter aircraft, while Russian and South Korean airliners are notorious for straying out of assigned air lanes.

Tunnel Vision

Over the last decade, sixty-two U.S. military helicopters have crashed, resulting in 134 deaths, because of the misuse of special night-vision goggles designed for use by ground troops. The heavy goggles, made by ITT, electronically amplify available light, such as moonlight, displaying images on two tiny screens, but severely restrict peripheral vision, are overwhelmed by sudden bright lights, and do not function well under cloud cover. As a result, helicopter pilots using the goggles while on low-level, high-speed flights have run into mountains, trees, power lines, and even other aircraft. Nevertheless, military helicopter pilots have been using them as a matter of course for many years. A high-ranking marine aviation officer defended their use on the grounds that "while they have their limitations, they give us more capabilities than we would have without them," while indicating that if pilots "had followed procedures" and "used common sense, the accidents would not have occurred."

There's Something About Russian Pilot-Training Methods. . . .

On August 6, 1988, the president of the African nation of Botswana was flying to Luanda, Angola, in his two-engine executive jet. As the plane entered Angolan airspace at an altitude of 35,000 feet, the pilot noticed one of the engines being blown off the aircraft. Desperate maneuvering and the fortunate appearance of an airfield below allowed all to survive the encounter with an Angolan MiG-21 fighter firing air-to-air missiles. The president of Angola apologized for the overzealousness of his Russian-trained pilot in the defense of Angolan airspace.

Russia's Vietnam Veterans

During the Vietnam War, it was widely believed by most people and known by some intelligence types, that Russian troops were actively serving as crews and advisers for North Vietnamese SAM (surface-to-air missile) systems. Officially, little was made of this by either government. However, one of the items to come out of the current Russian *glasnost* (media openness) is a story about the annual reunion some of Russia's Vietnam vets have been holding since the late 1960s. These graying vets tell stories of U.S. aircraft coming down in flames, and toast comrades who died in U.S. flak-busting raids. The several thousand Russian Viet vets are not as troubled as their U.S. counterparts. After all, the Russians were on the winning side.

The Unbearable Frightfulness of Low-Flying Jets

Even before radar came into use, flying 100–200 feet above the ground was a common technique for avoiding detection. But low flying has many drawbacks. For one thing, it's dangerous. The winds are less predictable down there, and a sudden loss of altitude can be fatal. There are also numerous hard-to-see obstacles, like power lines and large (5–20-lb) birds. Flying low also burns fuel faster and makes navigation more difficult because you cannot as easily see landmarks. Coping with all this adds another problem, pilot fatigue. To make matters even worse, low flyers are often ground-attack air-craft, so on top of all the other problems the pilot also has to find and hit a target while moving along at several hundred meters a second.

The only protection against these dangers is practice, which is in itself dangerous, particularly in Europe, where thousands of aircraft are stationed and the weather is often foggy or overcast. Most air-craft accidents occur while flying low-level training missions. Since the 1960s, several generations of increasingly capable and reliable electronic aids to low-level flying have appeared. But these gadgets cannot take all the risk out of flying on the deck. Moreover, they get more expensive as they get better. Indeed, the U.S. Air Force has admitted that just about any aircraft can be turned into a ground-hugging close-air support plane if enough expensive navigation sys-tems are added. It used to be that aircraft that just attacked ground units were basically cheaper than high-flying fighters. No longer. If you want an all-weather, low-flying, and accurate ground-attack air-craft, plan on paying at least as much as for an all-weather fighter, and probably a little more.

The Odd Couple

Since the 1950s, the U.S. Army has been forbidden to have fixed-wing combat aircraft, and the U.S. Air Force cannot have combat helicopters. This arrangement was meant to prevent future inter-service rivalries and duplication of effort. So the army proceeded to put thousands of attack helicopters in the air, and the air force increasingly pulled back from supplying fixed-wing ground-attack aircraft. Even though the air force assumes that 30 percent of its sorties will be ground attack, and 40 percent multirole (either air-to-air or ground attack), it has been reluctant to devote resources to building a replacement for the aging A-10 dedicated ground-attack aircraft. The air force would prefer to modify a fighter, like the F-16, into a ground-attack aircraft (called the A-16). The army resists.

However, exercises using army attack helicopters and F-16s fitted out for ground attack have shown curious results. The two dissimi-lar aircraft actually complement each other quite well. This was also seen with the slower A-10, but the results were even more dramatic with the faster F-16. The basic tactic is for the helicopters to find enemy units, which usually come lavishly equipped with air-defense weapons. The helicopters call in the F-16s. As the F-16s prepare to make their attack run, the helicopters pepper the enemy with rocket and cannon fire to disrupt the air-defense units. The F-16s, now possessing accurate target data, zip in at high speed, deliver up to seven tons of ordnance, and zip away. As the F-16s fly off, the army helicopters pop up again and hit the now-disrupted enemy with still more fire to cover the F-16s' escape and generally add to the damage and destruction. Such tactics enable the F-16s to do maximum damage and minimize losses to both helicopters and F-16s.

There are, however, several problems with this approach. One is that although the older A-10 is slower, it is armored and basically designed to take hits at low altitude and keep going. Russian divisions have nearly 1,000 heavy machine guns plus scores of antiaircraft cannon and missiles. Another problem with this coordinated approach is getting helicopters and aircraft enough opportunity to practice these tactics in order to make them work. The U.S. Marines can make this sort of cooperation work because the fighter-bombers that support marine units are flown by marines and belong to a marine aviation unit. The marine division commander can give orders directly to the commander of the marine aviation unit. An army division commander must go through several layers of command to reach the air-force unit commander with a "request" for anything. These different degrees of access make an enormous difference.

The Billion-Dollar Makeover

The B-2 Stealth bomber is an adventurous piece of engineering. Using the flying wing is more efficient in lifting weight, and this alone allows the B-2 to carry up to 50 percent more weight than a conventional aircraft of similar size. Over 50,000 people are involved in its design and construction. It was originally conceived as a high-altitude bomber shielded from enemy detection by shape and electronic countermeasures. Approved during the Carter administration, design work was completed in late 1983, shortly after the F-117A fighter became operational. It was then decided that the B-2 would be much safer if it could fly low-level missions. This meant a substantial redesign of the aircraft that cost $1 billion and took over a year. Actually, this redesign was prompted by more than just the need for a more robust airframe to withstand the added stress of low-level flying. The flying wing design is a notoriously unstable beast, and it's unknown just how well it will withstand the long-term wear and tear of operations. Strengthening the airframe, then, solved several potential problems. Low-level flying also requires design changes to deal with bird strikes: The engines must be modified and the pilot's windows reinforced. Provision for a third crew member was made in case the automation of the complex electronics did not prove adequate for a two-man crew.

Problems encountered during the redesign caused the first flight to be set for late 1987, then mid-1988, and finally early 1989. The earlier decision to deploy the B-1 provided an ironic assist: It relieved the pressure to rush completion of the B-2. Had it not been redesigned, the B-2 would have been a more fragile and less capable aircraft, with a much shorter life.

Royal Hangar Queens

The Royal Air Force claims that unreliable equipment grounds nearly half of its jet aircraft at any given time, and that in consequence expenditures on maintenance and upkeep are now running about $800 million a year, roughly double what is being spent on procurement.

Minor Details

Several hundred civil aircraft belong to what is called the Civil Reserve Air Force (CRAF). The idea is that in the event of mobilization, all those 747s, DC-10s, and L-1011s would be pressed into service to help ferry the troops over to Europe in order to stem the Red tide. This certainly sounds like a good idea. But it has one minor flaw: Who will fly these airplanes? It seems that a sizable percentage of commercial pilots are themselves reservists, and already have assignments should they be called to active duty in the event of a national emergency.

"How Are You Gonna Keep Them Down on the Flight Line? . . ."

Ever since the explosive growth of commercial aviation in the 1950s, most non-Communist air forces have had the problem of seeing their pilots lured away by higher-paying jobs with airlines. In the late 1980s, Finland found that it was going to lose a third of its 180 combat pilots all at once to the national airline, Finnair. So Finland passed a law preventing the state-owned Finnair from hiring Finnish Air Force pilots. This may only slow the process down. Most of these pilots also speak English or Swedish, so they have plenty of incentive to leave the country for foreign parts, as commercial pilots make $10,000–$15,000 more a year than fighter jocks.

Sortie

When a combat aircraft takes off to go on a mission, it is making what is called a "sortie." In high-intensity combat, the air force that can generate a higher rate of sorties, which involves refueling and rearming the planes quickly after completion of each mission to get them in the air as rapidly as possible (say, six times a day, as the Israelis seem to have done in 1967) is likely to prove more successful than one with a greater number of aircraft making fewer sorties— say, twice a day.

Dealing with Aircraft Cost Escalation

In the 1960s, an air-defense fighter cost about $3 million (in current dollars). In the 1970s, you could have F-4s for about $10 million each. In the 1980s, interceptors cost $30 million. Something has to give. Part of the problem, and part of the solution, is the constant upgrading of aircraft capabilities. An example is the U.S. F-15. Originally a high-performance interceptor weighing 28 tons and carrying only 1.5 tons of weapons, the current F-15E multipurpose version weighs 40 tons and carries 12 tons of weapons. These upgrades enable the F-15 to serve for another quarter of a century. Another upgrade is more radical, yet has a higher payoff. The U.S. Air Force needs a new ground-attack aircraft. Building a new aircraft would cost up to $15 million a copy. A cheaper solution is to rebuild the 337 thirty-year-old A-7s at a cost of $6.5 million each. The upgrade will include lengthening the fuselage four feet, replacing the single engine with two and vastly increasing the electronics load. These changes will keep the A-7 viable until 2010.

Air-Transport Blues

In the event of an emergency in Europe, the United States is committed to reinforcing NATO with the equivalent of about eight divisions within two weeks. These forces are intended to go by air, and, although some units have complete suites of equipment "prepositioned" in West Germany, most will have to take their gear with them. As a result, the possibility of bringing these reinforcements into Europe with sufficient speed and efficiency so as to have a positive influence on political and military developments appears problematic. The airlift of a fully equipped mechanized infantry battalion requires sixty-three sorties by C-141 aircraft plus two by C-5As, while an armored battalion requires twenty-four C-141 sorties and thirty-five C-5A sorties. To move a full mechanized infantry division by air requires 1,072 C-141 sorties plus 267 C-5A sorties, while that of an armored division requires 1,022 C-141 sorties and 299 C-5 sorties. Problem is, USAF has only about 270 C-141s, each having a net payload of about 34 tons or 150–200 troops, and 77 C-5As, each with a payload of about 102 tons, plus about 50 C-5Bs in the pipeline, though on mobilization the Civil Reserve Air Fleet would contribute about 30 Boeing 747-200Fs, with a payload of 120 tons, plus about 100 DC-8-63CFs (60 tons) and DC-10-30CFs (78 tons), all capable of carrying heavy equipment, plus about 220 passenger aircraft of 200 troops capacity.

Air Pollution?

There are, on average, 700,000 military flights a year in West German airspace, roughly 15 percent of total flights of all types.

Never Enough

The U.S. armed forces train 4,000–5,000 new pilots each year. These pilots are obliged to remain in the service for up to eight years. It costs $1–$2 million to train a new pilot. Training one flight leader to command small groups of aircraft in the air costs up to $6 million and takes about six years. The majority of pilots leave the military long before they become eligible for pensions after twenty years of service. The most common reason for a pilot's leaving is a better-paying job in commercial airlines. The commerical airlines recruit up to 6,000 new pilots a year and prefer military pilots, since they are already trained and have several thousand hours' experience.

Force Packaging

Long gone are the days when aircraft operated independently, with two or four fighters or fighter-bombers going off to defend some airspace or hit a ground target. Current tactics assume that the airspace over a ground target will be defended by enemy interceptors and SAMs. The bombers need fighters to take care of the interceptors and Wild Weasel electronic warfare aircraft to destroy or blind the SAMs. Putting together the right mix of fighters, bombers, and Wild Weasels for a mission is called "force packaging." Skill in putting these packages together becomes increasingly important as the potential strength of air defenses grows. Even the new U.S. F-117 Stealth fighter is part of this concept. Although capable of solo missions, the F-117 is also very capable as a Wild Weasel, as it can evade detection until it gets close enough to destroy enemy radars.

European Flying Weather

Ground-attack aircraft that cannot operate in darkness or low-visibility weather have only an average of 4.5 hours a day in which they can fly if they are fighting in Central Europe. This restricts them to only about two sorties a day. If they have an all-weather capability, they can fly about fourteen hours a day, limited only by maintenance needs. This allows for up to six sorties a day.

How to Use Mines Against Aircraft

Western air forces have a comprehensive array of weapons for destroying enemy airfields. The principal device is a cluster bomb containing hundreds of bomblets of several different types. Some are special penetrator bombs that crack the concrete surface of the airfield and create a crater. Not a big one, but a pothole that would be fatal to any aircraft landing or taking off. Another bomblet sits on the ground searching for and attacking moving aircraft. A third is basically an antipersonnel mine that keeps the repair and maintenance personnel nervous and much less effective. Another type of bomb explodes only after penetrating deep beneath the runway, thereby "heaving" up the ground, so the runway must first be dug up before it can be repaired. These cluster-bomblet containers are delivered by aircraft flying over enemy airfields, which although risky, insures that the airfield is hit. They can also be delivered by rocket or guided bomb. The Russians have similar devices, although probably not as effective, as these items depend a great deal on two technologies Russia has trouble with: electronics and miniaturization.

Trashing the Tarmac

The easiest way to destroy enemy aircraft is to get them on the ground before they can shoot back. This was a lesson learned over seventy years ago, shortly after air warfare began. While ground-based defenses such as guns or missiles can slow down or disrupt these attacks, they can't stop them. Interceptors are the only effective way to thwart these attacks. If one side obtains even temporary air superiority, the other side's air bases, and the aircraft on them, are at great risk.

The most common occurrence of this temporary air superiority is at the beginning of a war when one side makes a surprise attack. This was the case during the 1956 and 1967 Arab-Israeli wars. In each case, the Arab air forces lost heavily, with over 400 aircraft destroyed on the ground in 1967 alone. In the 1973 Arab-Israeli war it was the Arabs who attacked first. In addition, they had installed fortified hangars for their aircraft, which was the primary reason why they lost only twenty-two aircraft to ground attacks. While this preserved aircraft, constant Israeli attacks on the runways with bombs kept most Arab aircraft on the ground most of the time.

World War II and Korean War experience also demonstrated that you can destroy unprotected aircraft on the ground as well as rendering the runways unusable by bombing. In 1986 French bombers attacked a Libyan-controlled air base in Chad and closed it down for two days. Current doctrine strives to shut down air bases for as long as possible. Bombing maintenance, fuel, and repair facilities also degrades the ability of aircraft to sustain operations. Attrition will thus take place in the air as well as on the ground.

Silicon Bombs

Since the late seventies, Western air forces have used electronic scoring and recording devices to facilitate realistic training of fighter pilots. But it was not until the 1980s that ground forces began using similar setups and it became possible to electronically simulate bomb and artillery hits. All of this was made possible by smaller and smaller computers and communication devices. First, the training area is seeded with transmitters and receivers that detect the movement of all aircraft and vehicles. The attackers and their targets are also fitted with transmitters and receivers. When an electronic substitute for a bomb or artillery shell is sent in the direction of a target, a central computer calculates how close it comes. If a hit is achieved, the target's capabilities are suitably reduced. For bombing aircraft, it is also possible to accurately simulate the various dangers from enemy radars, missiles, and guns. The pilot receives feedback on all this, as well as on the performance of his own equipment.

This type of training is particularly useful for ground-attack aircraft, which previously needed large tracts of land on which to drop real bombs. If realistic targets such as vehicles or structures were to be used, the bombing range had periodically to be cleaned up to clear out unexploded munitions and replace blasted targets. This was dangerous and expensive. Moreover, few parts of the world had enough land for these ranges. People living nearby were rarely enthusiastic about the idea. Using "silicon bombs" makes it possible to practice bombing in a far greater variety of locations. Note that the pilots still periodically go out and drop real bombs, if only to maintain faith in the electronic substitute. Besides, it's not really the same if you can't make some real holes in the ground once in a while.

Viffing for Fun and Safety

The British-designed Harrier fighter, with its vertical takeoff capability, proved an immensely valuable aircraft in the 1982 Falklands War. But that brief conflict did not fully test the aerial combat capabilities of the Harrier, and, by implication, of several other similar aircraft. Harriers have the ability to move directly upward or downward, or at an angle, without moving forward, a phenomenon known as "viffing," derived from "vector in flight." At the onset of the Falklands campaign, much was made of the potential value viffing might offer in air-to-air combat: a Harrier with a hostile aircraft on its tail might suddenly rise or fall, permitting the enemy to overshoot, so that the Harrier would suddenly be on his tail. However, although the thirty-eight Harriers committed to the campaign accounted for at least thirty-two Argentine aircraft in air-to-air combat with no loss to themselves save from accidents or ground fire, not once did a Harrier pilot vif during combat. This was due to the nature of air combat in the Falklands, where Argentine fighters were operating at their maximum range, with little time for dogfighting, so that the Harriers served primarily as interceptors. As a result, the jury is still out on the full potential of the Harrier in aerial combat. However, peacetime exercises between Harriers and conventional fighters show that the Harrier is likely to change the rules of aerial combat.

Video Games

The U.S. Air Force paid $50 million each for three F-15E fighter-bomber simulators. The F-15E is the new, two-seat strike version of the F-15 air-superiority fighter, designed to operate primarily at night and in bad weather. The F-15E simulator contains a data base with 500,000 square kilometers of detailed terrain, an area equal to about 14 percent of the United States. Simulators in the U.S. Air Force have become so successful in preparing pilots for the real thing that the portion of aircraft devoted to training will be reduced from 25 percent to 12 percent. This will make more aircraft available for operations and eliminate the frequent training accidents that normally occur when pilots practice in an unfamiliar aircraft.

The Art of Flak-Busting

Once ground forces developed special weapons to shoot back at attacking aircraft, the air forces developed techniques for destroying their ground-based tormenters. The antiaircraft units were called "flak" (from a German term, *Fliegerabwehrkanone*) and taking out the flak came to be called "flak-busting." Currently, the flak consists of numerous radars and the guns and missile launchers they direct. Special aircraft called "Wild Weasels" carry heavy loads of electronic devices for detecting search and fire-control radars and, if possible, jamming these devices. These aircraft are the most expensive, because of their extensive electronic equipment, and are usually flown by the most skillful and audacious crews. Along with the Weasels are fighter-bombers. These carry bombs and antiradar missiles to take out ground-based radars and weapons. Usually, most of the damage is done by jamming the "eyes and ears" of the flak, namely the radars. In addition to jamming, ARMs (antiradiation missiles) home in on enemy radars. The ARMs don't always work, as radar crews can switch frequencies or even shut down their radars to neutralize them.

However, flak-busting missions attempt to come in fast and low and catch the radars by surprise. ARMs are launched 50–100 km from the radars, and will often hit the radars before their operators are even aware that they are under attack. It's very much a cat-and-mouse game, as the flak units will attempt to counter this by not having all radars on at all times. Just when the flak-busters think they're home free, on come several more radars. Because most ARMs must be fired in the direction the aircraft is flying, radars painting you from the side or rear are cause for alarm and rapid maneuvering. The radars need less than a minute to lock onto a target and let loose with missiles. The more capable Wild Weasels, ARMs, and flak radars are in the West, which makes things difficult for Russian-built flak units. The defender always has an extra advantage if the attacker has not carefully reconnoitered before sending in the Wild Weasels. Indeed, a common Wild Weasel mission is simply to gather information on enemy flak deployments and zip right out again. A game of cat and mouse with jet aircraft, electronics, and missiles.

Telegraphed Blows

The introduction of the "variable geometry," or "swing-wing" concept in the late 1960s led to a revolution in aircraft performance, for an airplane could now have all of the advantages of a full-sized wing on takeoffs, landings, and nap-of-the-earth flying, and quickly convert to a smaller wing in combat. However, not all swing-wing aircraft are created equal. Western swing-wing aircraft really can change the attitude of their wings to any degree the pilot desires. Russian-built swing-wing airplanes work differently. To be sure, they have the capability of changing the angle of their wings. However, wing attitude can only be locked at one of three or four fixed positions. As a result, some Western pilots claim they would be able to guess the intentions of their Russian opponents by watching their wings. This notion has been tentatively confirmed in combat, in some of the occasional actions between U.S. and Libyan aircraft.

Tanks Versus Aircraft

For nearly fifty years, tanks have been equipped with a machine gun atop their turret in a usually futile effort to provide some defense against aircraft. These decades of frustration have finally produced some quite different, and possibly effective, antiair weapons. In the early eighties, the Russians began to equip some of their T-64B tanks with guided missiles fired from the 125-mm smooth-bore gun tube. At first this was thought to be exclusively a long-range antitank weapon. But it was soon realized that such a missile could also be effective against helicopters and, under the right circumstances, low-flying jets.

The U.S. Army is testing a 105-mm tank round using an HE warhead and a heat-seeking fuze. If the shell comes close enough to the hot exhaust of a jet or helicopter, it explodes. More advanced antiaircraft shells for 105-mm and 120-mm tank guns are in development. None of these weapons really provides much protection against aircraft or helicopters that pop up out of nowhere firing rockets and missiles. U.S. tanks plan to attempt to hit Russian helicopters with their main gun, although this has not been tested in combat. But every little bit helps.

Air Support

The term "air support" is not a euphemism for "bombing." Rather, it is a technical term for the fine art of delivering aerial ordnance on targets designated by ground troops directly engaged with the enemy without hitting the ground troops themselves. Though not much favored by the flying fraternity, who would prefer dogfighting with each other, air support is greatly appreciated by the groundlings.

Taking the Anxiety Out of CAS (Close Air Support)

Using aircraft to bomb enemy positions in close proximity to your own troops has always been a heart-stopping experience. It wasn't until the Vietnam War that jets were effectively used in this role: In Korea the task had been left to prop jobs (propeller-driven aircraft). It readily became apparent that the faster speeds of the jets and the heavier bomb loads made the pilot's job much harder. The development of "smart" bombs helped somewhat, but they were more expensive and there was not always time or opportunity to use them. The increased number of antiaircraft weapons also made it necessary for jet fighter-bombers to use their higher speed to get in and out fast. Even though U.S. forces developed techniques for ground-based air controllers, the increased use of jamming made these links increasingly vulnerable. Finally, in the late 1980s, technology came to the rescue.

First the aircraft and ground forces got secure radio communications using frequency-hopping and burst transmission.

Then the aircraft got mapping systems that allow the pilot to have the coordinates broadcast to him and entered into his mapping system automatically. The HUD (head-up display) then shows how close the aircraft is to the target and indicates when to release the appropriate weapon.

Basically, the FAC (forward air controller), either on the ground or aloft in a light aircraft or helicopter, could use the ATHS (automatic-target handoff system) to keep track of several aircraft and artillery units at once with a minimum of confusion. Most important, it allows for greater accuracy and less chance of bombing friendly troops.

Missile Anxiety

Two things happened soon after guided missiles were first widely used in air combat during the 1960s. First, pilots quickly learned that by rapid and skillful maneuvering, they could avoid the missiles. Then they learned that while they were concentrating on avoiding the missiles, something else would get them. There was always a danger of collision with nearby friendly aircraft. Over North Vietnam, it was common for aircraft to zoom downward to get away from surface-to-air missiles. This would bring them low enough to encounter massive gunfire from all sorts of antiaircraft weapons. One anticipated problem was that an aircraft evading missiles would have to abort its current mission. For bombers, this meant releasing bombs immediately, often over politically embarrassing targets like hospitals, orphanages, and schools. To overcome these attacks of missile anxiety, Wild Weasel aircraft were developed, as was the "mission package" concept. This technique sent the Wild Weasels and fighter-bombers in first to take out the ground-based missile and gun defenses so that the bombers following would not be disturbed. Much of the current work on robotic "pilot associates" is being directed to take some of the stress off pilots suddenly confronted with an oncoming missile.

No Pain, No Gain

The U.S. Task Force 160 is a transportation unit for U.S. commandos. It has seventy-five helicopters and 900 men. It practices flying at night and in all types of bad weather, perfect flying conditions for moving commandos. This form of training is expensive. The unit has two or three flying accidents a month.

Best of Friends

"Only on the surface has the strategic-missile race reflected competition between the United States and the Soviet Union; the real struggle is between the U.S. Air Force and its archrival the U.S. Navy."—Samuel H. Day, Jr., peace activist

PART THREE

Naval Forces

Navies have been around nearly as long as armies. Ships were the original high-tech weapons systems, and in this century warships are only slightly less technologically sophisticated than aircraft and spacecraft. Nuclear submarines and aircraft carriers have redefined naval warfare and how it is fought. The newest technology must get along with some of the world's oldest warrior traditions. It's a strange world where individual ships cost billions, and sailors rarely even see the water.

Hearts of Oak

"Ships are to little purpose without skillful sea men."—Richard Hakluyt, sixteenth-century English maritime historian

"Take Her Down to 500 Feet, Mr. Spock."

Submarines are similar to spaceships in that they are airtight and depend on various sensors to determine where they are and how they're doing. Until now, one of the principal submarine sensors was the periscope, a long tube using mirrors to show the skipper what's at the end of the periscope sticking out of the water. For this reason, the sub's command center had to be where the periscope was, under the large "sail" that juts out of the sub's midsection. A British and U.S. R&D effort began in the late 1980s to change all this, and trials in a modified U.S. SSN 688 class sub took place in 1989. The new system uses various sensors in place of the periscope. In effect, the new "periscope" never has to break the surface of the ocean but can lurk just below it and still capture good images of what is out there. These images are displayed on a large screen (at least 6 × 4 feet) in a large room (at least 12 × 30 feet) in the more spacious forward portion of the nuclear sub. The large display can show what's on the surface, maps covering various amounts of sea area, or any other information. Along the sides of the room, various consoles and displays are manned by technicians. In the middle of the room, facing the large display, are another console and the captain's chair. Thus seated, the captain can absorb all necessary information and then issue orders to the rest of the crew on the "bridge." Rumor has it that this new-style "bridge" was inspired by a 1960s-era television science-fiction series. Take her to warp 3, Scotty.

Gray Ladies of a Certain Age

The very size of the Russian submarine fleet, at over 300 boats the largest in the world, is enough to give NATO strategists nightmares. However, many of the boats are rather long in the tooth. About 150 (41.1 percent), including many diesel-powered boats, are at least twenty years old, and about 115 more (31.5 percent), including a few diesel boats, are between twelve and twenty years old. This leaves only about 100 (27.4 percent) that are less than a dozen years old, of which about half are "boomers," city-busters armed with nuclear missiles, too valuable to send against shipping in a conventional war. By a slim margin, the U.S. submarine fleet is younger. Of about 140 U.S. submarines at the beginning of 1989, virtually all of which are nuclear-powered, 70 (50.0 percent) are twenty or more years old, while another 24 (17.1 percent), are between twelve and twenty years old, and 41 (29.3 percent) are less than twelve years old, of which about 75 percent are attack boats.

The Russian Naval Tradition

"The only successful Russian admiral was John Paul Jones."—Josef Stalin, Russian dictator during World War II. Jones, a U.S. Revolutionary War hero, became an admiral in the Russian Navy after the United States won its independence, and had no more need of naval heroes. The Russian Navy began World War II with the world's largest submarine fleet, and managed to achieve the unusual feat of losing more than one sub for each enemy ship sunk by its submarines.

Robot Warriors of the Ocean Floor

Naval mines have always been an effective means of sinking ships or blocking an area. In the past ten years, a new class of mines has come into use that are even more troublesome than past types. These new items are the enhanced pressure mines (EPMs). The original pressure mine was introduced over forty years ago and was activated by the increased water pressure created when a ship passed overhead. These have become more complex over the years, and the EPM version is the nastiest to date. An EPM uses acoustic sensors as well as pressure. Worst of all, it is microcomputer-controlled so that it will only detonate for certain targets. It is also more difficult to clear. Its shape resembles a flat rock, which can fool special sonars that are used to detect EPMs. They can operate in deeper water, up to 200 meters, putting more areas at risk. Around Britain, for example, this means that 5,000 km of 800-meter-wide shipping lanes are now vulnerable.

The technique for keeping these lanes clear is to patrol them continuously with special sonar, making a map of the bottom. Any unusual object on the bottom must be investigated with a remote-controlled minisub. This sub has a camera that allows for closer examination of the object. If the object looks suspicious, an explosive charge can be used to blow it up. It's tricky business, using sonar in coastal waters, because of the complex nature of the temperature layers, tidal waters, and detail on the sea floor. Usually, a mine-hunting sonar can spot an object on the sea floor at 500–1,000 meters' range. But it has to get within 200–300 meters to get a clear-enough look in order to attempt identification. Most mine hunters have to make two passes, one to locate everything on the sea floor and another to identify anything suspicious. The mine hunter will cruise along slowly, no more than 200–500 meters a minute. The key elements in this business are the power of the sonar computers and the skill and experience of the operators. Fortunately, the need to "map" sea lanes in peacetime gives operators plenty of practice. More modern equipment allows location and scanning on the same pass. Mine-hunting sonars can also be used from helicopters and towed underwater on a cable as a "sled." Soon the mine hunters will be as robotic as the mines they seek out. They will have to be, as the most recent bottom mines can go down as far as 2,000 meters and use a rocket to propel the warhead to the target on the surface. These deep-water mines can be laid by submarines, from their torpedo tubes, thus making subs with mines more effective against shipping than subs with torpedoes.

Whose Is Bigger?

There are several ways to calculate who has the largest navy. The U.S. Navy, with only 550 "warships," certainly has fewer ships than both the "People's Liberation Army Navy," with about 1,000 vessels, or the Soviet Navy, which has nearly as many. However, in a very real sense this is a matter of "apples and oranges," as are many issues in military affairs. Take those 550 U.S. "warships." Only about 450 of them are actually in the business of inflicting harm on other people—14 fleet carriers, 13 helicopter carriers, 4 battleships, over 120 submarines, about 80 cruisers, and 145 destroyer-types, plus about 32 smaller patrol craft and an equal number of mine warfare vessels. The rest? Well, there are over 45 amphibious warfare vessels. Then there are a lot of auxiliaries, such as ammunition ships, underway-replenishment ships, repair ships, submarine tenders, survey ships, floating dry docks, and the like. And then there are scores of vessels in the Coast Guard, many of which are destroyer-escort or patrol-boat types. And there are a lot of U.S. Maritime Commission ships, which provide logistical support for the navy. These all bring the USN up to over 700 ships. But that's still less than the Chinese or Russian fleets. Again, it's a matter of apples and oranges. The following tables look at the ten largest fleets in several different ways.

Total Number of Fighting Ships:

China	830		Egypt	126
Russia	655		West Germany	125
U.S.	450		Thailand	115
North Korea	354		Taiwan	113
South Korea	154		Philippines	105

Thousands of Tons of Fighting Ships:

U.S.	3,890		Japan	146
Russia	2,660		Italy	120
Britain	366		India	119
China	336		Taiwan	112
France	294		Greece	107

Thousands of Tons per Ship:

U.S.	8.7		Canada	3.1
Britain	4.2		Italy	2.6
Russia	4.1		Spain	2.1
France	3.8		Japan	1.9
Netherlands	3.1		Argentina	1.9

On the basis of these figures, the USN not only has the greatest tonnage, but also has the largest ships, which is an indication of seakeeping ability. Of course, these figures do not reflect such less tangible qualities as seamanship, which is a reflection of time spent at sea. It is likely that Britain's Royal Navy wins the prize in this category, though it is followed closely by the USN and several other NATO navies.

Gas Bags at War

After more than twenty-five years, the U.S. armed forces are getting back into the blimp business. Military experience with airships—both steel-framed, rigid zeppelins, and the nonrigid blimps—began before the turn of the century. During World War I, German zeppelins conducted numerous bombing raids over England, the first aerial bombardments in history. In the period between the wars, several powers continued to be interested in airships, but a series of disasters, of which that of the German *Hindenburg* was only the most spectacular, caused almost everyone except the U.S. Navy to lose interest. During World War II, 168 "oceangoing" U.S. Navy blimps—essentially giant, flexible helium gas bags—escorted nearly 90,000 ships across the Atlantic without a single vessel being lost to enemy submarines, and at a cost of only one blimp shot down in action.

Although the navy continued to operate blimps through the fifties, the program was ended in 1961, apparently because it represented an "obsolete" technology. For most of the nearly thirty years since, blimp technology was kept alive primarily by various commercial enterprises interested in their advertising value, plus a few hardened enthusiasts who saw potential for their use as heavy-lift air-transport vehicles or who were convinced of their military value. Finally, in 1987 the Department of Defense entered into a $170 million contract with an Anglo-American consortium, Westinghouse-Airship Industries, for the construction of what the bureaucrats have dubbed the YEZ-2A. The largest nonrigid airship ever built, the YEZ-2A will be 425 feet long—over 40 percent longer than a football field—and will be filled with 2.5 million cubic feet of helium, 67 percent more than any previous nonrigid airship, contained in two "balloonettes" that will be concealed by a Kevlar-reinforced gas-tight skin. In order to fulfill its military mission, the YEZ-2A will have a large radar mounted in the main envelope, and it will have antisubmarine- and antimine-detection equipment that can be lowered into the sea to be towed along at relatively leisurely rates.

A crew of fifteen will live in considerable comfort in a spacious three-story gondola, pressurized to permit altitudes up to 10,000 feet, which will allow operation for as long as six weeks, given refueling, which can be accomplished from surface vessels or through the retrieval of fuel cells parachuted into the sea. The navy has high hopes for the experimental design, and Britain's Royal Navy has expressed an interest as well.

Undersea Missiles

Long-range ballistic missiles fired from submerged submarines have long been an American specialty. In the early 1960s, the U.S. Polaris missile went into service. This was a fifteen-ton missile, thirty-two feet long and fifty-four inches in diameter. It carried one nuclear warhead that could land within 1,000 meters of its target. Range was 4,600 km. At about the same time, Russia put into service the SS-N-5, weighing a few more tons but otherwise about the same size. However, its range was only about half of the Polaris, and it was able to hit within only about 3,000 meters of its target. Worst of all, the SS-N-5 used liquid fuel, which required a lot of complex plumbing and was much less reliable than the solid fuel of the Polaris.

In the early 1970s came the next generation. The United States deployed the Poseidon, weighing thirty tons, thirty-four feet long, and seventy-three inches in diameter. Range was the same as for the Polaris, but accuracy was twice as good and it carried ten to fourteen warheads. Russia came out with the SS-N-6 for the older boats that were using the SS-N-5, and the SS-N-8 for the newer and larger boats. The SS-N-6 weighed twenty tons, was thirty-two feet long and sixty-four inches in diameter. The initial version had one warhead with about 50 percent better accuracy than the SS-N-5. In the next fifteen years, two new versions were introduced that eventually gave it three warheads with about twice the accuracy of the SS-N-5. The early version had a range of 2,400 km, later versions were 3,300 km. All used liquid fuel. The Russians began to phase out the SS-N-6, and the older boats carrying it, in the 1980s. The SS-N-8 weighed twenty-two tons, was forty-two feet long and sixty-four inches in diameter, with a range of 7,700 km and an accuracy of 1,000 meters. Later versions had up to three warheads. In the early 1980s, the United States came out with Trident C4, weighing thirty-two tons, with the same number of warheads, range, and size as Poseidon, but with slightly better accuracy and larger nuclear weapons.

In the late 1970s, Russia came out with the SS-N-18, which also stressed better accuracy and more warheads, achieving up to seven warheads per missile with a range of 6,500 km and accuracy of 500 meters. This was still a liquid-fuel missile. In the early 1980s came the SS-N-20, the first Russian solid-fuel undersea missile. However, throughout the 1980s there were constant problems with this missile, indicating that, although it was deployed, it was not working properly. In the late 1980s, the United States introduced the Trident D5, a fifty-five-ton missile with a range of 7,000 km. It is forty-four feet long and eighty-two inches in diameter, with ten to fifteen larger warheads and an accuracy of 250 meters. The longer range of many Russian missiles was seen as an advantage, but in practice it wasn't. The unreliability of their subs and missiles made it desirable for Russian boats to cruise close to their bases, so that maintenance facilities were always nearby.

Three Sheets to the Wind

Arguably the most unique "warship" in the world is the Swedish Navy's 250-ton *Sigrun*, the world's only laundry ship, which makes the rounds of various isolated coast-defense installations to attend to the needs of their personnel.

The World's Largest Antiship Missiles

Russia developed the first antiship missiles in the 1950s, using a jet fighter with the cockpit removed and a radar-guided automatic pilot added. It was big, it was bulky, and it worked, if the target did nothing to defend itself. In 1967 one of these missiles sank an Israeli destroyer. Western nations quickly got on the ball, defensively and offensively. In the 1973 Arab-Israeli war, none of the dozens of Russian-made antiship missiles was able to get past Israeli countermeasures. By the late 1970s, several Western antiship missiles appeared, most notably the French Exocet and the U.S. Harpoon. The contemporary generation of Russian missiles was somewhat smaller than the preceding one. Most curiously, the new missiles were built largely for use aboard specially designed submarines. The first of these was the SS-N-7, 23 feet long and 7,700 pounds. It had a range of 50 km and a 1,100 pound warhead (HE or nuclear). Guidance is similar to Exocet. This missile was introduced in the late 1960s and is used only on ten *Charlie*-class nuclear subs, with eight missiles each. Rather than having one missile with different versions for ships, subs, and aircraft, Russia built different missiles for ships and subs and none at all for aircraft. At the same time, the SS-N-7 came out for subs, the SS-N-9 came out for ships. Weighing 6,600 pounds and 27 feet long, it carries a half-ton warhead up to 100 km. Weighing four times as much as the later Harpoon and twice as long, it has a warhead twice as large and a guidance system probably half as effective.

The next generation of Russian missiles, contemporaneous with the first Western missiles, was the SS-N-12, introduced in the early 1970s. This beast is 37 feet long and weighs 5,000 pounds. It travels 550 km at supersonic speeds (2,500-plus km per hour) and has a one-ton warhead. This missile is carried on large surface ships and a few older nuclear submarines. Although not carried by aircraft, it is dependent on aircraft for targeting information. A missile with this long a range cannot go after targets identified by the ship that fires it. The missile's guidance system must be told where to go before turning on its search radar. Because a missile like this is only in the air for about fifteen minutes, search aircraft radio back the position of targets and then try to escape themselves. These missiles are intended primarily for use against U.S. carriers, which can be expected to be on the lookout for Russian recon aircraft. In the late 1970s, the SS-N-19, an updated version of the SS-N-12, was introduced. About the same size as the SS-N-12, it weighs 4,000 pounds, has a 500-km range, the same speed, and a more effective guidance system. In the early 1980s, the SS-N-9 was updated with the introduction of the SS-N-22. Except for its range (100 km), this missile is similar in performance to the SS-N-19.

Lacking the ability to manufacture large quantities of miniaturized electronics and other components, Russia has leaned more toward massive long-range missiles that, if they do hit, will do relatively more damage than the more accurate, but smaller, Western models. This puts the Russians on the wrong end of the situation. Their larger missiles are easier for the more effective Western radars to pick up, while their less effective radars will have an even harder time picking up the smaller, more ECM-resistant Western missiles.

The Ups and Downs of Naval Helicopters

Despite the obvious appeal of using helicopters at sea, progress in this area has been full of problems. Helicopters are complex beasts and require a lot of maintenance. Moreover, operating at sea exposes them to saltwater damage and generally more stress than land-based operations. Although naval helicopters are built with more anticorrosion features, they still require more attention. Space is at a premium, so ships must either give up a lot of space to store spares and mechanics or limit the hours helicopters can operate in order not to overload limited shipboard-maintenance capabilities. Another problem has been the relatively large size of helicopters. For this reason, most naval helicopters are operated from aircraft carriers, or smaller "helicopter carriers." Smaller helicopters operate from destroyers and cruisers, but under the maintenance limitations described above, which restrict their use to twenty to forty hours a month.

Most navies use a small utility helicopter similar to the UH-1 "Huey." These weigh six to twelve tons loaded and are small enough to land on the back end of a small warship. The major difference between these helos is the quality of their communications and ASW (antisubmarine warfare) equipment. The larger helos operating from carriers naturally have more extensive equipment. A big breakthrough in shipboard-carrier operations arrived in the early 1980s when the U.S. Navy deployed the SH-60 (LAMPS III) helicopter. An eleven-ton chopper using the same airframe as the army's UH-60, the LAMPS III included the latest electronics and communications equipment. Most important, though, was the sharply increased reliability of this helo. The SH-60 needed much less maintenance than previous helicopters and could regularly put in 100 hours a month, with the ability to go as high as 200 hours. This will have enormous significance in wartime, where ships will be in harm's way for days on end. Being able to have a helicopter available all through the combat period can be a decisive advantage. Moreover, the SH-60 has proven itself very capable in chasing down Russian subs. Military R&D doesn't always end up in embarrassing headlines. Often the troops get it right the first time around.

The P-3 Plus

For over thirty years, the P-3 Orion four-engine aircraft has been the backbone of Western ASW warfare. Despite regular upgrades, the 600 P-3s in service are in need of a yet more drastic upgrade. The U.S. Navy finally came up with one, the LRAACA (long-range-air-antisubmarine-warfare-capability aircraft, or the P-7). It looks like the P-3, as it uses the same basic airframe. But only

20 percent of the components are common to both planes. Many of the improved LRAACA components, however, could be installed on the older P-3. The P-3 will continue to be built (for $32 million apiece) and in the mid 1990s production will switch over to the LRAACA, hopefully at about the same unit cost, but don't hold your breath on that. The major improvements in all previous P-3s have been electronic, which increased their efficiency in locating submarines. This will continue with the LRAACA, with a major improvement being the increase of sonobuoy capacity from 84 to 300, although half these would be at the expense of Harpoons and some torpedoes. As submarines become quieter, the need for more sonobuoys increases. These bantamweight four-inch diameter sonars become more capable year by year as electronics become more miniaturized. For the last ten years, P-3s have carried Harpoon antiship missiles.

The LRAACA will also carry electronic countermeasures, enabling it to resist enemy antiaircraft missiles, but will still need a fighter escort if faced with enemy interceptors. Weight of the LRAACA will be eighty-six tons compared to seventy tons for the P-3. Payload will go from eleven to nineteen tons. Operating range and endurance (four hours, 2,800 km) will not change. The primary improvements are a more efficient and effective aircraft. Although jets were put forward as potential replacements for the P-3, a prop-engine design was chosen because the LRAACA must spend a lot of time moving slowly at low (200 feet) altitudes. Jets are not very efficient in this mode.

The Mighty Exocet

The extensive use of the French Exocet missile by the Iraqi Air Force in the Persian Gulf was the first sustained-combat use of this class of weapon. Exocets had been used a few times during the 1982 Falklands War. Nearly 3,000 were built by 1990. There are actually three Exocets, the MM.38, the AM.39, and the MM.40. The 38 version was developed during the 1970s for ship-to-ship use. The 38 weighs 1,650 pounds, is seventeen feet long and fourteen inches in diameter with a wingspan of thirty-nine inches. Speed is subsonic, at about 1,000 km per hour. Minimum range, providing enough time for the radar to find the target and arm the warhead, is 4–5 km. Maximum range is 42–45 km. The rocket motor only burns for about 100 seconds, leaving the missile to cover most of its journey on momentum. Normally, the missile's radar turns on when it is 12–15 km from its launching vessel. A radio altimeter keeps the missile at 100 m or less from the water to increase surprise. The fragmentation warhead weighs 363 pounds and is supposed to penetrate a warship before exploding in order to maximize damage. In the early 1980s, the AM.39 version was introduced for use from aircraft or helicopters. This version weighed 1,434 pounds, 13 percent less than the ship-launched version. Length is fifteen feet, other dimensions are identical to the MM.38. Because of air launch, the range was longer (50–70 km). The rocket burned longer (130–150 seconds) to improve control after the air launch. The guidance system was essentially the same as on the MM.38, while the warhead was identical.

The AM.39 was first used in combat in 1982, by Argentine pilots against British ships. Two things became apparent. First, not unexpectedly, the missile could be jammed or deceived if you acted promptly enough. Second, the fuze on the missile had some problems, as not all the missiles exploded after hitting a ship. Both of these problems surfaced again when the Iraqi Air Force fired over a hundred AM.39s in the Persian Gulf a few years later. To cope with these problems, a new warhead was introduced in the mid-1980s, along with a new model, the MM.40. This new version weighted 1,870 pounds and was nineteen feet long, but otherwise had the same dimensions as the earlier MM.38. Its range was now the same as the air-launched AM.39 (70 km) and was more accurate by virtue of a longer (220-second) burning engine. In the same period, a submarine-launched version, based on the AM.39, was introduced. During the Persian Gulf actions, yet another problem arose, that of the relative invulnerability of large commercial ships to hits from missiles designed to wreck smaller warships. Large crude-oil carriers did not have the "busy" superstructures of warships, and this tended to confuse the radar seeker of the Exocet. When hits were made, they were often in one of the many nonvital portions of the large tankers or cargo ships. Generally, missiles would injure large commercial ships but wreck small warships. This bodes well for large warships, which are better able to absorb missile damage than the several smaller warships that have been hit so far. Work is already under way on a replacement for the Exocet line. This new weapon, called the ANS, has the same weight and dimensions as the MM.40 with a range of 180 km and a top speed of over 2,000 km per hour. A more effective radar will be used and a heavier (484-lb) warhead fitted.

Russia's SOSUS

For over twenty years, the United States has deployed acoustic sensors (SOSUS) on the ocean bottom to monitor submarine and surface-ship movements. In the mid-1980s, the Russians finally began deploying their own version of SOSUS near their major naval bases in the Pacific and possibly under the polar ice pack.

More Gas

The Coast Guard recently signed a $42 million contract to procure three aerostats—balloons—that can be tethered 2,500 feet above a ship and, through the use of an onboard radar system, detect small surface craft and airplanes at more than fifty miles, thereby greatly enhancing the USCG's ability to conduct ocean surveillance against smugglers in peacetime and hostiles in war.

Jet-Propelled Subs

Propellers on nuclear submarines are a primary source of detectable noise. They also churn up the water in ways that make the sub easier to spot from the air. A solution pioneered by the British is the pumpjet propulsor. This design operates somewhat like a jet engine, which is basically a casing that surrounds a smaller set of propellers. With the pumpjet, water instead of air is drawn in and forced out the back. For the same amount of engine power, the pumpjet provides more push. The pumpjet is also heavier and more expensive than the conventional propeller setup. The advantages outweigh the disadvantages to the extent that all navies building nuclear subs are moving toward the use of pumpjets. The new U.S. SSN-21 class boats will have it, the French are using it, and the Russians have been working on it.

French SSNs

France pays some $400 million for their *Rubis*-class SSNs. Total program costs bring the per-ship expense to over $500 million. This is their first class of SSNs, which began entering service in the early 1980s. The French have offered to build Canada twelve similar, but upgraded, boats for about $490 million each, counting all program and operating costs. These subs are about half the weight (3,000 tons submerged) of U.S. SSN-688 boats, and somewhat less capable. They have a crew of sixty-six and are highly automated even for nuclear subs. The *Rubis* is very noisy.

Crowded Down Below

As large as U.S. attack aircraft carriers are, there is not sufficient space in the hangar deck below the flight deck for all the ship's aircraft. Typically, nearly half the aircraft must be stored on the deck. This is one reason why naval aircraft are so expensive, as special measures must be taken in building and maintaining these aircraft to control saltwater corrosion. Another problem with deck storage of aircraft is the amount of time and effort the flight-support personnel must take in moving the planes around during flight operations. However, these strenuous exercises are one reason why naval aviation is so efficient and effective. Just getting aircraft into the air and down again is a dangerous and exacting business. Actual combat is not much more dangerous than the risks endured during years of peacetime operations.

Captain Ahab's Friend

Although the French Exocet has got most of the press, it is not the most capable antiship missile around. Those honors more likely belong to the U.S. Harpoon. Nearly 5,000 Harpoons have been manufactured since it was introduced in the 1970s. It has not been used in combat as much as Exocet, but has performed as expected under fire. The Harpoon weighs 1,468 pounds for the ship-launched version (fourteen feet long) and 1,173 pounds for the air-launched version (twelve feet long). This is over 20 percent lighter than the Exocet. Harpoon range is 110 km, compared to 70 km for Exocet. Guidance systems are similar, although the Harpoon has a slight edge. The Harpoon has a larger warhead (500 pounds) and a turbojet with a fifteen-minute endurance. The Exocet uses a rocket that burns out after a few minutes. Harpoon is slower than Exocet, about 800 km an hour versus 1,000. The Harpoon also can be fired from submarine torpedo tubes.

ASW Sleds

The primary weapons in antisubmarine warfare (ASW) are electronic sensors. Once you find submarines, they are relatively easy to destroy or damage because they cannot long survive even light damage while underwater. One Western innovation in the 1980s was the Sonar Sled. Towed up to a kilometer behind a ship, this device contains passive and active sonar and other sensors. There are a number of advantages to this approach. First, the distance from the ship minimizes interference from the sounds of the ship itself. Second, any ship, even a tugboat, can operate the sled. Third, the sled can operate at great depths, up to several hundred meters, getting down below the temperature layers that make sonar contacts so unreliable. Russia is expected to deploy similar systems in the mid 1990s.

Boomer

A "boomer" is a nuclear submarine carrying ballistic missiles (SSBN). Usually a large boat, hence the name, as larger submarines return a louder signal when "pinged" by sonar. This name is something of a misnomer for U.S. SSBNs, as these are among the quietest nuclear subs ever built. It's extremely rare for a Russian ship or sub to find a U.S. SSBN and get close enough to use sonar on it.

Strategic Missile Submarines

Russia has about sixty-two nuclear subs (SSBNs) carrying submarine-launched strategic nuclear missiles (SLBMs). Over 85 percent of these missiles use liquid fuel, which is more difficult to handle than the solid fuel missiles that equip all U.S. SSBNs. About thirty-six U.S. boats carry 624 missiles with a total of 5,600 warheads, compared to 942 Russian missiles carrying about 3,000 warheads. U.S. boats are at sea about 60 percent of the time, compared to 15 percent for Russian boats. As a result, there are about 3,360 submarine-launched U.S. warheads targeted on Russia at any given time, as opposed to only about 450 Russian submarine-launched warheads targeted at the United States, giving the United States an eightfold superiority. Not that 450 nuclear warheads are anything to sneeze at. According to the U.S. Navy, the latest Russian SSBNs, four Delta IVs with SS-N-23 missiles, have suffered such severe reliability problems that as of 1989 none had gone to sea on patrol. At any time, about twenty U.S. boats are at sea carrying 3,360 warheads compared to about ten Russian boats carrying 1,500 warheads (including dockside launches). One of the U.S. Trident (*Ohio*-class) SSBNs carries 192 warheads, enough to destroy every large and medium-sized city in Russia. In addition, the United States is deploying sea-launched cruise missiles on attack submarines and surface ships and will have nearly 800 deployed by 1994.

Icebusters

Strategic missile submarines (SSBNs) have one major advantage over other subs; an SSBN does not have to get very close to its target. An SSBN's missiles can travel thousands of kilometers against targets with a known location. Cities and airfields do not move, while the SSBNs can. Russia was the first to notice that operating under the polar ice pack had more advantages than disadvantages. The advantages were:

- Aircraft could not drop sonobuoys, thus making the SSBNs more difficult to detect.
- Sonar did not function as effectively under the ice pack, because of the additional "clutter" provided by the irregular shapes of the overhead ice pack as well as the noise the shifting ice made.
- Aircraft could not drop torpedoes into the water to attack lurking SSBNs.

- The irregular shapes of the overhead ice pack gave the SSBNs additional places to hide from enemy subs.
- Surface ships could not chase SSBNs at all when the subs were operating under the ice.
- The polar ice pack is closer to targets in the United States than many open ocean areas. Russian land-based ICBMs must fly over the ice pack to reach the United States.

There were, however, some disadvantages:

- The SSBNs had to get through the ice to launch their missiles. There are numerous places in the polar ice pack where the ice is thin enough to be broken through by a suitably reinforced sub. The Russians have been building their subs to do this.
- While sonobuoys cannot be dropped through the ice pack, other sensors can be dropped onto the ice pack that can detect passing SSBNs.
- It's more dangerous maneuvering under the ice. While a careful sub commander will usually avoid accidents, there's a higher risk of unfortunate collisions with the ice.
- It's more difficult to communicate with subs operating under the ice pack. Lack of access to the surface as well as all the additional ice-generated noise contributed to this. This communication problem has been the major limiting factor for under-ice operations by SSBNs.

Increasingly, SSBNs are spending much of their time under the ice pack. At the very least, the boats under the ice are safer from Western ASW forces. From the Russian point of view, this provides them with a reserve of SSBNs that would more likely survive a determined Western campaign against their strategic missile boats. This factor alone makes under-ice operations worthwhile.

Undersea Friends and Relations

Although from 1977 to 1987 Russia virtually matched the United States in the addition of major surface combatants to its fleet (83 to

87), when the efforts of the European allies of the two superpowers are included, the Warsaw Pact added only 108 vessels while the NATO powers added 188. Adding in new Japanese, Australian, and New Zealand construction, about 30 ships, raises the U.S.-aligned navies to 218 new surface combatants, or slightly more than double the number added by Russian-aligned powers. Similarly, while Russia built nearly twice as many attack submarines as did the United States in this period (65 to 33), overall Warsaw Pact and NATO totals were much closer (67 to 62), figures which, with the contributions of the Pacific powers, rise to virtual parity (67 to 66).

Carrier Aviation Blues

Ten nations currently operate aircraft carriers of various types: Argentina, Australia, Brazil, Britain, France, India, Italy, Russia, Spain, and the United States. Argentina, Australia, and Brazil each have a single post–World War II vintage British-built light fleet carrier of some 16,000 tons, with a capacity for about twenty to twenty-four fixed-wing aircraft. France has two newer, domestically built vessels of about 22,000 tons, with a capacity of about forty aircraft, plus a helicopter carrier of about 10,000 tons, and will shortly begin building two much larger nuclear-powered ships. India has two of the older British types, one a postwar model acquired in the 1960s and the second a slightly larger, heavily modernized 1944 vessel that rendered excellent service to Britain in the Falklands, and will build a third. Britain has three 16,000-ton light-support carriers with a capacity of twelve to fifteen fixed-wing V/STOL—vertical/short takeoff and landing—aircraft, while Spain and Italy each have a somewhat smaller, similar vessel. The Russians currently have four 36,000-ton oddities capable of carrying perhaps thirty aircraft, two older 15,000-ton helicopter carriers with fifteen choppers, and are building three nuclear-powered ships of about 70,000 tons full load. The United States, of course, has more carriers than everyone else put together, fourteen leviathans of 65,000 to over 90,000 tons displacement, several of which are nuclear-powered, each carrying from eighty to one hundred aircraft, plus a dozen 10,000 to 25,000 ton amphibious assault carriers that, although officially designated "helicopter carriers" regularly operate the USMC version of the V/STOL Harrier, the AV-8.

There are a number of problems that confront countries operating aircraft carriers, particularly those with only one or two ships. Since carriers represent an enormous financial investment, they are expected to last a long time, forty years not being unusual. However, this means that as new equipment comes along, the older vessels must regularly be subject to often extensive, and expensive, refits. Moreover, as the ships get older, they become less capable of handling newer, heavier, aircraft, which are frequently larger in the bargain, thereby reducing carrying capacity. As if this were not enough of a problem, the limited number of carrier-capable aircraft required by all of these powers except the United States poses an enormous financial burden. The Argentine, Australian, Brazilian, and Indian carriers are all operating aircraft that are at least twenty-five years old, as are some of the French carrier aircraft. While this procurement problem may not bother the Russians, who do not much worry about cost accounting, even the French, with their advanced aviation industry and relatively enormous resources, has found the production of carrier aircraft prohibitive. They have secured some carrier aircraft from the United States, although national pride—and a desire to maintain a native design and production capacity—recently won out over Gallic parsimony when they decided to procure a "navalized" version of the Dassault Rafale as an alternative to purchasing 120 F-18s from the United States over the next decade or so to replace their aging F-8E Crusaders. Thus, only the United States, Britain, France, and Russia are producing fixed-wing carrier-capable aircraft. And given that it is unlikely the Russians will make available for foreign sale their V/STOL Yak-36/38, it appears that the British, with their Harrier, have a lock on the market for V/STOL aircraft, which is the airplane most suitable to the light carriers that constitute most of the flattop fleet not owned by the United States, Russia, or France. The result will likely be a considerable profit, which is why an advanced version of the Sea Harrier is currently under development.

Prerequisite

"The defeat of the U-boats carries with it the sovereignty of all the oceans of the world."—Winston L. S. Churchill, "former naval person," British first lord of the admiralty (secretary of the navy), 1911–15, 1939–40

The "New" Russian Submarines

Until the early eighties, Russian nuclear subs were considered something of a well-armed joke by Western submariners. But when the Russians finally caught on to the knack of silencing their boats, the situation was no longer funny. Whereas before 1980, U.S. subs could detect Russian subs ten times farther away (up to 100 km) than they could detect other U.S. subs, new Russian boats now could get within torpedo range (under 40 km) before being spotted. This allowed Russian subs to get off one of their own torpedoes if they detected the launch of a U.S. one. While this was by no means the end of the world for U.S. submarine supremacy, it simply made things more difficult and dangerous. In a perverse way, it actually helped U.S. subs, as it lit a fire under U.S. Navy R&D people and kept the submarine crews on their toes more than was usually the case underwater.

Moreover, as of 1989, there were only twenty-eight of these "new" Russian subs (*Akula*, *Sierra*, and *Victor III* classes). There are over a hundred Western boats of equal, or quieter, performance. U.S. boats also have much better sensors, largely driven by computing power far in excess of anything Russia has been able to produce. There are also techniques one can use to launch a torpedo quietly, although this involves more time and less maneuverability. Torpedoes are gaining new attention from the Russians, as they plan to introduce a larger-diameter model that could travel further using better sensors. This would allow a sub to fire torpedoes at carriers over 50 kilometers away. The "smart" long-range torpedo would then chase the wake of the large carrier. The larger torpedo has a larger warhead, meaning that one or two hits could cripple a carrier, and three or more hits could put it out of action. This torpedo, like their silencing efforts, has been a long-range project for the Russians. One point missed during the Toshiba propeller-milling machine scandal was that the quieter new Russian subs were actually using propellers made by French equipment received during the late 1970s. For a decade, the Russians have been working on silencing and have only achieved noticeable results since the late 1980s. Finally, keep in mind that finding anything underwater is very difficult, no matter how good your sensors or how loud your opponent.

Antiship-Missile Defense

There are five ways to prevent your ship from being hit by a modern antiship missile (ASM).

First, you can destroy the enemy ship or aircraft before it can launch the missile. For this reason, the United States has aircraft carriers and Russia has a lot of land-based naval aviation.

Second, if the missile is launched, the next line of defense is long-range (up to 100-km) surface-to-air missiles (SAMs), or air-to-air missiles like the U.S. Phoenix. Because most modern ASMs fly low and fast (a few feet above the water and at a speed of 40 km a minute), long-range SAMs have a low success rate.

Third, short-range SAMs. The most effective ones are designed for use against ASMs and are good out to 5–10 kilometers.

Fourth, automatic guns, firing hundreds of rounds in seconds, which are good from a few hundred meters up to a few kilometers.

Fifth, deception measures like flares, chafe, and other electronic trickery.

If all these measures fail, the ship gets hit. Most ships have only one or two of these methods available. There is also the problem of surprise. If the defender is not alerted to turn the defenses on in time, the defenses, of course, will not work.

Flying Fish

Exocet, the name of the French antiship missile, derives from the Greek *exokeitos*—"flying fish."

Saving the USS *Stark*

At 9:12 P.M., on May 17, 1987, over the Persian Gulf, an Iraqi aircraft fired two French-made Exocet missiles at the U.S. warship *Stark*. *Stark* displaces 3,700 tons, is 445 feet long and 45 feet wide, and 24 feet of the hull is below the waterline. She entered active service in October 1982.

The first missile hit amidships, about eight feet above the waterline. Instead of exploding, it largely disintegrated as it passed diagonally through the ship, leaving a gaping hole on the opposite side. The missile left behind several hundred pounds of burning propellant. This stuff burned at 3,500 degrees Fahrenheit, well above the upper limit of 1,800 degrees most ships expect to cope with.

The second missile hit thirty seconds later, eight feet forward of the first. This one exploded after penetrating five feet inside the ship. It did less damage, as most of the explosive force was directed away from the ship. Eighty feet of the level just below the main deck was now on fire. Two of the ship's three damage-control lockers, each containing essential damage-control gear, were blocked by the fire. Nearly 20 percent of the 200-man crew was dead or injured, as the missiles had done most of their damage in the living quarters. Just forward of the damaged area was the ship's missile-storage area. Aft of the damaged area were the galley [kitchen] and storage areas. Above were work areas, and below more living spaces. The explosion and fire disabled the forward fire main, cutting off water for fire fighting to the front end of the ship. For three hours, the fire spread upward into the ship's superstructure.

Four hours after the missiles hit, the damage-control teams ran out of air canisters for their breathing apparatus. Fortunately, a helicopter from another ship arrived less than half an hour later with more canisters and additional damage-control equipment. The fire was not put out until 5:00 P.M. the following day. Using equipment at hand and their damage-control training, the crew was able to get the forward fire main fixed. This was important because water had to be constantly sprayed on the forward missile-storage area to prevent an explosion that would have destroyed the ship. Water sprayed on the intense heat of the fire itself quickly reached the boiling point, which caused additional injuries.

For twenty hours, the crew systematically put out fires and pumped excess water out of the ship to prevent her from rolling over. Stark's previous damage-control training had been above average. This edge provided the margin of survival.

Submarine-Design Philosophies

The United States invented the nuclear submarine. Much of the pioneering work was ably supervised by Admiral Hyman G. Rickover. However, because of the nature of the U.S. military budgeting process and the high cost of nuclear subs, there has not been a lot of variety in the design of these boats. At present there are basically four designs: the attack boat (the current SSN-688 *Los Angeles* class is not much different from the preceding *Sturgeon* class), the big missile boat (The *Ohio* class, a new design for the current ballistic-missile boats being built), the small-missile boat (the original late 1950s design used into the early 1970s) and the new *Sea Wolf* design for attack boats (the most innovative one yet). Russia has over two dozen nuclear-sub designs. The Russian approach recognizes their technical inferiority and need to develop superior submarine designs by trial and error. Nearly half their designs are seriously flawed, but several of them have incorporated significant innovations.

But in some respects, Russian nuclear-submarine design practices backfire. The Russians' inability to miniaturize and produce consistent quality in their construction has resulted in boats that are prone to fatal accidents. In 1961, '68, '80, '83, '86, and '89, Russia lost nuclear subs due to internal breakdowns. The United States has lost only two subs in similar circumstance, in 1963 and '68. The large number of losses in the 1980s indicates that Russian engineers aren't getting any better. Only wartime conditions can reveal the true worth of the Russians' nuclear-submarine program. Peacetime operations do demonstrate steady progress for all their efforts, despite the accidents. However, they do keep their flawed designs in service, incurring substantial expense and dubious wartime value.

Russian Submarine Aircraft Carriers

Aware of their inability to match U.S. carrier forces, but still wanting to use air power at sea, Russia has built a fleet of 50 special missile-carrying submarines carrying nearly 500 cruise missiles. Unfortunately, many of these boats are over twenty-five years old and carry equally antique missiles. The most modern, five *Oscar*-class boats, each carry twenty-four SS-N-19 missiles (range—500 km). There is one *Papa*-class boat, originally built as an experiment, carrying ten SS-N-9 missiles (120 km). Six *Charlie* II boats each carry eight SS-N-9s. Ten *Charlie* I boats each carry eight SS-N-7s (60 km). Twenty-six 1960s-vintage *Echo* II boats each carry eight SS-N-12 missiles (500 km). The Echos are an exception to usual Russian practice, as they had their original SS-N-3A missiles replaced with a more modern SS-N-12. There are also two converted *Yankee* ballistic-missile subs carrying cruise missiles, which are not quite perfected yet. The basic problem these boats have is that their sensors cannot pick up a target more than 50–100 km away. To use the longer range of most missiles, they require friendly aircraft to do the spotting for them. The missiles are then programmed to fly to the designated target area where the missiles' sensors can pick up targets when these are a few kilometers ahead. If no targets are there, the missiles are lost to no effect.

Maybe We Should Try Bribery?

From 1983 through 1985, the U.S. Navy spent $57.5 billion on antisubmarine warfare, roughly $152.5 million for each Russian submarine, or rather less than $2 million per Russian submariner. On an annual basis, the U.S. Navy spends nearly a million dollars a week on ASW per Russian submarine.

Rule Number One

"He who commands the sea has command of everything."—Themistocles, Athenian politician and navalist, fifth century B.C. Athens, already a prosperous city, heeded Themistocles' advice to build a fleet and soon became the most powerful of the Greek city-states.

Deep Six

Deep Six is an old navy and marine expression for disposing of something, derived from the pre-EPA maritime custom of throwing things overboard.

We're Looking for a Few Good Sea Lions.

For over twenty years, the U.S. Navy has been training various sea-going mammals to perform combat missions. Dolphins, sea lions, and even small whales have been captured and trained much like dogs and homing pigeons in the past. There are at present about 100 dolphins of various types in the navy, as well as 25 sea lions and 3 beluga whales. Although some animal behaviorists claim the program is unrealistic, and many animal-rights advocates have raised objections to it, the program has met with some success, and over $5 million a year is spent on it. The animals and their trainers are permanently stationed in California, Hawaii, and Florida. First used in Vietnam, the marine mammals have most recently served in the Persian Gulf, guarding stationary U.S. ships against hostile divers. They will also be deployed to guard the Trident SLBM base on the West Coast. The animals are assigned to attack enemy divers in these situations, although the critters appear to have a broad interpretation of who is an enemy diver. Less aggressive missions include searching for mines and man-made underwater objects in general.

Nothing Like a Little Experience

Britain was a bit disappointed at the reaction of its ships to battle damage during the Falklands War. They should not have been surprised, as the same thing happened during the early naval battles of both world wars. Not wanting to be caught short in some future conflict, in 1987 they took an old destroyer, rebuilt it to resemble a more modern ship as far as protection went, recruited a crew of volunteers, and then proceeded to run a series of destructive tests. Rather than waiting for some enemy to bomb and generally shoot up the ship, they did it themselves, and carefully recorded the results. They also tested countermeasures and the numerous combinations of effects when so many systems are interacting during combat. From this experience, they expect to make modifications throughout the fleet and be better prepared the next time around.

Lessons of the *Stark* Incident

As a direct result of the experience of the USS *Stark* in the Persian Gulf on May 17–18, 1987, a number of fleetwide changes in fire control were quickly made. The supply of air-breathing apparatus was tripled, and the number of air canisters for each was doubled. More fireproof clothing was added to the damage-control lockers, as well as metal-cutting devices and viewing equipment that could see through smoke. Plans were made to increase the use of more fire-resistant materials in ship construction. The damage-control training aboard *Stark* had been exceptional, and other ships needed little urging to improve their own. Damage-control drills were made more complex and realistic as a result of the *Stark* experience. Even Hollywood helped out, and sold the navy a nontoxic special-effects smoke generator for use in onboard damage-control drills. Many ships had got into the habit, common during peacetime, of slighting damage-control training in order to attend to seemingly more pressing matters.

The *Stark* incident made everyone aware of how important all that damage-control training could be. There is still a problem in that the officer principally responsible for damage control is normally one of the more junior on the ship. This may be changed. Oddly enough, the *Stark* ordeal made more of an impression than the similar experiences of the British Navy off the Falklands in 1982. The British experience did not go completely unnoticed, it's just that the *Stark* incident was, well, closer to home. As a result of the Falklands, the British did what all modern navies should do, fired real missiles at a real ship and paid attention to what happened. Suddenly, most NATO navies are looking to improve shipboard sprinkler systems, electrical systems, fire-fighting equipment, and crew training. The thirty-seven sailors who perished when the USS *Stark* was hit did not die in vain. Many current and future sailors will owe their lives to them.

Submarine Spies

Sweden has long complained of Russian submarine incursions into her territorial waters. The Russians deny this, but were caught red-handed when a Russian diesel sub ran aground near a Swedish naval base in 1981. This didn't stop them: In the last six months of 1987, there were thirty reported submarine violations of Swedish territorial waters. The Russians have been less willing to complain about "foreign" subs in their own waters. Yet American nuclear subs regularly enter Russian waters to collect information. In the late 1970s, U.S. subs left behind two nuclear-powered listening devices attached to a supposedly secure underwater communications cable near a Russian naval base in the Pacific. These devices were only discovered when they were betrayed by an American intelligence officer who defected.

Civilians at War

So technically complex have modern warships become that all U.S. aircraft carriers and many other warships go to sea with dozens of civilian technical specialists aboard to service various esoteric pieces of equipment, usually under provisions included in procurement contracts. Generally treated as officers, and paid considerably more than navy personnel, these civilians occupy an ambiguous niche in the seagoing navy. Although officially they will be removed from the ships in the event of war, over the last eight years they have been aboard during the Lebanese, Grenadan, Libyan, and Persian Gulf operations, all of which involved combat by carrier aircraft, and sometimes combat pay to the crews. Their presence on men-o'-war during these combat missions constitutes a violation of the Geneva Convention. Other nations have solved this problem by having a class of troops called "officials," who basically fulfill the same function as the U.S. Navy's civilian technicians. The German Army, for example, used this approach extensively through World War II. Note also that the first artillerymen several centuries ago were civilian contractors. When the British battle cruiser *Hood* went down before the German battleship *Bismark* in 1941, there were a number of British civilian technicians aboard her running mate, HMS *Prince of Wales*. The problem of civilians handling high-tech weapons is nothing new.

Faint Praise

When Admiral Hyman Rickover, the "Father of the Nuclear Navy," was finally retired from active duty, he was informed that a new nuclear-powered submarine was to be named in his honor, to which he replied, "It should have been a carrier."

Marksmanship?

On October 20, 1984, an Irish fisheries-protection vessel came upon a 330-ton Spanish trawler poaching in restricted waters. The Irishmen ordered the crew into boats, and sank the intruder. Rather than prosaically knocking a few holes in the bottom, the skipper of the patrol vessel decided to do it in style, by opening up with his "main battery," a single 40-mm and a pair of 20-mm guns. The results were perhaps predictable, and the trawler went to the bottom, after taking 596 rounds. In 1988 U.S. Navy ships expended even more rounds while destroying an Iranian oil platform. In this case, the ships' captains saw the incident as a good opportunity to let the gun crews get as much practice as they could. The Irish may have had the same idea.

Brassy Boat

Aside from an occasional royal boat ride, the highest ranking ships' crew since some Galileans went fishing about 2,000 years ago was probably that of the fifty-three-foot British sail training yacht *Racer*, which in 1988 took part in a special Spain-to-England run to commemorate the 400th anniversary of the Spanish Armada. The crew comprised two commanders, two captains, and five admirals of the Royal Navy, skippered by yet another admiral, Sir John Woodward, who last gained some distinction by commanding the Royal Navy squadron in the Falklands.

Experience Counts.

"The best that science can devise and that naval organization can provide must be regarded only as an aid, and never as a substitute for good seamanship."—Chester W. Nimitz, American admiral, World War II

"Go Ahead, Make My Day!"

In a remarkable demonstration of how warm U.S.-Russian relations have grown recently, Marshal of the Soviet Union Sergei F. Akhromeyev, chief of staff of the Soviet armed forces, paid a formal professional visit to military installations in the United States during the summer of 1988. Most of the time Akhromeyev wore his uniform, which may have stunned some inveterate Cold Warriors when they ran into him at various bases, academies, and maneuvers. However, he donned civies for a meeting with the Joint Chiefs of Staff at the Pentagon. It was there that he had an interesting exchange with Admiral Carlisle A. H. Trost, the chief of naval operations. It seems that while swapping war stories with the U.S. brass, Akhromeyev suddenly turned to Trost and said, "You! You're the problem! You and your navy are the problem! You and your navy are too strong, you've got to get rid of your cruise missiles. You've got to get rid of some of those carriers." As Admiral Trost would later remark, ". . . in the words of a famous American, 'He made my day.' "

Fish Don't Vote.

The U.S. Navy once named its submarines after "denizens of the deep," so that they bore such designations as *Wahoo, Triton, Nautilus,* and *Sturgeon.* But in the late fifties, in an effort to stimulate support for its ballistic-missile submarine program, the navy cleverly arranged to have the SSBNs—nuclear-powered ballistic-missile submarines—named after various heroes of American history, paying careful attention to spread the goodies around to keep all the states and various ethnic groups happy. The result was a pod of boomers with names like *Ethan Allen, Theodore Roosevelt, Casimir Pulaski,* and *George Washington.* A number of anomalies turned up, so that one was named for Simón Bolívar, hardly a gringo, and another for George Washington Carver, one of the gentlest men in American history, while several bore the names of various "heroes" of the Confederacy, making the United States the only nation in history to name warships after defeated rebels, and one went to sea with what is perhaps the most ridiculous name ever borne by a ship, *Lewis and Clark*.

By the mid-sixties, the navy had abandoned its system for naming other vessels as well, so that carriers, formerly named for famous ships of the old sailing navy or great battles, are increasingly bearing the names of politicians, some of whom had only marginal association with the navy, while some cruisers, formerly named for cities, now bear names from the navy's heroic past, such as *Yorktown*, and submarines are now also being named for cities and states. When one old submariner inquired as to the reason for the change, he was bluntly told, "Fish don't vote."

Interservice Rivalry

The United States is the only country to have a service song that actually identifies an enemy, the navy's "Anchors Aweigh," which includes the words "sink the Army."

"Two if by Sea."

While the U.S. merchant marine has sunk to an all-time low of some 350 vessels, and the Maritime Administration maintains a "reserve" of 250 obsolete merchantmen in mothballs, it is worth recalling that nearly 98 percent of all military cargo landed in support of American operations in Vietnam went by sea, a figure that would not change much in any future war. While shipment of goods by sea takes over thirty times longer than shipment by air, a single merchant ship can transport dozens of tanks at a cost equal to that of sending a single tank by air over an equal distance, and that single ship can carry a lot more tanks than can all the aircraft capable of lifting such at any given time.

'Nuf Said

" 'Better' is the enemy of 'Good Enough.' "—Motto that hung on the wall of Admiral Sergei Gorshkov, head of the Russian Navy, 1950s–1980s, to remind him of the relative quality of the U.S. and Soviet fleets

Torpedo-Proof Ships

One interesting development of the Persian Gulf "naval war" of the late 1980s was the invulnerability of supertankers or VLCCs (Very Large Crude Carriers)—vessels of over 100,000 tons deadweight capacity—when hit by mines, and probably torpedoes as well. There are several hundred VLCCs in service, mostly controlled by NATO or other allied nations. Their protection comes from the fact that these ships are designed to carry large quantities of liquids, usually oil. When traveling empty, the oil tanks are usually flushed and filled with seawater to provide more stability in rough seas. Some of these ships have open decks more than 1,000 feet long. A few days' work by carpenters can cover the pipes on deck and provide space for 2,000 to 4,000 standard (twenty-foot) cargo containers. Hundreds of trucks and armored vehicles can also be placed on deck. As the British demonstrated during the Falklands War, containers can also be used to house and maintain troops. Also, with the right kind of jury-rigged decking, they can easily serve as improvised helicopter and V/STOL aircraft carriers.

The two major disadvantages of VLCCs are that they are slow and they are difficult to unload. Their top speed is only about twenty knots, about 38 km per hour. This is a result of the increase in oil prices during the early 1970s: VLCCs built after that time had smaller engines that used less oil. Most other merchant ships built during this same period also had slower speeds, so most convoys will be using the slower speeds.

The second problem is a consequence of their sheer size, which renders them unable to use most port facilities. This can be overcome by emptying most of the cargo in the tanks. The VLCCs would then ride high in the water and be able to dock. VLCCs can also be off-loaded in a harbor using cranes and barges. The VLCC can carry oil as well as cargo on deck. When going to dry areas, fresh water can be carried instead of oil. If hit by several torpedoes, a VLCC could stay afloat long enough for passengers and perhaps even cargo to be rescued.

The Cost of Prestige

For some years now, the Argentine Navy has been building a nuclear submarine. Although the government would like to scrap the project, the navy insists on continuing, so that Argentina will have the distinction of being the first Latin American power to own an atomic sub. Meanwhile, the project is sopping up so much money that in order to pay for it the navy is limiting warships to about twenty days of sea time a year. This approach will not enable the navy to do any better in a future war than it did in the 1982 Falklands conflict.

Smoke and Fire

In the seven months from September of 1987 to March of 1988, the British deployed three minesweepers in the Persian Gulf, during which period they found ten mines.

Russian Secret Submarine Missions

It's been known for years that Russian submarines have been used to scout the coastal waters of Sweden. There has also been a long history of such incursions in Norwegian waters. Between 1975 and 1987, there were 123 possible or probable incidents. The busiest year was 1983, at about the same time that activity in Swedish waters was at its peak. It is thought that Russian subs are testing Norwegian ASW defenses, practicing for wartime minelaying, and perhaps leaving behind sensors or even remote-control bottom mines. However, no underwater devices or mines have ever been found.

Russia's Secret ASW Weapon

In the early 1980s, the U.S. Navy noticed that the Russians had an uncanny ability to find U.S. subs. This was thought to be coincidence, or a secret Russian ASW technique that was able to locate subs better than anything in the West. Later it was discovered that the Russian technique was to read coded U.S. messages courtesy of code books obtained from the Walker spy ring. The United States thought its codes were unbreakable. So did the Germans, when, during World War II, their U-boats were consistently discovered by Allied ASW forces. You can never be sure of anything.

Canada's Nuclear Submarines

For several years, Canada was in the market for a couple of nuclear-powered submarines. Attempts to procure some in the United States were rebuffed on the grounds that should a U.S.-supplied Canadian atomic submarine have an accident, the blame would fall on us. As a result, the Canadians have been talking about buying some surplus British nuclear subs or some smaller French-built types. The Reagan administration attempted to block these deals by citing a hypothetical potential for ecological disaster, an odd argument coming from an administration not noted for its devotion to the environment. The real reason for U.S. reluctance to see the Canadians own a few nuclear submarines has to do with what they intend to do with the things: patrol their extensive arctic waters, which have hitherto been pretty much the exclusive domain of the U.S. Navy's nuclear subs, with an occasional "intruder" from Russia. In any case, the Canadians will probably not go forward with this project, as it would either consume an unhealthy chunk of the defense budget, or increase defense spending to uncomfortable levels.

Teething Problems

Developmental difficulties are nothing new in weapons programs. The introduction of the surface-to-air antiaircraft missile is a good case in point. By the early sixties, for example, the U.S. Navy had a number of ships equipped with Terrier and Tartar SAMs for air defense, and had decided to abandon guns as the principal air-defense weapon on its newest supercarriers. There were occasional difficulties, such as target-acquisition radar that could not distinguish friends from foes, or from migrating flocks of birds. There were also some unpleasant incidents when missile launchers occasionally slewed around as if to fire on ships running alongside. But, by and large, the navy was fairly satisfied.

Then a truly unfortunate incident took place. Shortly after John

F. Kennedy became president in 1961, the navy, aware of his love for the sea, figured to score some points by inviting him to a major review and demonstration. Things went pretty well until the time came for several drone aircraft to make "attacks" on carriers, so that they could be shot down by the navy's newest toys. There was many a red-faced admiral that day, for missile after missile missed. Seeing his brass becoming apoplectic, the president shrugged off the incident with a good-natured remark and suggested that it appeared some work had yet to be done to perfect the missiles. Shortly afterward, 5-inch antiaircraft guns began appearing on carriers that had not been designed to mount them.

Just What *Are* Nuclear-Attack Subs Good For?

There is an enormous difference in capability between the current nuclear-attack subs (SSNs) and the last bunch of diesel-electric boats to see combat in World War II. As in the past, SSNs are expected to go after subs and surface ships, but improvements in other technologies enable them to assume a number of new roles, one of which is reconnaissance. Nuclear subs can stay quietly on station for months at a time.

They have powerful passive sensors, which can be used in mine-clearing. SSNs have already demonstrated their ability to plant sensors. They can also launch recon-equipped cruise missiles; although most SSNs cannot carry more than one or two dozen, these can be effective if delivered onto the right target at the right time. In the United States, two older ballistic-missile subs were converted to carry several hundred commandos.

One nagging question remains: Why do so many nations continue to build diesel (SS) electric subs? These modern diesel-electric boats are in fact much more capable in terms of coastal defense than their World War II predecessors, and are smaller and quieter than SSNs. Although SS boats do not have the range of SSNs, they do carry capable sensors and torpedoes. In smaller bodies of water like the Baltic or Mediterranean, they are more survivable than an SSN. The main reason the United States, alone among major navies, has abandoned SS subs is because the U.S. Navy is primarily a high-seas navy. The SSN is the ultimate high-seas submarine.

Front End/Rear End?

The U.S. Navy has a rather peculiar pair of ranks among its flag officers. These are "rear admiral of the lower half" and "rear admiral of the upper half." Both types of rear admiral are commonly known as "rear admiral," wear two stars as their insignia, and have almost precisely the same uniforms, save for a little extra braid on the "upper half" cuffs. However, the "lower half" are paid at the rate established for brigadier generals of the other services, while the "upper half" earn the same salaries as do major generals. This unusual situation has its roots in military tradition. By ancient military custom, "flag officers"—that is, generals and admirals—are the beneficiaries of special privileges.

However, by equally ancient tradition the British Army, from which the U.S. Army derives its customs, had four grades of general—brigadier general, major general, lieutenant general, and general—plus field marshals, while the Royal Navy, parent of the USN, had three grades of admiral—rear admiral, vice admiral, and admiral—plus "admiral of the fleet" and an intermediate grade of commodore, ranking below rear admiral. While generals and admirals had the right to fly special flags, commodores, although paid the same as brigadier generals, could only "display" a broad pennant, and were also denied various other benefits of "flag rank," such as additional aides-de-camp, salutes, and the like. This made commodores very unhappy. In the late nineteenth century, the British resolved the problem in an economical fashion: They changed "brigadier general" to "brigadier," thereby demoting such persons from flag rank and putting them on a par with commodores. Not long after the beginning of the twentieth century, the United States took the opposite tack, virtually abolishing the rank of commodore except as a courtesy title for the senior captain of a flotilla of vessels, and created two tiers of rear admiral. As a result, the U.S. Navy has a lot of two-star officers, many of whom receive the pay of one-star officers in the other services. Of course, the question of privilege still lingered, as brigadier generals in the other branches occasionally found themselves saluting officers of equal or inferior seniority, that is, the "lower half" rear admirals. As a result, slight uniform changes were introduced, so that an "upper half" wears one 2-inch and one half-inch bit of braid on his sleeve, while a "lower half" has only the 2-inch stripe. In a further effort to clarify matters, "rear admirals of the lower half" were redesignated "commodore admirals" several years ago, which sounded so silly, it was almost immediately abolished. At that time, one congressman commented, "If that rank [commodore] was good enough for John Paul Jones, Farragut, and Peary, it is good enough for a bunch of people that I never heard of!" This bit of wisdom went unheeded, and the rank of commodore passed from the American scene, for the moment.

"*Quo Vadis,* Navy 21?"

The navy has recently concluded two studies that attempt to assess the needs of the service into the next century. "*Quo Vadis?*" ("Where are you going?" in Latin) tries to consider the navy's needs at the end of the century, while "Navy 21" looks forty years further. The studies attempt to pinpoint "immature technologies," which may be of importance to the high-speed fleet of multihulled and surface-effect vessels that the navy expects to have by 2040. Such technologies include particle-beam and laser weapons, submarine-launched antiaircraft missiles, Stealth technologies, nonmetallic construction materials, robotics, superquiet submarines, and virtually perfect satellite-navigation and intelligence-gathering systems. One senior officer justified the studies by observing that fifty years ago nuclear weapons, jet aircraft, computers, and radar did not exist, and that the navy must look ahead in order to be able to use innovative technological developments as soon as they become available. Curiously, however, both studies presuppose the continuation of a "Cold War" relationship between the United States and Russia, which also did not exist fifty years ago.

Submarine-Warfare Blues

Under certain conditions (if the layers of water temperature, etc., are just right), it is possible to detect a nuclear submarine by the noise it makes as much as 800 kilometers distant, even when deeply submerged, such as at 650 fathoms, about 4,000 feet (1,200 meters).

The Electrician's Nightmare

The average large warship has 50–100 tons of electrical cable installed. The stuff comes in all sizes, from telephone wire to thick power lines, several thousand kilometers of wires, most of which perform the traditional role of carrying electricity or voices. But more and more of it links computers with other computers and with automated ship's equipment and weapons. Keeping all this stuff sorted out, and not shorted out, becomes an ever-larger task for crews. While machines do more of the sailor's traditional work, someone has to look after the machines. Then, too, of course, although there is some "redundancy" in the systems, no one knows how effective this will be in the event of battle damage.

The Vast Ocean Spaces

Oceans cover 120 million square miles of the earth's surface. Less than 25 percent of this area would be a potential naval battlefield in a future war. On average, ASW (antisubmarine warfare) platforms (ships, subs, aircraft) cannot search more than 1,000 to 3,000 square miles per hour. No wonder submarines disappear from enemy view so easily. While ASW sensors have been getting better during the last fifty years, their prey have also become quieter and more difficult to detect. Although ASW sensors differ in their effectiveness, the larger and better ones tend to be carried on slower platforms. The slower the platform, the less area it can cover in an hour. For example, an aircraft flying at 400 miles an hour with a sensor that can only detect subs for two miles in any direction is going to cover only 1,600 square miles an hour. One reason so much effort is put into satellite ASW sensors is because these birds streak over the ocean at 10,000 miles an hour. Even a low-sensitivity sensor could be very effective at that speed. Fixed sensors, like the U.S. SOSUS system, can cover millions of square miles on a regular basis, but are vulnerable to destruction in wartime. For the foreseeable future, numerous ASW platforms will be the primary means of hunting down submarines in the vast ocean spaces.

The Third Battle of the Atlantic

In World Wars I and II, submarines attempted to prevent merchant ships from carrying troops and supplies from North America to Europe. In both wars, the subs failed, although it was touch and go at times. A third World War could see Russian subs attempting to do what German subs could not do the last two times around. This is unlikely, however. Although Russia has a fleet of over 200 attack subs, most of them are older, quite noisy boats. Unlike the Germans, who had bases on the Atlantic, Russian subs must transit from their bases in the White Sea, east of Norway. Moreover, most of their subs are assigned either to guard their own ballistic-missile subs (SSBNs), to attack enemy SSBNs, or to go after enemy surface warships. Not only does this leave few subs for attacking North Atlantic convoys, but it places those subs under some terrible operational restrictions. To reach the convoy routes, the subs must transit more than a thousand kilometers of hostile waters. Hundreds of enemy ASW aircraft patrol these waters, in addition to surface ships and underwater sensors. Nor would convoys be undefended, though NATO is a bit vague on just what sort of escort each convoy would get. Top priority in resources would be given to going after whatever Russian surface ships were on the high seas, as well as sealing off their northern naval bases. Most likely, each convoy would have no more than one to three escorts, plus one or more ASW aircraft, and possibly a new-model blimp.

Nuclear subs have several advantages over World War II types, especially in speed, sensors, and ability to cruise underwater indefinitely, which enables them to keep chasing and attacking convoys. In World War II, transports were faster than submerged subs and could outrun them. If Russian naval-recon satellites survive (unlikely), it would be relatively easy to mass available subs against convoys. NATO forces would require fifty or sixty shiploads of supplies per day after two to four weeks of combat. This would mean about two dozen convoys at sea at any given moment. Even without recon satellites, Russian subs would not find it difficult just to sit still in likely areas with their passive sensors turned on. However, nuclear subs make more noise at high speeds, which makes it easier for modern ASW forces to find and destroy them. NATO expects to deploy against the Russians two carriers, fifteen cruisers, and over sixty destroyers and frigates, plus more than three dozen subs. Even if a Russian sub did get a sustained run at an unescorted convoy, it only carries about two dozen torpedoes, some of which are nuclear. But if the Russians "go nuclear," they will find themselves on the receiving end of nuclear-depth charges and antisub torpedoes. There's no free lunch.

Getting from Over Here to Over There

Getting U.S. mechanized forces from North America to Europe is a major logistical operation. It takes at least twenty days from decision to deployment. About ten ships are required to do the moving: A typical U.S. mechanized infantry division requires 90,000 tons of shipping, and the average high-speed Ro-Ro transport can carry about 9,400 tons. It takes four days to get a division to the port. Another three days are spent loading the ships. Six days are required to cross the Atlantic, and three more to unload the ships. Two days are required to sort all the men and equipment into their normal organization. Finally, it takes two days to get from the port to the battlefield. A lot can go wrong, so in reality it could take another week to actually do the deed. And that assumes no attempts are made by the enemy to interfere. There is also the matter of warning time. Peacetime movements like the above usually require weeks or months of getting things in order before going through the twenty-day drill. In wartime, the preparation is cut quite a bit, but there the potential for foul-ups would still be great.

The Pains of Budget-Cutting

The U.S. Navy found its budget explosion of the 1980s coming to a halt by 1987. Few of the necessary reductions were without unpleasant side effects, such as the decision not to upgrade the radar on most carriers. Since the early 1970s, the principal air-defense radar has been the SPS-48C, used on carriers to control friendly air traffic and detect hostile planes. A new version, the SPS-48E, was introduced in the late 1980s. The 48E is practically a new system, using more efficient components, and is easier to use and maintain. In other words, it would break down less frequently and be easier to train new operators for. The 48E has half as many components as the 48C and requires 90 percent fewer adjustments to get it working right. But it would cost $11 million to upgrade each of the 48Cs on the ten carriers that did not already have the 48E. The navy's reasoning, on leaving the inferior 48C on the carriers, was that carriers are surrounded by ships carrying the 48E, as well as the even more advanced Aegis SPS-49 radar. Critics of the decision, primarily the SPS-48's manufacturer, ITT Corporation, claimed that the different radar signals coming from a 48C among all those 48Es would give incoming cruise missiles an easier shot at the carrier. Critics within the navy point out that the 48C is likely to be overwhelmed under combat conditions and leave the air-wing commander aboard the carrier incapable of effectively controlling his aircraft. The navy felt that there were simple ways to overcome these problems. ITT took its case to the public and Congress, creating another struggle for the navy. This is likely to become a fairly common event as budgets are cut back and systems dropped. The U.S. Navy pays $15 million for each new AN/SPS-48E shipboard radar system.

The 600-Ship Navy

Although the 480-ship navy that the nation maintained in the late 1970s was generally considered rather small, there is actually no consensus on or established basis for calculating the number of vessels that the navy ought to have. Nevertheless, the "600-ship navy," which proved so politically useful to the Reagan candidacy in 1980, has been adopted as an official goal, and the fleet has risen to about 550 ships in the last eight years. However, new construction, most of it Carter administration inspired, accounted for only about 80 percent of the increase; the rest was due to retaining older vessels in service longer than normal, and restoring to service several ships in "mothballs," such as four 1942-vintage battleships. A closer look at the present rate of construction suggests strongly that the fleet will fall far short of the official goal of 600 ships.

There is presently a six-year cycle for the construction of new warships. That is, every six years two new supercarriers are laid down, as well as three nuclear-powered ballistic-missile submarines, nine nuclear-powered attack submarines, three cruisers, twenty-one destroyers, twenty-one frigates, fifteen amphibious-warfare vessels, three mine warfare vessels, and nine auxiliaries. Thus, the navy is adding fourteen or fifteen new vessels to its fleet each year. Given the normal life expectancy of various types of warships, this rate of new construction would allow the core group of fourteen new or modernized supercarriers to be maintained well into the next century, but is insufficient even to maintain the total size of the fleet at its supposedly inadequate 1980 level, which would require about twenty new ships each year. To keep the fleet at its present strength would require about 23, while a 600-ship navy would require about 25 ships a year. Nor is the rate of construction likely to rise, despite intense lobbying by navalists, some of whom are advocating an "800-ship navy," which would require about 33 new ships a year. While widely touted financial concerns are one reason an increase in ship-building budgets is unlikely, the anticipated, though much less widely advertised, shortage of manpower that will begin to affect the armed forces in the next decade is a very serious additional limitation, not to mention the improving international climate.

Shanghaied into World War III

In times past, the lot of a merchant sailor was so bad that crews had to be filled out with unlucky civilians "shanghaied" (kidnapped) into service. This practice died out in the late 1800s, but a new version of it may well appear in the event of another major war. Since World War II, merchant-shipping business has, like everything else, gone to the low bidder. In this case, the ships have been built in places like Japan and Korea, while most of the crews have come from Third World nations. In consequence, the number of U.S. merchant seamen has fallen from 200,000 just after World War II to about 25,000 at present. For economic reasons, most U.S.-owned ships fly under foreign "flags of convenience." In wartime there would be some legal wrangling over government control of these ships. But legal obstacles tend to be less formidable in wartime, and there is little doubt that the U.S. government would put to use any merchant ships it got its hands on, regardless of the flag they were flying. The crews are another matter. Many of these merchant sailors, and their officers, don't speak English.

It's one thing to grab the ships, it's quite another to convince the crews to sail into a combat zone, in this case the North Atlantic. It is estimated that 2,400 ships a month would have to make round trips from North America to Europe to keep the war going. These would require crews totaling over 100,000 trained sailors and technicians. Only 16 percent of this shipping is for military needs; the rest is required to keep the civilians going on both sides of the pond. The first two months would see slightly higher military requirements. For the first five months of a European conflict, some 3 million tons of military matériel would be moved from North America to Europe. Much of it would be explosive and highly flammable goods. In winter, getting dumped into frigid Atlantic waters is fatal. Some inducements would be needed to convince non-American crews to ship out under these conditions. A combination of financial bonuses and, perhaps, a green card (right to immigrate to the United States) could do it. Recruitment would also be easier if the losses to Russian subs could be kept down.

Talking to Boomer

Submerged submarines have limited communications capability. They must come close to the surface and deploy an antenna to communicate with the outside world. This makes them more vulnerable. Such exposure can be reduced by using very low frequency signals, but this requires special sending and receiving equipment at each end. Russia uses a land-based system, which is vulnerable to attack. The United States also uses a land-based system, but in addition has an airborne system using C-130 aircraft. The current four-engine propeller-driven C-130 aircraft are being replaced by B-707 four-engine jets. Two of these jets will be in the air at all times and are hardened against the electronic effect of nuclear explosions. The aircraft deploy a 5,000-foot antenna behind them and a 25,000-foot antenna below them to communicate with the subs. In the event of a nuclear war, these aircraft will issue the firing orders to the boomers (ballistic-missile submarines). With airborne refueling, these jets can stay aloft as long as seventy-two hours. The jets will be based in Oklahoma and operate over the Atlantic and Pacific. Even though the aircraft have to travel over a thousand miles to reach the ocean, it's still cheaper to run the airbase in Oklahoma than in more expensive areas on either coast.

Sonar and the Inner Circle

The appearance of much quieter Russian subs in the 1980s caused the U.S. Navy to rethink its tactics for defending aircraft carriers from underwater attack. Each carrier has a half-dozen ASW helicopters. These can drop sonobuoys (passive sonar) or dipping sonar (passive and/or active). Going after quieter Russian subs appears to rule out using passive sonobuoys so close to the noisy task force. It is felt that the more powerful active sonars on escort ships now offer the best potential for catching subs that have got within torpedo range. Tests using U.S. subs show that quiet subs can easily get very close. Quiet subs, just sitting around in likely areas waiting for a high-value target like a carrier task force to come looming into torpedo range, are becoming an increasingly likely possibility.

Sea Power?

Although during the Reagan administration the navy grew from rather less than 500 ships to about 550, the U.S. Merchant Marine declined from nearly 800 active vessels to about 350, while government expenditures on the merchant marine average about $8 million a year, roughly the same as in the late 1940s, when the dollar was worth a lot more. Moreover, while new construction of warships has risen to fourteen or fifteen a year, no oceangoing merchant vessel has been completed in a U.S. shipyard since November of 1987, nor have any been ordered since: For the first time in the history of the Republic, there is not a single merchant vessel under construction in a U.S. yard. In addition, most of the fifteen major shipyards left in the country are in financial difficulties despite navy contracts for construction and repair, which are only benefiting about five yards.

One-Hit Wonders

In the last ten years, there have been several instances where modern warships have been taken almost entirely out of commission by just one hit. During World War II, similar ships took much more damage and were still able to operate some of their weapons. The reason appears to be the way modern ships were designed. Engineers sought to make the ships more resistant to component failure. A modern ship's components were designed to support each other in the event of a normal failure. Combat damage is not normal; it is unpredictable and usually catastrophic. Another problem is the replacement of many mechanical systems with electronic ones. The heavier mechanical systems were more robust and could withstand more battle damage. The distance ship designers have drifted from the reality of combat can be seen in the way their ships have fared once they've taken some combat damage. This makes the lessons of the Falklands and the *Stark* incident particularly valuable, as they keep the engineers and designers honest.

"And Ask Questions Later."

Violations of Swedish territorial waters by submarines of "unknown" nationality have reportedly resulted in orders that naval units and coast-defense personnel are to "shoot without warning" upon detecting the presence of underwater intruders.

Middle-Aged Ships

Most warships have a useful active life of twenty to thirty years. With regular modernizations, though, carriers and battleships can hang in there for a couple of decades longer. In 1988 the average age of the ships in the principal NATO navies was:

France	16.6 years
United States	15.6
West Germany	15.1
Italy	12.4
Britain	12.1

Indian Ocean Blues

The Indian Ocean is the only year-round sea route from Russia's Far Eastern provinces to Western Russia's Black Sea ports. The Arctic Ocean route and the Trans-Siberian Railroad have limited capacity and are often interrupted by harsh weather conditions. Some industrial and military equipment is more efficiently sent by ship, so the route from the Black Sea, through the Suez Canal, across the Indian Ocean, and into the China Seas and thence through the Sea of Japan up to Vladivostok is important. It is not a crucial route, but now that Russia has a large navy, it seemed reasonable to take some measures to secure these distant sea lanes. Moreover, these areas are of vital importance to many of Russia's potential enemies, so a Russian naval presence could have some significance in wartime.

It wasn't until the 1970s that Russia was able to establish any significant naval presence in the Indian Ocean. In 1968 the Russian navy managed about 1,000 ship-days in the Indian Ocean. This works out to two or three ships a day, although in practice the number of ships actually present was larger, as it included support ships carrying supplies. So for many days there were no Russian combat or combat-support ships there at all. Through the 1970s, this figure grew, until it peaked at 11,800 ship-days in 1980. This was the equivalent of over thirty ships continually in the area. Through the eighties, Russia lowered its ship-days at sea worldwide. But only minor cutbacks were permitted in the Indian Ocean. This was due to both the Iran-Iraq War and Russia's continued and unsuccessful desire to establish a naval infrastructure in the area. The Russians did have a major naval base in Somalia, but lost it in 1977 when they switched sides in the dispute between Ethiopia and Somalia. The Ethiopian facility is much smaller, and is guarded by a company of Russian naval infantry, and consists of one pier, a few warehouses, some fuel tanks, a communications station, a small floating dry dock, and housing for less than a thousand personnel. This is the largest Russian base in the area. Russia also has anchorage and fueling rights in South Yemen, the Seychelles islands, and, to a lesser extent, in India. In wartime, however, the twenty or so Russian warships in the area would either get out quickly or be forced to sacrifice themselves to damage as many Western ships and facilities in the area as possible.

Guarding the Gap

The key to control of the North Atlantic is Iceland, and the two channels from the Arctic Ocean to the Atlantic, which lie on either side. Iceland has no armed forces of its own, but it belongs to NATO and allows the stationing of U.S. Air Force units on its territory. There is a squadron of 18 F-15 fighters, plus 9 P-3 ASW aircraft, several AWACS and tanker aircraft, and several radar units. Additional aircraft fly in periodically to train. NATO nuclear subs patrol adjacent waters, and carriers can be brought into the area within a day or two. F-15s are always on alert, and can be airborne within five minutes. These interceptors carry two long-range Sparrow missiles and cannon. They can stay in the air for four hours and, after landing, can be refueled, rearmed, and airborne again in sixty-five minutes. Their primary opponent would be Russian long-range bombers. In peacetime they scramble several times a week to intercept Russian "Bear" long-range reconnaissance bombers. The Bears file no flight plans and fly through heavily used civilian flight paths without thought to the risk of collision with airliners. Each year there are several near-misses. So the F-15 intercepts serve an additional safety function: They greet about 98 percent of Russian flights. Those 2 percent were missed due to bad (and dangerous) weather, which would not stop the interceptors in wartime.

The Same, but Different

All nations with a coastline have some form of coast guard. Their primary purpose is usually to enforce laws concerning smuggling, fishing, and illegal entry or exit. Russia's Coast Guard is different. For one thing, it belongs to the KGB, the state security organization, a quarter-million-strong force charged with seeing that neither citizens nor armed forces get out of line. The 25,000 sailors in the "Maritime Border Guards" (MBG) answer to no one but the head of the KGB. To put it more clearly, a lieutenant commanding an MBG patrol boat can order any Russian warship to halt and then arrest its captain. In fact, this is one of the principal functions of the MBG, to prevent mutiny or defection by ships and sailors of the Soviet Navy and merchant fleet. Smuggling is a minor problem, as Russian currency is useless outside the country and there are few items Russia produces that are good (and small) enough to be profitably smuggled. Moreover, much of Russia's coastline is in arctic waters, and most of the remainder is adjacent to other Communist nations. What keeps the MBG busy is insuring that Russian citizens don't flee the country. Such flight is a criminal offense, and several prisons are full of Russians who attempted it and got caught by the MBG. The personnel for the MBG are selected carefully. Although two thirds are conscripts, these are chosen from among the most reliable Slavic candidates and are given special benefits and privileges to compensate for doing three years of service instead of two. These benefits extend into life after military service, as they have demonstrated that they are strong supporters of the government and thus worthy of choice job assignments and other privileges.

While many young conscripts are eager to be in the KGB, they soon discover that the service is extremely grueling if they end up in the MBG. For one thing, nearly half of the MBG is stationed in the Pacific. Except for a few hundred sailors stationed in Vietnam to keep an eye on Russian ships there, most Pacific MBG serve in the frozen north. Most of the MBG back west serve up near the arctic naval bases. Not only are normal MBG operating areas stormy and cold, but MBG ships are generally small, and out on the water most of the time. The MBG has over 200 ships, of which only 15 are over 1,000 tons, and about 150 are under 200 tons. Many ships have two crews, to make it easier to keep the vessels constantly at sea and spare the crews excessive wear and tear. The larger ships have the latest ASW equipment, to assist the navy in defending against submarines in wartime. Because of the three-year term for KGB conscripts, only a quarter of the personnel are replaced each year, allowing for a higher degree of training and effectiveness. Less than a third of the 25,000 MBG sailors are on ship's crews. The majority serve in support jobs on land, supply security detachments for guarding MBG bases, and keep an eye on suspicious foreign merchant ships or any Russian personnel suspected of disloyalty. The Russian Coast Guard looks after a lot more than the coast.

Union Shop

Britain's Royal Navy has permitted neither submariners nor aviators to command any of its three antisubmarine aircraft carriers. Such assignments have always gone to officers with surface navy credentials. This tradition is one reason why Britain, which pioneered carriers, did not develop carrier aviation as quickly or as effectively as the U.S. Navy. Although both navies got off to a good start in the 1920s, Britain kept the aviators in their cockpits while the U.S. Navy allowed naval pilots to advance to the command of carriers and fleets. This policy has been a key factor in the explosive growth of U.S. carrier aviation during the last fifty years.

"O Captain! My Captain!"

By ancient tradition, a ship may have only one captain. Nevertheless, it is now common for some U.S. warships to have four or five people with the rank of captain. A typical supercarrier, with a crew of 5,000, will have one captain serving as air-group commander, another as chief engineer, yet another as executive officer, occasionally a fourth fulfilling some technical function, and, of course, one more as the real captain, better known as the "skipper." The Russians get around this problem on their large ships by putting an admiral in charge. But the Russians do this because they don't trust mere captains in critical situations, their reasoning being that an admiral has more to lose.

Russia in Vietnam

It was not until 1980 that Russian forces in Vietnam reached a significant level, when Vietnam asked Russia to station some naval forces in Danang as a form of insurance against Chinese aggression. A year earlier, there had been serious border battles between Chinese and Vietnamese forces. Russia sent half a dozen ships and a few long-range recon aircraft. In 1983 the Russian Navy took over the old U.S. Cam Rahn Bay complex. In 1984 they completed building a new airstrip for heavy aircraft. In 1985 a major electronic intelligence-gathering complex became operational. That same year, anti-aircraft units were set up and a naval infantry battalion moved in. By 1988 sixty aircraft were stationed there permanently, including sixteen MiG-23 fighters. Nearly three dozen ships were stationed at Cam Rahn Bay and one or two dozen additional Russian vessels visit the port each month. Total Russian manpower at the base peaked at over 10,000, but has since declined considerably.

Life on an SSN

Many today consider the nuclear-attack sub (SSN) the principal warship. Five nations have them: the United States, Russia, Britain, France, and China. The SSNs average about 5,000 tons submerged and carry about two dozen torpedoes with a crew of about 100. Western boats spend about two thirds of their time at sea and one third in port undergoing maintenance. Every four or five years, a sub goes into dry dock for up to a year of overhaul and upgrades, including refueling the reactors. These boats can stay at sea for three or four months at a time, and are forced back to port only to resupply food, spare parts, and munitions, or for maintenance that cannot be performed at sea. The subs can be resupplied at sea, if need be, and can also operate even when some systems are not working properly due to lack of in-port facilities. (This would be a real possibility in wartime.) About a third of the crew works with the power system (nuclear reactor and engines), a third handles weapons and sensors, and a third takes care of housekeeping (food, paperwork, and maintenance). About 25 percent of the crew is normally "on watch" at any given time. Most of their time is spent running ship's systems and performing mandatory maintenance.

Fixing and upgrading instruments and electronics is a major ongoing task on these ships. The number of these systems is staggering. There are several sensor systems, several communications systems, several navigation systems, and complex control systems for engines, diving, and maneuvering. As a result of all this technology, there is always an upgrade going on. There are also additional crew members on board for training and civilian technicians to assist with the new equipment being tested or upgraded. Because there are so many people on board, it's common that there are not enough bunks to go around, so some junior crew must share a bunk, taking turns using it when not on duty. At any given time, there are about two dozen men operating the sub who, because of the nature of submarine warfare, must be capable of quickly performing combat operations. A high degree of automation makes this possible. Indeed, most of the crew spends the bulk of its time double-checking equipment and fixing even the most minor breakdowns. When off-duty, crew members have access to exercise equipment and excellent food, as well as recorded music and VCR tapes. Because most submarine crew are volunteers and technically inclined, they tend to spend a lot of their off-hours working with the subs gear or similar technical activities. Personal computers, including computer games, are a favorite way to spend time.

"Send in the Marines!"

Nearly forty-five countries possess marine corps or amphibious-capable troops of various types, for a total of nearly 850,000 troops, including reservists and personnel discharged within the last five years, roughly twenty-five divisions' worth of manpower. However, it is the USMC that essentially sets the pattern for marines worldwide. With its 85,000 reservists—who themselves outnumber any other marine corps—the four divisions of the USMC account for nearly a third (283,000) of all marines, comprising quite literally an entire army and air force in itself.

Actually, only the U.S., British, South Korean, and French marines are trained to storm hostile beaches. Other nations have what is basically naval infantry, sailors trained for ground combat. This is an important distinction when we speak of units that call themselves "marines." Besides the United States Marines, other sizable "marine corps" are those of:

Active/Reserve

Taiwan	30,000/35,000	Brazil	15,000/20,000
Vietnam	27,000/10,000	Indonesia	12,000/?
China	25,000/25,000	Philippines	9,500/6,000
South Korea	25,000/50,000	Spain	8,500/20,000
Thailand	20,000/10,000	Britain	7,100/3,700
Russia	17,000/50,000	Poland	7,000/12,000

Of course, sheer size is not the only criterion for measuring the abilities of a military force. Although small, the marine corps of several other powers are quite capable. Notable among these are:

Argentina	6,000/10,000
France	4,500/10,000
Netherlands	2,900/5,000
East Germany	2,100/5,000
Italy	800/2,000

The smallest marine corps is that of Madagascar, barely 100 men organized into a single company. The most unusual marine corps are undoubtedly those of Bolivia (1,000/1,000) and Paraguay (500/400), both landlocked countries. For most smaller powers, marines perform special combat duties, usually providing riverine assault forces, counterinsurgency troops, or security forces for naval bases and installations. Several countries find their marines useful as a counterweight to the army when it comes to political maneuvering and coup-plotting. The quality of the manpower, equipment, and training in most marine corps is rather high. Nevertheless, few powers have the experience, skill, and ability to effect a forced landing on a hostile shore. The problem is not so much the size and quality of the marine corps, but the availability of suitable sea lift and landing craft. Not even the United States can land a strategically significant force—say, 80,000 men—anywhere in the world. However, America does possess this capability in most areas in which it has significant interests, though only with some difficulty. Britain (who placed approximately 5,000 men—both marine and army—ashore in the Falklands) and France are probably the next most capable powers in this regard. A few other countries can do reasonably well in a regional situation, such as China, Taiwan, and South Korea, to mention the most prominent, though by no means with the bulk of their marine manpower. The Netherlands could probably effect landings with upward of 2,500 men in the North Sea or the Caribbean. The capacity of the Soviet bloc marine forces is largely confined to the Baltic, where a combined East German, Polish, and Russian operation could conceivably put 15,000 to 20,000 men ashore. In the Black Sea, European Arctic, and Russian Far Eastern areas, Russia might be able to land 4,000 men or so. A few of the other marine corps—the Spanish, Indonesian, Italian, Israeli, and larger

Latin American ones—have the ability to conduct landings or raids within a short distance of their homelands. None of the other powers could do more than conduct operations within their national territories, because their manpower strengths are too small. Some of these are:

Active/Reserve

Bulgaria	300/?	Morocco	1,500/?
Burma	800/?	Nigeria	5,000/?
Chile	5,200/5,000	Peru	2,500/5,000
Colombia	5,000/5,000	Portugal	2,850/1,000
Cuba	600/?	Romania	1,000/500
Dominican Republic	500/?	Saudi Arabia	1,200/?
Ecuador	1,000/2,000	South Africa	900/2,000
Greece	5,000/?	Turkey	4,000/5,000
Guatemala	650/500	Uruguay	400/?
Honduras	600/1,200	Venezuela	5,200/2,000
Israel	300/?	Yugoslavia	900/2,000
Mexico	3,800/2,000	Zaire	600/?

Too-Tough Training

Amphibious operations work because of specially designed ships that can get men and heavy equipment onto beaches quickly and in quantity. The most impressive of these vessels is the LST (landing ship tank) and its modern derivatives. There is a catch, however. These large ships, when run up on a beach, suffer damage. The ships are designed to survive this damage, at least for a few times. Eventually, extensive repairs are required. To spare the expense of these repairs, peacetime training often eliminates the run up on the beach. This plays havoc with schedules, as landing a shipload of men and equipment takes less than an hour if you run up on the beach and over two days if you off-load the cargo into smaller boats that can run up on the beach with less damage. How this will affect actual wartime amphibious operations remains to be seen.

It's Miller Time.

The U.S. Navy banished shipboard drinking of alcoholic beverages early in this century. However, in recognition of the privations of long-term overseas deployments, each sailor is authorized to have two cans of beer each time he spends 100 days afloat without shore leave.

Getting Better All the Time

Over the last twenty-five years, the noise signature of a nuclear-powered attack submarine has fallen by about 20 percent. Since Russian boats started out about 10 percent noisier, the U.S. ones remain considerably quieter than their potential opponents. However, the illegal transfer to the Soviet Union of U.S. computerized propeller-grinding technology and other improvements will probably narrow the gap in the next few years.

The Speed of Listening

Submarines are most effective when they can simultaneously move and listen with their passive (nonbroadcasting) sensors. However, the faster a submarine moves, the more noise it makes. At a certain point, the "speed noise" is so high that the sub's passive sensors can't hear anything. Right now, most Western nuclear subs can move and still hear at speeds up to about 10–12 km an hour. Russian subs prefer to move even more slowly, as their passive sensors are not so powerful. Ideally, a sub should move just fast enough to maintain control, or "way," a few km an hour, and still be able to listen with practically none of its own noise to interfere. The problem with this approach is that you do not cover much territory. The oceans are enormous, and there are never enough subs to cover the areas where your opponents are likely to be.

The Key to Successful ASW

Antisubmarine warfare is usually thought of as marvelous electronic devices pinpointing submarines lurking deep in the ocean. The gadgets are important, but it is often forgotten that they are only as good as their operators. The earliest sonars were crude underwater radars that broadcast a sound and then listened for it to bounce (or "ping") off an enemy sub. The operators used a combination of skill and art to interpret the "pings," and success was directly proportional to how good the operators were.

Modern sonars come in many different flavors, and are aided by magnetic detectors and an increasing number of more exotic sensors. Computers are used to collect and interpret all this sensor data, but it is still up to human operators to make the final decisions. Computers have not yet been capable of that. As a result, the chief limitation of a submarine hunt has become operator fatigue. Peacetime exercises against allied and Russian subs have demonstrated this, and wartime experience will probably be no different. Skill and endurance are the key attributes of successful ASW-equipment operators.

The Black Gang Goes Electronic.

The sailors who tend a ship's power plant have long been called "the Black Gang" in reference to all the coal they once shoveled, now replaced by equally dirty oil. As with the electronics wizards topside, the engineering crew has gone electronic. For example, *Spruance*-class destroyers have seven electronic consoles to control all their machinery. These contain over 1,200 electronic-component cards of three dozen different types. These cards are similar to the ones inside a personal computer. It's not enough to know your way around machinery anymore, you have to be able to debug and troubleshoot all the electronics as well.

Over the Beach Without Wet Feet

Although the U.S. Marine Corps has long organized and trained for storming defended shores, it has covered its bets by developing a considerable air-landing capability. The USMC's principal amphibious ships are basically helicopter carriers. In the early 1990s, the marines want to introduce hundreds of tilt-rotor aircraft that can cruise like fixed-wing aircraft and land like helicopters. Aside from avoiding the messiness and often bitter resistance encountered when assaulting beaches, air landings can reach farther faster, thus forcing the defender to spread his units around a lot more than might be desirable.

Marines *Do* Walk on Water.

The U.S. Marine Corps is paying $24 million each for air-cushion ("hovercraft") landing craft. Aside from the increased speed with which these craft can transport men and supplies from ship to shore, the air-cushion vehicle can also get over the soft sand and marsh covering much of the world's coastlines. This makes landings possible in areas that were previously too difficult, thus complicating the defender's job, as there is now a lot more coastline to be defended.

"Tell It to the Marines!"

A traditional nickname for marines is "leathernecks," derived from the leather stock that they wore in the early years of the Republic to prevent getting their throats cut when fighting hand-to-hand in defense of their ships. They are also less politely known as "jarheads," whether from the presumed hollowness of their heads or the fact that their extreme GI haircuts make their heads look like two-handled crocks. In retaliation marines have been known to refer to sailors as "swab jockeys," from a traditional nautical pursuit, swabbing—mopping—the deck. There is usually a bit of tension between sailors and marines on board ship. This is because one shipboard marine function is to provide security, and arrest any sailors they find misbehaving.

Ladies Hit the Deck.

Navy carriers frequently run out of key components that are needed in a hurry. Replenishment ships often do not carry the needed spare parts, or crucial replacement personnel. Thus, an early feature of carrier operations was the use of "carrier on-board delivery" (COD) aircraft. Female pilots occasionally fly COD missions, one of the few instances where women are allowed to operate aircraft from carriers, since COD is considered a noncombat assignment for which women are eligible.

Keeping It Quiet

Silence in a submarine is a lifesaving attribute, since the easiest way to locate a submerged submarine is by detecting the sounds it gives off. Strenuous measures are taken to keep things quiet. One of the more obvious methods is anechoical (sound-absorbing) tiles on the exterior hull. This was pioneered by Russia and Britain and is being adopted by other nations. The crew wear sneakers and are trained to do what they do quietly. The major machinery is made to an exacting standard to eliminate operating noise, and the British have pioneered floating the engines in oil to further dampen their sound. Even soft-drink vending machines were eliminated from U.S. subs because it was found that the noise of the can being delivered could be heard by sonar.

Aerial Mining

Naval-mine warfare is a highly neglected art, but relatively effective and fairly cheap. The most efficient way to deliver sea mines is by air. During the last months of World War II in the Pacific, over 20,000 mines were planted by army air-force B-29 bombers, completing the stranglehold on Japanese commerce already well begun by the navy's submarines. This was a prodigious effort, and only a small part of the over 300,000 naval mines used during World War II. But this experience was largely forgotten over the next twenty years. Then came the Vietnam War, and the mine-laying abilities of aircraft were rediscovered and used to mine the Red River and Haiphong Harbor. With that war over, the matter was again laid aside.

However, in the late eighties, there has been renewed discussion of the possibility of using the air force's large bombers as mine-layers in a conventional war, particularly given the extreme shortage of vessels suited to such work in the U.S. Navy, a result of intramural jurisdictional feuding among the navy's three principal "unions," submariners, aviators, and surface warriors. Moreover, the bombers can be operating on-station almost anywhere in the world within a day or so of orders being issued, whereas mine-laying vessels could take days or even weeks to arrive on-station, by which time the need may well have passed. Although the United States has several different types of mines, the most readily adaptable to aerial planting is the MK-36. A B-52 can carry about fifty MK-36s and eight Harpoon antiship missiles, while the faster but shorter-ranged FB-111 can carry twenty, and the B-1B a remarkable eighty-four. Though such use was probably never contemplated by the airmen and engineers who designed the B-1B, it may well be that the expensive airplane's most valuable role in a future war could be in mining hostile waters. The same benefit would be obtained with the F-117 and B-2 Stealth aircraft. Moreover, the Stealth aircraft are even less likely to be caught in the act and thus would enhance the surprise effect of mines.

Sea Duty

Personnel in Britain's Royal Navy spend about 75 percent of their time assigned to a ship. This rate is among the highest in the world, as most navies keep most of their personnel on land most of the time. Since the more time a navy spends at sea, the better it is, this makes the Royal Navy among the best in the business.

The Prime Directive

"No captain can do very wrong if he places his ship alongside that of an enemy."—Horatio Nelson, Vice Admiral of the White, victor of Trafalgar and the Nile, the greatest admiral in history, with a taste for low women

Join the Navy and See the World.

About 90 percent of enlisted personnel who become lifers in the navy will spend at least one year overseas in the course of their careers. The U.S. Navy maintains its qualitative edge by keeping its ships at sea constantly. The average U.S. sailor spends between 50–60 percent of his time at sea. About half of this sea time is overseas, often for months at a time.

End of an Era

On December 16, 1988, the destroyer USS *Edson*, launched in 1958, was officially retired, with the result that in the U.S. Navy there is no longer a single major surface combatant (defined as a warship in excess of 2,000 tons) armed exclusively with guns. All such vessels now carry a mixture of guns and missiles.

PART FOUR

High Tech

PART FOUR

High Tech

Nearly everything in the military is touched by some form of technology. But there is technology and then there is high tech (sometimes known as the "bleeding edge of technology"). Moreover, there are new technologies emerging from laboratories all the time, some of which are not usually thought of as a form of high tech. All of this new technology creates both opportunities and problems for military forces. This chapter covers some of the high points, and sometimes high comedy, of armed forces' coping with technology, as well as the potential for high tragedy.

Tough Enough

"There is no room in war for delicate machinery."—Archibald Wavell, British general, military writer, and poetaster

The Giant, Whale-Shaped Nuclear-Powered Computer

The Russian armed forces have fallen far behind in the race to enhance combat power with computers. Consider Russian progress in computerization. By 1960 Russia had only 120 minicomputers and mainframe computers, and the United States had 5,000. By 1970 the numbers were 8,000 and 40,000. By 1980 they were 25,000 and

400,000. By 1990, there will be about 125,000 in Russia and 1.4 million in the United States, plus over 24 million personal computers (PCs), many of which were more powerful than many of the Russian minicomputers and older mainframes. Russia, as is its custom, continues to use many twenty-year-old (or older) computers. Thus, the average Western computer is of more recent vintage and several times more powerful than the average Russian one. Moreover, the total computing power of all PCs in the United States exceeds the total computing power of all U.S. minis and mainframes. There are only about 300,000 PCs in Russia, most of them of Western design or manufacture. Although Russia is gearing up to produce more than 100,000 a year, it will be a long time before they get anywhere close to the U.S. numbers. The U.S. armed forces alone possess over 300,000 PCs and tens of thousands of minis and mainframes. Many of these larger computers are actually part of weapons systems, particularly in ships. In fact, the latest U.S. nuclear-attack submarines each possess more computing power than all the computers in the Russian Navy (okay, maybe it would take two or three U.S. subs, at most).

Microcomputers Go to War.

By 1988 there were over 300,000 personal computers in use throughout the U.S. armed forces, about one PC for every nine uniformed and civilian personnel. The value of these machines was over $1 billion. The number of personal computers will be doubling through the early 1990s. The army uses the machines for many of the same functions as do civilian organizations; for example: keeping track of people and equipment; scheduling events such as training and maintenance; and scientific and engineering tasks. Typical combat uses are information-gathering and analysis of possible enemy actions. Laptop personal computers are increasingly popular in the field because they are rugged enough to go anywhere the troops go. Even the space shuttle takes laptops into orbit, and aircraft and ship's crews have been taking PCs with them for years. Note that the laptops are the most powerful computers aboard the shuttle, as the other five computers use 1960s technology, kept in service "because they work."

Chip Race

Microprocessors are becoming ever more important in military equipment. More powerful "computers on a chip" are needed to handle the larger software programs that run them. For example, the software on the U.S. F-16 fighter is about 50,000 lines long. That for the next generation U.S. fighter (mid-1990s) is expected to be 5 million lines long. Currently, the U.S. military has a specially designed sixteen-bit microprocessor, the 1750A. The military has resisted moving to a more powerful thirty-two-bit chip because of the time and expense. It's estimated that it would take at least three years to get the project funded: one year to find a developer and two or even three years to actually do the work. Meanwhile, the French military has been using the U.S. civilian Motorola 68000-series sixteen- and thirty-two-bit chips used in Macintosh personal computers and scientific work stations. These chips are regularly upgraded every two or three years. The British also used commercial PCs to develop a sonar system equal in computing power to a modern U.S. system but at a fraction of the cost and weight. The U.S. military has been sneaking 68000-series chips into systems, despite the official policy of using only the 1750A. It looks like sheer need will overcome regulations and bureaucracy, and the civilian chips will eventually become the "standard."

Red-Hot Red Satellites

Radar ocean-reconnaissance satellites (RORS) are Russia's primary means of keeping tabs on the West's superior and more numerous naval forces. An RORS uses a nuclear-power supply for its radar but is still only able to cover a narrow band of ocean as it swings around the earth. Low altitude, limited nuclear fuel, and general unreliability limit the life span of the Russian RORS. Only a few have lasted more than a year. Two or three are needed in orbit at any one time to provide militarily useful information. Since the 1960s, nearly forty Russian nuclear-powered satellites have been launched. This has put nearly two tons of nuclear fuel in space. Russian radar ocean-reconnaissance satellites require a lot of electrical power, and they get up to ten kilowatts from a nuclear reactor. Satellites using batteries and/or solar panels rarely obtain more than a few hundred watts. The nuclear fuel used is 90 percent pure enriched uranium, sixty to seventy pounds of it.

One Russian nuclear satellite came down over northern Canada in 1978. Fortunately, the radioactive material was spread over a largely unpopulated area. Subsequent Russian nuclear birds had a special feature that launched the nuclear-fuel capsule into a higher orbit in case the satellite began to head earthward. In 1988 this device was put to the test and worked as planned. There is still, however, a high risk of collision between the dozens of spent nuclear birds and the thousands of pieces of debris in orbit. Such a collision could send more radioactive material raining down on earth. Attempts by the United States to use nuclear power in space have been blocked by public opinion. However, for SDI (aka "Star Wars") to work, dozens of nuclear-powered satellites would have to be launched. This would put several more tons of radioactive material in orbit. Note that these nuclear-powered satellites use the nuclear material as a heat source for a battery, not to drive a dynamo as in ground-based nuclear-power plants. In this way, the orbital nuclear material requires no attention from power-plant operators and is relatively safe from accidents, other than falling to earth.

Stealthy Ships

Submarines were the first Stealth ships. Submerging made them invisible. Lately they are made more quiet so that they cannot be detected by underwater-listening devices. Now, Stealth techniques are being applied to surface ships. This makes these ships harder to detect, particularly by attacking missiles, but also radar, sonar, and passive sensors. The new Russian *Kirov* missile cruisers, for example, have a rounded superstructure, which gives them the same radar signature as more conventionally designed ships one-third their size. A 7-degree slope on walls will also confuse most radars. Sonar is defeated by insulating all noisy machinery from the hull and ejecting air bubbles to muffle the sound of the propellers. Magnetic detection is defeated by regularly degaussing the hull. Infrared detection is made more difficult by rearranging the ducts inside the ship to spread heat from the engine, and other sources, more evenly. Ships train to operate without their active sensors, using passive sensors instead.

Soldiers, Sailors, Marines, Airmen, Butchers, Bakers, Candlestick . . .

The approximately 1.85 million enlisted women and men in the U.S. armed forces held the following jobs at the end of 1988:

Combat Specialists	282,822 (15.3%)
Electrical and Mechanical Repair Technicians	380,000 (20.6%)
Administrative and Clerical Personnel	288,400 (15.6%)
Communications and Intelligence Workers	173,700 (9.4%)
Electronic Equipment Repair Technicians	168,300 (9.1%)
Supply and Service Personnel	166,200 (9.0%)
Health-care Specialists	100,950 (5.5%)
"Craftsmen"	74,800 (4.1%)
"Other Technical Personnel"	42,500 (2.3%)
Other "Other Personnel"	170,900 (9.2%)

The combat specialists were outnumbered 6.5 to one by the clerks and electricians and plumbers and photographers. However, slicing the figures another way, about 1,060,000 of the enlisted personnel (57.3 percent) are in tactical and mobility forces, and in time of war would either be directly involved in inflicting harm upon an enemy or in enabling the other troops to do so. And in the event of mobilization, the number of "combat specialists" would grow rather more rapidly than that of some of the other categories.

The Forest or the Trees?

"The combination of professionalism and technology may also result in narrow-minded specialization more suited to a debating society than to an organization whose task it is to cope with, and indeed live in, the dangerous and uncertain environment of war."—Martin van Creveld, military historian

Off-the-Shelf Electronic Warfare

Armed forces have a long history of adapting civilian equipment for military purposes. In World War I, civilian shotguns were popular in the trenches, and were again in great demand fifty years later in Vietnam. When the U.S. Navy was deployed to confront Iran in the Persian Gulf in the mid-1980s, it was decided not to send the latest version of its EA-6 series electronic-warfare aircraft. The reasoning was that, since the Iranians did not have advanced electronic equipment, why chance losing one of the U.S. EW aircraft and take the risk that the Russians might get their hands on it? So older EA-6s were sent. However, the older version no longer had an adequate jammer, as the old jammer was no longer available and the new one was a little too new to be reliable. Then an enterprising officer discovered that one of the electronics manufacturers had developed a cheap and simple jammer for use in testing its own EW equipment. A number of these "test" jammers were acquired, and the fleet went off to the Persian Gulf fully prepared.

Spooks in the Land of the Nerds and Buffs

We usually think of the CIA as a bunch of secret agents and globe-trotting adventurers. In fact, some 95 percent of the CIA staff are technicians and academics. Or, as less charitable observers put it, "nerds and buffs." Less than 5 percent of CIA staff are involved with what is traditionally seen as spying and "covert operations." Most of the intelligence information is obtained from satellite photography and imaging plus many forms of electronic data-gathering. About half the CIA staff tends to all these sensors and computers. These are the nerds. Most of the rest are experts in various kinds of arcane information. For example, if you were an expert on Siberian geography, Indonesian politics, undersea topography, microwave propagation, and so on, the CIA would be interested in recruiting you. These are the buffs. The CIA's biggest customer is Congress, which received some 5,000 reports and hundreds of briefings each year during the late 1980s. Most of this data comes from the nerds and buffs. The spooks get more attention because few authors write exciting novels about the escapades of nerds and buffs.

Kentucky Windage

It is estimated that between 1988 and 1992 the U.S. armed forces will spend more than $19 billion in procuring new fire-control systems to enhance their ability to hit something.

Getting from Here to There Electronically

At a cost of $9 billion, the United States is completing a satellite-navigation system for ground troops and other personnel. When finished in 1991–92, this system will enable infantrymen equipped with special handheld receivers to read their location to within 100 feet. Similar devices can be fitted to ships, aircraft, missiles, and vehicles of all types. The system has been delayed by technical problems and space-shuttle unavailability. This has created a curious situation with the various receivers. The design of these items was frozen in the early 1980s. Since then, nondefense manufacturers have developed more compact and cheaper receivers for the civilian market. As of 1989, the military appears to be stuck with the larger, more expensive, less capable, and less reliable receivers they originally contracted for in the early 1980s. The Russians are building a similar system of satellites and have proposed to make receivers capable of receiving signals from either system. In wartime, the navigation satellites may be the first casualties. But maybe not, as these high-orbit satellites are not easy to destroy, and all participants may find it in their interest to keep the birds flying. If a major war goes nuclear, these satellites may be one of the few survivors of our civilization. Let later alien visitors try to figure that one out.

Nasty Surprises

New weapons, organizations, and tactics can often provide nasty surprises the first time they are tried in combat. World War II was full of such embarrassments. The Vietnam War, a large-scale conflict fought twenty years after World War II, contained a number of surprises. In the air, it was found that the new weapons (missiles) for the new high-performance jet fighters were not an improvement on older tactics but actually a hindrance. Corrections were quickly made. When antitank missiles were first used on a large scale in the 1973 Arab-Israeli war they were quite lethal. But in a matter of days, tank crews came up with simple countermeasures that severely limited the missiles' effectiveness. Not so fortunate were Israeli pilots who were told that the air force could not afford the expensive U.S. ECM (electronic countermeasures) for use against the new Russian radar-controlled guns and missiles their opponents now had. Many Israeli aircraft were shot down before the ECM devices could be hastily flown in from the United States. In the Falklands (1982) and the Persian Gulf (1988), sailors had to learn the hard way better techniques for dealing with the antiship missiles that had been around for over twenty years. Although the Israelis lost a destroyer to an antiship missile in 1967, and developed successful techniques to stop all the missiles fired at them in 1973, the 1980s missiles had got better more quickly than techniques to deal with them. You can't stand still in this business, even if you're not sure where you're going.

Electronic Guidance

The U.S. Air Force pays $102,000 each for inertial guidance systems that enable aircraft to know their location at all times without using a map or taking a "reading" from the sun or the stars.

Increasing the Tempo

"The accelerating pace of technical advance resulting from massive and systematic research and development programs is illustrated by the fact that it took forty years for self-propelled torpedoes to increase their range from 220 yards when first invented in 1866 to 2,190 yards in 1905, but only six to rise to 18,509 in 1913, whereas the range of the Polaris missiles, installed in U.S. submarines for the first time in 1959, increased from 1,200 to 2,500 miles in a mere five years."—William H. McNeil, American military historian

Blinded by the Light

The world's major armed forces currently possess hundreds of thousands of laser devices. Most are used for range finding, target designation, and fire control. Humans can be temporarily or permanently blinded by most lasers, and battlefield accidents are expected. They have already occurred in peacetime. The Russians are suspected of staging such accidents to test the possibility of using lasers in wartime to blind enemy pilots. They have already temporarily blinded several American pilots with their high-powered shipboard lasers. Iraq is believed to have tested such a device in combat against Iran, leaving thousands with severe eye injuries. Other nations are building weapons that will blind enemy troops and/or instruments with lasers. The next war may be quite a light show, though few who see it may be able to do so more than once.

Combat Microcomputers

The following item will only make sense to a bytehead. Ever since microcomputers became widely available in the late 1970s, troops have got their hands on them and taken them into the field. Microcomputers were made to be rugged, but bouncing around in a truck or armored vehicle made the micros unreliable unless treated with some care. Powerful laptop micros came into general use in the mideighties. These were a bit more rugged, but still vulnerable to the exceptional dirt and violence of the combat zone. Several modifications were made to off-the-shelf designs to maximize ruggedness and security. Hard and floppy disks are not used, but massive amounts of RAM; up to sixteen megabytes. One to three megabyte RAM cards can be inserted to change programs or add storage. The serial port is used to transfer data to and from conventional PCs. The unit is sealed, with heat dissipated by a heat ladder. Sealing protects against jamming, while emissions are damped with filter connectors. An industry standard 80386 thirty-two-bit processor is used. Power comes from an on-board battery or a variety of common battlefield power sources. The power and capacity of such a machine allows a wide variety of functions to be covered, from command and control to equipment maintenance and administration.

Is That Tough Enough for Ya?

The 1988 INF treaty stipulated that missile structures were to be crushed beyond use. The Russians interpret this to mean crushed flat. But the U.S. Pershing missile structure is made with Kevlar, a material noted for its durability. The crushed Kevlar structures sprang back to their original form. The Russians protested. Finally, a heavy-duty automobile crusher was brought in and the Pershings were finally put down, flat. Among other things, Kevlar is used to make the army's new "fritz" (because it looks like the German World War II helmet) headgear, a comforting thought.

Obtaining American Technology on the Cheap

One of the best ways to secure American military technology is to steal it. There is a proven technique for this. First, you monitor all U.S. military and scientific publications. All but a few top-secret U.S. military R&D projects are discussed in some detail in the open press. From this you will get a good idea of what's coming and when. At this point, you also alert your spies to look for American R&D people who can be bribed, blackmailed, or otherwise persuaded to deliver secret documents and components to your scientists. In many cases, you will string these people along until the project is near completion. Then you can get perfected components or plans rather than the more buggy versions available during development. Since U.S. military R&D projects take about fifteen years to complete, you can afford to watch and wait. Besides, developing illegal contacts within these projects takes time. A year or two after the American system is put into service, you begin development of your own version. Because of all the information you have gathered, plus observation of live examples in the field, it will only take two or three years to build your prototype. It will take only five or so years until you send your own version to the troops. Your version will not be as sophisticated, but it will be simpler and cheaper. You save 10 to 50 percent of your development costs because of your espionage efforts. Russia has been using this approach successfully for over fifty years. Dramatic examples are their obtaining technical documents for the KH-11 spy satellite and F-18 fighter. From Japan's Toshiba Corporation, they purchased machinery needed to make their submarines quieter. Their new systems take less than ten years to field as a result.

Anatomy of a Satellite-Launch Vehicle

The Titan 34D-7 is based on the old Titan liquid-fuel ICBM. They cost about $178 million each and can place 4.5 tons into GTO (geosynchronous, or geostationary—which means the same thing—transit orbit, a high stationary orbit for communications, etc.), or 14.5–17.6 tons into LEO (low earth orbit for spy satellites). The first stage is eighty-seven feet long and ten feet in diameter. Its two engines generate 248 tons of thrust using hydrazine and nitrogen tetroxide fuel as they burn for 200 seconds. The second stage, with the same diameter but only thirty-three feet long and with one engine, burns for 245 seconds with forty-seven tons of thrust. Two solid-fuel booster rockets (each 113 feet long and 10 feet in diameter) are attached to the first stage. Each of these weighs 269 tons, and produces a thrust of 627 tons for 120 seconds. Total first-stage thrust, with two liquid-fuel and two solid-fuel engines burning, is 1,502 tons. The final stage is up to 132 feet long (depending on the size of the satellite) and up to 16 feet in diameter. The final-stage engine generates 15 tons of thrust. A final maneuvering engine for the payload can generate 3.9 tons of thrust. The first two stages are fairly standard. The third stage and payload stage vary quite a lot depending on the payload and how high the bird has to go and what shape orbit it must achieve.

Thirty Years of Delta

The longest-running satellite-launcher development project is the U.S. Delta rocket. First launched in 1960, it has been continually developed and enhanced through fourteen distinct generations of systems. The Delta is the principal rocket used to blast U.S. satellites into high (GTO) orbit. It has been used nearly 200 times, and over the last ten years the success rate has been 98 percent. (Russian boosters, in comparison, have had over twice that failure rate.) The original Delta could only place about 100 pounds into orbit. The current Delta II can put over two tons into GTO orbit. Weightlifting capability grew regularly, reaching 400 pounds in 1965, 800 pounds in 1969, 1,600 pounds in 1973, and 2,400 pounds in 1980. The current Delta II was developed largely in response to the troubles with the space shuttle. The United States plans to launch as many as twelve Deltas a year in the early 1990s.

Star Wars Versus the Killer Bees

A minuscule solar-powered transmitter developed as a by-product of research on SDI (Star Wars) has been pressed into service in the battle against the so-called "killer bees" that are expected to invade the southern part of the United States in the next few years. The transmitters are so small that they can be strapped on the backs of bees without interfering in their normal activities, thus permitting entomologists to study migration routes, foraging areas, and nesting patterns in an effort to better understand the dangerous apians. This is an example of unexpected technological "spin-off" of high-tech defense and space projects. Such "spin-off" can often lead to the development of whole new industries, such as personal computers, "freezer-to-oven" dishware, and microwave ovens.

Ah, We Have Third-Stage Separation at T+1576. . . .

The most complex bit of satellite-launching is placing a bird in geostationary transit orbit (GTO). The process takes about half an hour. A typical launch would use a three-stage Delta vehicle. The first stage is a liquid-fuel rocket motor with nine solid-fuel booster rockets strapped on. Launch begins when the liquid-fuel motor and six of the boosters ignite. The boosters burn for 56 seconds and are then jettisoned in groups of three at one-second intervals. At T+59 (fifty-nine seconds after launch) the remaining three boosters ignite and burn for fifty-nine seconds and are jettisoned. The liquid-fuel motor burns for four minutes, twenty-five seconds. At T+265 the first stage is jettisoned, and thirteen seconds later the second-stage liquid-fuel motor ignites.

At eleven minutes, twenty-seven seconds into the flight, at an altitude of 298 kilometers, the second-stage motor turns off. At this point, the ground controllers can intervene if need be to change the flight profile. The vehicle is now largely free of the earth's gravity and the two remaining stages coast for nine minutes, thirty-six seconds, until they are astride the equator. Then the second-stage engines come on again for twenty-three seconds. The two stages now coast for another minute and a half, during which the second stage is jettisoned and the third-stage motor ignites. From about twenty-three minutes into the flight, the third-stage solid-fuel motor burns for three minutes, twenty seconds. Nearly half an hour has elapsed since the rocket lifted off. The capsule carrying the satellite is now separated from the third stage, and the satellite assumes its stationary orbit above the equator, assuming the on-board computer and navigation system did their job properly.

The Old Ways Still Work.

The Swiss Army maintains a reserve of some 20,000 carrier pigeons just in case radio, telephone, and telegraph communications systems become inoperable in a war. As one Swiss officer remarked, "They're cheap." Modern military radios cost from a few thousand dollars to over $20,000 apiece.

Our Shuttle Versus Theirs

In 1989, Russia conducted manned tests of its version of the U.S. space shuttle, named *Buron* ("Snowstorm"). Photos suggest that both shuttles are similar. They are, but only superficially so. The biggest difference is that the Russian shuttle does not have any engines and is little more than a reusable payload container. This has several advantages. For one thing, the Russian shuttle is launched on a more powerful rocket and has a greater payload, about 100 tons, than the U.S. shuttle's 30 tons. This is due to the absence of an engine on the Russian shuttle and the greater power of their current launcher rocket. The Russian shuttle could carry up to twenty people to the Russians' space stations, or carry heavier loads to build and maintain their space stations.

Russian Satellite Surge Capability

Long known for their crude but copious satellites, Russia has developed the ability to launch a large number of satellites when the situation demands it. Normally, they launch about two a week. But during the Falklands War in 1982, they increased the launch rate by 30 percent over an eleven-week period. Since then, they have increased their launch capability by another 20–30 percent. This has a modest bit of usefulness and a lot of disadvantages for the West. Any sudden increase in Russian satellite launchings would certainly indicate that the Russians were up to something. On the other hand, in wartime it won't be enough to shoot down Russian satellites. NATO will also have to go after the numerous replacements, or, given recent developments in conventional warheads for cruise missiles, they could attack the three Russian launch complexes.

A Jump Too Far

The latest thing in tactical radios are "frequency hoppers" that evade jamming and are more secure from overhearing. They do this by switching frequenices so quickly that no jamming equipment can keep up with it. Enemy monitors cannot follow conversations because they cannot switch frequencies quickly either. The two frequency-hopping radios synchronize their hopping so they can understand each other. As these radios came into use, an unpleasant side effect was discovered: The radios sometimes touch upon a frequency combination that jams other friendly radios. A solution to this is promised forthwith.

Universal Gadget Lust

"Western analysts seem consistently to underestimate the ability of Third World states to handle advanced technology."—Elliot A. Cohen, military analyst. But then, for every Chadian or Afghan who proves adept at handling modern missiles, there is a Third World tank gunner who never quite figures out how to use the fire-control system properly.

Software Support

The U.S. armed forces pays between $45 and $50 an hour for programmers to patch up and upgrade their computer software. For example, the U.S. Air Force annually devotes nearly 200,000 hours of programmer time to maintain the software at its North American Air Defense Command headquarters at Cheyenne Mountain.

The Military Consequences of the *Challenger* Disaster

When the space shuttle *Challenger* failed in early 1986, the U.S. military satellite program entered a period of crisis. By 1985 the Defense Department had committed itself to launching all of its major communications, navigation, and recon satellites via the shuttle. The manufacture of large rockets for satellite launching was stopped. *Challenger*'s failure halted the shuttle program for thirty-two months. Only four small military satellites were launched in 1986. In 1987 there were six launchings, and in 1988 there were seven. Over twenty satellites waited on the ground for larger rockets to be built or for the shuttle to return to action. With the shuttle back in full use in 1989, and large rockets available again, the United States planned seventeen military satellite launches in 1989 and nearly as many in 1990. Between 1986 and 1990, the United States had only one of the normally two KH-11 recon satellites available. And this single KH-11 was short on fuel and thus unable to move around a lot to observe what needed watching most. If a major war had broken out during this period, the United States would have been at a significant disadvantage because of its reduced satellite-recon capabilities.

Let the Chips Fall Where They May.

Millions of the computer chips that the United States uses in its defense equipment are manufactured abroad. In addition, many circuits made of domestically produced chips are actually assembled abroad, particularly on the rim of Asia, in countries such as Singapore, Thailand, Taiwan, and South Korea. A major internal upheaval in any of those countries could have serious effects on U.S. defense electronics.

Hiding in the Rain

In temperate and tropical climates, fog, mist, and rain are quite common. These conditions degrade many widely used sensors, notably heat, laser, and light. Normal radar does not really replace these sensors, particularly for slow-moving ground vehicles and helicopters. The only solution in the offing is millimeter-wave radar, which has short range and high detail. This technology depends on high-tech electronic components to work. And like all radars, it can be detected. In the West, millimeter-wave radars are being introduced for missile-guidance systems and helicopter sensors.

Which Way Do the Missiles Go?

Military satellites are usually launched in secrecy. However, some information can be obtained simply by watching the bird go up. If the missile goes off toward the east, it is probably an electronic eavesdropping satellite. If it goes east then veers to the northeast, it is going for a polar orbit favored by photo-recon birds.

"There's a Bug in Line 57,345,267, I Think."

It is estimated that the SDI—Star Wars—battle-management system may run to 100 million or more lines of computer code, making it the hands-down most complex program ever devised, requiring the efforts of thousands of programmers to develop, yet one that could never be fully tested. SDI advocates point to the millions of lines of computer code that successfully guide the national telephone system. The telephone-system software was built up over decades and put into service in stages after considerable testing. Although less than one percent of each day's calls are lost, a similar proportion of attacking missiles getting through would result in devastating losses.

The Price of Information

Secret U.S. expenditures for spy satellites and similar technologies designed to provide diplomatic and military intelligence are believed to run about $20 billion a year, or nearly $71.50 for every man, woman, and child in Russia. Of course, not all of this reconnaissance is just for Russia. Depending on the world situation, up to half of the recon effort may focus on other nations.

The Peaceful Side of Star Wars

The SDI (Strategic Defense Initiative), or Star Wars program, has generated a lot of controversy on a number of fronts. The idea was to use a system of sensor and weapons satellites to detect and destroy any attempt to attack the United States with nuclear missiles, which many scientists thought was technically impossible, or at least improbable. Many taxpayers cringed at the thought of trying to pay for it. Some diplomats wondered if the installation of such a system might trigger a nuclear exchange as a desperate Russia realized that it had to "use it or lose it."

While the budgetary and technical problems will probably prevent SDI from ever getting close to implementation, there will be some interesting spinoffs. For one thing, the SDI concept was created partially because the United States has had such great success in launching very capable recon satellites. By 1989, for example, the Lacrosse and KH-12 birds were in orbit, providing the ability to count the rivets on equipment coming out of Russian factories as well as seeing through darkness and clouds. Much of the SDI development work done to date has been in the area of sensors. If SDI falls by the wayside, its contribution to sensor development will make verification of a strategic-weapons-reduction treaty much easier to accomplish. This verification is crucial, as Russia has a large organization assigned to the task of "strategic deception." This bureaucracy exists solely to devise and implement new ways to deceive U.S. satellite reconnaissance. The Lacrosse birds can see through much of this, especially once several of them are up, and all parts of Russia can be observed at once. The complete Lacrosse system will cost over

$10 billion, including space-shuttle missions to supply and repair each of these eighteen-ton satellites. The contraction of defense budgets in the 1990s may prevent the entire Lacrosse network from being launched. The biggest argument in favor of Lacrosse under those circumstances is that with Lacrosse, a nuclear-weapons-reduction treaty can be more effectively monitored. In other words, the money saved from not building strategic weapons would go for building more Lacrosse systems.

The Dark Side of Black Boxes

The numerous electronic components (commonly packed in black boxes) filling modern aircraft usually have to do with electronic warfare. These devices either detect enemy radar and transmissions, or jam and deceive them. The weak link in these complex devices is the difficulty in testing them properly. The problem usually begins with the development of these systems: If all the necessary test equipment is included in the project, the higher cost could well result in project cancellation. Testing is complicated by the presence of a dozen or more sensors in the aircraft that are capable of dealing with thousands of different frequencies and many more combinations. All these sensors are tied together on the aircraft by complex systems of wires. In addition to possible electronic failures, any defects in the wiring can have catastrophic effects on system performance. Ultimately, any failures in the electronic-warfare systems would only be known when enemy systems were encountered under actual combat conditions.

Keeping Civilians at Bay

Many of the most effective military equipment items are also useful for civilian uses. Indeed, the military will often adopt civilian equipment instead of building special military versions because the civilian gear is more inexpensive and/or effective. Examples are motor vehicles, personal computers, and even some weapons, like shotguns and the first M-16 rifle.

But the military will try to keep civilians from reversing the process and using military equipment, or even restrict the use of civilian equipment after discovering it has a military application. For example, business needs a way to encrypt electronic information, such as banking transactions. When a standard encryption system (DES) was developed in the 1970s, the U.S. government promptly declared DES sensitive technology and liable to export controls. Until recently it was illegal to carry a disk with one of the many commercially available DES encryption programs out of the country without an export license.

Another example is satellite photos. Ever since the 1970s, the United States has sold low-resolution LANDSAT satellite photos. In the 1980s, France began selling higher-resolution SPOT satellite photos. The French photos are at a resolution that the United States considers militarily useful. Russia disagreed, and soon began selling high-resolution photos also. Undeterred, the U.S. military also proposes to exercise its right to lower the resolution of its satellite-based Global Positioning System (GPS), which is used by military and civilian ships and aircraft to more accurately determine their position. The system is capable of 30-meter accuracy, but the United States proposes to shift to 100-meter accuracy for civilian receivers in time of military emergency. The primary purpose of this is to deny Russian users of civilian receivers from taking advantage of the better accuracy for military purposes.

"We're Sorry, Phone Service Is Cancelled in the Event of a Nuclear Holocaust."

In the early 1980s, the United States decided that it was time to prepare for operations *after* a nuclear exchange. One of the more critical items was communications, especially communications that could survive the EMP (electromagnetic pulse) released by nuclear explosions. EMP ruins most communications signals and fries the electronics in unprepared electronics equipment. One pressing need was for communications immediately after an enemy surprise-nuclear attack, to tell U.S. troops to fire back. Part of the solution was a new series of communications satellites. The MILSTAR (MILitary Strategic, Tactical, And Relay) satellites would be able to send narrow signals to receiving stations.

As current owners of satellite receiving dishes know, existing satellites broadcast a very wide signal that can be picked up in an area hundreds of kilometers wide. The narrow MILSTAR beam could cut through the EMP interference and is more resistant to interception and jamming. It uses frequency hopping and encryption and could send voice, data, and fax. Special receiving stations were designed for army, navy, and air-force vehicles. The army receiver uses a sixty-six inch dish and takes about thirty minutes to set up. The air-force receiver is designed for large command aircraft and uses a thirty-six inch dish. The navy has two receivers, one for surface ships that uses a seventy-two-inch dish and one for submarine periscope masts with a four-inch dish.

The MILSTAR birds were to have gone up in the late eighties, but were delayed by space-shuttle problems (the *Challenger* mishap). The system will probably be in place by the early nineties. While MILSTAR may never be used to keep the lines open during a nuclear exchange, it will provide more reliable and secure military communication for nonnuclear operations. On a more familiar note, the U.S. government also has several billion dollars of new-design banknotes stored in an underground vault on the outskirts of Washington, D.C. In the event of a nuclear war, these new notes would replace the old ones to assist in economic reconstruction.

Alphabet City

NBC, nuclear-biological-chemical warfare, archaically ABC, for "atomic biological chemical", is sometimes called CBR ("chemical biological radiological").

Keeping the Nukes Fresh

You can't just manufacture a nuclear weapon, stick it on a missile or in an aircraft bomb bay, and forget about it. These things require maintenance. Nuclear weapons are complex mechanisms that contain conventional explosives (which degrade and become unstable over the years) and nuclear material (which degrades much less slowly). One item of nuclear material that does lose 5–6 percent of its strength each year is Tritium, which is used to boost the power of the other nuclear material. Then, too, a lot of electronic gear is included in nuclear weapons to insure that the complex detonation process works correctly, otherwise there is a conventional explosion that sends a lot of unexploded radioactive material into the atmosphere. The electronics must be tested regularly to insure that they still function correctly. The electronics run on batteries, which must be periodically replaced. Owning a nuclear weapon is like owning and operating an automobile, except that you only use the nuke once, if at all. Thousands of obsolete nuclear weapons are disassembled and rebuilt or discarded each year.

Nuclear Arsenals

Estimates for the number of nuclear weapons in the world usually revolve around the number 55,000. However, since about 30,000 of these are supposed to belong to the United States and a further 25,000 to Russia, what's left over for the rest of the world? Since by most estimates the "minor" nuclear powers have about 3 percent of the total nuclear weapons available, and since Britain has some 525 nuclear weapons, France about 475, and China as many as 400, plus perhaps 100 Israeli ones, to which may be added about 20 for South Africa and a few for India, we can put nonsuperpower nukes at around 1,500. Assuming this figure is 3 percent of the world total, then that total must be around 50,000 nuclear weapons, roughly 10 percent less than the generally accepted 55,000, which would leave the United States with only about 27,000 nukes and Russia with only about 22,500. To be sure, some estimates put nonsuperpower nukes at about 2,000, but if this is 3 percent of the world total it would mean that there are over 65,000 nuclear weapons, a figure that has never been suggested. Not that it matters much, since even the modest numbers held by Britain, France, or China would, if used, probably suffice to set the survivors back by a century or two.

Eggs and Baskets

The United States has about 12,600 nuclear weapons targeted on Russia by strategic delivery systems. Of these, about 4,700 (37.3 percent) are carried on approximately 400 strategic bombers, many of which are equipped with cruise missiles. Another 2,300 (18.2 percent) are carried on 1,000 ICBMs, which are housed in increasingly vulnerable silos. The thirty-six ballistic-missile-carrying submarines account for a further 5,600 (44.4 percent) warheads. In addition, there are perhaps 3,400 smaller nuclear weapons that could be delivered to targets in Russia by tactical aircraft launched from bases in Europe and the Far East or from aircraft carriers. There are thus a total of about 16,000 American nuclear warheads potentially deliverable on Russia, roughly one for every 540 square miles or 18,000 people. In contrast, Russia has about 10,000 nuclear weapons targeted on the United States by strategic delivery systems. About 600 (6.0 percent) of these are carried on approximately 160 strategic bombers, some of which are equipped with cruise missiles. Another 6,400 nuclear warheads (64.0 percent) are carried on 1,389 ICBMs. Russia's 62 strategic submarines, some of which carry cruise missiles rather than ballistic missiles, account for about 3,000 (30 percent) more warheads. An additional 500 (5 percent) or so nuclear weapons might be delivered to the United States by various tactical aircraft, assuming one-way missions. Thus, Russia could shower the United States with about 10,500 nuclear weapons, roughly one for every 344 square miles or 23,400 people.

So You've Been Gassed.

It only gets worse. To be treated, you have to be handled by other troops. These medical personnel have to be careful not to pick up the same nasty stuff that got you. Mustard and nerve agents can coat clothing as well as flesh and can be easily picked up by someone else. Doctors and nurses won't be so hasty in manhandling chemical-warfare casualties. Various techniques and special equipment have been produced or, more frequently, planned, to handle these tricky situations. Worst of all, there is no way to realistically train for these conditions. There you have one more reason for not wanting to get involved in chemical warfare.

It's the Thought That Counts.

"Taking an 'objective' point of view, it is not clear why the use of high explosive for tearing men apart should be regarded as more humane than burning or asphyxiating them to death."—Martin van Creveld, military historian and analyst

Ah, That's Much Better.

Nerve gas is a deadly weapon, often incapacitating or killing its victims within seconds. To date, the most effective antidote was Atropine. This was distributed to the troops in the form of an easy-to-use syringe. Within seconds of being hit by nerve gas, the troops had to plunge the syringe into a large muscle, usually in the leg. Unfortunately, there are many different flavors of nerve gas, and Atropine is not equally successful with all of them. Moreover, soldiers can become quite sick if they administer Atropine when they are not actually hit by nerve gas. To overcome these problems, the Atropine formulation is constantly being changed. One of the more successful has added Valium (a common tranquilizer) to the syringe. You may not feel better, but it will calm you down.

A Question of Intent

Several nations are engaged in research into biological warfare. This may, however, not be as sinister as it sounds, at least insofar as the major powers go. In the developed world, there appears to be a recognition that offensive use of biological weapons may actually be highly counterproductive: The germs are unlikely to be able to distinguish friend from foe, and in any case someone finding himself under serious biological attack is likely to retaliate with nuclear weapons. So the principal reason for biological-warfare research is defensive, to develop specifics against possible biological weapons. Moreover, this may actually be only a secondary consideration. The primary purpose of biological-warfare research may be to insure that one's army will be capable of operating in environments in which certain natural diseases are endemic. Biological-warfare research furthers preventive medicine, and most specifically in diseases that are not likely to attract the attention of institutional or commercial medical researchers, those plaguing the Third World.

American biological-warfare specialists have recently conducted experiments in China—which accused the United States of engaging in biological warfare during the Korean War—and Argentina. The Chinese experiments are intended to develop a cure for hemorrhagic fever, a viral infection that is endemic in Korea and China to the extent of about 100,000 cases a year. The Argentine study is intended to determine the value of a recently developed vaccine for two local variants of the same disease. Other recent experiments have focused on Lassa fever, dengue fever, anthrax, Q-fever, and other diseases common in various parts of the Third World.

However, questions about the validity of biological-warfare research are legitimate. In 1979 an accident at a Russian biological-warfare research facility at Sverdlovsk—or poor sanitation in the local meat-processing industry (take your pick)—resulted in an anthrax epidemic that caused about a thousand deaths, while there have apparently been "near-miss" accidents at the principal U.S. biological-warfare research facility at Fort Detrick, Maryland. And while 111 nations, including both the United States and Russia, have signed the "Bacteriological and Toxin Warfare Convention" of 1972, which bans the development, production, and stockpiling of biological weapons, though not research and development into defensive measures against them, not all of the signatories can be considered reliable.

U.S. officials suggest that at least eight other nations in addition to the superpowers are believed to be engaged in biological-warfare research, though declining to identify them. Two powers that are generally considered to be included in this number are Iraq, which used poison gas against Iran and may already have "field tested" typhoid fever against Kurdish rebels, and Libya, which has also not demonstrated a significant commitment to international order.

The Psychology of Biological Warfare

Biological warfare, deliberately causing disease within enemy populations or armed forces, is an ancient practice that has largely disappeared in this century. The primary reason for the decline of biological warfare is that it has become too easy to start and too difficult to stop. Germs and viruses are not as disciplined as soldiers and will attack any vulnerable victim they can reach. Aircraft and missiles make delivery easy to begin and difficult to stop. Unlike a nuclear attack, you can't be certain of destroying all of your opponents. Some will remain to retaliate, perhaps with nuclear weapons. Terrorists are reluctant to use biological weapons because the target nations may well become so enraged that they will retaliate by obliterating the known terrorist bases, including the large number of nearby civilians. Chemical weapons are far less likely to spread and harm friendly personnel. Biological weapons, including such deadly diseases as anthrax, bubonic plague, dengue fever, and several less lethal afflictions, are not likely to see use. But you never know. . . .

Who Guards the Guards?

A common problem since the introduction of precision electronic components into weapons systems is effective calibration. Periodically, the sensitive weapons components must be hooked up to even more sensitive devices that insure that all components of the weapon operate in unison. Under field conditions, particularly in the army, the calibration equipment takes as much of a beating as the equipment it calibrates. This results in the calibration equipment getting out of calibration and passing its error on to the weapons it supports. In theory, most calibration equipment can calibrate itself. But this depends on the diligence of the troops tending it, which is often lacking, so that weapons get out of order without anyone's knowing it until it's too late.

Déjà Vu All Over Again

In this era of high-tech weapons systems that are "over budget and behind schedule," it is worth recalling that the famed M-1 Garand semiautomatic rifle, which was introduced into the American arsenal early in World War II and continues to soldier on in some armies, required seventeen years to develop. Or that the "locomotive" torpedo, developed in the 1860s and first fired in anger in 1877, did not score a hit in combat until 1893. The Patriot surface-to-air missile system, whose development began in the early 1960s, was not deployed until twenty years later, and has yet to hit anything under combat conditions.

Weak Link in ECM

ECM (electronic countermeasures) are a key element in all forms of warfare. Success in ECM allows one to remain unseen, or to reveal enemy units who believe themselves to be undetected. The techniques involve complex electronic gear and, more important, computer software that runs the equipment. Also crucial are the actual capabilities of the ECM gear. Naturally, this stuff only works well if you keep the details secret from potential opponents. This is quite difficult. Special low-flying "ferret" satellites constantly pick up ECM gear as it is tested or used. Spies or traitors who obtain technical specifications of ECM gear are more dangerous. While the Russians may not have "ferrets" as effective as the Western models, they do have cash and access to greedy officials in the West with access to ECM secrets. In 1988 a Belgian Air Force colonel working in that nation's F-16 fighter program sold ECM details to the Russians. Fortunately, the CIA discovered the colonel meeting a Russian agent in Austria and passed the information back to Belgium. The colonel was caught, but many ECM secrets were still compromised. To maintain ECM effectiveness, millions had to be spent to change the software.

Time and Motion

Time and speed are weapons, as well as a defense against enemy weapons. For centuries, camouflage and deception were used to enhance the speed with which combat troops could use their weapons. Guerrillas are a classic example of this technique. Against larger and more powerful regular forces, guerrillas depend on remaining unobserved until they have the best opportunity to use their weapons and then make an escape. Combat aircraft similarly attempt to spot their opponents first, get off a shot, and then go to full speed to escape retribution from a possibly superior opponent. Electronic sensors and ECM (electronic countermeasures) have added new opportunities, and complexities, to this ancient game.

Active sensors like radar and sonar used against technologically advanced opponents are falling out of favor because these sensor signals can be detected long before they give the user any useful information. How long did it take leaden-footed drivers to respond to ambushes by police radar speed detectors? Sensors that look for heat (infrared) and listen for sound (acoustic and seismic) are becoming more popular. Their range is shorter, but if you are lying in wait for an opponent, the warning received is sufficient to allow you to fire the first shot. Similarly, these passive sensors can also give you a few seconds' warning that you are being approached by a missile or enemy vehicle. You can then use countermeasures or take (high-speed) evasive action. The opening battles in a future war will be full of uncertainty and surprises as the numerous untried sensors and countermeasures get put to the test for the first time under combat conditions. This situation is nothing new, but it is always nerve-racking for the participants.

The Art of ECM

Electronic warfare and its principal component, electronic counter-measures are, in practice, as much art as science. Jamming, or sending out a similar signal to deceive an enemy transmitter, also reduces your ability to monitor that transmitter. More advanced systems can switch between jamming and listening fast enough to allow both nearly simultaneously. But generally the attackers attempt to discover what transmitters they are likely to encounter and what frequencies will be used. Of course, the defender is aware of the situation and can usually switch frequencies on his radars and jammers. So it becomes a high-speed cat-and-mouse game as the defender attempts to maintain an unjammed radar signal long enough to get one of his missiles on to defending aircraft.

Off-the-Shelf High Tech

Those who insist that the export of seemingly innocuous consumer electronics to Russia would serve no military purpose should consider China's new tank-crew training simulator. It uses off-the-shelf video disk and microcomputer equipment, and a real tank turret. This indoor facility allows an instructor to display video-disk stored battleground scenery to the crew's view slits and fire-control equipment. The instructor's personal computer also controls the introduction of targets, and scores the crew's simulated firing of the main gun. This sort of indoor setup can be very cost-effective, allowing the simulated firing of hundreds of rounds of expensive tank shells each day. Russia may already have a system like this, using technology that can be bought off the shelf in most electronics stores. The only reason China announced the existence of its system was that the Chinese hope to sell it to equally bargain-minded Third World countries.

Foxing the Artillery Radar

The use of special radars to spot incoming shells and calculate the location of the guns has really come of age in the last twenty years. There are, however, problems. The radar computer makes some assumptions about the enemy shells, and if they use a different design, the gun's location cannot be accurately fixed. For example, longer ranges are being obtained from artillery shells by making them in different shapes. The new shapes sacrifice some accuracy and carrying capacity to obtain the additional range. It appears that the new shapes also change the flight patterns of the shells sufficiently to confuse most current artillery spotting radars.

"I Need Item 673/34a-7761, and I Need it Now!"

Faced with about 850,000 separate items available through its supply services, the British Army has developed a fully computerized catalog that permits continuous updating of items in stock, and includes utilities allowing consultation of standard tables of issue, a pictorial reference system, a schedule of which components constitute what equipment, and a number of other innovative features.

The United States and Russia have long had even more complex logistic systems. The U.S. Air Force, with the largest inventory of parts, became computerized over twenty years ago. As is common with such systems, the past twenty years have been well spent getting all the kinks out of the system. The computerized inventory systems in the U.S. armed forces are currently among the most efficient in the world. Russia is another case. Their lack of suitable computer hardware has given them serious problems in dealing with their growing military inventory problems. This is seen as one of their great weaknesses in the event of a major war.

The Electric Soldier

Twenty percent of United States enlisted personnel work in an electronics-related job. Training is commensurately expensive. The U.S. Navy spends nearly $200,000 each to train electronic-warfare technicians. Civilian job prospects are so attractive for such technicians that the military has a difficult time retaining them. Often, a military technician will leave the service and go to work for a defense contractor, where he will perform the same job, in the same type of military unit, but at a higher rate of pay.

GEOSAT

The U.S. Navy's GEOSAT satellite is officially described as intended to effect significant improvements in weather prediction, provide more accurate maps, and, by working in conjunction with research vessels, greatly improve sonar capabilities. Unofficially, it is believed that GEOSAT is intended to collect information about gravitational patterns and anomalies on a global basis in order to improve the accuracy of SLBMs.

"Over Hill, Over Dale, Over . . ."

The army has recently activated the U.S. Army Space Agency, to provide army input into planning for space-based systems that might be of value to ground forces, such as reconnaissance, surveillance, targeting, and navigation systems.

Hide, Seek, and Get Shot Down.

Since the 1970s, Russia has been putting nuclear-powered radar satellites in orbit. Their primary use is keeping track of ships at sea. The U.S. Navy, alarmed at the persistence of the Russians in this endeavor, feels that eventually these nuclear birds will become quite effective. At first the navy proposed having one or more of the missiles on its nuclear-ballistic-missile subs carry an antisatellite warhead. But in the late 1980s, it switched to a program that would place antisatellite missiles on surface ships. Whatever the outcome of these projects, the U.S. Navy appears determined to keep the Russians in the dark about ship movements.

Chasing Ditties

Copying Morse code characters manually is referred to as "chasing ditties," a fast-disappearing art as more efficient communications gear comes into use. One area where Morse code still has some use is in clandestine operations. These operators have traditionally been called "ditty boppers."

The Straw That Broke the Camel's Back

Warships and combat aircraft last a long time, which is just as well in this age of $500 million B-2 bombers and billion-dollar nuclear submarines. To make the most out of these investments, the ships and aircraft are continually updated with new weapons and equipment. There are drawbacks, however. As more items are added to or modified on ships and aircraft, their performance often suffers. Ships become top-heavy and less stable in rough weather. Aircraft become slower and less maneuverable. Sometimes the damage is more subtle. The British discovered that the stress on destroyers pulling new towed sonar arrays was literally tearing the ships apart. This was found to be the case in 1989 with their new Type 23 frigates. No doubt other navies will now check those among their own ships that drag these heavy sonar devices behind them.

Complete with Air-Conditioning

Although first considered a luxury, air-conditioning has increasingly become a feature of modern warships and combat vehicles. There are two reasons for this development, which actually began prior to World War II. One is the necessity of securing personnel against NBC (nuclear, biological, chemical) attack, thus requiring that ships and vehicles be airtight. In addition, the major powers, who may find their forces operating in environments as diverse as arctic tundra and tropical jungle, find that air-conditioning greatly enhances the durability of the troops: During World War II, many U.S. submariners and tankers fell victim to heat stroke, dehydration, and various skin disorders because a lack of air-conditioning often sent temperatures inside their "vessels" to over 100 degrees Fahrenheit. However, designing an air-conditioning system for a warship or combat vehicle is a fine art. After all, the purpose of a destroyer or a tank is to engage in battle, which means that any air-conditioning system designed for them must be capable of operating effectively even in the face of significant damage. Moreover, the many peculiar design features of military equipment, such as rotating turrets, sealed compartments, and breech exhaust, further complicate the design and installation of air-conditioning systems, driving costs up remarkably. By one estimate, it costs $35,000 to air-condition each heavy construction vehicle or prime mover.

The Flip Side of High Tech

"If you load a mud foot down with a lot of gadgets that he has to watch, somebody a lot more simply equipped—say with a stone ax—will sneak up and bash his head in while he is trying to read a vernier."—Robert A. Heinlein, American novelist

In the Realm of the Senses

With all the talk of electronics and sensors, we tend to forget that all these goodies are only as good as the human senses of sight, hearing, and touch are in coping with them. The fit has never been perfect. In the last fifty years, the number of devices with which the troops have to contend has grown enormously.

Even the infantry has a variety of electronic gadgets to cope with, including complex fire-control systems in many of their antitank and antiaircraft weapons. Sailors and pilots are overwhelmed by the data from dozens of instruments at once. Cathode ray tubes (CRTs) are a partial solution, as you can scan twice as much information if you do not have to glance across a control panel looking for a particular instrument. Unfortunately, these CRT-based instruments are designed by teams of experts, including programmers who must ultimately distill everyone else's work into the actual format of the image the user sees on the screen. Much is usually lost in translation.

What is known is that 50 percent of system failure are due to human error. Much of this error comes from operator confusion at not getting the right piece of information at the right time. The programmable-CRT approach does have the advantage of being easier to reprogram in order to change what is displayed, when to display it, and how it looks. Voice warnings are now more sophisticated. They no longer have to be tape recordings, and computer-generated voices are being used, like those that give you a phone number when you call directory assistance. Current systems can even accept voice commands. Tests have been made placing electric devices on pilot's forearms and chest, which would enable the pilot to feel changes in status of systems. This could give new meaning to the terms *heartburn* (fuel-pump failure), *foot's asleep* (landing gear inoperable), and *pain in the ass* (afterburner malfunction). However, this sensory approach could make an unexpected itch in the wrong place a potentially fatal event. Artificial intelligence techniques are being used to develop systems that will provide the operator with only the information needed for the task at hand. Future combinations of well-laid-out graphic designs and voice technology will provide a decisive edge in combat on land, air, and sea.

Whistle While You Work.

Although several Western observers at Soviet Army maneuvers in November of 1988 were amused to observe troops armed with the most modern infantry weapons being led by an officer who had "a wooden whistle hung around his neck with a piece of twine," it is worth noting that wooden whistles cost very little, are not easily broken, need very little maintenance, never have dead batteries, do not short out when wet, work in all atmospheric conditions, require very little special training to use, and are immune to electronic countermeasures. As General John Vessey, Chairman of the Joint Chiefs of Staff in the early eighties, once remarked regarding high-tech communications equipment, "In the next war we will still have to use runners" to deliver messages when the radios and telephones fail.

PART FIVE

The Human Factor

Technology doesn't win wars, people do. The individual soldier remains the ultimate weapon. Although the human factor often gets buried by the efficient marketing campaigns of the hardware suppliers, it is the troops who will have to use the equipment. And it is these men, and increasingly these women as well, who must bear the pressures of combat, with only their wits, and their training, and perhaps a touch of tradition, plus a few medals to help. As this chapter demonstrates, you can't get from here to there without them.

Ungrateful-Swine Department

"When a general complains of the morale of his troops, the time has come to look into his own."—George C. Marshall, American general, architect of victory in World War II, Nobel Peace Laureate

Rust on the Iron Curtain

Though the measure has gone largely unnoticed, in June of 1988 the Polish parliament revised the standard military oath used since the late 1940s, so that Polish recruits will no longer have to swear to "relentlessly safeguard peace in fraternal alliance with the Soviet Army and other allied armies," but rather merely to safeguard peace in conjunction with "allied armies." At the same time, they passed another law providing for conscientious objectors to do alternative service instead of going to jail. These two items are but the tip of the iceberg of the problems the Polish armed forces have suffered since the military coup in 1981. Ever since that event, morale in, and respect for, the Polish military has plummeted. As the largest (aside from Russia) and most professional (aside from East Germany) force in the Warsaw Pact, this indicated a sharp drop in Warsaw Pact military capability. Unlike other Warsaw Pact forces, Poland depends on volunteers for half its strength. Since 1981, the Poles have been having a hard time getting those volunteers. A more open economy and freedom to travel to the West have made military service even less attractive. The officers' schools have an increasing number of vacancies, and the number of long-term NCOs steadily shrinks. The personnel situation became so acute that several infantry divisions have had to be disbanded. Morale in the ranks is very low; the conscripts feel more sympathy for the Solidarity government than for the Russian-dominated officer corps. Both the Polish and Russian high commands recognize that Polish units would fight only reluctantly in any war. This dismal situation shows little prospect of changing in the near future.

Those Who Know

"War first got its bad name from soldiers."—D.J.R. Bruckner, historian

REMF

Rear-echelon motherfucker (pronounced "remf") is what the combat troops call everyone else. Human nature usually overcomes good sense in warfare, and it is common for the REMFs to enhance their lifestyle at the expense of the combat troops they are supposed to be supporting. The German Army, among a few others, has a long tradition of making every effort to get all amenities possible to the combat troops. If this meant that the combat troops were better supplied than the support troops, then the system was working. This paid tremendous dividends among the combat troops, who had one less misfortune to get depressed about.

Good Habits

"Discipline is the foundation of an army."—José Vilabla, Spanish Army officer and military writer

Mercenaries and Hessians in the Modern World

Mercenaries are soldiers who fight for anyone who'll pay them. While the mercs that get the attention are the free-lance Europeans and Americans who occasionally turn up in odd corners of Africa, sometimes trying to take over an impoverished country, most mercenaries go relatively unnoticed. There are perhaps 140,000 mercs in the world today, and they serve in just a handful of armies. The French have about 8,500 in their Foreign Legion, and the Spanish another 7,500 in theirs, though many of the men in both corps are native sons pretending to be foreigners. In addition, Britain has about 10,000 Gurkhas, recruited by arrangement with the government of Nepal, and there are perhaps 100,000 more Nepalese in the Indian Army and police, serving mostly as individuals. Finally, Oman and the United Arab Emirates regularly hire troops from Pakistan, while the Presidential Guard of Equatorial Guinea is recruited in Morocco, and South Africa, Israel, and Libya appear to have some nonnative troops on the payroll as well, though their numbers are undetermined. Then there are Hessians, named after the troops that Britain hired from Hesse and several other German principalities during the American Revolution.

Hessians are not mercenaries in the classic sense—that is, men who serve for whomever will pay them. Rather, they are serving an ally of their country, an ally who is paying the bills. This was, and remains, a clever way to maintain a viable army on a tight budget: Hire the troops out to someone who'll support them, and you, in the style to which you are accustomed. The number of Hessians in the world seems to be rather higher than that of proper mercs, but again figures are difficult to establish. The best example of Hessians today are the Cuban forces who have been active in Angola, Ethiopia, and other parts of Africa, currently running about 25,000–35,000 troops, but peaking some years ago at perhaps 65,000. The system works well. At the expense of Russia, which supports him and his troops to the tune of $5–$8 billion a year, Castro gets to play the role of an international revolutionary while solving a serious unemployment problem at home and securing some valuable combat experience for his army, which may come in handy should Uncle Sam decide to invade Cuba. France also has about 8,000 Hessians, including part of the Foreign Legion, stationed in the Central African Republic, Djibouti, Ivory Coast, and Senegal, with the bills partially paid by local governments, who find the French presence comforting. Likewise, French pilots are generally believed to have flown some missions for Iraq against Iran.

Until recently, Pakistan was heavily into the Hessian business, with more than 20,000 troops hired out to Saudi Arabia and several other Muslim powers in the Middle East, but it is currently cutting back. Though precise information is unavailable, during the Iran-Iraq War several Arab powers contributed a total of about 10,000 to 15,000 "volunteers" to the Iraqi Army. Even Britain is in the Hessian business, with one battalion of Gurkhas actually on the payroll of the sultan of Brunei. Perhaps the most surprising Hessians of all, however, are the 55,000-odd Americans in Japan who are partially supported out of Japanese funds, to the tune of about $45,000 a head per year.

Sound Advice?

"When you see a good war, go to it."—Rafael de Nogales Bey, Venezuelan mercenary, American cattle thief, and Parisian boulevardier

The New Generation in the Russian Army

Most Western armed forces retire their senior commanders in their fifties and early sixties. Thus, most of the World War II veterans passed from the scene in the 1970s. In Russia, it's different. Senior commanders hold on to their positions almost literally until they drop. This is partially due to custom and bureaucratic inertia. But it also has to do with the loss of so many comforts when one leaves a senior position. Retirement is not nearly as comfortable in the Soviet bloc as it is in the West, where money can actually buy something. So it was in the late 1980s that Russia's World War II generation of commanders finally passed from the scene. Currently, over 80 percent of Russian officers are under age forty. In other words, only a few percent served in World War II—or any war, for that matter. This development has serious implications for military and political affairs.

The officers who went through World War II experienced the most destructive war in Russian history. They also had parents or family telling them about how bad World War I, the Revolution, and subsequent Civil War were. Moreover, these soldiers also experienced Stalin's brand of terrorism. The subsequent generation, born just before or during World War II, knows little of this. Stalin and World War II are dim childhood memories. Except for some of the 100,000 who served in Afghanistan, these new commanders have not experienced combat. While most of those who were in Afghanistan didn't actually serve in combat, at least they were close to it. The Russian military press indicates that the Afghan experience was quite a shock for the post–World War II officers. This generation of leaders had been taught that the Russian Army walked on water and could do no wrong in combat. The failure of Russian troops to make much headway against a bunch of "bandits" has caused these officers to rethink what is going on in the Russian Army. And the current generation can think, as over 80 percent have university degrees and over two thirds are Communist party members. Another disturbing trend in Russia is that fewer of the "best and brightest" opt for an officer's commission. Most military posts are in dreary frontier areas, and Russian yuppies would rather stay in the large cities and take their chances with the "restructured" civilian economy. Expect a lot of changes in the nineties.

The Easy Way, the Hard Way, and the Army Way

"The price of victory is hard fighting."—Reuben Jenkins, military analyst

The "New Soviet Man" Becomes an Officer.

The nearly one million officers of the Russian armed forces are the core of Russian military might. Because the Soviet armed forces lack adequate numbers of NCOs and other long-service enlisted personnel, the officers play a larger role in holding everything together than in other nations. When Colonel General Vladimir A. Vostrov was appointed chief of the Military Educational Establishments of the Ministry of Defense, he made a shocking announcement that most instructors in his directorate were deficient in their methods and attitudes toward effective selection of officer candidates and officer training in general. He insisted that officer candidates be chosen on the basis of aptitude and ability rather than the amount of clout their parents had. Traditionally, Russian officers came from the nobility and military families. Apparently, this method has persisted under the Communists and has reached the point where too many officer cadets were flunking out, or just barely making it. Vostrov commented that many of those who passed their courses were inept, had bad attitudes, or both.

Nearly all Russian officers come from a network of military academies that provide the equivalent of a college education as well as military training. Many ambitious young Russians strive for an officer career because it's one of the few jobs that offers the Russian version of the good life. This is another ancient Russian tradition, and one that helped bring about the 1917 Revolution in the first place.

Experience

"He that makes war without many mistakes has not made war very long."—Napoleon Bonaparte, Corsican adventurer, 1769–1821

Women in Uniform

The approximately 221,000 women in uniform constitute somewhat more than 10 percent of the personnel of the U.S. armed forces.

	Officers 1000s	%	Enlisted 1000s	%	Total 1000s	%	Officers as % Women
Air Force	12.8	11.9	63.0	12.8	75.8	12.5	16.9
Army	11.6	10.7	71.7	10.8	83.3	10.8	13.9
Marines	0.7	3.2	8.9	5.0	9.6	4.9	14.3
Navy	7.2	10.0	45.5	8.9	52.7	9.2	13.7
TOTAL	32.0	10.5	189.0	10.2	221.0	10.2	14.5

Remarkably, women officers are statistically more numerous than total womanpower in the armed forces. Indeed, on the basis of all women in uniform, women officers are roughly proportional to the total number of officers in the armed forces, which is an impressive accomplishment for what is essentially a "minority group."

Ring Knocker

A "Ring Knocker" is an officer possessing military-academy credentials, with specific reference to one who has graduated from a certain small engineering school about 50 miles north of New York City, a place sometimes known as "Hudson High," but more commonly called West Point. The term derives from the studied disinterest with which such individuals are rumored to casually bang their class rings against glasses in the Officers' Club. The phrase is also a euphemism for an alleged sinister conspiracy among such individuals to insure their mutual advancement in the military service of the United States.

The Other Half Is Bigger Battalions.

"A bold heart is half the battle."—Latin proverb

Minorities in Arms

Roughly 23 percent of Americans belong to various racial minority groups. Approximately 12 percent of us are black and 7.8 percent of Hispanic origin, while about 3.2 percent of us belong to such groups as Native Americans, Eskimos, Aleuts, Pacific Islanders, and Asians. These groups contribute more than their share in active-duty military personnel, 590,000 men and women, or about 27.4 percent of active personnel, statistically well above the norm.

Military Service By Ethnic Minority

	Officers 1000s	%	Enlisted 1000s	%	Total 1000s	%	Officers as % of the Group
Blacks	20.8	6.6	398.0	21.6	420.0	19.5	5.0
Hispanics	5.4	1.8	79.7	4.3	85.0	3.9	6.4
Others	7.5	2.5	78.3	4.3	86.1	4.0	8.7
TOTAL	33.5	10.9	556.8	30.1	590.0	27.4	5.7

Both statistically and absolutely, the army has the highest proportion of minority personnel, nearly 35.0 percent of the troops being members of ethnic minority groups, while the navy has the lowest proportion, only about 23.7 percent.

Minority Personnel By Branch of Service

	Officers 1000s	%	Enlisted 1000s	%	Total 1000s	%	Officers as % of the Group
Army	15.6	14.5	254.0	35.3	269.6	35.0	5.8
Air Force	10.6	9.9	120.0	24.3	130.0	21.6	8.2
Marines	1.6	8.1	53.0	29.7	56.5	28.6	2.8
Navy	5.7	7.9	131.5	24.5	135.6	23.7	4.2
TOTAL	33.5	10.9	556.8	30.1	590.0	27.4	5.7

Black Americans represent the largest single ethnic minority in the U.S. armed forces. However, measured in terms of the proportion of members of the group who are officers, the most successful ethnic minority is the "others," almost 9 percent of whom hold commissions, a figure nearly approaching the normal officer-to-enlisted ratio in the service.

Black Active Duty Military Personnel

	Officers 1000s	%	Enlisted 1000s	%	Total 1000s	%	Officers as % of the Group
Army	11.1	10.2	199.2	28.2	210.3	27.3	5.3
Air Force	5.8	5.4	85.1	17.2	90.9	15.2	6.4
Marines	0.9	4.7	37.0	20.7	37.9	19.2	2.4
Navy	2.5	3.5	77.6	15.2	80.1	14.3	3.1
TOTAL	20.8	6.6	398.0	21.6	420.0	19.5	5.0

Hispanic Active Duty Military Personnel

	Officers 1000s	%	Enlisted 1000s	%	Total 1000s	%	Officers as % of the Group
Army	1.6	1.5	27.1	4.1	28.7	3.7	5.6
Air Force	2.2	2.0	18.4	3.7	20.6	4.0	10.8
Marines	0.4	1.8	10.1	5.7	10.5	5.3	3.8
Navy	1.3	1.8	23.9	4.7	25.2	4.4	5.2
TOTAL	5.4	1.8	79.7	4.3	85.0	3.9	6.4

Other Minority Group Active Duty Military Personnel

	Officers 1000s	%	Enlisted 1000s	%	Total 1000s	%	Officers as % of the Group
Army	3.0	2.7	26.9	4.0	29.8	3.9	10.1
Air Force	2.7	2.5	16.7	3.4	19.4	3.2	13.9
Marines	0.3	1.5	5.9	3.3	6.2	3.1	5.1
Navy	2.0	2.6	28.9	5.6	30.8	5.4	6.5
TOTAL	7.5	2.5	78.3	4.3	86.1	4.0	8.7

Excuses, Excuses . . .

"With two thousand years of examples behind us we have no excuse, when fighting, for not fighting well."—T. E. Lawrence (of Arabia)

Generalists Versus Specialists

Most businesses train their managers in certain specialties. A factory manager and an auditor do not normally switch jobs. In the military, this system is also used, sometimes. In the air force, pilots are selected early for fighter, ground-attack, bomber, helicopter, or transport work, and most of them stay for their career. In the submarine service, a similar system is applied to the various specialties on nuclear boats. On surface ships in the U.S. Navy, however, officers are frequently transferred from ASW to damage control to surface weapons to air defense. Some critics of surface-ship officers' performance versus aviation and submarines officers' hold this generalist approach to blame for the problems that affect surface warships, such as higher accident rates. Better, they say, for an officer to stick with either one specialty or at least one type of ship, such as destroyers, carriers, amphibious, and so forth.

Ring Knockers Need Not Apply.

Only about 20 percent of the generals in the U.S. Army are West Point graduates, most of the rest having received their commissions through ROTC, officer-candidate schools for enlisted personnel, and similar programs. For example, General Colin Powell, who took over the National Security Council after Oliver North's secret operations were discovered, and is now chairman of the Joint Chiefs, was a prominent graduate of the City College of New York ROTC program. Nevertheless, military-academy graduates are rather more numerous among the generals than among the officers as a whole. Academy grads account for only about 12–13 percent of the roughly 8,000 newly commissioned army officers each year, while ROTC brings in about 43–45 percent, OCS about 4–5 percent, and various other programs, including direct commissioning of medical specialists, aviation cadets, and the like, account for the balance. However, ring knockers make the service a career at a much higher rate than do other officers, who are primarily reservists.

Who Gets Things Done?

"Battles are sometimes won by generals; wars are nearly always won by sergeants and privates."—F. E. Adcock, British classical scholar

NATO's Distaff Warriors

Of the sixteen nations in NATO, thirteen have women on active duty with their armed forces, exclusive of paramilitary forces. The accompanying table lists them by the percentage of female active-duty personnel at the beginning of 1989:

Power	Number	%
U.S.	221,000	10.2
Canada	7,600	9.2
Britain	16,500	5.1
Belgium	3,500	3.9
France	17,500	3.7
Denmark	850	3.0
Netherlands	1,550	1.5
Norway	500	1.4
Greece	1,850	1.0
West Germany	141	0.03
Portugal	9	0.012
Turkey	63	0.0084
Luxembourg	2	0.0029

Two NATO powers, Italy and Spain, legally prohibit women from serving in the armed forces, and Iceland has no armed forces. The peculiarly small percentages of women in the West German, Portuguese, Turkish, and Luxembourgian armed forces reflects the very small number of women in the service. All West German women on active duty are medical officers. Turkish women in uniform are also officers, serving up to the rank of colonel in various technical branches, as is the case with Portugal's nine women. But Luxembourg's two women are both enlisted.

Veteran's Lament

"I hope to God that I have fought my last battle."—The Duke of Wellington, June 19, 1815, on the morrow of having defeated Napoleon at Waterloo

Troops

At the highest level of usage, the word *troops*—in the plural—refers to military manpower of any sort, army, navy, marines, or air force, as in, "Will we have to send troops?" Within a particular service, however, if used at all, it usually refers to enlisted personnel, as in, "What do the troops think about this?" *Troop*, in the singular, refers to a company-sized formation in cavalry units in the U.S. Army, and to platoon-sized mounted formations in the British Army, or, when used in collectives, such as "troop units," to the mass of soldiery as a whole. Occasionally, a poorly educated officer or military expert will be found using the word *troop* to refer to the individual fighting man, as in, "The needs of the individual troop must be considered." However, the term *troop* is used, for emphasis, when an NCO wants to get a wayward soldier's attention. For example, "All right, troop, let's get this area policed up." This does not count as a misuse of English as it is not, properly speaking, English at all, but rather a dialect peculiar to the military.

Tradition Preserved

During winter maneuvers in the 1960s, a Russian soldier froze to death on bivouac. In the normal course of events, such an "incident" might be counted among the unfortunate but relatively frequent deaths in training that occur in all armed forces. However, in this case, word of the man's death made its way up the chain of command until it reached a very senior officer, an old Marshal of the Soviet Union with many decades of service under his belt. The incident offended his innate Russianness, and he thundered, "Have Russian soldiers forgotten how to sleep in their overcoats . . . ?" or words to that effect. Within days, word went out ordering every division commander in the Soviet Army—over 175 generals—to Moscow for an emergency conference. Whatever it was that this pomposity of generals expected to hear—orders for World War III?—at this extraordinary meeting, what they got was quite different, a lecture on how a soldier can safely sleep in the snow in the coldest weather, by using his overcoat and a little common sense, a practice in which Russian soldiers had been well-versed for centuries. The generals were then ordered to carry this information back to their commands and disseminate it to their troops. And to insure that they did it right, the old marshal issued each of the generals an infantryman's greatcoat and ordered the lot of them out into the cold of a Moscow winter to practice the theory that they had just learned.

Chain of Command

"Generals speak often of their military duty to their superiors, but never of their duty to their soldiers."—Helmut Lindmann, German military historian

Mean 18

Golf is a favorite recreation for military officers in the Washington, D.C., area. There are several golf courses there run by the military, including one at Andrews Air Force Base just outside Washington. Officers in charge of procurement seeking to gain some relief from the constant badgering of arms merchants will find no escape on this golf course. The benches found near each hole are designed to hold advertising posters. The air force sells the space to any legitimate advertiser, and most of the advertisers on the golf-course benches are selling weapons to the air force.

Will the Real Marines Please Stand Up?

The thirteenth Marine Corps Marathon, run in 1988, was won by the USMC, taking the title from Britain's Royal Marines, who had held it four years in a row, a victory that means the USMC has broken the 5–5 tie between the two rival corps.

The Grunts

"The soldier is the primary and most powerful mechanism of war."—
José Vilalba, Spanish general and military historian

The Grass Is Always Greener. . . .

Armies share certain pathologies, one of which is a mania for neat-
ness. Thus, it was not surprising that, while being interviewed by
U.S. intelligence, a former Russian officer who had recently immi-
grated to the United States commented that he had once been ordered to spray-paint some brownish grass so that it would appear
green and healthy during an upcoming inspection. The tale made
the rounds for a while, much to amusement of the Americans who
heard it, until it reached a major who said, "Hell, I've seen that
done out at Fort——."

The Good Get Going

At ceremonies commemorating the second inauguration of President
Ronald Reagan, it was discovered that ninety-seven members of the
Salvadoran Army's *Batallion Ronald Reagan* had deserted.

Good PR

"Victory in war is the result of the successful organization of enthusiasm."—Raymond Carr, British historian

Oops!

In a recent survey of the role of women in NATO armed forces, a
feminist journal observed somewhat caustically that "Iceland has no
female military personnel," which, while true, failed to take into
account the fact that Iceland has no military personnel of any sex,
having no armed forces.

Jungle Lust

During the Vietnam War, the U.S. Air Force dropped acoustic sensors along the Ho Chi Minh Trail to detect North Vietnamese convoys so that the U.S. bombers could find their targets. Most of these sensors only picked up the sound of porters or trucks moving in the distance. One famous tape caught a North Vietnamese soldier and a woman taking a break from the rigors of war in a particularly passionate fashion.

Why Soldiers?

"The only reason for the existence of the soldier is to defend the principles that civilian society represents."—Georges *"Le Tigre"* Clemenceau, premier of France in World War I

Don't Tell.

The Russian penchant for secrecy extends even to denying the troops in the field regular access to accurate maps. As a result, the troops often get lost on maneuvers. Reportedly, on one occasion an American officer observing Warsaw Pact maneuvers in East Germany had to help a Russian unit find its position and objective. East German officers have been observed wincing when their "fraternal brother soldiers" from Russia stumble about. As one East German officer observed to an American officer, "That sort of thing does not happen with German troops."

On German Military Prowess

"Why study an army that has lost two world wars?"—Michael A. Palmer, U.S. Army officer

Crime and Punishment

Although the story sounds apocryphal, it was told by a Russian tank officer who claimed to have been a witness. A tank unit was out on maneuvers that involved defense against enemy attack helicopters. The exercise proved a frustrating one for the tankers. They were unable to evade detection, and, worse, the umpires constantly ruled that the simulated shots that they were taking at the target drones— the army budget for such being tight—were misses. Finally, one sergeant boiled over. Unbeknown to his superior, he took careful aim and cut loose with live ammunition, scoring a perfect hit and bringing the drone crashing down. The ensuing bureaucratic furor was resolved in perfect bureaucratic fashion. The powers-that-were decided to reprimand the platoon commander for the poor discipline in his outfit, but recognized the sergeant's marksmanship with a commendation.

Comrade Cadet

In one of the latest manifestations of the thawing of U.S.-Russian relations, the U.S. Military Academy at West Point will be sending Russian-speaking cadets to a Soviet military academy for two-week visits in exchange for visits from English-speaking Soviet military cadets.

Timing Is Everything.

"More than one general has redeemed faulty dispositions and won fame by a suitably glorious death."—John L. Stokesbury, military historian

General Expenses

At any given time, the United States has about 1,050 officers of flag rank on active duty with the army, navy, air force, and marines. The cost to the taxpayer for salaries, housing, standard emoluments, and other perquisites averages $79,814.50 per general or admiral. This does not include incentive pay, such as hazardous-duty, flight pay, and sea pay, which can add a few thousand more. Indeed, a general's pay and emoluments can be so lucrative that Congress has "capped" military pay so that generals and admirals—and all other federal employees—don't take home more than do senators, representatives, and the service secretaries, who make only $89,500. The actual cost of supporting and maintaining general officers varies considerably. The three dozen four-star officers (full generals and admirals) pull down about $85,000 a year, while the ten dozen three-star people (lieutenant generals and vice admirals), rake in some $85,500 apiece, the nearly 400 two-star folks (major generals and rear admirals "of the upper half") earn some $84,300, and the lowly one-star officers (brigadier generals and rear admirals "of the lower half") make only about $75,000. The anomaly of four-star officers averaging less than their three-star subordinates is due to the fact that most four-star folks serve in Washington, and therefore do not qualify for various additional monies for overseas and hazardous duty. Without the cap, four-star officers would earn about $90,700 a year, with salaries for other officers increased proportionally.

Note that British general officers are paid over 50 percent more than their U.S. counterparts, while Soviet generals are paid less— and that in rubles—but have much better perqs. Indeed, Russian colonel generals—the equivalent of four-star generals—are commonly called "princes" in recognition of their lavish lifestyle and enormous powers. And they're outranked by marshals.

They Have Long Memories.

"A general must be shot or befriended—but never hurt."—Salvador de Madariaga, Spanish politician and historian

A General Dilemma

On VE-Day, the end of World War II in Europe, the United States Army, including the Army Air Forces, had 8,267,958 men and women on active duty, of whom about 1,500 were generals (0.002 percent), or one general to every 5,512 other persons in the army. In 1989 the combined number of army and air-force personnel was approximately 1,376,800 men and women, of whom 730 were generals (0.006 percent), or one general to about every 1,750 lower-ranking people. In effect, the peacetime army and air force of 1989 had about 16.6 percent of the personnel, but fully 48.7 percent of the generals, of the army which won the Second World War. At the start of 1990, the U.S. armed forces had 1,056 generals and admirals on active duty. This means that one out of every 2,040.9 men and women in the armed forces was a flag officer. The breakdown by service was:

	Number	Troops per Flag Officer
Army	396	1,947.0
Air Force	334	1,775.4
Marines	70	2,828.9
Navy	256	2,273.4

Of this proliferation of generals and admirals on active duty, 36 (3.4 percent) had four stars, 122 (11.6 percent) had three, 368 (34.9 percent) had two, and 530 (50.2 percent) only one. The air force had 13 (36.1 percent) of the four-star people, while the army and navy had 10 each (27.8 percent) and the marines (which belong to the navy) made do with three (8.3 percent). On a statistical basis, this means that there was one four-star officer for about every 45,000 men and women in the air force, one for every 57,100 in the navy, one for every 66,008 in the Marine Corps, and one for every 77,100 in the army. Thus, in both absolute numbers and statistically, the air force wins the four-star officers' sweepstakes. Given the often acrimonious state of interservice relationships, it is a wonder that the army lets them get away with it. Surprisingly, there is reason to believe that these ratios, as excessive as they may seem based on World War II experience, are rather conservative when compared with those of other powers.

Now, We Know.

The official Defense Department Dictionary of Military and Associated Terms contains the line "Total Nuclear War.' Not to be used. See 'General War.' "

Why the Best Russian Defense Is a Quick Offense

The Russian military high command realizes that their Western opponents in NATO have economies more than three times larger than their own. Thus, a long war would tend to go against Russia once these larger economies started to turn out torrents of war materials. The only alternative to defeat in a protracted contest with such enormous economies is to build a large offensive capability and attack vigorously. This would give Russia a chance to cripple the superior NATO economies in Europe. Remember that Russia was forced out of World War I by the collapse of its economy and was on the ropes economically at the end of World War II. Another thing to remember is that Japan used the same "attack first and hard" doctrine against the West in World War II. Does Pearl Harbor ring a bell?

Gamblers' Disease

"To gain all, we must risk all."—Paul von Lettow-Vorbeck, arguably the most successful German general of World War I, who fought the Allies to a standstill in Central Africa

The Sukhomlinov Effect

Military historians have an amusing rule of thumb for determining which army is most likely to win a war, the "Sukhomlinov Effect." Named after General Vladimir Sukhomlinov, the imperial Russian minister of war at the start of World War I, this "rule" holds that in any given conflict the loser is most likely to be the side whose generals wear the better uniforms: Sukhomlinov himself was perhaps the most splendidly outfitted general in this century, with gold braid embroidery down to his knees. Consider the lessons of history: The barbarian invasions, the Dutch War for Independence, the English Civil War, the American Revolution, the French Revolution, the Napoleonic Wars, the American Civil War, World War I, the Russian Revolution, World War II, the several Arab-Israeli wars, the Vietnam War, and the Afghan War were all lost by the side that had the snappier uniforms. There is more than a coincidence here, though the suggestion of a "law" at work is perhaps a bit facetious.

The Sukhomlinov Effect describes a common pathology of armies. Particularly in peacetime, armies tend to concern themselves more with appearances and style than with fighting skill, which cannot, after all, be demonstrated. Men who "look" like generals—tall, ruggedly handsome guys with broad shoulders and splendid posture who wear the uniform well—are more likely to be promoted than those who may have a real talent for war, since the latter may not meet the peacetime criteria. Although lots of fine commanders have been short, and fat, and slovenly, they had to wait around for a war before they could prove themselves. There is no known way to pick the able generals in peacetime. As a result, despite a few notable exceptions, the generals who command at the onset of a war are rarely still in charge by its conclusion.

The Usual Method

"Military history, when superficially studied, will furnish arguments in support of any theory."—Bronsart von Schellendorf, imperial German officer and military historian

Red Alert

In early November 1983, KGB headquarters sent an urgent order to all its agents outside Russia to suspend current operations and shift their efforts toward gathering information about an impending nuclear strike by the United States against Russia. The Russian leadership, in a fit of paranoia and misinterpretation of NATO military maneuvers, was certain that within two weeks a torrent of nuclear warheads would fall on them. Of course, this happened at the height of Ronald Reagan's "evil empire" campaign. Apparently, the KGB has no sense of humor about these things. Nevertheless, this potentially disastrous incident had highly beneficial consequences. Not long afterward, feeling the breath of the KGB on his neck, a well-placed Russian intelligence official in Britain, a man long on the MI-5—British intelligence—payroll, defected. Information that he supplied on this incident, considered in the light of other intelligence, led to a major reassessment of Soviet intentions, and convinced British prime minister Margaret Thatcher that the new Russian leadership was sincere in its desire for a reduction in international tensions. As a result, Maggie convinced Ronnie, and both began to get along famously with Mikhail.

How Do You Raise the Defense Budget
When the Threat Is Shrinking?

In late 1988, Russia announced a 10 percent reduction in armed-forces strength. The Russians would like their potential adversaries to make similar cuts, and they will probably get their way. China has been cutting its armed forces and defense budget throughout the 1980s. This allows Russia to lower its guard on its Chinese frontier areas. The United States and other NATO countries had been increasing their forces and spending throughout the eighties. They did this in response to a Russian buildup in the sixties and seventies, during "détente." Now that the Russian threat is scheduled to shrink throughout the 1990s, there will be much less support for increasing NATO spending and loud calls for reductions from the taxpayers. Another factor that will speed this trend along is the increasing openness of the Russians about their own armed forces. A large part of the perception of Russian military strength comes from the lack of information about exactly what they have and what shape it's in. It is becoming apparent that the Russians are neither as well-equipped nor as well-prepared for a major war as was previously thought. The scare tactics NATO defense planners have used so frequently in the past appear ready to backfire as a clearer picture of the Russian "threat" comes out.

Losers Lament

"We will do better next time."—Edward Braddock to young George Washington, on the occasion of "Braddock's Defeat," 1755

Competitive Strategies

In the mid-1980s, the United States began to develop a military strategy based on its strengths against Russian weaknesses. The doctrine was called "Competitive Strategies." Examples of competitive systems are Stealth aircraft, robotic weapons, superior sensors, precision guidance systems, and computing power in general. Stealth aircraft severely degrade the enormous Russian investment in air defense. Robotic weapons, whether land, sea, or air versions, negate Russian advantages in numbers of weapons systems. Superior sensors make it difficult for Russian weapons to get close enough to do any damage. Precision guidance systems allow Western weapons to do more damage to key Russian targets at less expense to the West. The substantial Western advantage in designing and building computers of all sizes drives most of this high-tech arsenal. The Russians are quite worried about all this, as they have used the same technique for decades and believe in it.

Deep Kimchi

"Deep kimchi" means big trouble, from a Korean delicacy whose principal ingredient is very hot peppers.

From the People Who Brought You "Protective Reaction"

The United States Army has recently been detected avoiding use of the word *combat*, preferring the euphemism *violence processing*. In a similar vein, the New Action Army does not *attack* targets, it *services* targets. You might think of the army as the ultimate service industry.

But It Helps.

"Bravery does not of itself win battles."—H. H. Wilson, British naval historian

Part-Time Soldiers?

In the event of a national emergency, approximately 35 percent of the immediately available mobilization strength of the armed forces would come from the 1,150,000 members of the reserves (18 percent) and National Guard (17 percent). The service with the highest proportion of its mobilization strength composed of part-time warriors is the army, with 49 percent of its personnel being either reservists (20 percent) or guardsmen (29 percent). The Coast Guard—in wartime part of the navy—is a distant second, with 26 percent of its mobilization strength composed of reservists, just ahead of the air force, which would be 24 percent reserve (14 percent) or National Guard (10 percent) on mobilization. About 20 percent of the navy and 17 percent of the Marine Corps would consist of reservists in a national emergency.

Things Don't Change.

"We trained very hard, but it seemed that every time we were beginning to form into teams we would be reorganized. I was to learn in this life that we tend to meet any situation by reorganizing. And a wonderful method it can be for creating the illusion of progress while producing confusion, inefficiency and demoralization."—Attributed to Petronius Arbiter, Roman hedonist, about A.D. 60. A current example of this is taking place in the Russian Army. After World War II, the Russians reorganized their combat units and basically adopted the same divisional organization of the Germans they had just defeated. Russia's World War II mechanized units had a unique organization called a tank (or mechanized) corps, similar to an overstrength Western armored (or mechanized infantry) division. What made the tank corps different was its use of brigades instead of regiments. The brigades were a bit stronger than regiments and had more support units attached. These brigades were thus capable of more independent action. This was well-suited for the fast-moving breakthrough and exploitation operations the tank corps were normally assigned. After forty years of using the German-style organization, they are now reorganizing into the World War II tank corps setup. The reason: The tank-corps organization is better suited for breakthrough and exploitation operations. Petronius was certainly a visionary.

Over There . . .

The total U.S. military deployment abroad amounts to nearly 900,000 people, of whom only about 485,000 are uniformed personnel, and the rest civilian employees and dependents. Surveys consistently find that many of the military personnel are planning to put the welfare of their dependents first and shirk their military duties until they have seen to the safety of their kinfolk.

Not a Pretty Picture

During 1986, 380 South African national servicemen attempted suicide, and 18 succeeded. The government had no comment on this matter. Note that suicide among conscripts is common in other armed forces. This is particularly true if the duty is unpleasant. Few statistics are released on this subject, although it is known that the U.S. annual rate is 6 per 100,000 troops. For Spain it is 9, Israel and South Africa 18. Russia's rate is thought to be higher still.

Never Volunteer?

A recent survey revealed that while the bulk of the personnel in the armed forces of the NATO nations are volunteers (men and women who have elected to join the service, or chosen to remain under arms upon expiration of their statutory military obligation), the bulk of the personnel in the Warsaw Pact armed forces are conscripts fulfilling their service obligation. Generally, the higher the proportion of volunteers, the more effective the military force is as a whole. Having fewer conscripts means that less time is spent on teaching basic skills and more on developing better combat skills. The ideal is to have small units that have the same people working together for many years. Ironically, the best examples of this are in the trained reserves. The United States and Israel have reserve armor units containing tank crews that have worked together for a decade or more. Such crews have proved much more effective in combat than newly formed conscript crews. Fully seven of the NATO powers recruit at least half of their personnel voluntarily:

Britain	100%	Portugal	76%
Canada	100%	Denmark	70%
Luxembourg	100%	Belgium	67%
U.S.	100%		

This stands in marked contrast to the situation in the Warsaw Pact, only one member of which, Poland, has as many as 50 percent volunteers in the ranks. The worst showing in the Soviet bloc was that of Russia itself, with volunteers amounting to only 18 percent of the troops, though this was better than the lowest NATO figure, that for Turkey, 11 percent. Figures for the other powers fell between these extremes. In NATO:

West Germany	47%	Greece	24%
France	37%	Italy	19%
Netherlands	36%	Norway	18%
Spain	26%		

In the Warsaw Pact:

Poland	50%	Romania	32%
Hungary	42%	Czechoslovakia	30%
East Germany	41%	Bulgaria	24%

The low figure for Norway reflects the militialike character of its armed forces. Iceland has no armed forces. In the late 1980s, increasing numbers of senior Russian officers could be heard advocating more volunteers and professionals. Part of this attitude comes from their envy of major Western armed forces. But the Russians also note the higher efficiency of East European armies that have a higher proportion of volunteers than they do.

"Re-Up"

"Re-up" is military slang for reenlisting, in order to "go career," or become a professional soldier, a "lifer."

The Impossible Dream

"The professional soldier likes his wars clean, short, and decisive."—Geoffrey Parker, British military historian

Looking Good Versus Being Good

A common problem in armed forces during peacetime is a tendency to place more emphasis on meeting administrative requirements than getting the forces in shape for combat. In a war, the correct priorities are quickly established: combat effectiveness, taking care of the troops, administrative efficiency. In peacetime, these priorities tend to get reversed. The troops' morale is watched, lest they leave the service or attempt to take over the government. The last thing attended to, if it all, is how effective the troops will be in combat. This reversal makes a lot of sense to the peacetime commanders. Lacking actual combat to settle disputes over which doctrine, equipment, and tactics are best, two things happen. First, compromises are made. In effect, the most senior, opinionated, or persuasive leaders lay down the "regulations," and everyone quickly realizes that advancement in the organization depends on successful adherence to these regulations. Next, the measures of excellence become increasingly bureaucratic rather than practical. For example, it becomes more acceptable to have a lot of good-looking weapons than fewer weapons that are more effective in combat. Nation's with a free-market economy tend to lose their most able and results-oriented officers and troops because these people see better opportunities to prove they can get results by competing in the commercial sector. It's no coincidence that in wartime many of the most able combat leaders were also superior competitors in civilian life. This flight from the peacetime military is particularly acute with expensively trained specialists like pilots. Despite substantial cash bonuses paid to keep these pilots, many nations often end up losing the best ones anyway and end up retaining many pilots who are apt at looking good and lack the initiative to seek better opportunities in civilian life. Navies that spend a lot of time at sea, and air forces that let pilots fly often, suffer somewhat less from these problems because the realities of sea-keeping and flying impose restraints on how off-the-wall habits can become. But this is no guarantee that a nation's pilots and sailors will be as well-prepared for combat as another nation's. Actual combat invariably brings everyone up short. The Russians are carefully digesting their experience in Afghanistan, while the United States is getting large doses of reality from its lifelike electronic combat simulators and training systems. But most armed forces never break out of this peacetime paper-pushing syndrome. When change comes, it comes slowly, for better or worse. The good armies tend to stay good, and the bad ones never completely shake off their long-lived reputations for looking good and performing poorly.

Winning *Is* Everything

"Nothing brings a military establishment into such disrepute as the inability to win."—Claude C. Sturgill, American military historian

At Home Abroad

About 5,000 U.S. military reservists actually reside in Europe, primarily as employees of the U.S. government or of private firms, or dependents of U.S. military personnel. These troops perform regular reserve duties at reserve centers or with units in Europe.

And Stay Away from the Local Women . . .

Iceland is the smallest member of NATO, and the only one without any armed forces. Comprising one very large and several very tiny volcanic islands in the North Atlantic, Iceland lies in crucial sea routes, particularly for the Russian Northern Fleet heading for the open seas. Personnel totaling no more than about 6,000, including troops and their dependents, are provided by several other NATO nations, primarily the United States. So as not to offend the sensibilities of the 250,000 Icelanders, strict rules are imposed on the foreign troops. Unmarried male soldiers must observe a curfew. No one may live outside the NATO bases unless he is married to an Icelander. The troops are reminded that the Icelanders are the descendants of Norse Vikings and still speak the original Viking language, the implication being that these descendants of Norse marauders might react with beserker fury if anyone took liberties with their womenfolk.

"We're Looking for a Few Good [Manly] Men."

Defense Department statistics suggest that the Marine Corps has discharged far more women than men on charges of committing homosexual acts. Since 1977 an annual statistical average of about 35 enlisted women out of every 100,000 have been discharged for homosexual acts, in contrast to an average of about 4 enlisted men out of every 100,000. The pattern is particularly marked in the last five years, with the comparable figures being 44 women discharged for homosexual acts out of every 100,000 as against 4.4 men, a rate only one tenth of that for the women.

"Remember the Regiment!"

Ugandan president Yoweri Museveni's name means "Son of a Man of the Seventh," his father having had a distinguished record in the 7th King's African Rifles during World War II.

"The Old Lady Shows Her Medals."

Once given out rather sparingly, decorations have become somewhat less than uncommon, at least in the U.S. armed forces. Indeed, of late one even receives a medal just for enlisting. During the Vietnam War, the liberally dispensed National Defense Service Medal became known as the "warm body award," after its primary qualification. In 1986, the most recent year for which figures are available, Uncle Sam awarded his approximately 2,145,000 nieces and nephews on active duty 186,899 major decorations, or roughly one for every eleven people in uniform, counting only the Distinguished Service Medal, the Legion of Merit, the Meritorious Service Medal, and the Commendation Medal of each of the individual services. It was most difficult to avoid getting a decoration in the air force (593,000 on active duty), which gave out one for every 7.6 men and women under arms, followed by the army (771,000), which distributed one for every 7.9 of the troops. The sea services, in contrast, were rather less generous, the navy (582,000) being positively stingy, with one decoration for every 60.1 men and women, and the marines (198,000) absolutely niggardly, with one for every 86.7. This means that someone in the air force was about 1,110 percent more likely to get a decoration than someone in the marines, and over 700 percent more likely than someone in the navy, but was only 1.4 percent more likely to get one than someone in the army. When questioned about this, one leatherneck was heard to remark that the corps "doesn't pay a lot of attention to volume."

Rules We Kill By

The Geneva Convention, a series of agreements dating back to before World War I attempting to "humanize" warfare, contains a number of prohibitions. You aren't supposed to kill prisoners, but this is routinely done when there is no way to guard them, an action that the convention suggests may be permissible. You aren't supposed to use chemical weapons, but it wasn't the Geneva Convention that led nations to refrain from chemical warfare after World War I. Bullets that fragment after entering a soldier are forbidden, but most weapons in use today do just that at the normal short combat ranges. The most curious prohibition is of shotguns. Yet these were great favorites during World War I trench fighting. During the Vietnam War, soldiers at the lead ("point") of a patrol customarily carried a shotgun. No other weapon was more effective in fending off an unseen ambusher. The people who drafted the Geneva Convention were of good heart, but they should have studied their history. Several hundred years earlier the (then-more-influential) Roman Catholic Church attempted to ban the use of the crossbow. This met with much resistance, so the prohibition was lifted as long as the crossbow was used only against non-Christians. That didn't work, either.

Encouragement

"Give me enough ribbon and I'll give you an army of heroes."— Napoleon Bonaparte, dispenser of many medals

World-Class Warriors

There exists a series of military competitions—in effect, sporting events—that permit the armed forces of the world to "strut their stuff" without having to go through the unfortunate necessity of getting involved in a war. Thus, there is an annual Strategic Bomber Championship, in which various air forces demonstrate the accuracy of the bombardment techniques, with SAC or Britain's Bomber Command usually coming up the winners, and there is also a tactical-fighter competition, the Tiger Meet, held regularly in Belgium, and the World Reconnaissance Air Meet at Bergstom AFB, Texas, every other year. For ground forces, there are three important competitions. The Canadian Army Tank Gunnery Competition, held every two years, usually involves twenty to twenty-four tank platoons from various central-front armies, all competing for the "Canadian Cup." The Boeslager Challenge Cup, held annually by Britain, is a reconnaissance competition that usually involves twenty to twenty-five teams from as many as ten NATO powers engaging in various reconnaissance exercises. Then there are the World Helicopter Championships, which rotate among several NATO countries and involve choppers from as many as a dozen powers. These are, incidentally, all in the "NATO League," the Warsaw Pact having its own version of these activities.

In recent years, the U.S. Army has tended to dominate all three of the ground-forces competitions. In 1987 the United States swept the field, coming in first in all three, just eight years after being last in the first two and not even bothering to compete in the third. The principal reason for this remarkable turnaround appears to have been the introduction of more realistic training techniques, most notably at the National Training Center at Fort Irwin, California. On the other hand, the British, who were once consistent winners of the "Canadian Cup" for tank operations, have failed to finish at all in the last few years due to a poor tank. For more traditionally inclined soldier-athletes, there is also an annual military modern pentathlon that usually involves a half-dozen or so countries, including several of the European neutrals.

Rank and Privilege

From time to time, revolutionary armies have attempted to abolish the notion of hierarchical rank and the privilege attached to it. For many years following their respective revolutions, both the Soviet Workers' and Peasants' Red Army and the Chinese People's Liberation Army had no officers, but merely commanders: platoon commander, company commander, battalion commander, and so forth, right up to front commander. There was very little difference in uniform—the Chinese officer's tunic had four pockets instead of the two the enlisted men got by with. Rank badges and privileges were reduced to a minimum: At times in the history of both, the Red Army and the PLA officers even shared quarters, messes, and recreational facilities with the troops. But eventually even the most revolutionary armies revert to the more traditional patterns of officer/ enlisted man distinctions, as the PLA has recently begun to do, after several decades of revolutionary purity. There are a number of reasons for this. Functional rank titles—division commander, platoon commander—are satisfactory for personnel actually performing such duties, but are not particularly useful for officers performing administrative or logistical duties: Several European armies with "general of division" and "general of brigade" in their rank structure get around this by using special titles for officers not actually commanding such units. Similarly, the restoration of rank badges comes with increasing professionalism: Anyone wearing the badges is an officer and is to be obeyed, whereas in a badgeless army it's hard to tell the officers from the troops. Privilege follows logically as well, to suggest that the officers really are superior beings who ought to be obeyed. Besides, officers really do like the fancy uniforms.

The Rare Breed

"Under a good general there are no bad soldiers."—Chinese proverb

The Filipino Veterans Fairness Act

Filipinos have served in the U.S. armed forces for over ninety years, first as U.S. nationals and later under a special provision of the base agreement between the United States and the Republic of the Philippines that permits them to enlist even though they are neither U.S. citizens, nationals, nor resident aliens. Although many thousands of Filipinos have taken advantage of this provision and rendered long and faithful service—90 percent of them reenlist upon completion of their first enlistment—it turns out that because they are not resident aliens, they do not become naturalized American citizens upon completion of their first enlistment. As a result, the Filipino Veterans Fairness Act has been introduced into Congress to provide special immigrant status to anyone, not merely Filipinos, who properly completes an enlistment in the U.S. armed forces.

A Dangerous Job

During the Second World War, the German Army had to refill each officer slot an average of 9.2 times. In other words, the average unit went through more than nine commanders in the course of the war. Actually, the turnover in the combat arms was much higher than in support units. Adjusting for the distribution of casualties by branch, command of an infantry company changed due to death or injury at least once a month during the sixty-eight months Germany was at war. There is no reason to assume that the life expectancy of officers in any future major war will be much different.

Good Advice

"A soldier cannot afford to be pessimistic."—Maxwell Taylor, American general, World War II to Vietnam

Attention, All Hands! Stat!

In a classic illustration of a military "turf" battle, many years ago senior officers of the United States Navy Medical Corps engaged in a lengthy bureaucratic struggle with the navy in an effort to secure tactical command of hospital ships.

The Empire Is Secure. . . .

The British recently obtained a century's supply of one of their most critically important strategic materials when they purchased from China twenty kilograms of yak hair, which will be dyed scarlet in order to provide the plumes for officers of Her Majesty's Foot Guards.

But at Least Great-Grandpa Could Buy Something with It.

A recruit private in the Soviet Army currently earns about 5 rubles a month, roughly $8.00 at the official exchange rate, though as little as $1.20 at the black market rate. By either calculation, this rate of compensation is less than that which Ivan's great-grandfather received from the Tsar in 1914, about $11.00 a month on a "constant dollar" basis. And in "gold" rubles at that.

"Make Mine a . . ."

The American Seventh Army, which is stationed in Bavaria, the holy land of brewing, regularly consumes more cases of Miller, Coors, and Budweiser, shipped from the United States than it does of the headier local brews.

Regimental Reunion

Since the coup of General Ne Win in 1962, the government of Burma has been largely in the hands of veterans of the general's old regiment, the 4th Burma Rifles.

Real Uniformity

The Swedish Army has recently adopted its own brand of after-shave and a line of leisure wear in an effort to improve its image going into the trendy nineties.

La Mode Militaire

Like almost everyone else, soldiers are into fashion, and there are global trends in uniform style. At times this is complicated by military alliances. In the late nineteenth and early twentieth centuries, it was all "fuss and feathers," with oodles of gold braid and brass and plumes. Those nations friendly with Germany frequently adopted the pickelhaube helmet—with the spike on the top—while those on friendlier terms with France picked up the pillbox kepi, and those who admired Britain emulated the peaked cap. This admiration was often based on a nation's success at war. After the Germans trashed the French in 1870, the United States dropped the French-style uniforms and adopted the German models. After World War I, uniforms became more austere and businesslike, with virtually everyone adopting the British "Sam Browne" belt, which forced a man to brace as though he were a West Point cadet, and the peaked cap, introducing a homogenizing trend in uniforms that led to a monotony of appearance broken only by the French-style pillbox cap worn by a few Southern and Central European armies and by the pointy caps of the Red Army in the immediate post-Revolutionary period.

World War II led to a trend toward the American style in the Western bloc, and the Russian in the East, though on both sides the beret made an appearance, while the French clung to their pillboxes. In the 1960s, Maoism and Fidel Castro's successful revolution in Cuba, coupled with the Vietnam War, led to a global trend toward the wearing of the "revolutionary" fatigue uniform, which eventually infected even the "imperialist" powers, who came to favor its "rough-and-ready" macho image, though not the Russians, who remained quite formal. Lately, however, the trend seems to be back toward a more "soldierly" appearance. Curiously, the pacesetters have once again been the supposed revolutionaries. Castro has long since given up his fatigues for a well-tailored uniform with touches of gold braid, a practice in which he has been emulated by Daniel Ortega of Nicaragua and Muammar Qadaffi of Libya, while the U.S. Army has introduced epaulets on sweaters. And recently the Chinese People's Liberation Army, which abandoned insignia of rank and uniform adornments of any kind more than thirty years ago, announced that such will be reintroduced. Will the twentieth century go out with armies once again outfitted in gold and brass and plumes?

Battlefield Fashions

"I don't care how they dress so long as they mind their fighting."— Sir Thomas Picton, British general killed at Waterloo, 1815, when questioned about the slovenly appearance of his troops

Just How Tough Is She?

For most of 1987, the assistant adjutant of the 6th Queen's Own Gurkha Rifles was Second Lieutenant Anne Whittaker, the first woman officer to be assigned to the Gurkhas.

Bruised Dignity?

Ancient rules of protocol prescribe that visiting political, diplomatic, and military dignitaries be saluted upon their arrival and departure by various numbers of cannon shots and "ruffles and flourishes," drumrolls and trumpet blasts. Thus, the president or a visiting head of state will receive a twenty-one gun salute, four ruffles and flourishes, and the appropriate national anthem upon arrival or departure. The secretary of defense, and those of the army, navy, and air force, receive nineteen guns, four ruffles and flourishes, and an appropriate march or anthem upon arrival or departure, honors that they share with the members of the Joint Chiefs of Staff. This may seem reasonable, but why then do a number of at least equally important dignitaries, such as the vice president, the speaker of the House, the president pro tempore of the Senate, the Chief Justice, and all the other members of the Cabinet, as well as ambassadors and prime ministers, receive the nineteen guns, the four ruffles and flourishes, and the march only upon their arrival?

Yeah, but the Job Can Be a Real Killer.

The General Accounting Office has calculated that, including only pay, medical, and retirement benefits, military compensation is now 27 percent higher on average than that of comparable federal civil-service employees, who, moreover, lack PXs, dependents' allowances, and similar benefits, though they are not subject to certain occupational hazards common to the military persuasion.

Where the Boys Are

Of the approximately 2,140,000 U.S. military personnel on active duty at the end of 1988, about

1,330,000 (62.2%) are stationed in the 48 contiguous states,
46,900 (2.2%) are in Hawaii,
21,500 (1%) are in Alaska,
8,970 (0.4%) in Guam,

3,650 (0.2%) are in Puerto Rico, and

142 (0.001%) are on Johnston Island, in the central Pacific. Of the rest, about

190,000 (8.8%) are stationed afloat, based in U.S. territorial waters

54,000 (2.5%) are stationed afloat overseas, beyond U.S. territorial waters. Also, at any given moment, nearly

48,000 (2.2%) U.S. military personnel are in transit from one station to another. The balance, about

451,000 men and women, are stationed in several dozen different countries, in 21 of which there are actual U.S. bases. The largest contingents are in:

West Germany	250,000 (11.7% of all troops)
Japan	55,000 (2.5%)
South Korea	43,900 (2%)
Britain	29,700 (1.4%)
Philippines	16,300 (0.8%)
Italy	14,900 (0.7%)
Panama	10,400 (0.5%)

While many of the places where U.S. personnel are stationed are fairly exotic, such as Thailand (115) and Bahrain (120), and some undoubtedly a secret, it is unlikely that many troops can have a more curious situation than the 2,500 in Cuba.

School Days

In an average year, about 6,300 foreign military personnel, mostly from NATO or other allied nations, are in training in the United States.

Lifers

Lifers are the professional cadre of the armed forces, people who are making military service a career. Lifers are often considered a most peculiar and miserable life form by new enlistees, whom they continually entice into "reupping" so that they, too, can become lifers. The term *lifer* comes from prison slang for someone doing a life sentence. Many terms regarding military service are derived from prison slang. Make of that what you will.

Re-Up Rates

Statistically, nearly half (49.25 percent) of first-time enlistees in the U.S. armed forces reenlist for a second term. Not everyone who wants to reenlist is allowed to. The military can raise or lower the standards for reenlistment depending on how many volunteers they are getting and/or how many people Congress allows them to have on active duty. Thus, personnel strength can be maintained by varying the overall quality of the troops. The air force has the highest reenlistment rate, about 65 percent, followed by the navy, with 55 percent, and the army, with 42 percent, while the marines trail behind with 35 percent. Among career-enlisted personnel—that is, men and women who have served two or more enlistments—the reenlistment rate is nearly 85 percent. The army leads with 92 percent, followed closely by the air force, with 89 percent, while the marines are third with 80 percent, and the navy last with only 77 percent. Nearly all of those who reenlist a second time will stay for twenty years and thus qualify for a pension equal to half their active-duty pay. Such long-term volunteers must maintain a good record. They are expected to maintain their technical skills, which are tested periodically. They are also expected to qualify for promotion after a certain number of years in each grade. Promotions are made based on the number of open slots there are in each grade. There are nine pay grades for enlisted personnel, three grades of private, and six of NCOs. To make twenty years, you have to reach at least grade six, midway up the NCO ladder.

And Safest, Too

"Those who have not yet realized danger are generally the bravest soldiers."—Colmar von der Goltz, German field marshal, World War I

"How Do You Say That in . . . ?"

Despite its being the "Nation of Immigrants," mastery of foreign languages has never been very widespread in the United States. Most secondary schools and many colleges do not have a foreign-language requirement for graduation. This creates a particular problem for the armed forces, which stand in need of people fluent in many languages. In a survey of over 100,000 officers in the army, Army Reserve, and National Guard, only 11.6 percent were found to have "any recorded proficiency in a foreign language, and only 0.5 percent were classed as having or exceeding "limited working proficiency"—the middle level on a five-point scale from "no proficiency" to "functionally native proficiency"—in listening and reading skills. In an attempt to remedy this situation, the Defense Department operates one of the most extensive language schools in the world, the Defense Language Institute, at Monterey, California, which provides basic and advanced instruction in various languages of which military personnel are likely to find themselves in need, such as Persian, Malay, Polish, Korean, and Russian, and about two dozen others. The school does not always succeed as well as it would like to. CIA linguists often disparagingly call the graduates "Monterey Marys." Aside from a large block of officers whose linguistic skills are of unknown origin, of those with "any recorded proficiency," about 23 percent acquired it at the DLIC, and of those with "limited working proficiency," about 10 percent acquired it at the DLIC. Of course, the most sought-after linguists are those who grew up with a foreign language. Fortunately, the United States has a large number of immigrants who enlist and find themselves getting paid to use their mother tongue.

Bye-Bye, Happy Hour

In an effort to reduce drinking and alcohol dependency among military personnel, the U.S. armed forces have banned so-called "happy hours," during which the price of drinks is greatly reduced, at all clubs on military bases. This comes on the heels of bans on cursing and on smoking. The only bad habit left that's still acceptable is occasionally shooting foreigners.

Chiefs Versus Indians

As of September 30, 1988, the authorized strength of the active elements of the U.S. armed forces was 2,137,300 men and women, of whom 304,695 "may be officers," which gives a ratio of six "other ranks" for every officer. Although the actual number of officers and "other ranks" on active duty is usually lower than this, the official figures give the Marine Corps, with 177,080 enlisted personnel and 20,120 officers, an enlisted-to-officer ratio of 8.8:1 the best record of any of the services. The navy, with 510,590 enlistees and 72,610 officers, is close behind at 7.0:1, trailed by the army's 664,873 enlistees and 106,927 officers for 6.1:1, and the air force, which at 470,062 enlisted personnel and 105,038 officers, has an extraordinarily low ratio of only 4.4:1, just half that of the marines. Note that the Russian armed forces, which lack an adequate supply of NCOs and enlisted technicians, use officers to replace many of these two enlisted functions. Even with this, the enlisted-to-officer ratio is only 6:1. This is partially due to the Russian adoption of the German attitude toward officers, which stresses quality over quantity.

How's It Look, General?

One of the "good news/bad news" aspects of new communications technology is the ability of senior commanders to keep in direct touch with the troops at the front. The good news is that the generals are less likely to lose touch with reality, as often happened in World War I. The bad news is that many senior commanders take advantage of the technology to direct small units like companies, platoons, and squads. This happened frequently during Vietnam. Radio contact from the White House to a rifle platoon north of Saigon is one thing, but now you can instantly send pictures. In the late 1980s, the U.S. Army began using a system that allowed TV pictures taken by scout helicopters to be sent back, as still photos, by regular military VHF-FM radio. Each picture takes about half a minute to transmit and can immediately be displayed on a TV monitor. The received picture can also be blown up and manipulated in other useful ways. In addition to TV images, heat sensors can also transmit their images straight back to headquarters.

Actually, this technique can be a big help if the senior commanders resist the temptation to second-guess the commanders lower down the chain of command. This will be difficult, because the senior commanders have access to more equipment than their more mobile juniors. What will happen is that the division commander will sometimes have a better view of the frontline situation than the platoon, company, or battalion commanders at the scene. As it may have been ten to twenty years since the division commander led one of these smaller units, you are likely to have a clash of opinions on how to deal with the situation. In limited-war situations, this massive array of communications capabilities does have its uses. During the Persian Gulf operations in 1988, Pentagon commanders were often in instant communication with the ship captains on the spot. This allowed for many politically sensitive moves to be referred back to Washington. Fortunately, the answers were usually quick in coming. But in a larger war, the situation would be much more complex, and less politically sensitive. Many of these potential problems won't be clarified until there is an actual war in which to try out all these new gimmicks.

Intellectual Failure

"In war, the qualities of the character are more important than the intellect."—Fritz Halder, German Chief-of-the General Staff, 1938–42, who failed the test of character

The Dark Side of Military Tradition

In most Western armed forces, new recruits fresh out of basic training join their units still somewhat bewildered by it all. The older troops, particularly the ones with only a year or so of military experience themselves, are quick to help the newcomers find their way around. This attitude is another of those "military traditions." But in the Russian armed forces, at least since the early 1950s, the approach to rookies is somewhat different. The Red Army troops call it "dedovshchina" (dominance of the old-timers) and the purpose is not to help the new guy out but to make him do your dirty work. In systems like this, there are two things going on. First, the new troops only have to put up with it for about a year, then they can pull the same thing on the next group of new recruits. Second, the officers tolerate the practice either because they don't care to rock the boat or because "it toughens the troops." The only places in the West where this sort of thing was regularly practiced was in U.S. military academies.

Well, times change. During the 1970s, the academies assiduously began to try to change these exploitative attitudes. The reasons were straightforward: The "hazing" caused a lot of cadets to leave the service in disgust, and no one was able to prove that all the abuse had any positive effect. The Russians didn't have as much of a problem with the oppressed troops leaving the service prematurely as these fellows were conscripts, in for two or three years whether they liked it or not. And their officer candidates are less likely to leave the academies, because there are few better opportunities in the civilian sector. The major problem in the Russian forces has been morale and efficiency, both of which suffered under the "domination" system. Moreover, the increased percentage of non-Russians (mostly Asiatic Moslems) in Russian combat units was adding racial overtones to the exploitation. Many of the non-Russian troops found themselves on the short end of the stick for their entire period of service. Often this domination resulted in injuries from beatings delivered by the "grandfathers" to maintain their privileges. These injuries are listed as "accidents," and of late the Russian military press admits that these numerous "accidents" are the result of troops fighting each other. In the late 1980s, the Russian high command began to take official notice of the exploitation tradition that had existed in the Russian forces for many generations. They soon discovered that talking about it was a lot easier than doing something about it.

How *Not* to Evaluate
Unit Readiness for Combat

Most nations have some system for inspection and/or testing to determine unit readiness and capability for combat. This procedure usually consists of a written exam as well as drills to demonstrate troop knowledge of their skills and the unit's ability to perform its combat mission. In light of how this is usually done, here are a few pointers on how to insure that it won't work (it usually doesn't):

1. Don't allocate a lot of importance to combat-capability evaluation. It's much more important that the equipment and troops look

good and that all those administrative items be in top shape. After all, you have to live with noncombat items every day, and a war may never come: Real soldiering is a peacetime profession.

2. Make sure the troops have memorized a lot of facts about weapons characteristics and procedures. This knowledge is easy to evaluate. Don't bother taking a lot of time working on the questions; take them right out of the technical manuals. The troops should be reading these things constantly anyway instead of spending a lot of time working with their gear and finding ways to wear it out.

3. Don't worry if the troops are able to get a copy of the tests beforehand. This will allow them to brush up and make a good showing. Don't sweat it if the officers coach the troops on how to respond to questions and drills to be used. This will make the training officer's job much easier.

4. Don't worry if the test is not realistic. Realism is too complicated and will just muddy the waters.

5. The only score that is important is the one for the entire unit. This way you can have a few ace troops carry all the duds. It's too much trouble to get all the troops up to speed anyway.

6. These evaluations are such a hassle that they should be run infrequently. Not quarterly, semiannually, or yearly, but every few years.

7. Make sure that commanders are so intent on making a good showing on the standardized evaluation that they neglect any special training to reflect their particular mission or location. Let's keep everything neat throughout the armed forces.

Sad to say, most armed forces follow the spirit, if not the letter, of the above seven items.

The Big Picture

"Soldiers are close students of tactics, but only rarely of strategy and practically never of war."—Bernard Brodie, American defense theoretician

Draft-Dodging in Russia

At age nineteen, nearly every healthy Russian male goes into the military for two years (army and air force) or three years (navy and security forces). Those in college must train for an officer's commission and eventually serve in the reserve. Some youths have always managed to avoid service through real or faked disability or through family influence. Until *glasnost* came along, the positive patriotic aspects of service were played up, and the negative aspects were ignored. It was not considered good manners for those who had been in the armed forces to be too frank about how bad military life was with young lads who had not yet gone in. Now, the Russian media have made a minor industry of revealing how uncomfortable service actually is. Not only is there more draft-dodging among the Slavic half of the population, but such evasion has reached serious proportions among the non-Slavic half. Particularly in Central Asia, over 20 percent of the expected draftees somehow don't make it to the induction centers. Now, the Russian media is doing a lot of stories about draft-dodging, no doubt giving even more exposure to one of the less-pleasant aspects of Russian citizenship.

Career Versus Family

Women attempting to make a career in the armed forces suffer very much the same life choices as do women trying to make a career in the business world. A recent study revealed that only 21 percent of navy women married to civilians had children, in contrast to 70 percent of navy men.

AIDS

By early 1988, the U.S. armed forces had completed testing virtually everyone on active duty for the HIV virus, with the result that nearly 3,400 of the 2.1 million men and women in uniform were found to be infected by the AIDS-causing virus, which is statistically 1.6 cases per 1,000, a rate approximately twice that prevailing in the general population, but one not unreasonable given the gender and age profile of persons in military service.

"Please Follow Washing Directions Carefully."

The U.S. Army's standard polypropylene winter long underwear—irreverently nicknamed the "PP underwear" by the troops—shrinks if washed in hot water, placed in a heated dryer, or exposed to the heat of a fire. This last circumstance is a typical way of drying wet clothing under combat conditions.

Recruits

The U.S. armed forces consist wholly of volunteers. To maintain a strength of 2.1 million men and women, over 60,000 new recruits must be enticed to join each year. Toward the end of the 1980s, this became more difficult. The military is able to overcome these shortfalls by trading quality for quantity. Normally, the military does not want to recruit any of the two lowest of five mental classes. No Category 5 volunteers are allowed in, and the Category 4 people have limited employment opportunities in the service, being more expensive and difficult to train. The army and the navy can absorb a larger number of Category 4 troops, up to 15 percent before suffering any noticeable damage. The air force cannot absorb even 10 percent Category 4. The marines manage to avoid taking Category 4, because they are the smallest service and their glamorous image attracts a larger number of volunteers.

Officer-Training Patterns

Although all nations give their prospective officers some university-equivalent institutional education, there are essentially three basic patterns of officer training in the world. The most common, which may be termed the "European" tradition, is to take young men just out of secondary school and run them through a trade school–type military academy for one to four years, with a curriculum that concentrates on professional subjects to the virtual exclusion of anything else except the social graces. The "American" pattern resembles this, except that the U.S. military academies are essentially engineering and liberal-arts colleges with a heavy emphasis on things military, even granting academic degrees, and in wartime anyone with a university degree can become an officer with ninety days' training. The third pattern, which may be termed the "German" model, requires a minimum of one year's service in the ranks before attendance at a military academy, which in wartime becomes one year's service at the front before an academy. The European model is used by most European countries and their former dependencies, while the American model is primarily limited to the United States. The German pattern is used by Germany and Israel, which requires two years' service in the ranks from officer candidates. In terms of professionalism, the German pattern produces the best troop leaders, though history demonstrates that the product may perhaps be focused too narrowly on professional concerns.

The Perfect Warrior?

"Any fool can obey orders."—Sir John "Jackie" Fisher, architect of the World War I British Navy

The Grandsons of Beau Geste

The French Foreign Legion still soldiers on, with some 8,550 troops scattered worldwide, from Polynesia to Africa to South America. They comprise the largest purely mercenary army in the world, with three battalions of infantry, plus one each of parachutists, light tanks, and engineers, plus three providing various types of technical support or services. Terms of service are still the traditional five years, and discipline is still tough, but the French seem to have little difficulty finding recruits, there apparently being more than enough adventurous—or heartbroken—souls to fill the ranks of the Legion, which has 350 officers, including—what would Sergeant Markov say!—at least 1 woman, 1,400 noncommissioned officers, and 6,800 enlisted men. A recent survey revealed that the largest group in the Legion was ethnic Germans, totaling 11.3 percent of the troops, followed by Spaniards, numbering 3.4 percent, Belgians, 2.5 percent, and Italians, 2.1 percent. Britons and Irishmen together totaled 3.5 percent, while Canadians and Americans accounted for only 0.9 percent, fewer than the supposedly unromantic, pacifistic, and far less numerous Scandinavians, who totaled 1.0 percent. Other "nationalities" represented were Eastern Europeans, 5.0 percent, Middle Eastern Arabs, 2.5 percent, North African Arabs, 2.2 percent, Latin Americans, 1.4 percent, and Sub-Saharan Africans, 0.7 percent. However, fully 63.5% of the men in the Legion are classified as "other," most of whom are probably French, technically barred from serving in the Legion.

The Angolan Foreign Legion

In 1988 South Africa and Cuba agreed to withdraw support for the warring Angolan factions each had backed in the fourteen-year-old Angola civil war. This conflict began when Angola became independent from Portugal in 1975, and the country promptly lapsed into a civil war between two allegedly Communist revolutionary groups, FAPLA and UNITA. FAPLA got to the cities first and established a government. Before UNITA could run them out, several Communist nations rushed in with aid and a grab-bag of troops. By the late 1980s, this Foreign Legion ran to more than 70,000 troops, consisting of:

> 50,000 Cubans (possibly more)
> 2,500 North Koreans
> 2,000 Russians
> 1,000 East Germans
> 600 Portuguese (possibly more)
> 7,000 SWAPO rebels from Namibia
> 1,400 Katangan rebels from Zaire
> 10,000 ANC guerrillas from South Africa (possibly half as many)

The African groups, although there primarily to support insurgencies in their homeland, generally wore FAPLA uniforms and pretended to be government troops. Sometimes these foreign African troops were engaged by UNITA troops, but this was an exception. The FAPLA forces consist of 80,000 regular troops and 60,000 part-time local-defense forces. The opposition UNITA forces control about a third of Angola's territory and use 28,000 full-time troops to hold this area, while another 37,000 guerrilla troops operate in FAPLA-controlled territory. Because the FAPLA was hostile to South Africa and gave sanctuary and support to South African rebel groups, UNITA received substantial military aid from South Africa. Large amounts of ammunition and equipment were supplied by the United States from dumps in Zaire.

UNITA has been successful in shutting down the country's transportation system. The railroads are useless, and truck convoys between major urban areas operate only once every one or two months. These convoys consist of hundreds of vehicles and thousands of troops plus aircraft and helicopters. Even so, they are often attacked. FAPLA uses its more lavishly equipped forces to go after UNITA infrastructure, which is hidden away in remote areas. In the past, when major FAPLA forces got too close in these major drives, South Africa committed its own forces. The withdrawal of the Cubans, South Africans, and other nonlocals as a result of a U.S.-sponsored peace plan may significantly alter the character of the war: Hitherto, in many cases combat was largely between Cuban and South African troops, with FAPLA and UNITA forces looking on.

The Russian Tradition of "Scientific Warfare"

Each nation has its military traditions, and these usually go back for centuries. Russia picked up a lot of its ideas from the Germans, whom they have been fighting for over a thousand years. One concept the Russians acquired from the Germans in the 1800s was the use of quantitative "norms:" They count the activities going on during military operations and deduce average "norms" for each of these activities. For example, troops require a certain number of hours to prepare trenches in certain types of soil in a particular season. Most Russian officers carry a little book of norms in their pocket. Troops are intensively drilled to execute activities in a certain way within a certain amount of time. All armies use this approach to a certain extent. Gun crews of all armed forces and all branches of the service (land, air, and sea) learn a precise drill for operating weapons. The Russian angle is to apply these drills to just about everything. In this way, a division or army commander can give orders with reasonable assurance that his subordinate units will perform these tasks within a predictable amount of time. The Russians still recognize less predictable factors, such as the abilities of enemy troops and the actual performance of their own troops. The Russian military press is always complaining about the failings of many officers and inadequate training. What it comes down to is that in Western armies the lowest-ranking troops and officers have leeway for initiative and imagination, while in the Russian Army one must become a general before one is allowed to deviate from the drills.

From One Who Knew

"If men make war in slavish obedience to rules, they will fail."—Ulysses S. Grant, Union Army commander, 1864–65

Dreamland

"Fortunate is the general staff which sees a war fought the way it intends."—Richard M. Watt, military historian

Purging the Bozos

One valuable lesson of military history is the importance of getting rid of the worst officers and troops. This is not really a problem in peacetime, even though these folks tend to rise in the military establishment. In war, however, they can prove a handicap. Combat usually gets rid of them, but as long as the inept are still in charge, a unit continues to take excessive losses. Inept troops are a real danger to their more-skilled companions. Often units do not survive the weeding-out process in combat, since it usually takes place when units enter combat for the first time. It's not unusual for units to be wiped out in their first combat. Peacetime armies have a very difficult time identifying and purging the inept among them. Meanwhile, a likely solution has appeared. The United States has developed a large-scale version of laser tag in which entire battalions can "fight" each other under very realistic conditions. This has exposed a significant number of officers and troops who fall apart under such realistic stress.

Two serious problems uncovered were officers who didn't sleep through the several-day exercise and became so punch-drunk toward the end that they were unable to function. Another problem was the officer who would try to do everything and end up with massive disorganization. Any officer found to have either of these traits now has rather bleak career prospects. Although the official policy is not to penalize officers and troops found wanting during these exercises, in practice careers are being made and unmade during these electronic combats. In Russia, many officers back the announced reduction in armed forces' strength as an opportunity to purge the less enthusiastic of their members. There is no easy way for the Russians to ferret out their less-capable officers, but everyone knows there are a lot of them.

The Value of Bozos

"One bad general is worth two good ones."—Napoleon Bonaparte, emperor of the French, who won most of his battles, except for the last few. Made a career of finding, and defeating, inept enemy generals.

Equal Opportunity

"Battles are not always fought by efficient soldiers."—Rafael de Nogales Bey, Japanese spy, Nicaraguan muckraker, and Turkish general

Weekend Warriors?

Although the members of the reserve components of the armed forces are generally considered part-time soldiers, of somewhat more than 1.1 million men and women in the reserves and National Guard, 71,595 (6.1 percent) actually serve full time, for "the purpose of organizing, administrating, recruiting, instructing, or training the reserve components," and they are not counted as part of the active armed forces.

The Long Arm of Conscription

Nations whose armed forces are filled with conscripts take a dim view of citizens who leave the country to avoid military service. The usual drill is that anyone leaving while still liable for service will inform the conscription bureaucracy beforehand. If the individual's number comes up, he or she will be told to return from abroad and join the ranks. Failure to return causes varying amounts of trouble for the reluctant draftee, depending on the nation's circumstances. In most cases, draft dodgers are subject to arrest if they eventually return, followed by a choice between the military or prison. In some cases, the authorities get downright nasty. In early 1989, Iran announced that all Iranians who had left the country, legally or illegally, to avoid conscription had until March 8, 1989, to return. Failure to do so would result in the miscreants being declared deserters. The penalty for desertion in Iran is death.

Get Me Some Armed Fools.

"None but fools can deny that they are afraid in battle."—John Gibbon, American Civil War general

Betting on a Winner

A Russian tank company has three platoons of three tanks each, and a command tank. During training it is not unheard of for company commanders to funnel all their training allotments of fuel and ammunition to the three most efficient crews, and then to use those tanks to take the proficiency tests for the entire company, thereby raising the overall unit performance. This technique is not unknown in many other armed forces as well.

Up and Out in the Russian Army

Westerners get the impression that the Soviet armed forces are full of elderly officers and surly teenage conscripts. While the young conscripts are not particularly enthusiastic, only the senior officers are senescent, and most of the rest of the officers are quite young. Division commanders are frequently in their thirties. The majority of officers retire to a second civilian career after twenty or thirty years of service. The small percentage of officers who prove they are exceptionally capable are retained, often into their sixties and seventies. Once officers have achieved senior rank, they are faced with two problems. One is the enormous amount of power and physical comfort given them. These generals and admirals are truly a privileged class. Human nature being what it is, many of these "princes" become more concerned about hanging on to the goodies than in using their power to improve the forces under their command. The second problem is that senior commanders, unlike their subordinates, are expected to use considerable initiative and imagination in the maintenance and use of their forces. This is how Russia wins its wars. But in wartime, it's easy to see who is screwing up and who isn't. During World War II, several hundred Russian generals were executed or imprisoned for poor performance. Echoes of that Draconian approach can still be seen, as when the young German pilot Mathias Rust landed a single-engine aircraft in Red Square in 1987. Soon thereafter, several very senior Russian Air Force commanders went into early retirement. Similar, less visible flubs have even resulted in executions and imprisonment.

Advice and Consent

In the course of the Hundredth Congress, 1987–88, the U.S. president submitted the names of 81,805 men and women for commissioning or promotion as officers. By the end of the second session of the Congress, October 22, 1988, 81,795 of the nominations had been confirmed, a rate of virtually 100 percent. Of the remaining ten nominees, four had not been confirmed, four had been returned for reconsideration, and two had been withdrawn by the president. The air force had the lion's share of the nominations, 31,015 (37.9 percent), followed by the army, with 24,944 (30.5 percent), the navy, 22,258 (27.2 percent), and the marines, 3,578 (4.4 percent).

Academic Interlude

The total enrollment at the five U.S. military academies averages about 15,700 men and women. The U.S. Naval Academy at Annapolis is the largest, with about 5,400 midshipmen, followed by the Air Force Academy at Colorado Springs, with some 4,350 cadets, and the Military Academy at West Point, with 4,250 cadets. The Coast Guard Academy at New London and the Merchant Marine Academy at Kings Point each have about 850 midshipmen. Total faculty, many of whom are civilians, runs to about 1,860, with Annapolis having the largest number, about 600, followed by Colorado Springs, with about 575, West Point, with 500, New London, 110, and Kings Point, 75. Most U.S. officers come from ROTC programs, special air-cadet programs, OCS for former enlisted men, and direct commissioning of medical and other technical specialists. In contrast, Russia gets almost all its officers from military academies, which have an enrollment of over 200,000.

A Bit Worse Than Calculus

"No art or science is as difficult that that of war."—Henry Humphrey Evans Lloyd, eighteenth-century British military analyst

Ring-Knocking, the Distaff Side

Although they wash out at slightly higher rates than do male cadets, female cadets have had about the same degree of success at each of the three service academies. Both the Air Force Academy, which admits about 180 women each year, of whom about 101 graduate, and West Point, which admits 148 annually, of whom about 83 graduate, have the same dropout rate for female cadets, 43.9 percent, while Annapolis admits an average of 107 women each year and graduates only 63, for a slightly better failure rate of 41.2 percent. At all three institutions, the dropout rate for male cadets is about a third.

Women Warriors

The United States has the highest proportion of women on active service in the armed forces of any major power. There are approximately 221,200 women on active duty, comprising slightly more than 10 percent of the total active force. Proportionally, women comprise:

1.9% (10) of the brigadier generals and rear admirals "lower half"
2.2% (327) of the colonels and navy captains
4.3% (1,426) of the lieutenant colonels and commanders
8.3% (4,441) of the majors and lieutenant commanders

12.8% (13,567) of the captains and navy lieutenants

14.3% (6,608) of the first lieutenants and navy lieutenants j.g.

15.8% (5,449) of the second lieutenants and ensigns

 2.2% (432) of the warrant officers

 1.2% (632) of the senior NCOs

 8.5% (63,312) of the junior NCOs, and

11.8% (124,936) of the other enlisted personnel

The service with the greatest proportion of women on active duty is the

Air Force	75,000	(13.5%), followed by the
Army	83,000	(10.1%)
Navy	57,000	(9.3%)
Marines	6,200	(4.8%)

Women in the Trenches

Although still legally barred from taking part in combat, women in the U.S. armed forces have been getting closer to the front all the time. Nurses, of course have long served under fire. More recently, a number of women took part in the Grenada and Panama operations, many going in virtually with the first waves of the invasion forces. Women are now qualified to fly AWACS and SR-71 aircraft, both of which must go "in harm's way" in the performance of their duties, and, most recently, have been permitted to "man" ICBM silos, initially on an all-female, but now on a mixed-sex basis. The army wants to expand the role of women further, and has conducted experiments to study the performance of women in a variety of combat situations and roles.

Women and Weapons

Although women are increasingly insinuating themselves ever more deeply into the fabric of military life on a global scale, few countries are giving them more than a passing familiarity with the tools of war. Although many Third World countries make a show ot conscripting women and putting them through regular military training, it is the more developed nations that have been the most progressive in this regard. Denmark has gone the furthest. Perhaps because of widespread pacifism, the Danes allow women, who must volunteer for military service, in all combat roles, including tank-crew members, warship captains, and combat pilots, with the curious omission of fighter pilots. Israel, which is the only important power to draft women in peacetime, trains women in the use of a wide variety of weapons, but no longer permits them to fight, as was the case in the War of Independence (1948–49). The United States is probably next, and while most women receive only basic-weapons training, some are being commissioned as officers in the combat arms and being assigned closer and closer to the front, as demonstrated in Panama, and are now permitted to fly reconnaissance aircraft. Cuba enrolls women in the air defense artillery and provides a wide range of infantry training. A few other countries give women training in a variety of infantry weapons, but little or no tactical training beyond basic self-defense. These include Canada, France, the Netherlands, and Sweden, as well as Greece and Russia, both of which also draft women in wartime, the latter having made extensive use of women in certain combat roles—military police, signals, snipers, pilots, artillery—in World War II. Surprisingly, Switzerland, the home of the citizen-soldier, provides weapons training for women only if they specifically volunteer for it.

They Should Know.

"Nobody dislikes war more than warriors."—Daniel James, Jr., military analyst

Underground Sex

After a yearlong trial by volunteer personnel, and over the objections of military wives, the air force has decided to permit mixed male and female crews to stand tours of duty together in the underground control rooms of ICBM installations. Out of fear of sexual "misconduct" and under pressure from service wives, air-force policy had long prohibited the mixing of men and women in the two-person crews, who are locked up together in the control rooms for twenty-four-hour stretches. However, this policy caused numerous difficulties. If one member of a two-woman crew was unavailable for duty, her partner had to be relieved as well, since she was prohibited from serving with a male replacement. The result was that male officers sometimes found themselves serving extra duty. While women in the air force have welcomed the move as career-enhancing, air-force wives remain concerned.

Turning Russian Civilians into Soldiers

In Western nations, the traditional method for turning civilians into soldiers is to put them through a traumatic process known as "basic training" or "boot camp." This is two or more months of intense physical training and instruction in weapons, military customs, and other skills. In Russia things are different. There is no basic-training period. When a young man is called up, he spends a few days getting his uniform and attending lectures, and is then flown to East Germany, one of the other satellites, or some distant part of Russia to join his unit. Nearly half the new recruits are sent to a school for special training. For example, 15 percent are selected for a six-month NCO course, and others go to schools for technical subjects, usually for only a few months. But most of the combat troops go straight to combat units.

However, Russian conscripts are not totally unprepared for military life. There are various paramilitary youth organizations, which about 90 percent of students join shortly after they begin school, and there is some "premilitary" training in high school. Many of the activities of these organizations are similar to scouting in the West. The major difference is that the older kids are trained to handle a number of weapons. The high percentage of youth enrolled is partially due to social and academic pressure and the fact that these organizations control most of the sports facilities and programs. Besides, most teenage boys are quite keen on playing with real weapons. Unfortunately, the quality of the military training in these youth programs varies considerably throughout Russia.

The non-Russian half of the population receives very uneven pre-conscription military training. This, combined with the inability of many of these non-Russians to even read or speak Russian, presents the combat-unit commanders with severe training problems. Conscripts are called up twice a year for two or three years' service, and constitute about 75 percent of the troops in combat units. Thus, every six months a combat unit loses 18 percent of its best-trained troops, which are replaced with increasingly raw recruits. The percentage of non-Russian and poorly prepared conscripts grows each year. By the turn of the century, it will be nearly 60 percent.

The Old Guard

The most experienced pilots and ground crew in the U.S. Air Force are the part-timers of the Air National Guard. The only squadrons with combat veterans and pilots with thousands of hours of flight time are in the Guard. Equally important are the experienced ground crews, many with over twenty years' service and a number who are aircraft mechanics in their civilian lives. National Guard squadrons frequently outperform regular air-force units in joint exercises. Guard pilots are usually regulars who resigned in order to keep flying aircraft instead of desks. In the air force, pilots are expected to rotate into nonflying positions from time to time. Really eager pilots would rather just fly their high-performance jets. In the National Guard, pilots can do just that on weekends, and clean up as commercial pilots in the bargain.

And Lots of Money

"War is a complicated business that can be mastered only by intelligence and application."—Gordon A. Craig, American military historian

The Navy Family

With 80 percent of career personnel married, and 25 percent of junior enlisted personnel, the navy finds that there are 1.2 dependents for every person on active duty. Anticipating increased morale problems, the navy, assisted by the Marine Corps, convened a three-day conference to review the needs of service-connected families.

Among particular concerns were how to help young service couples adjust to military life, how to deliver services to the dependents of personnel on extended overseas deployments, day-care needs of service families, and improved procedures for informing dependents of news concerning their sailor kinfolk in the event of hostilities or accidents. Of particular concern was the problem of "child-development centers." Since military personnel are on call on a twenty-four hour basis, there is a need for such "day-care" facilities to be operated around the clock. As one officer observed, "The days of the attitude of 'If we wanted you to have a family, we would have issued you one,' are over." The assistant commandant of the Marine Corps said, "Mission-readiness is not limited to equipment repair and supply availability. A marine with his or her mind on family concerns is not giving 100 percent to the job at hand."

The Military Family

There are about 1.3 dependents for every man and woman on active duty with the armed forces, for a total of about 2,850,000. The army has the largest number of dependents, about 1,050,000, or roughly 1.4 for each soldier. The air force follows, with about 885,000 dependents, nearly 1.5 per man or woman on active duty, statistically the highest rate of all the services, while the navy, with about 706,000 dependents, has only 1.2 per person in uniform. The marines, which has a relatively small professional cadre, has only 215,000 dependents, statistically less than 1.1 per leatherneck.

The Educated Soldier

About 93 percent of first-time recruits in the armed forces have a high school diploma, with the air force having the highest proportion of high school grads among its recruits, 99 percent, followed by the Marine Corps, with 96 percent, and the army and navy, each with 91 percent. If there are fewer volunteers for military service, a likely event in the 1990s because of the shrinking pool of young people, the military can simply take more nongraduate volunteers.

Soldiers and Sailors, and Poets, Too

It may come as a surprise, but the only U.S. military journal to publish verse on a regular basis is *Leatherneck*, which frequently contains poetic paeans to the Marine Corps or the military life.

Sex, Drugs, and Rock and Roll in the Red Army

Well, two out of three ain't bad. Russian troops are still kept away from women as much as possible. But since the 1970s, conscripts have had more access to rock music. And since the 1960s, army service was often a means of being introduced to recreational drugs. Since the 1960s, Russian troops stationed in Central Asia have had access to hashish and similar drugs. Such drugs have long been produced in that area, largely for export. A long-standing Russian custom sent conscripts from Slavic areas to non-Slavic regions.

Afghanistan, with a less repressive government, had an even larger drug-producing operation. When Russian troops invaded Afghanistan, they found themselves in the midst of a vast outdoor pharmacy. Supplies of vodka were short, so hash took up the slack. The Afghans would take military equipment in payment instead of money. By the late 1980s, it was discovered that 27 percent of drug users had begun in the army, and most of the others picked it up from pushers or friends who had first got high in uniform. At that point, there were about 500,000 drug users in Russia. This is small compared to the millions of alcoholics, but Russia doesn't need yet another debilitating vice. Drugs in the military have been around for a while. In the 1950s, a regulation was put into effect prohibiting the sending of parcels from Russia to Russian troops in Eastern Europe because of the contraband found in many parcels, including drugs.

Safe Sex

Russian conscripts are kept in their barracks most of the time when not performing their military duties. But sexual urges remain a problem. Although homosexual activity is not exactly rampant, it does exist, as much as a form of domination as for sexual gratification. The army finally decided to confront the problem in the late eighties, and began publishing articles in soldiers' periodicals on the benefits of masturbation.

"Coffee, Tea, or . . .?"

One of the peculiarities of modern military life is the "doughnut dolly," a female Red Cross or similar volunteer who hands out coffee and doughnuts to the troops in an effort to boost their morale, when what they really want is the volunteer.

Canvas, or Toke That Tent

The name of that militarily useful substance "canvas" is derived from the word *cannabis*, which is the genus for the hemp family of plants, as in *Cannabis sativa*, another substance that has occasionally been found to be militarily useful.

Russian "Blue Suiters"

In 1948 the U.S. Air Force was created from the old Army Air Forces. The devil-may-care "flyboys" soon became technically inclined "blue suiters." In Russia a similar event occurred in 1959, when the army lost its strategic missile units, which went to form the Strategic Rocket Forces as a separate service. This shows one of the differences between the two nations. Russia considers the army the primary service, and artillery as a favored branch. Russian artillery forces are among the most technically competent. It was the artillery forces who developed Russia's first atomic bombs and ballistic missiles. This made some sense, as it kept the aircraft units under the control of the army (although aviation units are technically part of a separate service, in the field they answer to the local army commander), where the fliers would not be distracted from their primary task of supporting the ground troops.

Unfortunately, Russia also created a separate service in 1948 for strategic air defense. This included antiaircraft guns, and later missiles and interceptors. As one would expect, this led to duplication in aircraft-design efforts. The Air Defense Force and the army air force frequently create duplicate designs for aircraft, weapons, and other equipment. The strategic rocket forces are not without their problems, as the navy also has its own strategic missiles and the air force has some strategic bombers. These bombers, although administratively a part of the air force, are controlled directly by the general staff. This points up still another difference with Russian forces. Many of the best officers are recruited into the general staff, which has no branch orientation. Once in the general staff, you are no longer an infantryman, pilot, or sailor, but a member of the general staff, the organization that runs the entire armed forces. The army also surrenders its nine airborne divisions to general-staff control. Last, in a practice U.S. armed forces could well copy, the Russian Army is the sole developer of weapons used by ground troops. Thus naval infantry, or air-force security troops, all use the same weapons as the army's infantry. The same applies for armored vehicles, trucks, radios, and so forth.

It's Their Environment.

"Soldiers are prone to exaggeration."—Leon Trotsky, Russian revolutionary leader, founder of the Red Army, and official Soviet nonperson

Real Gun Bunnies

A study conducted by the army in the early eighties concluded that there was no significant difference in the performance of 155-mm howitzer crews composed entirely of women as compared to the performance of all-male crews.

Military Mobility

About 20 percent of all Americans relocate every year. In contrast, some 28.8 percent of those on active duty with the armed forces move at least once each year. Officers relocate somewhat more frequently than do enlisted personnel, about 29.3 percent moving every year in contrast to about 28.6 percent of enlisted personnel. Since frequent change of residence is a disincentive to military service, Congress is rather generous in providing relocation allowances to military personnel. For enlisted personnel, this ranges from $1,500 for a dependentless recruit to as much as $14,500 for an E-9 (sergeant major or master chief petty officer) with dependents. Warrant officers get between $10,000 and $17,000, depending upon rank and dependent status. The figures for officers are comparable, with lowly second lieutenants and ensigns getting $10,000 without dependents and $12,000 with, while those ranking O-6 (colonel or captains in the navy) and above get $18,000 regardless of dependents, though this compensation is rolled into their overall pay and is subject to legislation that caps military and bureaucratic remuneration at somewhat less than the $89,500 earned by members of Congress, the service secretaries, and federal judges. Despite these generous allowances, the military is trying to cut down on the constant personnel movement, to make units more effective by reducing personnel turnover and thus improving morale. Another reason is, of course, to save money.

Military Fashion

The U.S. Navy has joined the army and air force in permitting uniformed personnel to use umbrellas, requiring only that the latter be black and carried in the left hand, so that the right will be free to deliver salutes.

Housing Expenses

The 1989 defense budget included authorization for the construction of housing for 1,273 army-connected families, which, at an average of about $86,000 per unit, was nearly the $88,000 median cost for a single-family home in the United States in 1988.

Higher Education?

About 700 British servicemen are currently assigned to provide military training to personnel of non-NATO countries, while about 4,000 non-NATO military personnel are engaged in training in Britain each year.

Did They Learn That in Afghanistan?

In 1988 Russian paratroopers celebrating in Moscow became overly exuberant and required over a thousand police to restore order. Fortunately, the paratroopers were not armed, although the police were. Several hundred arrests were made.

Boys Will Be Boys.

Even during the bitterest periods of the Cold War, the occasional contacts between U.S. and Russian military personnel frequently resulted in a remarkable degree of camaraderie amid the hostility. Thus, "hot-line" staffers regularly transmit test messages back and forth, with the Americans preferring bits and pieces of popular culture, such as rock lyrics or the latest baseball scores, while the Russians have a penchant for poetry, though both sides appreciate a good joke or a bit of pornography from time to time, and it is rumored that a hot chess game has been played on occasion. Troops in Berlin have been known to swap items of uniform or insignia when no one's looking. Pilots and air-crew members on both sides have refined this informal contact to the point where Russian long-range reconnaissance air-crewmen regularly expect to be treated to glimpses of the latest centerfold attraction from various "men's" magazines by intercepting U.S. fighter aircraft. Though an occasional "better dead than Red" American or a devoted "hero of the proletariat" Russian will sometimes indulge in an obscene gesture, this is considered rather unsporting.

Bachelors, Take Heed.

Young men who find themselves having difficulties finding "Miss Right" might consider improving their chances by enlisting. By the time they reach E-5 rank—sergeant or petty officer second class—an average of 68 percent of enlisted men in the U.S. armed forces are married, a higher rate of marriage than that for U.S. males of comparable age—early and mid-twenties—as a whole. Figures for the individual services vary greatly. Only 54 percent of navy E-5s were married and only 59 percent of those in the marines, in contrast to 70 percent in the army and a remarkable 82 percent in the air force. Figures for officers indicate that 78 percent of them are married.

Mama-san

A "Mama-san" is a female brothel keeper, a madam, derived from Japanese occupation experience and carried over into Korea during the Korean War (1950–53).

Adding Insult to Injury

As a cost-cutting measure, the armed forces are now charging recruits for their induction haircut, with rates varying illogically from $0.95 to $2.46 per shearing, depending upon the particular recruit-training center.

"We Met in a Foxhole . . ."

With women constituting about 10 percent of the armed forces, the number of military marriages has increased. About 6.5 percent of career enlisted personnel in the army are married to military personnel, including members of other services. For lieutenants and captains, the figure rises to 10.5 percent, but falls to 4.2 percent for majors and colonels. Figures for generals married to military personnel were not available, but may be presumed to be lower still, given that it has only been in the last fifteen years or so that women have begun to constitute a numerically significant proportion of the armed forces.

The Lonely Soldier

About 15 percent of married enlisted personnel and 10 percent of married officers in the U.S. armed forces experience protracted separations from their spouses due to military service. The lowest rate of such separations is in the air force, where only 8 percent of enlisted personnel and just 4 percent of officers have experienced such. The marines have the highest rates, 23 percent for enlisted personnel and 10 percent for officers.

Youth and Enthusiasm Versus Age and Experience

The average company commander in the U.S. armed forces is a captain of twenty-six to twenty-seven years of age who has perhaps five years experience in the service, in contrast to the British armed forces, where company commanders are majors of thirty-three to thirty-five years of age and ten or more years in uniform.

Triumph of Hope

"The only way to win a war is to destroy the enemy's forces, which presupposes an efficient army of one's own."—Anthony Kemp, British military historian

Midnight Requisition

"Midnight requisition" is a military term for supplementing one's official issue of something through surreptitious means. This is usually not for personal gain but to obtain some item that is otherwise tied up in paperwork or regulations, preventing its release to the unit that needs it. Also known as "liberating" equipment, midnight requisition is usually practiced by veteran NCOs who know each other, and the system, well. These "midnight" arrangements might better be called barter, as NCOs will trade favors and equipment outside official channels. Knowledgeable officers are aware of this system and will casually request one of their NCOs to pursue a needed item in this way. This military institution has been played up in the media, as it does have entertainment potential. (Radar, a character in the TV series *M*A*S*H*, is a good example.) However, there can be a more sinister side to this. Midnight requisitions can be for private gain. During the Vietnam War, some senior NCOs made millions of dollars by combining this technique and a flourishing black market. The same thing has happened in every war.

Extra Help

"The Lord mighty in battle will go forth with our armies and His special providence will assist our battle."—Field Marshal Sir Bernard Law Montgomery, victor of El Alamein, 1942

PART SIX

Logistics

Wars cost money. And most of that money is for logistics, the art and science of supplying the troops with fuel, ammunition, food, medical supplies, and thousands of other items. In the broadest sense, logistics includes the development and procurement of equipment, the care and feeding of the troops, and all the housekeeping details necessary to maintain a military force in fighting trim. Though frequently slighted by commanders, historians, and journalists alike, not to mention the general public, it is arguably the most important aspect of the art of war. When logistics are ignored, military operations suffer, not to mention the troops. It may not be a sexy subject, but it is a vital one.

The First Principle of War

"The sinews of war are infinite money."—M. Tullius Cicero, first-century B.C. Roman politician. One reason the various Roman empires lasted a thousand years was because they paid attention to dreary details like logistics and finance.

Tonnage War

An American armored or heavy infantry division can expend about 5,000 tons of ammunition a day while consuming 2,700 tons of fuel, or about 555 pounds of ammunition and 300 pounds of fuel per man.

About That Coffeepot

The famous $7,000 coffeepot that the air force purchased for use on C-5 transport planes is frequently cited as a classic example of waste in military spending. However, while there certainly is a great deal of waste and suspicious overcharging, the coffeepot should not be included. Deliberately designed for use on the huge transports, which can carry over 300 troops, the coffee urn was "overengineered" as a safety measure. Especially reinforced to be "crash-worthy," it will not burst should the aircraft make a belly-landing or in the event of explosive depressurization, thus preventing many gallons of scalding coffee from splattering around the cabin and adding to the problems of the passengers and crew. Only 150 or so are being produced, which adds considerably to the cost. Similar devices for commercial aircraft are equally expensive.

Protecting Helicopters from Heat-Seeking Missiles

Systems that scatter and generally suppress the hot exhaust from army UH-60 helicopter engines, thus making it very difficult for heat-seeking missiles to find them, cost $56,000 each. Most modern combat helicopters now use such devices, including Russian models.

The Cost of Power

The U.S. Army pays $193,000 each for the 1,500-horsepower gas-turbine (jet-engine) power plants for the M-1 tanks. These items are commonly called "power packs," and are designed to be replaced in a vehicle rapidly in the field. This makes it possible to return a damaged vehicle to service quickly.

The Cost of Tanks

Current "rollaway" prices—without spares parts or extra ammunition—for main battle tanks are:

U.S. M-1 Abrams	$4.0 million
M-60A3	$1.5 million
M-48A5 basic	$1.0 million
M-48A3 updated	$1.5 million
West German Leopard 1	$1.8 million
Leopard 2	$2.8 million
British Vickers	$3.0 million
French AMX-30	$1.5 million
Leclerc	$5.0 million
Russia T-72 basic	$1.0 million
T-55 updated	$0.9 million

Light tanks are cheaper: a British Scorpion costs about $0.35 million and a U.S. Stingray only $0.16 million, while a German Gepard antiaircraft tank runs about $0.6 million. Prices for Soviet bloc tanks depend upon a number of factors, such as whether the seller is Russia or a power that has Soviet equipment in its inventory, such as Egypt or Israel, as well as how desperate the buyer is. It also depends on how friendly the Russians feel toward you: Favored powers can get enormous discounts. The cheapest MBT around is the Russian World War II-vintage T-34, new versions of which—the Russians never throw anything away and have lots of unused ones around—can be had for around $35,000 apiece. Of course, for this you get a very obsolete vehicle, but that may be all you need, and old T-34s have turned up with both the Greek and Turkish militias on Cyprus, with various factions in Lebanon, and in a number of impoverished African states.

Tankflation

When adjusted for inflation, the cost of tanks per ton has not increased markedly since 1918, particularly considering the enormous increase in firepower.

Do You Smell Something?

Chemical-warfare detectors are complex devices and currently cost the U.S. Army $50,000 each. Despite the complexity, these gadgets are only designed to detect known chemical agents. Russia is suspected of developing new chemical agents whose primary purpose is to surprise the victims with slightly different effects and fool the chemical detectors completely.

Where's the Fire?

Damage control on ships requires finding the fire amid a lot of thick smoke. To assist this process, special infrared heat detectors are used. These cost the U.S. Navy $10,500 each.

Where Are We?

Seagoing aircraft are highly dependent on accurate navigation, and are aided by specialized computers. The U.S. Navy pays $500,000 each for navigation computers on its SH-2G helicopters.

Smoke My Heat Detector.

Special smoke grenades that defeat heat-detecting devices cost the U.S. Army thirty-three dollars each. Battlefield heat-detecting devices have been in wide use for over a decade, primarily in the West. These gadgets are not perfect and have their quirks. Even a skilled operator will sometimes get a false reading. These grenades would be more valuable to the Russians, who have more tanks and fewer heat detectors. There probably are Russian versions of these grenades.

Seagoing Helicopter Engines

A special navy version of the UH-60 helicopter, the SH-60B Seahawk, uses engines that cost about $462,000 each. Helicopters, like fixed-wing aircraft, are basically built around their most expensive component, the engine. Naval helicopters tend to have more powerful, and expensive, engines in order to provide an extra margin of safety when operating over water or making landings on ships in bad weather. These engines are also more expensive because they are modified to resist saltwater damage.

Rocket Pods

The U.S. Army pays $16,000 each for rocket pods used on helicopters. This includes some of the electronics that connect the pods to the helicopter's fire-control system.

Naval Helicopters

The U.S. Navy pays $1.5 million each for SH-60F Seahawk ASW helicopters. These are similar to the SH-60B, which is assembled by a different contractor.

Missile Warning

The U.S. Navy pays $85,000 each for AN/AAR-47 missile-warning systems for use on its aircraft.

It's All in the Transmission.

Much of the cost of light armored vehicles goes into the transmission, which must deal with the complex integration of engine and track-laying mechanism. The U.S. Army pays $53,000 each for transmissions for its M-113 armored vehicles.

Hoist Me Up, Scotty.

High-performance hoists for U.S. Army UH-1 and UH-60 helicopters cost $93,000 each.

Gold-Plated Clay Pigeons

Special drone targets for testing the U.S. Navy's Aegis ship-defense system cost between $215,000 and $234,000 each. The U.S. Air Force pays up to $400,000 each for drones.

Chain Guns

The U.S. Army pays $32,000 each for 25-mm automatic cannon for its M-2/3 infantry fighting vehicles, one of which is in the turret of each vehicle. The cannon are also called "chain guns" because of the ammunition feed mechanism used.

Aircraft Guns' Cost

The U.S. Air Force pays $30,000 each for M61A1 20-mm automatic cannon used in aircraft. This weapon has been around for over three decades, proving itself reliable, effective, and relatively inexpensive.

Bradley Muscle

The U.S. Army pays $30,000 each for diesel engines for its Bradley M-2 infantry fighting vehicle (IFV). Note that this is one-sixth the cost of the gas-turbine engine used in the M-1 tank, which has three times the horsepower of the IFV diesel.

Cost of Extended Range

A 230-gallon fuel tank and associated fittings for U.S. Army AH-64 attack helicopters cost $45,000 each, about $195 for each additional gallon of fuel.

Cost of New French Tank

As with most other nations, France has problems controlling costs of new weapons. Their new Leclerc tanks were originally estimated to cost $4.2 million each. By the beginning of 1990, the estimates had escalated to $5 million each. The Leclerc is roughly similar to the U.S. M-1, although not so heavily armored.

How Do You Spell That?

The traditional military term for all the supplies necessary to make war is *matériel*. The lethal stuff—guns, bullets, etc.—is traditionally known as *munitions*. The stuff that actually hits the enemy—bullets, shells, rockets, missiles—is known as *ammunition*.

Ramses Rides Again!

In need of new main battle tanks (MBTs), Egypt has decided to procure, and possibly locally assemble, some U.S. M-1 Abrams tanks. However, since the price of new MBTs is truly impressive—$1.5 to $3.0 million apiece—the Egyptians have also decided to stretch their MBT budget by modernizing the 900 Russian-built T-55s already on hand. Since the hull, armor, and chassis of a tank age rather less drastically than the engines, controls, tracks, and weaponry, the frugal Egyptians will be able to field a fleet of relatively modern MBTs at about half the cost of completely new vehicles. The projected refit includes a stabilized 105-mm gun with an advanced Teledyne fire-control system, a new engine and transmission, and nuclear/biological/chemical protection, plus a new hydropneumatic suspension system and new tracks. While the Ramses II tank will not be a match for a completely new vehicle with a properly trained crew, the only power in Egypt's neighborhood that possesses such is Israel, with which war is unlikely, and which, incidentally, also possesses some hundreds of modernized T-55s, that have proven valuable. Libya, the only other neighboring power with more modern tanks, has not demonstrated an ability to make much use of them.

Making a Better Russian Mousetrap

Many Third World nations initially sought and stockpiled Russian arms, and then, disenchanted with the political strings attached, broke their close links with Russia. This left a lot of orphaned Russian equipment, too expensive to replace but in need of spare parts and upgrades. Western companies came to the rescue, reverse-engineering the Russian systems and providing replacement components that were usually superior to the original. Improved replacement components were eventually offered, resulting in a system significantly superior to the original Russian armored vehicle, aircraft, or whatever.

The Men in the
Gray Flannel Combat Fatigues

Wars cost money. Even revolutionary wars and insurgencies are expensive. Because not everyone involved in a revolution has seen the light, even confirmed sympathizers of revolutionaries like some hard cash in exchange for hardware and services. The Irish Republican Army (IRA), which appears to have an operating budget of $7.5 to $8.0 million a year, probably has the most well-developed system for raising funds of any revolutionary group in the world. Although the IRA still occasionally knocks over a bank or post office, or engineers a profitable kidnapping, such high-visibility activities appear to be relatively counterproductive, since innocent bystanders may get caught in the crossfire, thereby generating adverse publicity. This would cause security forces to react rather more energetically than normally, and, also, divert the movement's limited manpower from more important objectives.

Widespread extortion brings in a fair amount of money, and provides employment and training opportunities for recruits. A "tax" on the illegal gambling that flourishes throughout Northern Ireland brings in a lot of cash. Fraud is also fairly lucrative, with IRA supporters frequently claiming unemployment benefits and welfare under several different names. The IRA also has its fingers in organized crime, an activity in which it operates on the principle of "Let's divvy up the loot now and kill each other later," generously splitting up "territory" with such radical Unionist foes as the Ulster Freedom Fighters. Then there are legitimate businesses that are controlled by the IRA through covert loans, so that long-term income can be. realized. Finally, there are foreign sources of funds. Some evidence suggests that the IRA may be involved in counterfeiting operations in the United States, which may be more profitable than Noraid, the U.S.–based fund-raising front, which apparently contributes only about $250,000–$500,000 a year.

Russia, Cuba, Iran, and Libya appear to provide most of their aid in the form of training. Thus, the IRA seems to be largely self-supporting. This is not an unusual development in revolutionary movements. It is generally believed that in the mid-1970s the Farabundo Marti National Liberation Front in El Salvador had a war chest of some $35 million, of which it lent several millions to the Sandinista movement in Nicaragua, an investment that has since paid off in Sandinista support for FMNLF activities. Similarly, the PLO has an investment portfolio variously estimated at between $2 billion and $5 billion. The revolution has come a long way from the days when Stalin knocked over banks for the cause.

Perseverance

"He who has the last piece of bread and the last crown is victorious."—Gaspard Jean de Saulx-Tavannes, sixteenth-century French soldier

Sustaining the Fight

On the basis of its experience in World War II, Korea, and Vietnam, the U.S. Army has established that 104.05 pounds of equipment and supplies must be shipped each day for every soldier overseas in an active theater of operations. Packaging accounts for about 20 percent of the overall total. This figure breaks down to 6.7 pounds of rations, 3.26 pounds of clothing, personal equipment, and administrative supplies, 3.2 pounds of so-called "personal demand items," which means such "luxury goods" as toothpaste, cigarettes, chewing gum, razor blades, and, in the "New Action Army," feminine-hygiene products, 47.8 pounds of petroleum products and chemicals, 8.50 pounds of construction supplies such as cement, 31.29 pounds of ammunition, 4.27 pounds of heavy equipment such as tanks, artillery pieces, and bulldozers, 0.35 pounds of medical supplies, and 1.52 pounds in miscellaneous spare parts. While some of the items seem odd—after all, what can you do with 4.27 pounds worth of tank?—it is important to remember that these figures exist so that the army can have a basis for calculating material requirements during active operations. Thus, 10,000 troops involved in active operations for one week will require 3,641.75 tons of supplies, including about three new tanks ($4.27 \times 10,000 \times 7$ = about 150 tons).

Note, incidentally, that the requirement for petroleum products is over 50 percent greater than that for ammunition and nearly 700 percent more than that for rations: In modern war, an army marches not on its stomach, but on its wheels.

Poor Man's (Red) Army

While the Soviet Union is touted as having the world's largest, and arguably strongest, armed forces, often overlooked is the question of just how poor Russia itself is. Economists calculate a nation's wealth with a technique called the gross national product (GNP), or the total value of all goods and services produced by a nation in a year. To compare one nation's GNP to another's, GNPs can be calculated in terms of U.S. dollars. The value of each nation's currency to another's varies from year to year and day to day. But all nations that allow their currencies to be converted to another currency constantly trade money back and forth so that the value of their currency in U.S. dollars is realistic. Russia, however, does not allow its currency to be legally converted to dollars. It arbitrarily sets a conversion rate ($1.60 = 1 ruble) that no one pays any attention to outside the USSR. Or inside it, for that matter. On the "street" you can get a ruble for ten to twenty cents, sometimes less. At the official rate, the GNP per person in Russia is about $7,500. Using the more realistic "street" rate, the per-person GNP is more like $750–$1,800. This puts Russia right down there with many Third World nations.

Reliable financial data is hard to come by in Russia. Russian military leaders say they are not sure exactly what their military budget is because it is so complex. In fact, Russia uses more of a barter system internally, as they apply different exchange rates for their currency for transactions between different Russian factories and raw-materials producers. The state owns most assets, and most of the GNP goes through the government. It's a mess they are just now beginning to address. Military strength doesn't come cheap. In this case, the cost has been the impoverishment of the world's largest nation.

You Play, You Pay.

Syria, one of the largest importers of arms in the world, has armed forces totaling about 500,000 men, plus about 100,000 active reservists. The Syrian armed forces are among the most lavishly equipped in the world. The army, with a mobilization strength of about 430,000 men in the equivalent of ten divisions plus support units, has about 4,000 tanks, including about 1,200 T-72 and T-74 types, plus 1,600 armored personnel carriers, several hundred armored cars, 2,800 artillery pieces of 122 mm and larger, including a fair number of self-propelled weapons, as well as numerous antitank and antiaircraft weapons, about 50 surface-to-surface missile launchers, several dozen MRLs (multiple-rocket launchers), thousands of mortars, and lots of small arms, plus 36 helicopters. The air force, with a war footing of nearly 85,000 men, has about 550 combat aircraft, 100 combat helicopters, and over 300 other aircraft and helicopters. The navy, though numbering only about 7,500 in wartime, has two frigates, four missile corvettes, 22 missile fast-attack craft, 8 torpedo boats, 6 patrol boats, 3 amphibious warfare vessels, 5 mine warfare vessels, and 18 antisubmarine helicopters. Virtually all of this equipment is from the Soviet bloc. And thereby hangs a tale, for Syria appears to owe Russia about $10 billion and several other Warsaw Pact powers another $14 billion, debts incurred primarily as a result of the procurement of all that hardware.

Given a GNP of no better than $20 billion, Syria is not likely to be able to pay its debts, at least not in money or trade goods. But there are other ways. Since about 1987, the Russians have been building what appears to be a large naval base near the port of Tartus, about twenty miles north of the Lebanese-Syrian frontier, a valuable installation from the Russian point of view, since they have no secure local basing facilities for their Mediterranean squadron, and from the Syrian perspective as well, since the arrangement will not only help ease the Syrians' debt situation, but a Russian presence may prove useful in the event of future hostilities with Israel or Iraq, which Syria opposed in the Iran-Iraq War. This arrangement is not all smooth going, as Russia withdrew its military advisers in early 1989 because of more disputes on how to discharge Syria's huge debt.

Militarized R&D

Along with the world's largest economy, the United States has the highest expenditures for research and development (R&D), about $130 billion a year. Half comes from the U.S. government, with about 60 percent of that coming from the military ($39 billion). Over $25 billion comes from the Department of Energy (including nuclear-weapons research) and NASA (including support of military space programs). After deducting the military R&D, the United States falls behind Japan and Europe in purely civilian R&D. While there is some spin-off to the civilian economy from military research, these results can be obtained more quickly and cheaply if the research is done as civilian research.

Front-Loading

A common technique armed forces use for getting more money is to buy many new weapons systems and ignore the high costs of maintaining and operating them. This works particularly well in Western nations, where the defense budgets tend to be year-to-year affairs. In Communist nations, defense budgets are drawn up for a minimum of five years, and major projects are planned out in detail over even longer periods. In Western nations, the military can't get away with this, because the politicians change every few years, as do the military leaders. But the senior officers know that if they front-load now, as officers did for them in years past, it will pay off for some future officer. Eventually, the users of these new weapons systems can go to the legislature pleading insufficient funds to operate and maintain all these new goodies. The legislature is usually reluctant to take the heat from the public when stories get out reporting expensive weapons' rotting from lack of funds to keep them going.

Cost of War in Lebanon

The various militias in Lebanon are not composed solely of volunteers. Most of them are hired troops. For example, in the late 1980s, the Amal Moslem militia paid new recruits $78 a month to start, plus housing, clothing, medical care, school tuition for children, and a pension fund. New officers start at $120 a month, along with the same benefits troops get, plus the use of a car. Officers usually receive formal training in Algeria or Syria. Even the Afghan Mujahedin fighters get about $40 a month. Nothing is free in this life, not even irregular troops.

Paying the Market Rate

With high salaries in the civilian sector enticing experienced specialists to leave the service, Congress has authorized special financial incentives to convince pilots and physicians to stay with the colors. A pilot who agrees to remain on active duty for one or two years beyond his initial commitment will receive a $6,000 bonus for each year, while one willing to serve a total of fourteen years earns a bonus of $12,000 a year. Medical officers receive a $20,000 bonus for each year they agree to remain on active duty beyond their initial commitment.

Creative Accounting

Glasnost in Moscow has elicited comments from Russian economists that the Soviet economy was neither as large nor as efficient as previously thought in the West. The effect was to indicate that Russian military spending consumed over 20 percent of GNP, rather than 14–15 percent. Interestingly enough, a similar examination of the U.S. military budget would reveal that, including interest on the national debt (largely a result of defense spending, especially since 1980), the Veterans' Administration, and NASA support of military operations, the U.S. military spending goes from 6–7 percent of GNP to over 10 percent.

Cost of Missiles: 1989

U.S. Missiles

Titan 34D-7 satellite launcher	$180 million each
MX Peacekeeper ICBM	$68
Trident II sea-launched ballistic missile (SLBM)	$25
Tomahawk cruise missile	$1.3 (these have gotten cheaper, in constant dollars, since introduction in the 1970s).
Harpoon antiship missile	$1.3
Phoenix self-guided air-to-air missile	$1.2
ATACMS surface-to-surface missiles	$1.1
Patriot surface-to-air missile	$960,000
AMRAAM radar guided air-to-air missile	$644,000
SM-2 MR ground-attack missile	$460,000
HARM antiradar missile	$240,000
RAM ground-attack missile	$204,000
Chaparral surface-to-air missile	$155,000
Sparrow radar-guided air-to-air missile	$153,000
Maverick ground-attack missile	$113,000
Sidewinder heat-seeking air-to-air missile	$64,000
Stinger surface-to-air missile	$40,000
Hellfire air-to-ground antitank missile	$35,000
TOW 2 ATGM	$12,000
MLRS surface-to-surface rockets	$8,100

Bare Minimum

"We can get along without anything but food and ammunition."—Richard S. Ewell, Confederate general

Teeth-to-Tail

Combat equipment comprises only 15 percent by weight of the total basic allotment of matériel to be transported for an army unit involved in Rapid Deployment Force-type operations, while 70 percent is composed of noncombat motor vehicles and engineering equipment, and only 15 percent food and sundries.

Time Out!

For those who find the current levels of defense spending, about $290 billion a year, difficult to comprehend, it is worth noting that the United States spends about $9,200 a second on defense, roughly $551,750 a minute, $33.1 million an hour, $795 million a day, $5,561.6 million a week, and $24,153 million a month.

Doug Knew.

"To maintain in peace a needlessly elaborate military establishment entails economic waste."—Douglas MacArthur, "Defender of Australia, Liberator of the Philippines, Conqueror of Japan"

Flight Pay for Civilians

Better test results are obtained when new ballistic missiles are flown over land rather than ocean ranges. Although most U.S. missiles are tested over the Pacific, occasionally one will be flown over a sparsely inhabited range in Utah and New Mexico. To compensate the few civilians living under the flight path, they are sent checks in advance so they can move into hotels on the day of the test. Most recipients simply pocket the money and ignore the test. There is a scientific basis for this practice, as early models of missiles, or modified ones in need of testing, can behave erratically. In the fifties and sixties, it was quite common for ballistic missiles under test to do all sorts of strange things. Some of the accidents were due to human error. In the early 1960s, one ballistic missile crashed in Mexico when the officer in charge erred by 180 degrees while programming the flight path. The Mexicans were not amused, even though no one was hurt. After profuse apologies, American troops were allowed to collect what wreckage the souvenir seekers had not grabbed. A more serious problem is that ICBMs are expected to fly over the North Pole, and no one is actually sure they'll work in an environment where unusual magnetic properties plus increased and variable cosmic and solar radiation could seriously effect—"bias"—the navigational systems. Nor, for obvious reasons, can anyone do a test firing.

Weapons for Free

Between 1977 and 1986, the United States gave away $120 billion in weapons, training, and military construction to over 100 nations.

The Gold-Plated Eighties

The 1980s were a period of unprecedented peacetime military spending in the United States. Unfortunately, much of what was bought was so expensive that it could easily be called gold-plated. When compared to per-unit costs of the seventies, the weapons of the eighties were much more expensive. This was especially true in the air force, where a 75 percent increase in spending bought only 8 percent more aircraft. Missiles were worse: A 91 percent escalation in cost bought only 6 percent more missiles. The army spent 147 percent more on tanks, and got 30 percent more vehicles. The navy did somewhat better, increasing its spending on ships by 53 percent to build 36 percent more ships. There is some justification for the increased costs. Inflation is one, as the rate from 1975 to 1985 was about 100 percent. The other inflation was in capabilities, a quality that is rarely revealed until combat.

The Gold-Plated Nineties

Over $1 trillion was spent on the U.S. military during the 1980s. Of that, about $280 billion was for new weapons. Due to a little deception on the part of Pentagon planners, many expensive weapons were begun without letting the legislators know exactly what their eventual cost would be. The completion of these weapons systems will cost over $900 billion in the 1990s. The money is not likely to be there. Most of the projects are for aircraft and missiles. Over $250 billion is for strategic—nuclear—weapons alone. While some may be considered essential, the money won't be there for all of them, and something will have to give. Some of these systems will have to be dropped or cut back. Likely outcomes are listed below, with pro-jected cost in billions of dollars.

- SDI ($70b) stands a good chance of being dropped completely.
- B-2 Stealth bomber ($69b) will have production slowed down and numbers cut.
- The ATF (Advanced Tactical Fighter) ($64b) is supposed to replace the current generation. However, there are already upgrade programs for the F-15 ($12b) and F-16 ($17b). The navy wants to build its own ATF ($35b), as well as upgrading the F-14 ($23b) and F-18 ($12b). Something will give.
- The LHX ($37b), the army's program for a new attack heli-copter, includes plans to retire a lot of still-functioning 1960s vintage choppers, and may be cut or reduced.
- The C-17 ($31b) and V-22 ($24b) transport aircraft programs, are already under pressure.
- AMRAAM ($12b), Midgetman ($36b), Trident 2 ($20b), and Maverick ($5b) missile programs will also be at risk.
- Several DDG-51 destroyers ($21b), Trident subs ($7b), SSN-21 subs ($35b), and a new aircraft carrier ($7b) will be under pressure to be "stretched out" or cut back.

Operations and maintenance is another area traditionally at risk when money runs short. The 1989 budget proposed a 12 percent cutback in munitions purchases, and most of the programs canceled involved artillery munitions. Although most officers and troops rec-ognize that cuts in this area simply make current forces much less effective and defeat the purpose of having armed forces, the cuts are usually made anyway. Something has to give in the nineties, and it will most likely be combat capability of existing forces because of insufficient funds for training and maintenance, not from a lack of new weapons.

Guns, Butter, or Cows

The classic choice is between "guns" (defense spending) or "butter" (nondefense spending). It's a little more complex than that. A more apt way to put it is "guns, butter, or cows." An example of each is

Russia (guns), the United States (butter), and Japan (cows). The "cows" category stands for investment in productive resources. Without such investment, you cannot have any guns or butter. Russia has been spending 15–20 percent of GNP on defense, 50–60 percent on consumption, and 20–30 percent on investment. The United States has been spending 6–7 percent on defense, 70–80 percent on consumption, and 15–20 percent on investment. Japan spends 1–2 percent on defense, 65–70 percent on consumption, and 25–30 percent on investment. An economy's future strength is based largely on how much it invests in new productive capacity. To a lesser extent, consumption contributes to economic growth, as it enhances the educational level and well-being of the people who make the whole system work. Japan's economic strength comes largely from its highly educated and generally well-cared-for population. Russia suffers from the poor treatment its population gets, even though the country has an extensive education system. Greater defense spending also tends to weaken economic growth because a higher proportion of scarce research-and-development capabilities are devoted to generally nonproductive weapons projects.

Ike Knew, Too.

"The military establishment, not productive of itself, necessarily must feed on the energy, productivity, and brain power of the country, and if it takes too much, our total strength declines."—Dwight David Eisenhower, commander, Allied Forces in Europe, 1942–45, president of the United States, 1953–61

Spin-Off

It is estimated that 20,175 new jobs are created for every $1 billion expended on guided-missile production, while the same investment in motor-vehicle production will create 30,394 new jobs, and would create 32,000 new jobs if invested in public transportation. Moreover, if this sum were left in public hands, to be spent on consumer goods, it would generate about 51,000 new jobs, and if it were spent on educational services, it would generate 71,550 new jobs, over three times the number created by arms production. The differences generally reflect the more highly skilled, and paid, personnel in technical projects as well as the high material and capital costs for manufacturing. Teachers rarely earn as much as defense workers, or even automobile assemblers. The educational-services industry also includes a large number of less-skilled, and thus less well paid, teacher aides and support staff.

"Save Fort Puttee!"

The presence of a military installation creates 500 civilian jobs in an area for every 1,000 people on the base. Many of the people on the base are local civilians, as for every two people in uniform there is one Department of Defense civil-service employee. A large number of contractor personnel also work on military bases. The troops spend most of their pay locally, and the base purchases many items from local suppliers. Many large bases are in rural areas, making them the major economic activity in the area. Most base closings result in reuse of the facility for civilian purposes, and often result in greater prosperity. But the process is painful and expensive for the locals. It's also politically explosive. Senators and representatives who normally vote down every military budget become very hawkish when there is talk of closing a base in their constituency. The base closings that were authorized in 1988 had to be determined by an independent commission, so no representative of the people would have to take the heat.

Something for Everyone, a Comedy Tonight!

"Military spending plays an important role in 'pork barrel' politics."—Robert W. DeGrasse, defense analyst. This is the accepted wisdom. A comparison of the voting records of the representatives from the ten congressional districts that receive the most defense-related contracts with the ten that receive none supports this conclusion. While the representatives from the top ten districts average a "pro defense" voting record of 47.6 percent on a list of defense issues, those from the bottom ten averaged 10.8 percent. Nevertheless, the representatives from the top three districts averaged a "pro defense" rating of only 8.7 percent, so there are clearly other factors at work as well.

Daddy Warbucks, Come Home.

The long Iran-Iraq War proved a tremendous boon to arms merchants, generating an estimated $40 billion worth of new business, a boom in which some forty-two nations shared, some of which sold equipment indiscriminately to both sides. The United States was one of the nations that sold matériel to both sides, the Iranian sales being kept secret until revealed as the Iran-Contra scandal. Various nations offered every type of weapon and equipment in existence except nuclear weapons.

Cost of Unrest

The Palestinian uprising in Gaza and the West Bank areas is costing Israel an estimated $1 million a day in defense outlays and lost revenues due to a weakened tourist industry. Lebanon's ongoing civil war costs between $5–$10 million a day, over a million dollars in artillery ammunition alone. Most of the rest goes for destroyed property and the cost of maintaining the numerous partisan militias.

Almost as Much as a B-2 Bomber

The U.S. Navy's new class of Arleigh Burke destroyers are to cost about $750 million each. These ships are actually smaller versions of the navy's complex ($1 billion) Aegis type antiaircraft cruisers fitted in the smaller hull of the Spruance class destroyers. The air force is spending between $500 million and $600 million each for their B-2 Stealth bombers. The destroyers will be much more costly to operate, as they have a crew of over 200 men. While the B-2 has a flight crew of only two, the ground crew will amount to several dozen expensively trained airmen.

The Impending Veterans' Crunch

At present the Veterans' Administration handles about 3.8 million cases a year, mostly in the form of pensions and hospital services to some 2.8 million veterans and their dependents, for an expenditure of nearly $27.0 billion annually, or roughly $7,100 per case, including both benefits and the administrative costs of maintaining some 240,000 employees, 172 hospitals, 231 clinics, 117 nursing homes, and 27 domiciles. However, the total veteran population of the country is about 27.4 million, with some 53 million dependents. Over the next few years, the VA will have to contend with increasing demands for pensions and services from post-1940 veterans, who constitute all but a handful of the total. Virtually all of the 9.6 million world War II veterans—some of whom are already being served by the VA—will be over 65 by 1993, thereby becoming eligible for pensions and more extensive medical benefits. By the end of the nineties, 4.0 million Korean War–era veterans will attain wider eligibility for services. Thus, even given normal attrition due to age, by 2001 the VA could easily have 15 million cases. Even at the 1989 cost-per-case, the expenditure would amount to $106.5 billion and would require a staff of nearly 1 million. There is at the moment no evidence of any long-term planning being done in anticipation of this situation.

The Cost of Testing

Complex electronic systems require a lot of testing, both for individual components as well as the entire system under combatlike conditions. About 30 percent of the total development budget of the U.S. Navy's Aegis air-defense system was spent on testing.

Who Gets What

For the 1987–88 fiscal year, a typical year, the ten largest defense contractors were:

Firm	DoD Contracts	% of Sales
McDonnell Douglas	$7.7 billion	c. 20.6
General Dynamics	$7.0 billion	75.3
General Electric	$5.8 billion	24.8
Lockheed	$5.6 billion	49.6
General Motors	$4.1 billion	4.0
Raytheon	$3.8 billion	49.4

Firm	DoD Contracts	% of Sales
Martin Marietta	$3.7 billion	65.4
United Technologies	$3.6 billion	20.9
Boeing	$3.5 billion	22.7
Grumman	$3.4 billion	97.1

These together account for $47.4 billion, or about 16.3 percent, of the defense budget. Note that percentage of corporate gross sales are based on figures for calendar year 1987, while the defense budget in question was that for fiscal year 1987, which begins in that year and runs into 1988, so that the figures do not correspond exactly.

The Ideal Customer

"Nobody ever went broke supplying an army."—Fletcher Pratt, American author and military historian

More Bang for the Buck or the Pound

The United States has an extensive network of trained reserve units. Maintaining these units costs less than $20 billion annually, about 6.8 percent of the defense budget, yet they supply half the combat power after mobilization. The British Army's experience is very similar, with territorials—national guardsmen—accounting for about 23 percent of the combat power of the army, but only 4.7 percent of its budget and a mere 1.6 percent of total defense expenditures.

"How Much Do You Really Spend, Tovarich?"

The official defense budget of Russia hovers in the vicinity of 20 billion rubles, or about $30 billion at the official exchange rate, or roughly 30 percent more than what is spent by Britain, which has about 20 percent of the population, about 6 percent of the active duty manpower, 7 percent of the aircraft, 2 percent of the tanks, a lot less heavy equipment, only 2 percent of the nuclear weapons, no ICBMs, and a lot smaller navy. At the unofficial rate, which is all anyone will give you for rubles outside of the reach of the Soviet

Army, the figure is much lower, about $8 billion, which is nearly $2 billion less than what is spent by Italy, which has only 20 percent of the population, about 8 percent of the manpower, 4 percent of the combat aircraft, 3 percent of the tanks, much less heavy equipment, no nuclear weapons, no ICBMs, and a much smaller navy. Estimates of real Russian defense expenditures range up to about $250 billion. The actual figure is anybody's guess.

In fact, the Russians themselves don't know what their "defense budget" amounts to. The announced figure is apparently primarily for personnel costs. Other expenses are subsumed by the budgets of various ministries, such as the Ministry of Medium Machinery, which makes the nuclear weapons. Unfortunately, none of these ministries publishes a detailed budget. To make matters worse, prices that various enterprises must pay for raw materials, semifinished goods, machine tools, and other resources vary according to official schedules: In effect, a firm making military equipment pays less for things than one making civilian goods, but it also depends upon the priority given to the equipment. The official schedules are subject to negotiation, with politics and not economics playing the major role. So there is really no way of determining what the Soviet Union spends on defense, except by estimating what their equipment would cost to produce in the West. Unfortunately, this practice, while common, is also inaccurate, since in the West labor costs more than goods, and money has real value, while in the East the opposite situation prevails.

The Soldier's Usual Diet

"Soldiers' bellies are not satisfied with empty promises and hopes."— Peter the Great, seventeenth-century Tsar of all the Russias, reformer, shipwright, tourist, and gadget buff

Thrifty Competition

U.S. military procurement policy long held that "sole source" buying was more efficient because it would allow for a larger production run and less duplication of effort. However, in 1984 Congress passed the Competition in Contracting Act because of suspicions that a little competition—a little capitalistic market pressure?—might improve matters. It did. For example, by 1988 the army increased the competitive bids for its ammunition purchases 20 percent and gained an overall 20–30 percent reduction in costs.

What Now, Mahatma?

About 20 percent of India's national budget is spent on defense, some $8 billion to $9 billion a year.

The Price of Leadership

In most major nations, a senior official runs the defense establishment. There are significant differences in how these officials are compensated. Among the lowest-paid is the U.S. secretary of defense, receiving about $100,000 in salary and benefits. In Britain the minister of defense receives about twice as much. In the major Communist nations, the official pay is much less than what Western officials receive. However, because there is such a scarcity of things to buy in Communist nations, their senior officials receive something more valuable than cash: access to luxury goods. Spacious houses and apartments, chauffeured limousines, private aircraft, and just about anything else is available to these officials in lieu of pay. This is one reason senior Communist officials resist retirement. When they lose their position, they lose all the goodies that go with it.

The Defense Litigation Reporter

The increasing number of defense contractors who have been subjected to legal proceedings for shoddy workmanship, fraud, and corrupt practices has sparked the publication of a journal aimed at firms that anticipate difficulties with the federal government. *The Defense Litigation Reporter*, which comes out twice a month, is predicated on the assumption that "the Justice Department has declared open season on defense contractors." In conformity with the trend in defense-related matters, a one-year subscription runs to $654, which is presumably tax-deductible.

The Cost of the Gulf War

It is believed that Iran and Iraq spent a combined total of about $40 billion, not to mention nearly a million of their sons, in the course of their eight-year war, of which about $27 billion was spent on hardware from foreign sources. Iraq probably spent more than Iran, much of it borrowed money, while Iran came out of the war with no debt: Lenders were available, but Iran refused to borrow. Iraq also made generous payments to the survivors of dead soldiers, which did not show up as defense expenditures as such. From available information, it appears that these payments may have exceeded $10 billion.

Skeet-Shooting

Sometimes, improving military effectiveness can cost money in unexpected ways. In mid-1987, the British Army found that its new Javelin shoulder-launched antiaircraft missile was so effective that losses of its Skeet Mark II aerial target, a drone miniairplane, were much higher than anticipated. As a result, a new batch of Skeets had to be ordered at a cost of several million pounds.

Holy Land?

Over the past decade, countries in the Middle East have imported over $145 billion in arms, roughly 50 percent of total arms deliveries to the Third World.

Gas Guzzlers

Modern tanks with gas-turbine engines use about as much fuel standing still as when they are moving. Tanks spend most of their time stationary when they are operating. Successful tankers found that it's safer to wait for someone else to move into their gun sights.

Full Kit

The cost of weapons aside, it now costs about 800 pounds sterling ($1,400) to equip one British Tommy with all the necessary uniforms, gas mask, sleeping bag, first-aid pack, and other "nonlethal" equipment you normally see combat soldiers draped with. The collection of gear is commonly called the soldier's "kit." Then you have to add in the price of weapons.

Dollars per Round

The U.S. Navy pays fourteen dollars per round for the 20-mm ammunition fired by its Phalanx antimissile system. Several hundred of these rounds are expended each time the Phalanx is fired. A similar round is used in a similar cannon on jet fighters.

Bill It to Your Grandchildren.

Fully 125 years after Appomattox, federal pensions are being paid to about a dozen widows of Civil War veterans—all of whom had been involved in "May-December" marriages in the early part of this century—including the widows of former Confederate veterans, eligible under an act of 1959, who are in some cases also collecting pensions from states of the *soi-disant* Confederacy: Another few dozen pensions are being paid to surviving children of Civil War veterans. If the Civil War pattern holds true for subsequent conflicts, the last Spanish War pensions will probably be paid out sometime around 2030. Similarly, World War I will still be costing the taxpayers money until about 2050, World War II until about 2075, Korea will be with us until about 2080, the Vietnam War until sometime around 2110. The pension burden for the current "peacetime" armed forces will not run out until at least 2125, given the gradual increase in life expectancy.

As Good as . . . Well, Not Quite

The B-2 Stealth bomber costs about $580 million dollars and weighs something in the vicinity of 130–135 tons, which means it runs to about $137.30 an ounce, roughly twenty-two times more precious than silver, or about a third as valuable, per ounce, as gold. The U.S. M-1 tank, by the way, costs only $2.15 an ounce and the U.S. Navy's *Aegis*-class cruiser goes for $3.12 per ounce.

Armed Poverty

The Third World's share of world military expenditure rose from 19 percent to 25 percent during the 1970s, while that of the United States fell from 32 percent to 24 percent and that of Russia fell from 25 percent to 24 percent.

Foreign Relations

In an average year, the United States spends only about $4.5 billion to pay for military hardware, supplies, and troop maintenance abroad, mostly to the NATO powers, one or two of the European neutrals, Japan, Korea, Australia, and Israel, just about 1.5 percent of the total defense budget. Many expenses are picked up by the host nations, and a lot of material is shipped from the United States, including large quantities of food and fuel.

Guns, Butter, and Reality in Latin America

One of the more peaceful regions of the world, at least in terms of formal warfare, is Latin America. Most nations maintain small forces and low military budgets. Consider the major nations and their troops as a percentage of the population, and military spending as a percentage of GNP in the late 1980s:

Nation	Troops	Spending
Argentina	.25%	2.0%
Brazil	.21	.7
Chile	.78	2.8
Colombia	.23	.9
Cuba	1.71	9.1
Ecuador	.36	2.3
Mexico	.31	.5
Paraguay	.43	1.7
Peru	.54	3.6
Venezuela	.36	1.5

Several things become readily apparent. The largest nations in the list, Brazil and Mexico, devote the smallest proportions of their population and GNP to the military. Those nations with the largest proportion of people in uniform tend to be either repressive or fighting off rebellion. In other words, these armed forces tend to spend more of their efforts against their own populations than against any foreign threat. In Argentina, where the disastrous 1982 war with Britain exposed the ineffectiveness of the military, the military dictatorship subsequently fell, and the citizens promptly cut military spending in half and conscript calls by more than half. The threat, or reality, of unemployment, left a lot of angry officers. In a pattern common to the region, the military threatens to take over again in order to get their goodies back. After all, who else can defend the country from . . . whom?

Good Comrades All

Of the Soviet bloc's annual $7.5 billion—90 percent from the Russians—in arms transfers—including both sales and donations—to the Third World, only about 29 percent has gone to countries that are avowedly Marxist, including Cuba, Vietnam, North Korea, Angola, Ethiopia, and Afghanistan, while fully 70 percent goes to just three powers, Iraq, Syria, and Libya. These three do, however, have a better capacity to pay for their arms, and do so in U.S. dollars.

Don't Overlook the Footnotes.

The official Defense Department recipe and specifications for making, packaging, and storing fruitcake are eighteen pages long. Such attention to detail paid off in this case, as it eliminated ambiguities, detailing nutritional, shelf-life, and packaging requirements as well as itemizing the recipe. This considerably reduced the cost of fruitcake to the armed forces, to about $1.50 a pound, half the price on the civilian market. In a similar vein, the military specifications for chewing gum are fifteen pages long. On the other hand, the specs for condoms are only thirteen pages long. Among the reasons for the apparently absurd detail in military contracts and specifications is the fact that contractors have been known to cheat. In addition, the armed forces are mandated to demand that contractors comply with minimum-wage, child-labor, environmental-safety, conflict-of-interest, and civil-rights laws; international embargoes; and other legislation. An additional problem is that there's a tendency to get carried away when writing specs: Try explaining tic-tac-toe in writing.

Who Spends What?

The argument about who is shouldering the heaviest defense load among America's principal allies generally revolves around how much each country is spending. Figures for the period 1986–87 show what each nation spent per capita for defense.

Nation	Defense % GNP	Per Capita Defense	Per Capita Income
U.S.	6.6%	$1,200	$18,000
Greece	6.3%	237	3,752
South Korea	6.0%	108	1,800
Australia	4.6%	470	10,282
Britain	4.5%	416	9,256
France	3.5%	370	10,566
Turkey	3.4%	45	1,305
West Germany	3.0%	328	11,073
Netherlands	2.8%	276	9,762
Norway	2.7%	375	13,837
Italy	2.6%	161	6,100
Canada	2.6%	288	11,083
Portugal	2.5%	62	2,450
Belgium	2.5%	248	9,877
Denmark	2.0%	245	11,941
Luxembourg	1.0%	106	10,371
Japan	1.5%	154	10,266
Iceland	0.0%	0	10,216

Thus, both proportionally and absolutely, the average American spends more on defense than does any of his allies. On the other hand, the allies don't have nearly 30,000 nuclear warheads or a navy more powerful than all the others combined. And, by and large, the allies do contribute more manpower to the relationship, albeit usually by means of cheaper conscription, while several are also burdened by the presence of considerable numbers of American troops on their soil. No one knows what Russian defense spending is, but most estimates generally put it at a bit less than that of the United States, which would work out to some $1,100–$1,500 per person, with a percentage of per capita GNP figure being possibly as much as 20 percent, though this is difficult to determine given the nature of the Soviet economy.

You Can Say That Again!

"To carry on war, three things are necessary: money, money, and yet more money."—Gian Jacopo Trivulzio, Renaissance man

Underwater Budgets

In the 1990s, the U.S. Navy pays $800 million each for SSN-688 class nuclear attack subs and $1.5 billion each for the new SSN-21 class attack boats. The Trident class nuclear ballistic-missile boats cost $1.3 billion each. Each boat carries twenty-four Trident II sea-launched ballistic missiles costing $29 million each, bringing the total cost to nearly $2 billion per fully equipped boat.

Cost of Aircraft: 1989

U.S. Air Force

F-15 Fighter	$31 million each
F-16 Fighter	$15 million each
C-17 Transport	$226 million each (initial buy, they'll get a little cheaper in the future)

U.S. Navy/Marines

EA-6B Electronic-Warfare Aircraft	$41 million each
AV-8B Harrier STOL Fighter	$20 million each

F-14 Fighter	$66 million each
F-18 Fighter	$28 million each
CH-53E Amphibious Assault Helicopters	$13 million each
SH-60 Utility Helicopter	$17 million each
E-2C Early Warning Aircraft	$52 million each
T-45 Trainer	$16 million each

U.S. Army

| AH-64 Attack Helicopter | $12 million each |
| UH-60 Utility Helicopter | $3.3 million each |

Note that a late-model civilian B-747 jumbo jet costs over $100 million. Civilian versions of the UH-60 helicopter can cost almost as much as the military versions, depending on options.

Hot Markets

In 1988 the largest importer of military equipment in the world was India, which took a 14.8 percent share of the approximately $40.0 billion annual international sales of arms. Iraq, which in 1985 had led with about 24 percent of total arms imports, had by 1988 fallen to about 10.0 percent of the world market. Egypt accounted for 6.3 percent, Saudi Arabia, 4.8 percent, Israel, 4.6 percent, Japan and Syria 3.7 percent each, Turkey and Czechoslovakia for 3.4 percent each, while Angola and Spain took 3.1 percent apiece, and Canada and Australia 1.9 percent each, trailed by Taiwan, with 1.7 percent, and South Korea, with 1.6 percent. The balance, 31.9 percent, went to all the other countries in the world.

Where It All Goes

Of the roughly $290 billion the United States expended on defense in Fiscal Year 1989, $77.8 billion (26.8 percent) was spent on the army, including some $1.5–$2.0 billion on civil engineering projects such as flood control and port development, $96.4 billion (33.2 percent) on the navy and marines, and $97.2 billion (33.5 percent) on the air force. Of the balance, $18.6 billion (6.4 percent) was spent on various Department of Defense agencies, such as the Joint Chiefs of Staff, the National Guard Bureau, and the Selective Service System, and about $700 million (0.2 percent) was spent on the actual operation of the Department of Defense.

The Two-Billion-Dollar Petty Cash Account

Of the approximately $290 billion defense budget for 1989, $78.4 billion (27.0 percent) went to people, including the approximately 2.1 million men and women on active duty (some $34 billion, $16,000 each), plus the 1.1 million in the National Guard and reserves ($5.5 billion, $5,000 each), plus the million or so civilian employees of the defense establishment ($26.5 billion, $26,000 each), plus services and pensions to those among the 27.4 million retirees and veterans and their dependents who are eligible for such ($18.7 billion, on average $682 each). Another $85.6 billion (29.5 percent) went toward operations and maintenance. Procurement ate up about $80 billion (27.6 percent), while research, development, and testing accounted for another $38.6 billion (13.3 percent), and construction, including nonmilitary port and navigation improvements, for $5.7 billion (2.0 percent). Approximately $2 billion (0.7 percent) was allocated to miscellaneous things like a small cash reserve and various trust funds.

The Ministry of Oversight

The United States is cursed with a truly cumbersome defense-procurement bureaucracy. Within the services themselves, there are tens of thousands—20,000 in the air force alone—of officers who decide what has to be bought and what characteristics it should have. Some 135,000 Defense Department employees then go out and do the actual purchasing, to the tune of about $160 billion a year. But every cent they spend is carefully scrutinized by 535 elected senators and representatives, who are organized into over 50 congressional committees and subcommittees, each with an extensive staff of its own. Then there are some 1,100 auditors supported by about 26,000 staff members, who use more than 4,000 separate laws and over 30,000 pages of regulations, to examine the details of these purchases and offers to sell by vendors. Major projects often generate over ten tons of documents from a manufacturer just for a bid to do the work. Each year, the average senator or representative makes over a thousand inquiries of the Defense Department. It's a wonder anything gets done, or purchased.

The Arms Trade

The international trade in weapons does not leave the clearest of paper trails. The numbers take a while to collect, but they don't change much from year to year (or rather, their pattern doesn't). Some nations are not covered here because they must keep their activities secret for diplomatic reasons (Taiwan, South Africa). But included are the major players. Note that Iran and Iraq scaled back their purchases since the cease-fire in 1988. Well-armed nations sorely in need of hard currency (dollars) are maintaining their lead in the trade. In 1985 the following nations traded arms in the following millions of dollar amounts:

Nation	Import	Export
Angola	$1,200	$0
Australia	800	0
Brazil	70	120
Britain	575	700
Bulgaria	725	370
China	140	1,100
Cuba	1,500	0
Czechoslovakia	460	1,100
Egypt	825	50
Ethiopia	310	0
France	170	3,800
Germany (East)	525	220
Germany (West)	260	410
India	2,800	0
Iran	1,800	0
Iraq	4,900	0
Israel	450	20

Nation	Import	Export
Italy	170	250
Japan	675	20
Libya	1,200	60
Poland	650	1,100
Russia	1,100	18,000
Saudi Arabia	2,900	0
Sweden	60	190
Syria	1,100	20
U.S.	450	7,600
Vietnam	1,600	0

Practice Isn't Free

The U.S. Army pays $7.50 each for 25-mm cannon practice rounds. Regular rounds, depending on type, cost over $10 each. The 25-mm cannon is mounted on the M-1/2 infantry fighting vehicle.

You Can't Be Too Well Defended.

Although the United States and the Soviet Union have only about 11 percent of the world's population, and a third of the world's GNP, they account for about 25 percent of world military expenditures apiece. All this money has bought Russia about 35 percent of the main battle tanks in the world, nearly 25 percent of the combat aircraft, about 30 percent of the warship tonnage, 16 percent of the military manpower, about 44 percent of the nuclear weapons, and perhaps 80 percent of the chemical weapons. The United States has bought about 10 percent of the tanks, about 17 percent of the combat aircraft, about 50 percent of the warship tonnage, about 6 percent of the military manpower, about 53 percent of the nuclear weapons, and perhaps 15 percent of the chemical weapons. The principal allies of the two superpowers—some two dozen countries with about 8–9 percent of world population—account for another 25 percent of the world's military expenditures, while the rest of the planet, over 140 countries with about 80 percent of the population, accounts for the remainder.

Foreign Aid

While most Americans generally think Uncle Sam spreads their money around pretty generously, over the last decade or so over 50 percent of American military aid to foreign powers has gone to just two countries, Egypt and Israel, who, along with Saudi Arabia, Taiwan, and Pakistan, also account for about 75 percent of U.S. sales of arms.

Federalism at Work

Of 871 military installations in the United States, the state with the highest number is California, with 105 (12.1 percent), while South Dakota has the least, just two (0.02 percent), figures that are roughly comparable to the percentage of the U.S. population that lives in those states. On the other hand, California receives about 20 percent of defense-contract dollars each year, while South Dakota gets about .09 percent, so that both are doing better than their population percentages.

Defense Expenditures?

In addition to spending about $290 billion a year on its own armed forces, the United States provides roughly $3.5 billion in defense-related foreign aid, and about $60 million to support various peace-keeping operations, mostly in the Middle East.

Caveat Vendor!

The Department of Defense (DoD) actually *is* cracking down on corrupt practices in military contracting. Audits of U.S. military contractors reveal that more than a third had overbilled, for an average of 2–3 percent. Moreover, there were a number of cases where overcharges ran more than $100 million, monies that were recovered by the government. These sums are extracted through the efforts of the 22,400 auditors, investigators, and inspectors in the Defense Contract Audit Agency. This operation costs about $1 billion a year and recovers about $7 billion in overcharges annually. During the course of the year that ended in September 1988, the DoD's own internal investigative agency, which has over 1,100 investigators, uncovered $2.1 billion worth of probable overcharges, 50 percent more than had been uncovered in the previous year. Such overcharges amounted to nearly 2 percent of the approximately $124 billion that the nation invests in procurement, research and development, and construction for defense-related purposes. In addition to such practices as padding payrolls and overcharging or double-charging for materials and services, the investigators discovered numerous instances of misappropriation of government-purchased materials and many cases of outright bribery, such as civilian and military officials' letting contracts in return for financial or other consideration. Numerous cases are still under investigation or proceeding through the courts. During that year, however, the DoD won 299 convictions, resulting in a number of lengthy jail sentences plus fines and penalties amounting to nearly $300 million. The total cost of the investigations amounted to about $84 million, so the DoD got back over $3.50 for every dollar it invested in policing military contracts.

Pervasive Problem

The United States is not the only country plagued by questionable business practices in connection with defense contracts. During the course of 1987, Britain recovered 235 million pounds sterling ($420 million) in overcharges from defense contractors as a result of careful investigation into "accounting irregularities."

Out of Africa

When Angola, Cuba, and South Africa agreed to make peace in 1988, the terms included Angola's paying to send the 50,000 Cuban troops and their equipment from Angola to Cuba. The first Angolan estimate of this cost was $800 million, or $16,000 per soldier. The heavy equipment includes over a thousand tanks, APCs and artillery pieces. Based on this cost estimate, Angola pleaded poverty and asked for donations. It was pointed out that there were many transportation firms that would do the moving for a fraction of the Angolan estimate. The Angolans said they would review their estimates.

Investing in the Future?

About 69 percent of U.S. government expenditures for research and development is devoted to defense-related projects, in contrast to only 12.5 percent for West Germany, and a minuscule 4.5 percent for Japan.

Guns and Butter on the Installment Plan

For fifty years, the conventional wisdom was that wars, and defense spending in general, helped the economy. It is slowly becoming apparent that this is not the case. The United States was able to pay for World War II and enjoy thirty years of increasing prosperity thereafter. This was largely because the war had destroyed the economies of the other major industrial nations, which enabled the United States to grab and exploit numerous world markets. In 1945 the United States possessed about 50 percent of the total world GNP. Now that the devastated World War II economies have been fully rebuilt, competition is more even, and the U.S. GNP is down to perhaps 25 percent of world totals. It's now realized that defense spending, although necessary, is at the expense of economic growth and competitiveness. The rule of thumb is that for every percent of GNP devoted to defense spending, you lose half a percent of annual GNP growth. The United States has managed to avoid this slowdown in growth during the 1980s by borrowing heavily, but this only delays the day of reckoning as the debt builds up and the interest payments eat into the capital.

Dem Ol' Red Stamp Blues

U.S. defense manufacturers complain about not being able to enter into joint ventures with firms in friendly countries because of the large number of American technologies that are classified and not eligible for export. As technology development capability spreads and the U.S. advantage in military R&D shrinks, these restrictions merely accelerate the decline of the U.S. edge in making and marketing top-of-the-line equipment.

"Water, Water, Everywhere . . ."

Although not generally noted by the public, water supply has always been an important consideration in military planning. Depending upon the environment, water supply can be a major logistical problem. In the heat of a desert or tropical environment, minimal water requirements per man can run about six gallons a day, roughly fifty-three pounds, which increases his minimum per capita daily supply requirement by about 50 percent. Even in a relatively salubrious temperate climate, troops cannot long survive on short water rations: At temperatures below 77 degrees Fahrenheit, dehydration will become a problem within about two weeks if troops are limited to a quart of drinking water a day. For hospitals, the minimum demand is ten gallons per bed per day, nearly ninety pounds. Moreover, there may be difficulties in providing potable water to the troops even in areas such as Western Europe, where supplies are adequate for civilian needs, due partially to the destruction of local wells and aqueducts, and partially to the enormous size of modern armies. During operations in Lorraine in 1944–45, the U.S. Army was supplying about a million people with water every day. Armies have addressed the problem of water supply in various ways. The Israelis have well-organized columns of tanker trucks that accompany line units into combat. The U.S. Army maintains well-drilling units, purification units, and distillation units, and provides the troops with water-purification tablets as well. The British are proceeding with the development of the "Aquastraw," a disposable straw that filters and purifies water as a soldier drinks impure water through it.

Sharing the Burden

Since 1970 the European NATO powers—with the exception of France—have increased their defense budgets by about 34 percent, while the United States has gone up only about 15 percent. This discrepancy is largely due to the fact that, save for Britain, European powers all rely on cheaper conscripts, which reduces their dollar costs. In addition, several European powers shoulder a good deal of the maintenance costs for U.S. troops stationed on their soil. West Germany, for example, absorbs about $1.3 billion in annual rental expenses for U.S. installations, which have a market value of some $16 billion. In addition, West Germany covers all costs arising from damage to person and property contingent upon maneuvers and military operations on its soil, about $50 million a year. And in the event of war, some 90,000 West German reservists would be assigned as logistical and service troops to the U.S. Seventh Army.

"Merely Return the Unused Portion for a Full Refund. . . ."

Dissatisfied with the quality of some new equipment, Britain has recently begun requiring defense contractors to provide guarantees that their products will work as specified for at least two years.

Russia's Strategic Position

The Warsaw Pact, Russia and its erstwhile allies, have a total population of 396 million, a GNP of $3.3 trillion, and military spending of $350 billion. They are surrounded by a formidable array of sometimes unfriendly states. To the west, they face the NATO alliance with a population of 646 million, a GNP of $9 trillion, and military spending of $450 billion. To the east, they face China with a population of 1.1 billion, a GNP of $500 billion, and military spending of $10 billion. In addition, there are nations like Japan and Australia in the Pacific that would probably get involved in any eastern war.

Colonial Enclave?

Nearly 2 percent of West Germany's 95,975 square miles is occupied by military installations, about 1,580 square miles, an area larger than that of Rhode Island or the combined areas of the West German states—*länder*—of West Berlin, Bremen, and Hamburg.

A Lot More Than a Face-lift

One acronym often found in defense budget explanations is SLEP, for service life-extension package. This is a refitting of existing equipment such as aircraft or ships, amounting to a virtual reconstruction. All obsolete and worn equipment is discarded and replaced with new and usually better parts, while electronics and life expectancy are enhanced.

Food for Thought

The world is currently spending an enormous amount of money on defense each year. What can we do with it now that peace seems to be breaking out? To begin with, it's an incredible sum: The total annual world expenditure on defense is about a trillion dollars— that's $1,000,000,000,000—or roughly 75 percent of the total external debt of the Third World that so troubles international bankers. Some other possible trade-ins follow: For what the world spends on defense every 2.5 hours, about $300 million, smallpox was eliminated worldwide back in the late seventies. For the price of a single new nuclear-attack submarine, $726 million to $1 billion, we could send 5–7.5 million Third World children to school for a year.

For the price of a single B-1 bomber, about $285 million, we could provide basic immunization treatments, such as shots for chicken pox, diphtheria, and measles, to the roughly 575 million children in the world who lack them, thus saving 2.5 million lives annually.

For what the world spends on defense every forty hours, about $4.6 billion, we could provide sanitary water for every human being who currently lacks it.

Looking at it another way, the roughly $290–$300 billion that the United States plans to spend on defense in 1990 is greater than the total amount that Americans contribute to charity each year, about $100 billion, plus total federal, state, and local, public, and private expenditures for education, roughly $150 billion, plus NASA's entire budget of $7.6 billion, plus federal and state aid to families with dependent children, $16.3 billion, plus the cost of the entire federal judiciary and the Justice Department combined, $5.5 billion, plus federal transportation aid to state and local governments, $17.5 billion. Some notion of how expensive things really are may be gained by noting that a single Stinger missile costs about $40,000, or roughly 30 percent more than the income of the average American family, nearly twice more than the income of the average black American family, and about 400 percent more than the so-called poverty line, or that the price of 2,000 rounds of 7.62-mm rifle or machine-gun ammunition, about $480.00, is slightly more than what the average Social Security beneficiary receives every month.

But Winning Is Still Better Than Losing.

"War does not pay."—Douglas MacArthur, American general, World War II

PART SEVEN:

War and Society

Military affairs are not something separate from the human experience, but an integral part of it. War, and the potential for it, affects us all constantly. Moreover, military forces necessarily reflect the character of the societies that create them. Thus, their strengths and weaknesses are essentially the strengths and weaknesses of their society. For better or for worse, we get the armed forces we deserve. And while the nations of the world have a lot of armed forces, they often do not seem to derive any real sense of security from them. As a result, disarmament is becoming increasingly central to the political and diplomatic life of the principal powers. This chapter will look at the way society influences, and is influenced by, the doings of the armed forces.

Among Other Things

"When news of war is proclaimed, wisdom is thrust aside."—Quintus Ennius, Roman poet

The "Ignobel" Prize for Military Adventurism

Leaving aside imperial powers in the process of being thrown out of their erstwhile colonies, notably Britain and France, the post–World

War II belligerency champion is Israel, with six wars (Independence, Suez, Six-Day, Attrition, October, and Lebanon), plus an ongoing internal-security campaign (Palestinians), one "accident" involving a foreign airliner and one involving a foreign warship (the USS *Liberty*), and numerous "punitive," "rescue," "protective reaction," and "preventive" operations (Entebbe, Osiraq, etc.).

In a surprise showing by a reputedly pacifistic power, India is first runner-up, with four wars (three with Pakistan and one with China), plus one "peacekeeping" operation (Sri Lanka), four forced annexations (Hyderabad, Kashmir, Sikkim, and Goa), one "liberation" (Maldives), and five internal security "problems" (Kashmir, Mizo, Nagas, Bodos, and Sikhs). Historically, an empire, with the usual imperial ambitions, India seems to be moving back to its historical paternalistic attitude toward its neighbors.

Egypt follows as a close third, with six wars (Israeli Independence, Suez, Yemen, Six-Day, Attrition, October), two "rescue missions" (Cyprus and Malta), one "training" mission (Western Sahara), and one "border incident" (Libya).

Fourth place is held by yet another Third World power, Iraq, with four wars (Israeli Independence, Six-Day, October, Iran), several "border incidents" (Kuwait, Syria, Turkey, Iran), a long-running internal-security campaign (Kurds), one "incident" with a foreign warship (USS *Stark*), and one "revolution," plus several coups.

Pakistan comes in fifth, with four wars (three with India, plus Bangladesh Independence), one series of "border incidents" (Afghanistan), one "advisory mission" (Oman), one long-running internal security problem (Baluchis), and a couple of coups.

The United States and Russia, widely considered favorites for the title, have in fact made rather poor showings. Since 1945 the United States has had only two wars (Korea and Vietnam), plus one "liberation" (Grenada), four "peacekeeping" operations (Dominican Republic, Lebanon, 1956 and 1983, and the Gulf, which includes one "accident" involving a foreign airliner), plus a series of "incidents" (all with Libya), two "rescue missions" (Mayaguez and Iran), and one "drug bust" (Panama), while Russia has had only two wars (Hungary and Afghanistan), one "liberation" (Czechoslovakia), two "peacekeeping" operations (Berlin and Poland, 1953), several long-running insurrections (the Baltic States, Ukraine, 1945–53, Armenia), a "volunteer expedition" (Iran, 1945–46), and a series of "border incidents" (China), plus a number of "accidents" involving foreign airliners and "incidents" involving foreign military aircraft.

Of course, this sort of thing can be measured in other ways, such as on the basis of the "body count." Looking at the matter in terms of the loss of human life puts China, with one civil war, one "cultural revolution," two wars (India and Vietnam, 1979–present), one "pacification" (Tibet), two "volunteer expeditions" (Korea, Vietnam, 1964–75), and a series of "border incidents" (Russia, Matsu and Quemoy), the body count for which—including all deaths on all sides from all war-related causes—runs to about 35 million. In an upsetting surprise, the United States's wars come in with the second-highest body count, about 6.1 million, including some duplication of the Chinese totals, while Russia's warlike adventures since 1945 run to "only" some 1.5–2.0 million war-related deaths, a figure exceeded by that for Cambodia in its war against itself. The accumulated body count of the other powers do not even come close to a million, unless the enormous "unauthorized" massacres that occurred as a result of the partition of British India are counted, which would give India and Pakistan a death toll between that of Cambodia and the United States.

Soviet Civil Defense

The Chernobyl nuclear disaster in 1986 and the Armenian earthquake in 1988 put the spotlight on one of the most misunderstood aspects of Russian military power: civil defense. Since the early 1970s, American defense officials have pointed to a large and capable Russian civil defense organization of 25,000 uniformed personnel as an indication that Russia was prepared to fight a sustained nuclear war and survive it. That's probably true, as this attitude is consistent with long-standing Russian doctrine. But like most things in the Russian armed forces, when put to the test they perform much less effectively than expected. The performance of their civil defense organization was no different. Although some still insist that Chernobyl was handled fairly efficiently, an examination of the Russian press indicates that this was not the case. Lack of organization, shortage and inadequacy of essential construction equipment, and failings in the performance of nuclear defense troops from local army units were the norm. As with many things in the Soviet Union, and large bureaucracies everywhere, more effort was put into appearance than performance. The Armenian earthquake in late 1988 provided an even more graphic example of Russian civil defense inadequacies. And this time there were thousands of foreign relief volunteers and journalists on the spot as witnesses.

Red Sun Rising

The third largest military budget in the world belongs to a country that, technically, has no armed forces. That nation is Japan, whose post–World War II constitution mandates the armed forces to be called "self-defense forces." Whatever the name, Japan's forces consist of highly trained volunteers armed with the latest weaponry. Ground forces contain thirteen divisions, the navy has fourteen submarines plus sixty destroyers and frigates. There are also seventy long-range naval patrol aircraft. The air force has over 300 modern jet aircraft. All the quarter-million troops are volunteers. Annual defense spending is statistically small, about 1.5 percent of GNP, but it's an enormous GNP, and the resulting defense spending was somewhere around $30 billion in 1989. France, West Germany, and Britain have budgets of about the same size, but theirs are not increasing as swiftly as Japan's. Keep an eye on this development. Japan's nervous neighbors certainly are.

The Long Peace

Although the post–World War II period has generally been considered one of enormous international tension and crisis, it is worth noting that there has not been a war between the Great Powers in Europe since the surrender of Nazi Germany on May 8, 1945, a peace that, at the time this volume was published in late 1990, has lasted over forty-five years. This is the longest period of major-power peace in Europe since before the fall of Rome. The second-longest such period of peace among the European Great Powers was that stretching from the armistice that ended the Franco-Prussian War, signed on January 31, 1871, to the Austro-Hungarian declaration of war on Serbia, on July 28, 1914, which signaled the outbreak of the First World War two days later, a total of forty-three years, five months, and twenty-eight days. In effect, since November 5, 1988, every day that the European Great Powers have not been at war with each other has set a new European regional—and pretty much a world—record for the duration of a peace.

NATO Far Afield

One little-discussed aspect of the fact that many NATO nations sent warships to the Persian Gulf in 1987–89 is that they did so at all. These deployments demonstrated that NATO nations other than the United States, Britain, and France have the practical capability of projecting military power far afield. In addition, the non-"Big Three" NATO nations have many battalions of marines, airborne, and air-portable ground troops available, plus substantial naval and air forces. These capabilities must be taken into account during any future political crisis outside of Europe that threatens the interests of NATO nations.

The Man Who Liked Dark Places

"The beginning of a war is like opening a door into a dark room."— Adolf Hitler, leader of Nazi Germany. He ties closely with Josef Stalin as the individual responsible for the most deaths in this, or any other, century.

The Civilianization of War

An ominous trend in twentieth-century warfare is the increasing proportion of deaths among noncombatants. In World War I, the ratio of deaths among military personnel to those among civilians was about 20:1, a figure that fell to 1:1 during World War II, to 1:5 in the Korean War, and to 1:13 in Vietnam, a ratio that may be even worse for the Afghanistan war. A future nuclear war would see this trend spiral upward, with hundreds of civilian deaths for each military one.

Peaceful Intentions

"A conqueror is always a lover of peace."—Karl von Clausewitz, German military philosopher

Terror's Toll

The State Department estimates that from 1979 through 1986 some 3,856 persons were killed and an additional 8,137 were injured in acts of international terrorism. In 1987 and 1988, about 650 people were killed each year, with about twice as many injured. No figures are available on the number of terrorists killed or injured in the course of their activities, nor on the casualties caused by retaliatory actions on the part of aggrieved powers. On the other hand, consider that normal (i.e., nonterrorist-caused) aircraft accidents killed and injured more people during the same period: In these same years, nearly 1,500 people died in aircraft accidents in the United States alone.

Casualties of the Long Peace

It is probable that 40–50 million people have died as a result of all the wars that have taken place since 1945.

The Male Outlook?

"War is the mother of everything."—Heraclitus, ancient Greek philosopher. The Greeks also believed that the brain existed merely to cool one's blood supply.

Obviously

The English word *war* is etymologically a cognate of the Romance *guerre/guerra*, both deriving from the Old High German word *werra*, meaning "brawl" or "tussle," which in turn derives from the Old Teutonic *firwerran*, meaning "confusion."

The Ukrainian Liberation Front

The current ethnic unrest in Russia reminds us that the USSR is a nation of many nationalities, some of whom would prefer to be independent. In the late 1940s, there were nearly 50,000 armed anti-Russian guerrillas operating in the Ukrainian portions of western Russia. It was not until the mid-fifties that these were finally put down, using massive army operations. The U.S. Central Intelligence Agency stopped parachuting agents into Russia to support these groups in 1954. But in the Ukraine, the memory lingers, and by some accounts the infrastructure as well. A visit to the Ukraine by Gorbachev in 1989 was met by large Ukrainian independence demonstrations. This made the Russians quite nervous, as there are over 50 million Ukrainians. Russia knows well just how serious many Ukrainians are about their independence. Shortly after the visit and the demonstration, a statement was issued on nationwide TV that Ukrainian independence was unacceptable and would be resisted with every possible means. Aside from the economic advantages of controlling the industrialized, mineral-rich Ukraine, its kindred Slavic people helps strengthen Russian control over a nation in which only about 140 million people are ethnic Russians, barely 50 percent of the population.

Why Russia Needs Eastern Europe

Despite Russia's enormous scientific, technical, engineering, and manufacturing resources, there are still many important items of military equipment that Russian industry cannot produce as well as foreign firms can. Some of these high-tech companies are in Eastern Europe. In the area of optical and precision instruments, many notable firms have always existed in Eastern Europe. Czechoslovakia, East Germany, and Hungary still have a world-class capacity to produce these devices. Despite its desire to maintain self-sufficiency in military equipment, Russia has become dependent on Eastern Europe for several key items, such as gyroscopes and optical devices for strategic missiles and fire-control systems. Unless the Soviet Union can successfully restructure and improve its industry, this dependence will continue. The only alternative is to fall further behind the West in the area of high-tech armaments. So Eastern Europe has done its part in the "international division of labor." But don't call it imperialism.

Most Common Cause of War

"If we cannot secure our needs for survival on the basis of law and justice, then we must be ready to secure them with army in our hands."—Mihaly Karolyi, Hungarian revolutionary leader, 1848–49

Top Secret!

In recent years, approximately one out of every thirty Americans— including several members of the Walker family—had some sort of defense-related security clearance: About 2.6 million military and civilian personnel of the Defense Department, 400,000 National Guard and reserve personnel, and about 1,400,000 civilians engaged in defense production. Experience has shown that one out of every few thousand of these people can be expected to compromise the secrets he is entrusted with. Some need money, some can be blackmailed, some are disgruntled and want revenge, and some are just sloppy. The Russian KGB spends a lot of time beating the bushes looking for these weak links. With over 4 million clearances, there are over a thousand potential traitors. All the KGB has to do is identify them and make a deal, which is precisely what happens periodically.

If You Thought Iraq Was Bad . . .

About the same time Iraq began to use chemical weapons against Iranian troops in the early eighties, North Korea began to deploy similar material in tunnels near the South Korean border. This was largely coincidence, as North Korea has been working on manufacturing its own chemical weapons since the early 1960s. They made little progress until the 1970s, when Russia began to provide technical assistance and samples of their own chemical weapons. Much of the raw materials, and some of the manufacturing equipment, was obtained from Japan in the form of material for producing insecticides. Nerve gas, for example, was originally developed in the 1930s for use against insect nervous systems. The Japanese assistance was quite innocent, as the chemicals and equipment shipped were typical for supporting agriculture. The Russian assistance was also strictly commercial, as large amounts of chemical protection equipment was also sold to the North Koreans. The Russians, however, knew that the North Koreans were building a chemical capability. North Korea has also developed a number of biological-warfare agents, although in small quantities.

It Also Gets You Killed.

"War alone brings up to its highest tension all human energy and puts the stamp of nobility upon the people who have the courage to meet it."—Benito Mussolini, dictator of Italy, 1922–45

Who Can Resist a Man in Uniform?

About fifty countries, nearly a third of the total, are currently ruled— more often misruled—by military regimes.

U.S. Mercenaries Guard Japan.

Japan's thriving economy has been fueled by several factors, one of the more important being a low defense budget. Spending only 1.5 percent of GNP on defense versus 7 percent in the United States, Japan has that much more money to invest in more efficient factories and infrastructure. Helping to guard this growing Japanese wealth are 55,000 U.S. troops stationed in Japan or attached to the U.S. Seventh Fleet. Of the $6.5 billion annually it costs the United States to maintain troops in Japan, the Japanese pay for 40 percent. In effect, Japan is hiring U.S. troops, at a sharp discount, to protect Japan. Normally, foreign troops are stationed in a country either to keep it in line politically, or to serve the interests of the host country. The Russian forces in Eastern Europe have served largely to assure those nations' loyalty to Russia. The U.S. forces in Japan play no such controlling role. The only threat the United States can make to Japan is to withdraw U.S. troops. Japan would then have to replace them at its own expense or allow Japan's defenses to weaken accordingly. The U.S. approach to stationing troops in foreign nations is unique in history, and makes these troops, in effect, mercenary forces serving largely to defend the host nation with very few strings attached.

This arrangement is even better than a straight mercenary deal, where the mercenaries you pay for are all the ones you will have when the chips are down. With American troops in Japan, the Japanese could depend on even more lavish assistance if these U.S. troops were attacked by a foreign power. Best of all, these additional forces would cost the Japanese nothing. It's a strange world.

Unfinished Business

Even if peace were to "break out" immediately, it would be a long time before people would stop dying. There is an incredible amount of lost military equipment lying about, much of it still lethal. In 1972, over a century after Appomattox, the United States Naval Ordnance School issued a special manual on Civil War ammunition to assist in the disposal of the untold thousands of unexploded rounds that still can be found on many of the old battlefields. Thousands of tons of poison gas are believed to be buried somewhere in the vicinity of Spandau, near Berlin, where the Third Reich maintained a major gas-production installation during World War II. Late in 1987, a large cache of World War I–era phosgene gas was uncovered in an old ammunition dump in Britain. Construction crews in London regularly unearth live bombs left over from Hitler's blitz, and several years ago two live 8-inch shells of 1917-vintage were dredged out of the East River, virtually in the shadow of the Brooklyn Bridge.

The situation is not strictly academic or a matter for the bomb-disposal squad, for the old ammo can still kill. On June 7, 1917, British forces detonated about 500 tons of explosives under Messines Ridge in northwestern France, annihilating several German divisions. Two mines, with perhaps twenty-five tons of explosives apiece, failed to explode. One went off spontaneously in 1955, killing several local farmers and some cattle. The other remains lost.

Each year the casualties from the old wars increase. No one keeps statistics, but from time to time incidents turn up in newspapers, usually as fillers. Thus, in 1984, the only year for which any figures are available, five French school children died in a hamlet near Strasbourg when an old shell with which they were playing went off. In the Ukraine, a long-lost World War II shell went off near a school, killing three children. Over thirty Danish fishing trawlers were contaminated, and many fishermen were injured by mustard gas, from a cache of some 100,000 tons of German gas shells and grenades that the victorious Allies had dumped into the Baltic in 1945.

The extent of the problem may be imagined by noting that approximately 1,500 tons of unexploded ammunition left over from World War II is discovered annually in West Germany, an area of about 96,000 square miles. Assuming that the rest of Germany was bombed and fought over with an equal intensity during the war, an additional 650 tons probably turn up in East Germany every year and an equal amount in the formerly German areas annexed to Poland and Russia after World War II. Then consider what lies beneath the ground in other areas over which there was heavy fighting, such as France, Belgium, Italy, Poland, Hungary, the western republics of Russia, and North Africa, where the old Alamein battlefield in western Egypt is still largely closed to tourists as a result of leftover ordnance. Moreover, recent wars have tended to exacerbate the problem. Casualties in Vietnam due to mines left over from some forty years of war are so common that a volunteer group of Americans who served there as engineers has arranged to help remove the mines, which in some cases they had planted in the first place. During the 1982 Anglo-Argentine War, the Argentines scattered 15,000 land mines indiscriminately, most of which still litter the barren terrain of the Falkland Islands, though fortunately fatalities have been primarily confined to the local sheep. Then consider the tremendous number of mines and shells expended during the Afghan and Iran-Iraq wars.

No *Perestroika* for the Revolution

Despite moves to reduce nuclear and conventional forces in the late eighties, during this same period Russia continued to operate facilities within its borders that trained as many as 6,000 guerrillas and terrorists each year.

Just How Dangerous *Are* the Russians?

Nations tend to develop working habits that extend to all aspects of their existence. Take safety. *Glasnost* opened up Russian civil-aviation accident statistics somewhat, and revealed that the Russian accident rate was several times higher than Western rates. Then the USSR released automobile accident rates. On a per-mile-driven basis, a driver is fifty times more likely to be in a fatal automobile accident in the Soviet Union than in the United States. For several decades, Western nations have been monitoring Russian radio traffic in the air over East Germany. Although the compiled stats are secret, the anecdotes coming out of Western intelligence agencies indicate that their military pilots are about as safety-conscious as their civilian automobile drivers. All of this indicates that the historically higher rate of accident losses for Russian vehicles and aircraft has not changed much.

Gas Masks for Kids

Israel, confronted by belligerent neighbors possibly armed with chemical weapons, made a second attempt in 1988 to distribute chemical-protection equipment to civilians. This time, special equipment for babies and small children was provided. The kits are easier to use and include medication as well as masks. Some 37,000 kits were distributed in two towns. Kits may eventually be distributed to the rest of the population. Currently, there is not enough equipment on hand for the entire population. Chemical weapons used against unprepared populations can produce casualty rates of over 80 percent, nearly half of which will be deaths. Protective gear can cut these losses by over 90 percent.

No Nukes

CBW, military shorthand for chemical and biological warfare, is a recognition of the fact that while nuclear warfare might be avoided, biological and chemical weapons are cheaper. Chemical weapons have been used frequently in this century, and biological ones occasionally. When used against a nonchemically capable foe, chemical arms generate little more hostile reaction than a condemnation in the press or the United Nations.

Birds of a Feather . . .

Three international outcasts, Israel, South Africa, and Taiwan, have increasingly taken a cooperative approach to solving their common problems with regard to acquiring modern weapons and related materials. Of the three, only Israel has legal access to Western (largely U.S.) technology. But South Africa has raw materials, and Taiwan has cash and technology to offer in return.

A good example of how this works is the development of the South African Cheetah fighter. This is a thorough upgrade of the twenty-five-year-old French Mirage. The Israelis shared their experience from upgrading their own ancient Mirages with South Africa in the early 1980s. When Israel was forced to halt its development of the Lavi fighter (an F-16 clone), many of the Lavi R&D staff went to South Africa, where jobs in the same technical areas were available.

South Africa also has a thriving arms industry, and freely copies the technology of nations that refuse to trade with it. Taiwan is also developing a new 1990s technology fighter, and it is reasonably certain that Israeli engineers will be on the payroll.

"I've Got a Secret."

There are presently about a trillion U.S. government documents classified as secret, nearly 4,100 for every man, woman, and child in the United States. Many are not secret, at least not originally. If unclassified material is incorporated into a classified document, then the formerly open material also becomes secret. Often, material available in the open is classified when it is discovered that there is some reason or another for making it a secret. Generally, the attitude appears to be, "When in doubt, classify." And since more people have the power to classify than to declassify, the result is an enormous increase in classified documents. Unfortunately, a policy of "When in doubt, declassify" is not easily instituted. Foreigners who have assisted in intelligence operations over the years, even when they are not spies, may be subject to severe retribution if their connection with a U.S. intelligence agency is ever found out. Often foreign citizens may be at risk if their parents or even grandparents were found to have been so involved. For this reason, there is great reluctance to declassify secret documents without checking for unpleasant side effects.

The Multiparty System in Russia

There has always been at least one political party in Russia: the military. Even before the Communists took over in 1917, the military was such a large presence that the government had to pay close attention to its needs and feelings. The Revolution created another party, the Communist party. These two parties lived in uneasy peace for almost twenty years. Then, in the late 1930s, Stalin slaughtered most of the armed forces' senior officers in order to purge the troops of any independent ideas. To accomplish this, he created yet another political force, what is now the KGB, building on older, less omnipotent institutions. This outfit is the secret police, a sort of FBI, CIA, and more rolled into one organization. When the army responded loyally a few years later and defeated the invading Germans, Stalin reciprocated by eliminating the Zampolits, Communist party representatives present in military units down to the company level to ensure army loyalty. Stalin also gave the army all the new weapons and equipment it wanted after the war. But the KGB also had a network of informers in the military, which was never withdrawn.

When Stalin died in 1953 and Khrushchev took over, the military was brought to heel. Forces were cut, as was the defense budget. Generals in senior government positions who resisted were removed. Krushchev also shot the head of the KGB, an old Stalin crony named Beria, who had been responsible for large-scale massacres within the KGB during Stalin's reign. Less bloody-minded KGB officers were promoted to head the organization, which won the loyalty of the KGB "party." But the military resistance did not cease until Khrushchev himself was ousted in 1964 and a new arrangement was put in place for the army. The Zampolits were restored, giving the Communist party assurance that the military would not get out of hand.

In return, the military got a blank check for arms and equipment. Troop strength was rebuilt to over 5 million. This understanding lasted until the economy was near collapse and Gorbachev took over in 1985.

Now, the Communist party wants to cut back the military once more. The military resists. Who will prevail? Unlike 1955, when the economy was growing over 10 percent a year, the 1990s look grim. But also unlike 1955, there are several million active or retired officers, plus millions more in the defense industries, who see a large armed forces in more personal terms. Yet the KGB has not been touched, and Gorbachev says little about cutting it down to size. The KGB remains at the top of the social, political, economic, and legal pecking order. Gorbachev's rise to power was aided by senior KGB officials who saw a need for reform. The KGB are aware that their tsarist predecessors survived the 1917 Revolution. They are a relatively small group compared to the military and the Communist party. The KGB operates as something akin to a tie-breaker between the two other "parties": the military party and the Communist party. And it's election time.

The First Russian Disarmament

The 1989 Russian pledge to unilaterally reduce the strength of their armed forces and number of units in foreign nations is not a first for them. From 1955 to 1958, Russia underwent a significant reduction in the size of its armed forces, from 5.7 million to 3.5 million troops. Ground combat divisions declined from 175 to 139. This was largely driven by the fact that the massive deaths and disruptions of Stalin's 1930s terror and World War II had reduced the annual conscripts available to less than half the normal 2.5 million. The armed forces, over two thirds of whom were conscripts, had to be cut. Seventeen divisions were withdrawn from foreign nations, partially because they cost twice as much to maintain as units based in Russia. Only two divisions were withdrawn as a result of international negotiation (Austria), and the rest were pulled out unilaterally. These included one in Finland, two in Romania, three in East Germany, four in Manchuria (China), and five in Mongolia. In addition, twenty divisions were stripped of nearly all their personnel and continued to exist only as warehouses containing divisional weapons and equipment.

From Those Wonderful People Who Brought You . . .

It was during the Korean War (1950–53) that Japan's industrial economy got its start in rebuilding from the ravages of World War II. UN forces in Korea desperately needed a wide range of military equipment, so Japan, right across the Tsushima Straits from Korea, was pressed into producing various military items. Although barred by law ("guidelines," actually) from exporting weapons, there is no prohibition against exporting other military equipment or components like computers or sensors that can become parts of weapons systems. The Japanese defense industry expects to be allowed to export weapons sometime during the 1990s. Until the 1970s, there was not a lot of additional activity in the defense-production area. But having captured much of the world market for consumer electronics, Japan began to turn its attention to weapons. For example, one of the more innovative items they came up with was a radically new type of sensor for portable antiaircraft missiles. Their sensor "sees" the image of the target aircraft and memorizes it in terms of both shape and heat. Once the missile is fired, it starts looking for the image of its target. The U.S. Army plans to use this technology in the 1990s.

Adventure

Intelligence work consists largely of gathering information. Most of this is currently done by satellite. But there are some things satellites cannot pick up: The insides of equipment and structures elude them. So do landlines signals, which are plain old telephone wires, or more complex cables. To find out what information is on a landline, you have to tap it physically. In East Germany, there is a treaty dating back to World War II that allows U.S., British, and French officers to snoop around as much as they can get away with. Landlines in Eastern Europe and even Russia can be tapped with the help of friendly locals. But in Korea, things are different. North Korea is run by a fanatic dictator who enforces Draconian discipline

throughout the country. Moreover, North and South Korea are separated by a two-kilometer demilitarized zone (DMZ), which is further covered by mines and heavily armed guards. Undeterred, various
U.S. intelligence agencies initiated an aggressive information collection program in the 1970s, called Operation Adventure, which it
certainly was. Several U.S. intelligence specialists were shot while
attempting to tap into North Korean landlines. Eventually, the more
dangerous aspects of this project were turned over to the KCIA (Korean Central Intelligence Agency), a particularly rough and humor-
less group who relish sticking it to their northern cousins. When the
North Koreans got too rambunctious, the Korean Marines were called
in. This bunch are even more adept in the roughhouse department
than the U.S. Marines, who taught them the basics. Through the
late 1970s, there was something of a minor war going on in the DMZ,
with gunfire and explosions a common occurrence. Eventually, Operation Adventure was shut down and replaced with quieter programs (like Guardrail, but that's another story).

Casualties of War

About 9 percent of the population of Afghanistan has died in the
war against the Russians and their puppet government, a figure
marginally higher than the 8.6 percent dead suffered by the Russians during World War II. As with the Russian World War II experience, the Afghans suffered extensive damage to their
infrastructure. Agricultural production was reduced by 50 percent.
Half of the livestock was destroyed, and 70 percent of the paved
roads were damaged. This, apparently, was one reason why more
Russian troops were not sent in. There are no railroads in Afghanistan, and without adequate roads there was no way to supply a larger
force. Some 44 percent of the population was displaced, most to
Pakistan or Iran. A third of the villages, where most of the population lives, were destroyed. About 13.5 percent of the male population of Afghanistan has died. The biggest killer appears to have been
air attacks, which accounted for about 46 percent of the 1.3–1.5
million dead, followed by bullets, 33 percent, artillery fire, 12 percent, mines, 3 percent, and "other," an ominous category that includes gas, flame throwers, and the like, 6 percent. About 80 percent

of those killed by air attacks, and many of those killed by mines, were noncombatants who just happened to be in the way.

The European War

"If we go to war tomorrow, 90 percent of the land forces and three-quarters of the air and navy will be Western European. After 30 days of mobilization, under the most optimistic conditions in the United States, still 75 percent of the land forces and 50 percent of the air and 30 percent of the navy will be West European."—Bernard Rogers, American general, Supreme Allied Commander in Europe, 1984

Forces Abroad

Though figures are rather elusive, it appears that in the spring of 1989 there were about 1.9 million military personnel stationed outside of their immediate national homeland, either in overseas possessions or on foreign soil, representing about 5.6 percent of total active military personnel in the world. Excluding military attachés and the like, there were military personnel from forty-six countries stationed abroad, and personnel from a number of guerrilla organizations: the Palestine Liberation Organization, the African National Congress, and the Nicaraguan Contras. These troops were in ninety-one separate countries, over 50 percent of the total, plus a number of overseas territories such as Gibraltar, Guam, and Tahiti. Nine countries accounted for almost 90 percent of the total forces stationed abroad, as listed below, with the percent of their active-duty troops stationed abroad in parentheses:

Russia	718,000 (14%)	Vietnam	100,000	(9%)
U.S.	485,400 (23%)	India	50,000	(4%)
Britain	95,500 (30%)	Syria	30,000	(7%)
France	93,800 (20%)	Belgium	27,300 (31%)	
Cuba	55,000 (35%)			

Considered in terms of the proportion of a nation's active military forces that were serving abroad, the figures were:

Fiji	1,100 (41%) peacekeeping
Cuba	55,000 (35%) mostly in Angola
Belgium	27,300 (31%) in West Germany
Britain	95,500 (30%) mostly in West Germany
Zimbabwe	12,000 (29%) in Mozambique
Canada	6,000 (24%) mostly in West Germany
U.S.	485,000 (23%) mostly in Europe, Japan, Korea
France	93,000 (20%) half in West Germany
Russia	718,000 (14%) mostly in Eastern Europe

Several countries were the hosts of truly enormous foreign military contingents, who in some cases outnumber local forces, even including insurgents, as can be seen from this list of countries with 50,000 or more foreign troops on their soil:

Power	"Guests" 1000s	As % Locals	Origins
East Germany	420.0	244	Russia
West Germany	405.5	83	U.S., Br., Fr., Belg., Neth., Can.
Czechoslovakia	78.0	40	Russia
Cambodia	65.0	56	Vietnam
Hungary	65.0	66	Russia
Poland	60.0	19	Russia
Mongolia	55.0	224	Russia
Japan	55.0	23	U.S.
Sri Lanka	53.0	94	India

If one considers the matter proportionally, the figures can be even more impressive:

Power	"Guests" 1000s	As % Locals	Origins
Iceland	3.1	infinite	U.S., Neth.
Maldives	0.5	250	India
Belize	1.5	246	Britain
East Germany	20.0	244	Russia
Cyprus	16.0	226	UN, Greece, Turkey, Britain
Mongolia	55.0	224	Russia

Power	"Guests" 1000s	As % Locals	Origins
Laos	50.0	96	Vietnam
Sri Lanka	53.0	94	India
Panama	10.5	94	U.S.
Djibouti	4.23	90	France

Given the current trend toward friendlier international relations, the number of troops stationed abroad is declining, and will probably continue to do so through the 1990s.

Tail Wagging the Dog

"A political problem thought of in military terms eventually becomes a military problem."—George C. Marshall, American soldier, statesman, humanitarian

A Hundred Million Bayonets

There are approximately 5.1 billion people in the world. Of these, about 700 million may be considered to be eligible for military service under the traditional qualifications for such, being of the proper sex (male, despite all the efforts of women to secure recognition of their equal capacity to inflict bodily harm), age (15–45), and physical abilities (debatable). Of these, about a seventh are already committed to military service, for, including active forces (some 34.0 million, including those involved in guerrilla wars against their own governments), fully mobilizable reserves (about 34.1 million), and paramilitary personnel (34.9 million), the armed forces of the world total about 103 million: 57.5 million serve in, or in support of, ground forces, including marines; 3.6 million serve in naval forces; 7.0 million in air forces, including naval air forces; and 34.9 million in internal-security forces. Thus, one out of every seven "eligible" men is already in uniform, about 1.5 percent of the human race.

The Military Consequences of AIDS in Africa

Although there has been little comment on the matter from anyone, Cuba, which has a Draconian policy toward persons infected with the AIDS virus, imprisoning them for life, is likely to suffer a serious public-health catastrophe given that over the last decade or so some 500,000 of her troops—about one Cuban in twenty-one—have done tours of duty in Angola, which abuts Zaire, one of the principal foci of AIDS infection in Africa. According to the World Health Organization, there are about 2 million people with AIDS in sub-Saharan Africa and a further 5–10 million infected with the HIV virus, figures considered conservative by some. Satellite photos revealed, and ground surveys later confirmed, that large rural areas of Central Africa had been depopulated by the depredations of "Slim," the African term for AIDS. In some areas, such as Uganda, almost all of the prostitutes have been found to harbor the HIV virus. Statistics in some parts of West Africa are almost as bad. Long-haul truck drivers, a relatively recent development in Africa, have also helped spread the virus throughout sub-Saharan Africa. Any army considering operations in this region may have to face an enormous potential health disaster, and Cuba's is no exception.

AP Mines Forever

Most of the wars since 1945 have seen large-scale use of smaller and smaller antipersonnel mines. Most of these mines are not cleared after the shooting stops and continue to injure civilians for decades afterward. One of the most massive examples of this will be seen in Afghanistan, where it is estimated that the Russians placed over 20 million mines on the ground. Most of these were small, camouflaged antipersonnel mines intended to maim (remove feet and legs). They were often dropped in large quantities from aircraft and helicopters or in artillery rockets and shells. Russia has expressed some desire to assist in clearing these mines, but the most numerous and difficult to clear of these mines are the ones scattered in large quantities from the air. While most of these air-dropped mines were designed to self-destruct after a few days, given the usual Russian quality control in munitions, over 10 percent of them are probably still active, littering the Afghan countryside with several million "foot-buster" mines. This is why there are still civilian mine casualties in Afghanistan. Ironically, the British efforts to clear the 15,000 mines Argentina left behind on the Falklands may make a considerable contribution to this Afghan effort. The British developed special boots weighing eight pounds a pair that protect mine-clearing troops from these small mines. This can be an enormous help in clearing these mines, as the usual means Afghan Mujahedin used to clear the small mines was to walk carefully through mined areas and spot the mines before they stepped on them. The mines could then be disposed of. Using the special boots, mine-clearing Afghans could go through areas faster and with less stress. Despite these efforts, no one knows how long most of them will remain uncleared and active, but the Afghan people are certain to find out in the coming decades.

ZPG

Whatever the social, political, economic, and environmental advantages of zero population growth (ZPG)—a condition in which gains from births and immigration merely balance losses through emigration and deaths—it may lead to serious military problems. Nations achieving ZPG will find themselves running out of manpower in militarily desirable age groups. This is already a problem for those countries that have attained, or soon will attain ZPG, and is especially so for those that are actually experiencing a net decline in population. Among the countries involved are several NATO and Warsaw Pact powers. Indeed, it is estimated that the overall NATO manpower pool will decline by 12 percent from the late eighties to the end of the century. Within fifteen years, the number of West German males between twenty and twenty-four years of age will fall by 40 to 45 percent, Belgians about 27 percent, Italians 23 percent, Danes 17 percent, and Frenchmen 13 percent. Britain's population is actually declining by about 0.01 percent a year, and West Germany's by about 0.02 percent. Greece and Luxembourg both are now at ZPG. The only NATO powers to have positive growth rates are Norway, 0.2 percent, Portugal, 0.3 percent, the Netherlands, 0.4 percent, Spain, 0.5 percent, Iceland and Canada, each at 0.8 percent, the United States, running about 0.9 percent, and Turkey, with an impressive 2.8 percent a year: at this rate, by the end of the century, Turkey will be the most populous nation in NATO after the United States.

Although figures are difficult to come by, the situation is even worse in the Warsaw Pact. East Germany, which became the first country to achieve ZPG in 1969, was by the mid-eighties the first country to experience "negative growth," which is now also a problem for Hungary. Of the other Pact members, Czechoslovakia is at ZPG, Bulgaria is increasing at only 0.1 percent and Poland at 0.8 percent. While the growth rate of the Soviet Union, 0.8 percent, is adequate to maintain its armed forces at their present level, most of the growth is among unreliable non-Slavic Caucasian and Central Asian elements, who, though constituting less than 20 percent of the population, account for more than a third of military-aged manpower. Several European neutrals, notably Austria, Switzerland, and Sweden, are also at ZPG. Different countries have adopted different strategies to deal with the immediate problems created by their declining manpower pools. Several have introduced modest increases in the length of compulsory service.

A number of powers, such as Italy, France, and Spain, are reducing the size of their armed forces. Russia has adopted this method, in addition to increasing the liability of the more desirable Slavs. The United States, Canada, and Britain, already in the business of enticing people into their volunteer armed forces through high pay and extensive benefits, are increasing these still further. One alternative is to place greater reliance on reservists, who number nearly 10 million in NATO, including over 800,000 officers. However, for a long-term solution to the problems that the shrinking pools of military manpower pose—particularly in view of the fact that in the Third World such pools are growing—witness the increasingly amiable state of relations between the Western and Eastern blocs.

The Spirit Is Willing, but the Bureaucracy Is Not.

Although students in Soviet secondary schools are supposed to fire sixteen rounds from an assault rifle as part of their senior-year preinduction military training, many schools never receive their official supply of ammunition. As Soviet conscripts are sent directly to their units, this in-school training is designed to substitute for the two or three months of basic training that Western nations give new recruits after they enter the service. Army officers complain regularly of how ill-prepared the conscripts are for military service. After the navy, rocket force, air force, security forces, and technical services grab all the more able conscripts, the army combat units have to cope with what's left, which, apparently, is not much.

Warrior Is to War

In most languages the word for *warrior* is derived from the word for *war*, implying that the latter necessitates the existence of the former. Thus, of course, there is the English *warrior* from *war*, the German *krieger*, from *krieg*, and the Romance *guerrero/guerriero/guerrier* from *guerra/guerre*. In Russian, however, the reverse is true. The word for "war," *voyna*, derives from the word for "warrior," *voin*, the linguistic implication being that since we have warriors, we might as well have a war.

Not Enough Technology to Go Around

Many Third World nations decline offers of high-tech weapons because they simply don't have enough skilled manpower to operate and maintain them. *Perestroika* (restructuring) in Russia is likely to severely injure Russian military technology. Russia is beginning to encounter the problem of insufficient numbers of technical personnel, along with a number of uniquely Russian contributing causes. Russia has two economies: military and civilian. The military industries get the best of everything and are shrouded in secrecy. As the technical complexity of their weapons has increased in the last twenty years, they have found their pool of technical workers unable to keep pace. Part of this was caused by the secrecy in the defense industries. Factories and institutes did not communicate very well, and many organizations held on to people they did not need because the number of warm bodies they controlled was one way the senior bureaucrats kept score. There was no market mechanism to shift scientists, engineers, and technicians from one project to another. Moreover, these technical personnel could not shop around for jobs they wanted but were often kept where they were because of "national security." The students coming into the technical schools were not always the best qualified, as bribery and influence-peddling were often the final determinants of who got into what school. Things are likely to get worse for the military as *perestroika* takes hold. The civilian economy will now be able to attract talented people, and fewer people will want to enter the military sector because of all the secrecy and restrictions. Peacetime military industries are never efficient, and Russia's is no exception.

Holy Writ

"National defense, the 'sacred slogan' of the twentieth century"— Seki Hiroharu, Japanese historian

The Japanese Military-Industrial Complex

Although Japan has the world's third largest defense budget, it was only during the 1980s that its own defense industries began to expand significantly. Over two thirds of Japan's defense production is aircraft and missiles. The remainder is one-third combat vehicles and two-thirds ships and naval weapons. Current trends are expected to continue, which will see missiles and associated electronic equipment comprising over 50 percent of production in the 1990s. Local designs are becoming more common, which makes it easier for Japan to export these systems without having to obtain permission from foreign patent holders (especially the United States). Although Japan's laws currently prohibit exporting weapons, components can be sold abroad, or just the technology. The law itself may be changed if Japan needs the export business badly enough. Most major Japanese defense manufacturers obtain over 25 percent of their work from arms manufacturing. Many of these firms are also affiliated with large trading organizations. This gives the weapons companies access to the latest technology and manufacturing techniques. Before the end of the century, the most effective, and least expensive, weapons in the world will be from Japan. While Japan is barred by its own constitution from going to war, this is no impediment to its supplying the warlike impulses of others.

A Continent in Arms:
The Armies of Europe on the Eve
of the World Wars of 1914, 1939, and 19??

Europe has prepared for the "Big One" three times in this century: once in the generation before World War I; the second time, and rather hastily at that, on the eve of World War II; and the third time since the late 1940s, in anticipation of the ultimate "Big One." The first two times, the enormous hosts with which the combatants began the war proved insufficient to the need; wartime mobilization would greatly increase the size of the armies. While a direct comparison of the scale of such preparations is not possible, and, indeed, precise figures are actually difficult to come by, an idea of the magnitude of these preparations may be gained by looking at the approximate size of the forces available for combat in Europe during each period. Figures below are for forces ready for combat in Europe, or available for such within sixty days, and, in the case of the two world wars, include the "M-Day"—Mobilization Day—strength of powers that did not immediately get into action.

The Real Wars, 1914 and 1939

	August 1914				September 1939				
	MEN	DIVS	A/C	Q	MEN	DIVS	TANKS	A/C	Q
Allied Bloc	6,336	261.6	550	1.0	8,400	421.0	12,000	12,000	1.0
German Bloc	4,185	204.2	250	1.3	4,000	192.6	5,400	5,200	1.6
Neutrals	1,005	41.0	75	0.6	2,400	120.0	400	1,000	0.7

"Men" indicates troops in thousands, "Divs" refers to divisions of 10,000 or more men, with smaller formations, such as cavalry divisions and separate brigades, averaged into the totals. "A/C" refers to aircraft and "Tanks" to tanks of all types available for immediate combat service. "Q" is an overall indication of relative quality of the divisions available to each bloc, averaging all armies within the bloc together. For 1914 the German bloc includes Germany, Austria-Hungary, Bulgaria, and Turkey, while the Allied bloc includes Britain, France, Russia, Belgium, Serbia, Montenegro, Portugal, Romania, Italy, and Greece, the last four of which did not enter the war until some time after it had begun. For 1939 the Allied bloc includes Britain, France, Poland, Denmark, Norway, the Netherlands, the Soviet Union, Yugoslavia, and Greece, while the German bloc includes Germany, Hungary, Romania, Bulgaria, and Italy. As in the case of World War I, several of the powers involved did not actually enter the war until it was well under way, and as a result the figures given suggest an initial Allied bloc advantage that was in fact considerably less pronounced.

The Expected Wars, 1949, 1964, and Today

	NATO Formed, 1949					NATO Matures, 1964				
	MEN	DIVS	TANKS	A/C	Q	MEN	DIVS	TANKS	A/C	Q
Allied Bloc	1,000	26	2,500	2,000	1.2	3,760	94	12,000	3,000	1.5
Soviet Bloc	1,430	75	12,500	4,500	1.0	3,240	162	23,000	5,000	1.0
Neutrals	1,200	60	600	800	0.7	2,000	80	5,500	1,200	0.6

As Things Stood, 1989

	MEN	DIVS	TANKS	A/C	Q
Allied Bloc	4,500	115.0	28,200	6,100	1.3
Soviet Bloc	6,800	192.0	49,800	7,120	1.0
Neutrals	2,335	40.3	2,300	1,215	1.0

The Allied bloc includes NATO members as of the following years: in 1949, the United States, Britain, Canada, France, Belgium, the Netherlands, Luxembourg, Portugal, Denmark, Norway, and Italy; in 1964, Greece, Turkey, and West Germany; in 1989, Spain, though France and Spain are not integrated in the NATO military command structure. The Soviet bloc in 1949 included the Soviet Union, Poland, East Germany, Czechoslovakia, Hungary, Romania, Bulgaria, and Albania, and all but the latter since, though Romania is no longer integrated into the Warsaw Pact command structure, and the whole Pact is falling apart. Note that figures for 1949 differ from contemporary accounts, which, due to a paucity of information and faulty intelligence estimates, had Soviet bloc strength considerably higher than was actually the case: One estimate gave the Russians— excluding satellites—10 million men under arms in 1948, at a time when they claimed only 2.8 million and are now believed to have had over 4 million if certain paramilitary troops were counted; there were a lot of nationalist guerrillas running around in Russia at the time, and special local militias were set up to help deal with them. Note that the "1989" figures are as of mid-1989, and considerable changes have since taken place.

Don't Pick On Someone Your Own Size.

"The capacity of any conqueror is more likely than not to be an illusion produced by the incapacity of his adversary."—George Bernard Shaw, British playwright

Peacetime Combat Training for Military Doctors

Because of the smaller, and different, medical needs of the peacetime military, it is difficult to properly prepare for wartime medical needs. For combat, doctors in the reserves would be called up and civilian doctors drafted. Unfortunately, most nations do not provide realistic training for their reserve doctors. One proposal is to have U.S. reserve doctors spend their weekend training in emergency rooms. There they could observe, and even participate in treating, the most numerous collection of gunshot wounds, burns, and other warlike injuries found outside a war zone. Some estimates put probable U.S. casualties during the opening weeks of a conventional "Big One" in Europe at 50,000.

More Is Not Always Better.

Russia has more scientists and engineers, and devotes more resources to developing military equipment, than any other nation. Why, then, do much smaller nations surpass the Russians in the speed and quality of developing military technology? It all has to do with organization. In Russia military technology is developed through a tangle of independent and secretive organizations. Research institutes do basic research on technology, and design bureaus design the equipment. Then factories build it, and the military bureaucracies specify what is needed in the first place. Each category of equipment has its own collection of these entities. In some areas, such as missiles, there is even more fragmentation. There are separate organizations for land-based ballistic missiles, sea-launched missiles, solid-fuel missiles, liquid-fuel missiles, and so on. While there is some cooperation, it is the exception rather than the rule. Russia's mania for secrecy discourages free exchange of information between these hundreds of organizations. One of the major objectives of their *glasnost* (openness) campaign in the late 1980s was to break down these artificial walls and eliminate much of the inefficiency. This will not be easy, because the many bureaucrats controlling these organizations will not willingly put themselves at risk of elimination through consolidation. In contrast, the United States has a wide-open system, with millions of researchers tied together through worldwide computer networks (ARPANET, MILNET, etc.). Western weapons manufacturers design and build equipment in their own factories and often propose new systems to the military rather than waiting for orders. And they reap the profits of their labors. This approach allows small nations like Sweden, Norway, and Israel to produce very advanced military equipment more quickly than Russia.

Falling Out of Fashion

"Today, while war between organized forces remains a favorite third world sport, the mass center of public opinion in the first and second worlds seems no longer to regard deliberate resort to conflict as an acceptable instrument of policy."—Richard Simpkin, British military analyst

Terrorism Profiled

According to the U.S. State Department, there were 832 terrorist incidents worldwide in 1987. This figure was about 7 percent higher than that for 1986, but by factoring out incidents in Pakistan, plagued by the activities of the Afghan KGB, the rest of the world experienced a 10 percent decline in such incidents. Total casualties for the year were 633 dead and 2,272 injured, including both victims and terrorists. Nearly half the deaths and a third of the injuries were related to the politics of the Middle East, though not necessarily perpetrated there. Bombings were the most common type of incident, accounting for 56.7 percent overall, followed by arson, 18.0 percent, armed attacks, 15.9 percent, kidnappings, 6.4 percent, sabotage, 0.7 percent, and skyjackings, 0.1 percent, with a "miscellaneous" category of 2.2 percent. Regionally, 45 percent of the incidents were in the Middle East, 20 percent in the rest of Asia, 18 percent in Western Europe (almost a third of which were Middle East–related), 13 percent in Latin America, and 4 percent in Africa, with only a handful in North America, and just one incident reported from Eastern Europe. Preliminary figures for 1988 appear to be quite similar, with 658 deaths attributed to international terrorism. Note that the State Department is highly selective in its listing of terrorist organizations, excluding a number of groups that may be said to be serving friendly interests, makes no mention of governments that sponsor antiterrorist terrorism, and even went so far as to assert "there is no evidence that the South African Government was a willing accomplice in the perpetration of massacres and the targeting of civilians" by South African–sponsored terrorists in Mozambique.

The Fifty-first State?

Although a number of bases are scheduled to be closed in the near future, there are about 870 military installations in the United States, plus about 20 more in U.S. territories, commonwealths, and possessions, for a total of about 26,000 square miles, an area larger than that of eleven states (Connecticut, Delaware, Hawaii, Maryland, Massachusetts, New Hampshire, New Jersey, Rhode Island, Vermont, and West Virginia). There are, in addition, about 350 somewhat small U.S. military installations overseas, totaling a few hundred additional square miles.

Just Being Human?

"What is Man, that he can give so much for war, so little for peace?"—John Masters, British officer and author

Apples and Oranges

One of the principal strategic issues confronting world leaders is the question of the balance of forces between NATO and the Warsaw Pact. In approximate figures, NATO argues that the balance is:

	NATO	Pact	Ratio
Tanks	16,500	51,500	.3:1
Artillery	14,450	43,400	.3:1
Combat Aircraft	4,000	8,250	.5:1
Troops	2.2 mil	3.1 mil	.7:1

Overall, the NATO figures certainly suggest an enormous imbalance in favor of the Warsaw Pact. Of course, the other side claims the figures are rather different. The official Russian view is that the balance is:

	NATO	Pact	Ratio
Tanks	30,700	59,500	.5:1
Artillery	57,100	71,600	.8:1
Combat Aircraft	7,100	7,900	.9:1
Troops	3.7 mil	3.6 mil	1.0:1

If one accepts the Russian figures, one must certainly conclude that there is, at best, a marginal Warsaw Pact advantage in equipment. Certainly, the situation is by no means as clear-cut as that suggested by the NATO figures. Of course, the obvious question is, "Who's lying?" And the highly unobvious answer may be "Nobody!" For, to a considerable extent, the differences may be a matter of trying to compare apples to oranges. Each side is using a different basis for calculation. NATO counts only "main battle tanks" (MBTs), on the reasonable ground that light tanks are unable to slug it out with the MBTs. Similarly, they include only artillery pieces of 100-mm caliber or greater, on the equally reasonable grounds that only such are capable of doing in MBTs or delivering decisive volumes of fire. And NATO figures generally exclude most naval forces, on the very logical assumption that these are devoted to activities in the North Atlantic, which, while they might have an effect on the lines of communication of NATO forces back to the United States and Canada, are not necessarily directly involved in activities on the European mainland.

This all sounds quite sensible until we see it from the Russian perspective. The Russian figures include light tanks along with the MBTs on the reasonable grounds that many of these tote tank-caliber weapons, and after all a tank is a tank. They also include guns down to 50 mm, on the equally logical grounds these can generate a lot of firepower and are capable of doing in light tanks, APCs, and similar vehicles. In addition, Russian figures include naval forces that, after all, not only support NATO but could readily project considerable air power into Central Europe, and just about everything that flies in the United States that might make it to Europe, while lowering the number of their own aircraft possibly because they intend to commit the balance in other theaters, or perhaps merely because NATO overestimated the number that they have. One potential solution to the dispute would be to attempt to develop a broader set of categories so that, while multiplying the statistics, some mutually agreed-upon set of figures could be evolved. Thus, accepting each side's estimate for the others' air forces, one could rework the above data to read:

	NATO	Pact	Ratio
Tanks: Battle	16,500	51,500	.3:1
Light	14,200	8,000	1.8:1
Artillery: 100mm+	14,450	43,400	.3:1
<100mm	42,650	28,200	1.5:1
Combat Aircraft: Wave 1	4,000	7,900	.6:1
Wave 2	3,100	350	8.9:1
Troops: Committed	2.2 mil	3.6 mil	.7:1
Supplemental	1.5 mil	0.5 mil	3.0:1

Of course, these figures are not necessarily accurate. Indeed, some estimates set NATO's mobilized manpower at 4.5 million and the Pact's at 6.0 million. There's also the very real problem of the political reliability of the allies on both sides. Nevertheless, only by reaching such a mutually satisfactory listing could the really difficult work of negotiating a proportional reduction of forces begin. One major stumbling block will be an analysis of qualitative factors. For example, assume Warsaw Pact divisions equal "1" and NATO divisions about 1.3 by the NATO version of the data, and 1.7–2.0 by Russian figures. On this basis, total "combat power" would be 192 Warsaw Pact versus 150 by NATO figures, a Pact superiority of about 28 percent. By Pact figures, however, the total would be 192 versus 196–230, that is, virtual parity or a NATO superiority of about 20 percent. The biggest difference would be due to aircraft. Both sides unofficially recognize a NATO qualitative superiority. There is no agreement on exactly what the extent of this difference is.

Because They're Lousy Shots

There are about 670 active military personnel, but only about 85 physicians, for every 100,000 people in the world.

I Can't Understand You, Comrade Sergeant.

Throughout the eighties, the ethnic situation in the Soviet armed forces worsened. Nearly half of the Soviet Union's 280 million citizens are not in fact Russian, and don't speak Russian at home. Many of them don't even speak any Russian at all. In the armed forces, these "minorities" troops are first taught a vocabulary of a few dozen crucial commands and then given menial tasks. Many are not even accepted because of the language problem. But the declining pool of conscripts and the growing need for technically literate recruits in the air force and navy, plus the declining birthrate among the Russian-speaking population, have combined to increase the ratio of non-Russians in the politically sensitive combat regiments. Moreover, 5 percent of the most politically reliable recruits are taken for the KGB, national police, and border guards. You see, over the centuries the Russians have learned that it is a good thing to have the most politically reliable people in the combat and security units. But from the early 1980s to the end of the decade, the number of non-Russians in the combat regiments went from between 20 and 30 percent to nearly 40 percent. The result, as reported in the Russian military press, has been increasing morale and efficiency problems. Many combat units now have over one-third non-Russian speakers. This may well be a major reason for the 1988 decision to reduce armed forces strength 10 percent. Other proposals urge a switch to an all-volunteer force backed up by the traditional Russian militia, similar to the U.S. National Guard. This solution would be enormously expensive, as the regular troops would have to be offered pay and benefits similar to those now available to officers. Moreover, Russia has always shown more trust in quantity than quality.

But the current situation makes the Russian-speaking leadership of the Soviet Union very nervous.

Keeping It All Together on the Home Front

Several hundred years of diligent empire-building have given Russia vast border regions populated by people who don't much like Russians and often don't even read or speak Russian. Their loyalty is something the Russians don't take for granted. The Russian Empire peaked in 1914, when almost all the current territory plus Finland, parts of Poland, and a bit of Turkey belonged. Currently, the major minorities are 7 million people in the Baltic States, 10 million Belorussians ("White Russians"), 50 million Ukrainians, 1 million Moldavians, 16 million in the Caucasus, and over 40 million Moslems in Central Asia. Many millions of additional non-Russians are spread throughout the Russian Republic, which stretches from Leningrad to the Black Sea and thence all the way to the Pacific. From the Russian perspective, the biggest danger of *glasnost* (openness) and *perestroika* (restructuring society and the economy) is the stirring up of long-suppressed nationalistic feelings among the non-Russian populations, such as the Armenians, Lithuanians, and Georgians. This will be causing a lot more discussion in the government than what appears on the evening news, and certainly more than the availability of consumer goods and groceries. Not only are the non-Russians antagonistic toward the Russians, but often have longstanding grievances against neighboring minorities. If anything can tear the Soviet Union apart, it is the rebelliousness of the conquered and unassimilated non-Russian populations.

There Is Nothing Constant in the Universe.

In late 1988, a special mixed brigade was raised jointly by two NATO members who have historically been on less-than-friendly terms. The new outfit, which will not be under direct NATO command, consists of a binational command and service battalion, two French and two West German infantry battalions, a French light infantry battalion, and a West German artillery battalion. Officers close to this operation consider it something of a joke, but it does have considerable political and diplomatic potential. It also enables many French and German troops to improve their foreign-language skills.

ERA

More women serve as officers in the U.S. armed forces, about 32,000, than serve in any capacity as active-duty uniformed personnel in the armed forces of any other nation.

Getting the Mercedes Past the Tank Jam

For over thirty years, West Germany has been the maneuver area for army and air force units of more than half a dozen foreign nations. Citizens complain about the roar of low-flying aircraft and helicopters, particularly at night and in bad weather. At least once a week, one of these aircraft crashes. Several times a year there are major maneuvers by ground units. Thousands of armored vehicles tear up roads, fields, and anything else in the way, while often causing traffic jams that delay civilian travelers. While all these foreign troops are in West Germany primarily for the defense of that nation, West Germans are becoming less fearful of a Russian invasion and more intolerant of all the military activity in their own neighborhoods.

Who Really Pays for NATO (European View)?

The United States maintains nearly a third of a million troops in or near Europe for the defense of European NATO-member nations. This costs the United States over $20 billion a year. In the last fifteen years, the United States has periodically called for greater contributions from other NATO members to reduce U.S. expense in this area. Yet European NATO nations point out that since 1970 their per capita spending has increased 21 percent, while U.S. spending has actually declined 3 percent. Total military manpower among European NATO nations increased 5 percent during the same period while U.S. strength declined 30 percent. Total European NATO defense spending went up far more in this period than U.S. spending. European NATO members criticize U.S. inability to spend its money wisely or run its economy efficiently. The debate rages on.

Odd Bedfellows

There does seem to be some truth to the old saying "Politics makes odd bedfellows." Two of the strangest are undoubtedly the United States and Cuba, who officially get along infamously, but sometimes have had quite a cozy relationship. In Angola, Cuban troops guard U.S.-owned oil fields and coffee plantations from attacks by guerrillas partially sponsored by the United States. Meanwhile, in Central America, both Cuba and the United States have offered assistance to Belize should an ambitious Guatemala decide to make good some antique territorial claims.

Glasnost at Work

NATO and the Warsaw Pact have recently been coordinating military operations in the Arctic, where the Norwegian and Russian border patrols are cooperating to prevent tourists from stealing Russian frontier marker signs, which are decorated with the coat-of-arms of the Soviet Union.

Constant Budget

In terms of 1982 dollars, the U.S. defense budget has averaged $198 billion a year since 1961. From 1961–68, the average was $207 billion, largely because of Vietnam War expenses. From 1969–76, it averaged $189 billion. From 1977–80, it was $158 billion, and from 1981–88 it averaged $216 billion per year. This is uncharacteristically high, as without the Vietnam expenses the annual budget for the 1961–88 period would have been closer to $180 billion per year.

Trotsky Lives!

Several years ago a distinguished American military historian was invited to deliver several lectures at the Frunze Military Academy in Moscow, the nerve center of Soviet military intellectual endeavor. There was a major social event scheduled during his visit, to which he was courteously invited. Upon his acceptance, a senior Russian officer volunteered to give him a ride, saying, in effect, "I'll give you a lift to the Bronstein." The American apparently looked puzzled at this remark, and so the Russian added, with a sly smile, "After all, we know who really founded it," referring to Lev Bronstein, better known as Leon Trotsky, who, though Lenin's right-hand man in the Revolution, and the founder of the Red Army, has been persona maxima non grata in Russia since being driven out by Stalin in the late 1920s.

The Proper Spirit

"There's no sight more inspiring or heartwarming than troops marching out to battle when you ain't going with them."—Brigadier Sir Harry Paget Flashman, V.C., K.C.I.E., etc., etc. [George MacDonald Fraser]

Thanks, but No Thanks

When then–Chief Justice Warren Burger was notified that a place had been reserved for him in the government's secret underground fallout shelter, situated in the foothills of the Appalachians some miles west of Washington, he inquired as to what arrangements had been made for his wife. Learning that she was "nonessential" to national recovery from a nuclear war, the Chief Justice notified the appropriate authorities that so was he.

Let's Swap.

In another of the increasingly common signs of a deepening thaw in East-West relations, in July of 1988 a British Army tank museum traded an old Conqueror tank to a Soviet Army tank museum in exchange for a Josef Stalin II heavy tank, the very vehicle that the Conqueror was designed to fight, so that both museums would have a more complete collection.

They Did Make the Lowest Bid.

Construction at seventy-one allegedly secret bomb-proof hangars, which NATO was building to shelter aircraft scheduled to reinforce the Royal Danish Air Force in the event of war, ground to an abrupt halt one day early in November of 1988 when trucks bearing East German markings were discovered on several of the building sites. An investigation soon turned up the fact that an Austrian subcontractor had hired the East Germans to transport construction materials to the installations. A spokesman for the prime contractor is reported to have said, "Someone somewhere must have been fast asleep." Construction details were to have been kept secret lest a potential enemy develop more effective plans to destroy them.

The Top Ten

While the standard of living in Russia is quite low, not all Russians share these unpleasant conditions. About 10 percent of the population lives quite well. There are a million military officers and professional NCOs, plus their families. The middle-grade and senior government officials number several million, plus their families. The KGB and other security forces add another million or so officials and dependents. There are also several million who do quite well outside the system, either legally or illegally. The largest group of privileged citizens are those associated with the defense industries. There are over 10 million defense workers and researchers, including dependents, who share in a wealth of benefits to keep them motivated. One of the major problems of converting military production to civilian use is weaning these privileged workers away from the perqs and benefits to which they become accustomed. The majority of less well-off workers tolerated these luxuries in the name of national defense. The average Russian will not be so quiescent if defense workers produce the same civilian goods they do and still retain defense industry-level benefits.

Overkill?

It is generally believed that in the event of an all-out war, the United States has identified sixty separate targets in Moscow for nuclear obliteration. Similarly, New York City is believed to be targeted by several dozen Russian nuclear warheads. Unlike Moscow, there are no major military targets in the Big Apple, but the Russians do have over 5,000 nuclear weapons, and U.S. targeting specialists assume that the Russians will want to do something with all that firepower.

Just Imagine.

The CIA estimates that by the year 2000 there will be nuclear-power plants in about fifty countries, and the total amount of fissionable material in the world will be approximately 6 million tons. As it only requires about thirty pounds of fissionable material to make a small nuclear weapon, this would be sufficient to produce about 400 million modest-sized nuclear holocausts. More realistically, the conversion and diversion of less than one percent of this fuel to unauthorized uses would allow construction of several hundred weapons. Such diversion of small amounts of material has already enabled several smaller nations to build nuclear weapons.

Why the Thaw?

Russia is presently suffering, and the United States will soon begin to suffer, manpower shortages as both countries approach zero population growth. In addition, the United States and Russia are the only developed nations that border on Third World countries, with their impoverished, rapidly growing populations and increasing access to high-tech weaponry, which already makes the Soviet Union vulnerable to several Middle Eastern powers and is likely to make the United States vulnerable to several Latin American nations in the near future. Then, too, decades of massive defense outlays have seriously impaired the U.S. economy and brought that of Russia to virtual collapse. Meanwhile, Islamic fundamentalism not only threatens the stability of Soviet Central Asia, but, should it spread along the belt of Muslim states stretching from India to the Atlantic, it would effectively threaten Europe's southern flank. Finally, there is the rising industrial power of the Pacific Rim, which, if coupled with the enormous resources of China, would not only threaten the industrial future of the United States but the political survival of Russia. The truth will out.

Iran-Iraq War Postmortem

The 1980–89 Iran-Iraq War reaffirmed a number of ancient lessons. The first was that it's quite difficult to invade a neighboring nation, even if it's being torn apart by civil disorder. That was Iraq's mistake.

The second lesson was that it's risky to attempt overcoming equipment deficiencies with masses of fanatic infantry. That was Iran's error.

The third lesson was that possessing high-tech weapons does not mean you can put them to use in combat. It took Iraq five years before it got its air force trained well enough to be used regularly in combat. Iran never got its air force in shape, largely because its equipment was American and they were cut off from steady sources of spares and support.

Iran's antagonistic diplomacy also cut them off from many other nations that could have supplied them with needed equipment. Iraq was much more successful in keeping on good terms with needed arms suppliers. Although Iraq stopped the Iranian counteroffensives with diligent defensive measures, they were only able to force Iran to give up the war when Iraqi forces successfully attacked. Over 1,000 missiles and rockets were fired at each side's towns and cities, mostly in the last year of the war. This made it difficult for Iran to ignore the declining morale of its population.

The Small Print

The apparent end of the Cold War may signal a substantial reduction in armaments, but this may not necessarily be reflected in lower costs to the taxpayer, for the various disarmament agreements will have to be monitored. Thus, citing a need to verify the INF (Intermediate-Range Nuclear Forces) agreement, the Defense Department has convinced Congress to spring for six Lacrosse spy satellites, at a cost of $1 or $2 billion apiece. This will be in addition to the cost of American on-site inspections of various Soviet facilities, permitted under the INF treaty, which will average about $200 million a year. Should the widely discussed START (Strategic Arms Reduction

Treaty) ever be signed, on-site verification costs could easily run to another $200 million a year, if not more, since unlike INF, which eliminated an entire class of delivery systems, START would institute across-the-board proportional reductions in all delivery systems.

Reciprocity

In what may well have been among the most unusual nuclear-weapons tests ever conducted, in middle and late 1988 Russia and the United States jointly held two underground weapons tests in order to help calibrate "national technical means," or detection equipment, to be used to keep tabs on each other's testing programs.

Nuclear Winter Prototype

The massive forest fires in the United States during 1988 provided an opportunity to see what effect such fires, similar to those expected in a nuclear war, would have. One study conducted in northern California found that the clouds of smoke and ash blocked so much of the sun's heat that ground temperature fell as much as 36 degrees for as long as a week.

NATO's Other Strategic Nukes

A point often ignored by Americans, but not by Russians, is the existence of significant strategic nuclear weapons among non-U.S. NATO nations. Britain and France both possess nuclear-tipped ballistic missiles. Britain has four ballistic missile-carrying nuclear subs (SSBNs), each carrying sixteen U.S.-built Polaris missiles. France has six SSBNs, each carrying sixteen French-built missiles. France also has sixteen similar missiles fired from land-based silos. Thus, at any given time, the French have eighty 4,000-km range missiles aimed at Russia. The British have two subs and thirty-two missiles at sea at any time. An increasing number of the French and British missiles have multiple warheads. France is updating five of its six subs to carry six warhead missiles. Britain is building four new subs to carry 6,000-km Trident missiles, each with eight warheads. These should be in service by the mid 1990s. These two nations currently have, on short notice, over 200 warheads capable of hitting most of Russia west of the Urals. In addition, Britain and France have over a hundred nuclear-capable fighter-bombers able to reach targets in Western Russia. Thus, if the American nuclear forces disappeared tomorrow, there would still be enough potentially hostile nuclear weapons in Western Europe to devastate the Soviet Union.

Anyone Want My Share?

The combined nuclear arsenals of the world contain the equivalent of 3.5 tons of TNT for every living man, woman, and child.

The Odd Couple

"This soldiering thing sadly deadens that very good thing, humanity."—Lewis Wallace, Civil War general, author of *Ben-Hur*

World War I Lives

Belgium was the scene of the most intense fighting of World War I (1914–18). Millions of tons of artillery shells were fired by both sides. World War II added more shells and aircraft bombs. Anywhere from 5 to 10 percent of these munitions were duds, and did not explode when they hit the ground. As late as the 1990s, over 200 tons of unexploded bombs and shells are discovered each year and must be disposed of. This is a tricky business. In 1986 four Belgian soldiers were killed as they unloaded an old bomb from a truck. Several dozen bomb-disposal workers have been killed since 1945. To make matters worse, about 10 percent of the World War I–era artillery shells contain poison gas, usually mustard. The mustard gas is still potent after all these years. In the early 1990s, Belgium is spending over $4 million to build a special facility to safely dispose of these seventy-year-old chemical weapons.

Serving International Socialism

About 16,000 Soviet military advisers serve in various non-communist Third World countries (1989).

Rush Hour at the Golan Heights

Many Israeli units guarding the border with Syria are composed largely of reservists doing their one to three months a year of active duty. Because Israel is such a small country, numbers of these troops commute to their posts each day. When there is an alert, they may have to stay at their military posts twenty-four hours a day, but most of the time they can drive home to the wife and kids after a day of patrolling the border.

Population Density

There are almost 500,000 German and about 400,000 NATO troops in West Germany, which has an area of 95,975 square miles, about as large as Wyoming, with a population of 60.2 million, or about one soldier for every sixty-six civilians in the country, or nine soldiers per square mile. In East Germany, which has an area of 41,768 square miles, about that of Virginia, with about 16.7 million people, there are about 240,000 German and 420,000 Soviet troops, about one soldier for every twenty-five civilians and nearly sixteen per square mile.

One Might Say There's a Pattern Here.

In 1984 the University of Oslo and the Norwegian Academy of Sciences calculated that since 3600 B.C., there had been 14,531 wars resulting in 3,600 million deaths. Peace prevailed for only 292 years of the 5,584 studied, about 5 percent of the time. These rare instances of peace are probably due to inadequate historical records.

No Foreigners Need Apply.

The U.S. military technology advantage is based on the quality and quantity of its engineers. Fueled by forty years of heavy defense spending, excellent employment opportunities abound for U.S. engineers. In the last twenty years, these opportunities have been so attractive that senior engineers have declined lower-paying positions in teaching. As a result, over half the engineering faculty are now foreign-born. Even a green card or obtaining citizenship will not always get foreigners the security clearance they need for high-pay-ing defense work. Until 1988 foreigners had to be residents of the United States for ten years before they could even be considered for a clearance. Another fear is that a foreign-born engineer with U.S. defense experience could return to his native land and take his knowledge of U.S. defense technology with him. This has actually happened quite often. Thus, many highly trained foreign-born en-gineers take academic positions that Americans increasingly decline.

The major problem with this is that it is more difficult to do de-fense-related research in universities because of the large number of foreign-born faculty. It's not that the foreign-born must have secu-rity clearances in order for their American-born colleagues to do defense work, but the senior faculty must be aware of what their subordinates are up to. More and more, the senior faculty are for-eign-born and thus barred from any access to defense-related work. Another problem is that these foreign-born faculty have no defense-industry experience and tend to prefer research over applications. This attitude has caused the number of advanced engineering de-grees (masters and doctorates) to become overwhelmingly a province of the foreign-born. By 1985 nearly two thirds of engineering doc-torates went to foreign-born students. Although some 60 percent of these remain in the United States for the rest of their careers, the defense industry is increasingly being closed off from much of the best available engineering talent.

Make Love and War?

In Greek mythology, the illegitimate offspring of Aphrodite, goddess of love and beauty, and Ares, god of war, are Love, Passion, and Harmony.

Lawyers—1, Gunships—0

West German citizens have long been torn between gratitude that hundreds of thousands of foreign troops guard them from the Red Army and the annoyance of all the tank columns and low-flying air-craft. When it was announced in 1987 that U.S. units in West Ger-many would receive the new AH-64 "Apache" helicopter gunship, something snapped. The AH-64 is certainly one nimble aircraft, and normally practices right down to the roof and treetops, no matter how bad the weather. Every once in a while an AH-64 crashes on a training mission. German voters complained to their elected representatives. Some hired lawyers to sue the U.S. Army to keep the AH-64 out of Germany. As of early 1989, the AH-64s were barred from Germany. The U.S. Army has appealed the judicial decision.

In the Name of Peace and International Brotherhood

Since 1955 an average of slightly more than 2,700 Third World military personnel have been trained each year in Warsaw Pact countries, for a total of about 90,000 officers and men. About 75,000 (83 percent) of these troops received their training in the USSR, with the balance, 15,000 (17 percent) going to other Pact countries. In regional terms, about 18,000 (20 percent) of the troops involved were from sub-Saharan Africa, nearly 48,000 (50 percent), from North Africa and the Middle East, a little more than 25,000 (27 percent) from South and East Asia, and less than 2,000 (2 percent) from Latin America, excluding Cuba. The actual number of trainees has risen from a handful each year in the 1950s to several thousand in recent years. While this training gives these officers a Russian attitude toward military matters, it also tends to sour them on most other aspects of Russian society and culture.

Humanitarian Gesture

The Draft Protocol Concerning Non-Detectable Fragments, initialed by 81 countries during the 1978–80 UN Disarmament Conference, is perhaps the shortest arms-control agreement ever concluded, reading, "It is prohibited to use any weapon the primary effect of which is to injure by fragments which in the human body escape detection by X-rays."

The Fall Guy

"Let us not get so preoccupied with weapons that we lose sight of the fact that war itself is the real villain."—Harry S Truman, American president, 1945–53, and artillery captain in World War I

Glasnost?

Under the terms of the INF treaty, the United States and Russia are permitted to station personnel at various sites in each other's territory in order to monitor compliance with treaty provisions. A number of restrictions apply to the people in question. Thus, upon approval of the host country, the observers may travel, under escort, within a thirty-one mile radius of the installation to which they are assigned. In the United States, the organization charged with supervising Russian inspectors, the On-Site Inspection Agency, has indicated that the Soviet monitors may visit "public places, such as churches, schools, or just about any civic organization you can think of." However, in a masterpiece of bureaucratic asininity, they are not permitted to visit private homes on the grounds that such "makes guaranteeing their safety too difficult." As a result, the Russians have had to turn down numerous invitations to go to that most dangerous of places, the American home, where they have been invited to dine with American families, particularly around Thanksgiving and Christmas.

Doing Everything, and Nothing

The United States and to a lesser extent Russia suffer from the problem of trying to do too much in weapons development and not cooperating effectively with their allies. The United States attempts to produce all its own weapons, even though some of its NATO allies have demonstrated that they can produce some items better and cheaper. This approach also forces the United States and its NATO allies to produce uneconomically small runs of the same classes of weapons. The Russian problem is a little different, as the Russians have no reliable allies and are reluctant to share any of their defense-production secrets with those allies they do have. Russia does, however, allow its East European allies to produce some of the simpler systems, though not to any great extent. And Russia is reluctant to use many innovations developed by its East European allies. Finally, none of its East European allies have defense industries as large and well-developed as those of the NATO European nations.

Disarmament Moves the Russians Can Live With

NATO nations focus on large Russian ground forces in discussions about reducing conventional weapons in Europe. The Russians look at high-performance NATO aircraft and U.S. naval forces operating off the coasts of Europe. According to Russian calculations, NATO air forces in Central Europe account for half of NATO's combat power. The U.S. aircraft carriers are seen as capable of delivering significant combat power while being difficult to find and hit. An equitable reduction in conventional forces, for the Russians, would involve removing many U.S. aircraft from Europe and forbidding U.S. carriers to enter the North Sea or Mediterranean. In return, the Russians would move half a million men, including most of their combat-ready divisions, back behind the Ural Mountains. The idea behind this is that the United States could move aircraft and carriers back to Europe at least as quickly as Russia could move its divisions into Eastern Europe.

Civil Defense

The United States currently spends about $148 million a year "for the purpose of carrying out the Federal Civil Defense Act of 1950," which works out to an expenditure of about sixty cents for every man, woman, and child in the country.

But Soldiers Wear Snappier Uniforms.

There are approximately 34 million active-duty military personnel in the world but only about 28 million teachers. On this basis, the United States is actually doing better than the world average, having nearly 2.25 million classroom teachers for only about 2.1 million troops.

Old Wisdom

"The decisive means for politics is violence."—Max Weber, pioneer sociologist

At War with America

We don't usually think of the United States when the subject of insurrection comes up. Yet, there are a great many groups in the United States who regularly resort to violence in the furtherance of their political goals, or who reject with armed force the authority of the U.S. government. During one six-month period in recent years, the FBI reported 362 bombing incidents—299 explosive devices and 63 incendiary ones—in the United States, most of which appear to have been with criminal intent in mind, but with a fair number of politically motivated ones as well. These caused ten deaths, forty-four injuries, and $3.6 million in property damage. The total number of incidents was slightly below average for the last decade or so. In 1986 alone, there were over eighty-five violent attacks on family-planning clinics, including window breakings, sackings, beatings, arson, and bombings. While the number of incidents perpetrated by rightest movements seems to exceed those committed by leftists, who appear rather less well organized and financed than their rivals, there are a number of groups that do not fall into the traditional left-right dichotomy of political activism, including extremist factions of otherwise legitimate movements, as can be seen in the accompanying list.

> American Republican Army
> Animal-rights extremists
> Anti-Arab extremists
> Antinuclear power extremists
> Antipornography extremists
> Anti-Semitic extremists
> Arizona Patriots
> Armed Resistance Movement
> Aryan Nations
> Black Liberation Army
> Committee of the States
> Ecology/antitechnology extremists
> Irish Republican Army
> Islamic extremists

Japanese Red Army Faction

Jewish Defense League

KKK

Los Machateros Puerto Rican Nationalist Group

May 19th Communist Movement

Mormon polygamist extremists

Native American extremists

Neo-Nazi organizations

Organization of Volunteers for the Puerto Rican Revolution

Posse Comitatus

Puerto Rican National Liberation Front

Red Guerrilla Resistance

Religious extremists

Revolutionary Fighting Group

Right-to-Life extremists

White Patriots Party

United Freedom Front/Sam Melville-Jonathan Jackson Unit

The actual number of people who are "at war with America" is difficult to determine. Many of the groups involved are extremely small; some, such as the United Freedom Front or the Native American extremists, running to fewer than two dozen members. Some groups are larger, neo-Nazi "skinhead" groups, for example, total an estimated 2,500. A complicating element is the fact that some people are members of more than one group—during the civil-rights movement in the early sixties the FBI found one racist activist who was a member of thirty-five different hate groups—so that merely totaling up the estimated membership of various groups only inflates their numbers. Moreover, some groups, particularly leftist ones, operate under several different names. All things considered, however, it is likely that, common criminals aside, the number of people in armed opposition to the laws of the United States total from 3,000 to 4,000, or 60–80 per million population.

At War in America

Aside from domestically rooted political groups engaging in violence, there is some violence taking place in the United States that is inspired by, and occurs on behalf of, foreign nations or political movements for their own domestic purposes. Various unsavory regimes have been known to strike out at exiled dissidents in the United States, and there are internecine conflicts abroad that occasionally find expression in violent acts committed within various immigrant communities. In addition, several groups find committing violent acts in the United States against representatives of countries that they oppose a lot safer than operating in those countries. Groups and governments that have committed violence in the United States for reasons not involving American policy include:

> Armenian nationalists
> Bulgaria
> Chile
> Chinese political factions
> Colombian political factions
> Croatian nationalists
> Cuba and Cuban political factions
> Eritrean nationalists
> Ethiopia
> Greek nationalists
> Iran
> Iraq
> Israel
> Irish nationalists
> Islamic extremists
> KGB
> Kurdish nationalists
> Libya
> Mexican political factions
> Nicaragua and Nicaraguan political factions
> North Korea
> South Korea
> Pakistani political factions
> Philippines and Filipino political factions
> PLO
> Salvadorean political factions

Sikh extremists
South Moluccan nationalists
South Africa
Turkish political factions
Taiwan
Vietnamese political factions
Yemen Arab Republic

There are no figures available on the amount of foreign-inspired political violence in the United States. However, occasional items culled from newspapers suggest that the number of incidents may total several dozen a year.

Arms Embargoes

Widely regarded as a powerful diplomatic tool with which to exert pressure on recalcitrant nations short of resorting to military force, the embargo has never actually proved of particular value. The most notable recent failures have been embargoes placed on the sale of arms to South Africa in the late 1960s, to protest apartheid, and on Chile in the early 1970s, to protest widespread human-rights violations. Neither country has found the embargo a handicap in procuring arms. Covert sales, particularly by powers who need all the friends or dollars that they can get—such as Israel and Taiwan—are easy to arrange. More important, however, is the fact that arms embargoes stimulate local military industry. In Chile, existing installations devoted to the maintenance and repair of aircraft and mechanized equipment have gradually expanded into credible design and production facilities. South Africa, which formerly produced only small arms, now produces a wide range of equipment, including armored fighting vehicles, combat aircraft, helicopters, and warships. Many of these items are exported. For an arms embargo to work, it must be imposed in an immediate "war-imminent" situation, and even then, covert sales are likely to prove a problem.

And Teachers Don't Draw Combat Pay.

The average annual salary of an American teacher, who in most states must have a master's degree, is $26,704, only about 65 percent more than that of the average member of the armed forces, who only needs a high school diploma, who also gets about $10,000 a year in room, board, and medical benefits.

Those Practical Germans

In recognition of the many types of traffic found on West Germany's crowded highways, West German traffic signs have three speed limits listed: one for cars, one for trucks, and one for armored combat vehicles.

Tradition Pays Off

Tradition is widely considered one of the things that keeps a military force going. As a result, most armies pay at least lip service to traditional ceremonies, uniforms, and music. In one army, this has also proved to be rather profitable. The former East German Army was, in drill, ceremony, and music, something of a reincarnation of the Imperial German and Royal Prussian Armies. Indeed, the army band is so skillful in the reproduction of traditional Prussian and German military music that it has cut a number of records, which are sold to military buffs in the West. And by some accounts, the band once also held a recording session behind closed doors, so that it could cash in on sales to Neo-Nazis as well.

Fame

"The thirst for military glory will ever be the vice of the most exalted characters."—Edward Gibbon, historian

Peace Delayed

In April of 1986, the Council of the Isles of the Scilly Islands, a British archipelago thirty miles west of Land's End in Cornwall, concluded a treaty of peace with the crown of the Netherlands, thus ending a technical state of war that had existed since 1651, when the Dutch got tired of having their ships victimized by Scillian "false-lighters," who would erect decoy beacons to mislead ships onto the rocks, so that they could become wrecks suitable for plundering. At about the same time that the Scillians and Dutch were talking "peace," the mayor of Rome concluded a similar agreement with the mayor of Tunis, the latter acting as surrogate for the city of Carthage, wiped out in 146 B.C., thus concluding hostilities that had first begun in 264 B.C., as a result of commercial and territorial rivalries. And Greece and Albania recently agreed to end a technical state of war that had existed for some forty years.

Wisdom of the Ages

"There never was a good war nor a bad peace."—Benjamin Franklin, American revolutionary, scientist, diplomat, publisher, rake, and philosopher

Bureaucratic Obstacles

Early in 1989, Congress discovered that, due to an obsolete bureaucratic regulation, some 60 percent of the more than 120,000 World War I veterans are ineligible for old-age pensions and other benefits because they have incomes in excess of $6,200 a year. This amount is now over $50,000, adjusted for inflation since the time the law was passed. This action came shortly after the Congress managed to correct a Reconstruction-era law that prohibited veterans from paying more than ten dollars for legal assistance in disputes with the Veterans' Administration. Again, inflation would make the ten-dollar amount several hundred dollars in current value. Lawyers' fees have inflated much faster than general inflation.

A Season for War . . .

Despite the increasing mechanization of armed forces, the weather still remains a critical determinant in military endeavors. Excluding guerrilla wars and colonial affairs, of fifty-five conflicts involving one or more of the Great Powers between 1840 and 1988,

> 18 (32.7%) began in the spring (Apr., May, June)
> 16 (29.1%) began in the summer (July, Aug., Sept.)

12 (21.8%) began in the autumn (Oct., Nov., Dec.)

9 (16.4%) began in the winter (Jan., Feb., Mar.)

Fully forty-eight percent of the wars began in April, May, June, or July, the four months most favorable to campaigning by ancient tradition.

Wretched Excess

"In war you have to pay for your mistakes."—William J. Slim, British field marshal, World War II

A Different Drummer

The original version of the 1988 U.S. budget included a 4 percent increase in funding for military bands, to $154 million, and a 12 percent cut in funding for the National Endowment for the Arts, to $144 million.

Exchange Rates

The only real test of a military policy is that of the battlefield. And on that basis, the Russian style in warfare appears to be seriously flawed. The October War in the Middle East in 1973 was essentially a test between the Israeli military system, a modified form of the German variant of the Western model, and the Soviet model used by Egypt, Syria, and Iraq. Israel committed to the war about 30 combat brigades, some 1,700 tanks, and 500 combat aircraft. Omitting small contingents from several other nations, the Arab bloc committed about 78 combat brigades, 4,500 tanks, and 960 aircraft. In the course of eighteen days of fighting, the Israelis lost the equivalent of about four brigades (13.3 percent), 840 tanks (49.4 percent), and 120 aircraft (24.0 percent), while the Arabs lost 16 brigades (20.0 percent), 1,330 tanks (29.6 percent), and 368 aircraft (38.3 percent). Thus, the Arabs lost roughly 4.0 brigades, about 1.6 tanks, and nearly 3.1 aircraft for each one lost by Israel, certainly a telling indictment of Russian methods and equipment. But the story does not end there. The Arab power that was most heavily oriented toward a Soviet model was Syria, which lost 6 out of 28 brigades (21.4 percent), 600 out of 1,600 tanks (37.5 percent), and 165 out of 300 aircraft (55 percent). Iraq, also strongly influenced by the Russians, committed only a part of her forces, three brigades, which were in action from only the fourth through the tenth days of the war before having to be withdrawn, managed to lose 80 of the 400 tanks (20.0 percent) and 21 of the 60 aircraft (35.0 percent) involved, with all three brigades effectively destroyed as combat formations (100 percent). In contrast, Egypt, which a year earlier had expelled her Soviet advisers and instituted changes in weapons, tactics, and organization, lost 7 out of 47 brigades (14.5 percent), 650 out of 2,500 tanks (26.0 percent), and 182 out of 600 aircraft (30.3 percent), and Jordan, with a British-pattern army, committed only three brigades, lost not one, and only lost a handful of tanks.

And in Living Color

"I have never heard music as fascinating and grand as that of battle."—Lew Wallace, American author and politician

Military Participation Ratios

A military participation ratio (MPR) is the percentage of the population that is serving in the armed forces in some capacity. The present world MPR, for example, is about 0.6 percent in "peacetime" and about 1.7 percent upon mobilization. This means that roughly 0.6 percent of the people in the world—about one in 155—are serving in an active uniformed military capacity or are available for service within forty-eight hours, and about 1.7 percent—one in 55— will be available within about sixty days, if full mobilization reservists and paramilitary personnel are included. Excluding countries actually at war or just standing down from such—Iran, Iraq, Nicaragua, etc.—the five countries with the highest active forces military participation ratios (MPRs) are:

Israel	12.1%
Switzerland	9.8%

Sweden	8.2%
Singapore	4.3%
North Korea	3.8%

The first four of these have militia-type armed forces. By the sixtieth day of mobilization, the standings have changed considerably:

Switzerland	17.8%
Cuba	17.3%
Sweden	15.4%
Finland	14.5%
Austria	14.1%

The four European countries listed have well-organized, heavily armed militia systems, while Cuba has a large paramilitary contingent that could be expected to perform internal-security duties in the event of a war with the United States. These countries have so organized their defenses to make their maximum potential military manpower available on short notice. Most other powers could match these figures only after several more months of mobilization. Europe is, as expected, the most heavily armed region in the world, with a combined MPR of 1.1 percent within forty-eight hours and 3.4 percent within sixty days. The combined MPR for all sixteen NATO powers—including the United States and Canada—is 0.9 percent—one in 115—for available forces, which rises to 2.1 percent upon mobilization—one in 48. NATO MPRs are:

	Active	Mobilized
Greece	1.7%	6.8%
West Germany	1.2%	2.3%
Turkey	1.1%	2.9%
Spain	0.9%	3.9%
U.S.	0.9%	1.4%
Belgium	0.9%	1.7%
Norway	0.9%	10.5%
France	0.8%	1.8%
Netherlands	0.8%	1.9%

	Active	*Mobilized*
Denmark	0.7%	3.5%
Italy	0.7%	2.4%
Portugal	0.6%	6.6%
Britain	0.6%	1.1%
Canada	0.3%	0.5%
Luxembourg	0.2%	0.3%
Iceland	0.0%	0.2%

The combined figures for the seven Warsaw Pact powers are 1.2% active and 4.2% mobilized. Pact MPRs are:

	Active	*Mobilized*
Bulgaria	1.8%	6.5%
Russia	1.3%	4.1%
East Germany	1.9%	6.8%
Hungary	1.0%	3.2%
Czechoslovakia	1.0%	4.0%
Poland	0.8%	4.2%
Romania	0.8%	3.8%

The European neutrals are actually more heavily militarized than either bloc, with an active force MPR of 3.2 percent and a mobilization MPR of 12.4 percent. Indeed, three of the European neutrals—Switzerland, Sweden, and Finland—are among the five powers with the highest active MPRs, and four—Switzerland, Sweden, Finland, and Austria—are among the top five mobilized powers. While Singapore holds the record for Third World active force MPR, 4.3 percent, Cuba has it for mobilized forces, 17.3 percent. Aside from Israel (12.1 percent and 12.3 percent), the United Arab Emirates at 3.4 percent have the highest active MPR in the Middle East, but Libya has the highest mobilization MPR, 4.4 percent. Curiously, some powers actually at war have lower mobilization MPRs than do some at peace: Thus, including insurgents, Ethiopia has a mobilized MPR of only 1.3 percent and Angola only 1.4 percent, though El Salvador's mobilized MPR is 2.6 percent and Nicaragua's 6.9 percent. Also of interest is the fact that several authoritarian or military regimes have relatively low MPRs, such as South Africa, 0.5 percent,

Sudan, 0.3 percent, and Paraguay, 0.4 percent. These figures can be expected to change over the next few years if current international trends continue.

Plus the Body Count

During the 1973 Arab-Israeli war, combined losses for all sides averaged one tank every fifteen minutes and one airplane every hour.

Practical Advice

"If there is one thing that you can count on in war it is that there is nothing you can count on in war."—Richard M. Watt, military historian

Manpower Pool

In July of 1980, Congress approved a resumption of draft registration, but not actual conscription, for young men upon attainment of their eighteenth birthday. In the following eight years, 14.6 million men were signed up, and the earliest registrees have now passed their twenty-sixth birthdays, the upper limit of draft liability under existing legislation. Adding in about 10 percent for those on active duty and those who have failed to register, the number climbs to about 16.1 million. This is essentially the national reservoir of military manpower into the next century, as the country approaches zero population growth. However, this figure is basically a limited-war mobilization pool. For a serious effort, comparable to that of World War II, when over 16 million men passed through the ranks out of a population of 130 million (12.3 percent), the United States should be able to mobilize some 30 million men. Stretching the draft limits to forty, a measure that permitted Britain to mobilize about 16 percent of her people in World War II, would yield about 40 million men. Moreover, during World War II, less than 1 percent of the U.S. military-aged womanpower was mobilized.

What Makes China Great

"A country's wealth is the number of its men."—Frederick the Great, eighteenth-century Prussian king, composer, military innovator, patron of the arts, and general

Depends on How You Slice It

The total Department of Defense budget projected for 1989, something around $290 billion, was about 5.7 percent of the Gross National Product, 26.1 percent of total federal outlays, and 17.0 percent of total public spending in the United States.

And No Place to Park

According to official Department of Defense figures, the Pentagon has parking for precisely 9,849 vehicles, which must create problems, since over 24,000 people work there, and the place is visited by several thousand more people each day.

The Myth of Warsaw Pact Standardization

Many East European nations, such as Czechoslovakia and East Germany, have historically had higher levels of technology than Russia. Other East European nations, such as Poland and Hungary, have also enjoyed more developed economies and living standards than Russia. Once these nations were roped into the Russian orbit in the late 1940s, and into the Warsaw Pact in the fifties, their established arms industries were subordinated to Russian arms production. For economic, military, and political reasons, Russia insisted that East European nations buy their weapons from Russia. The East Europeans resent this, and resist the high prices and shoddy workmanship of much Soviet equipment. As a result, to a large extent noncombat equipment is of local manufacture, or purchased from other East European nations. APCs are increasingly produced locally. Attempts to produce Russian equipment under license are usually frustrated by unreasonably high license fees. The end result is that there is not as much weapons and equipment commonalty among Warsaw Pact nations as the Western press would have us believe. Because the East European nations spend much less of their GNP on defense and the Russians demand high prices for new weapons, most East European armies have weapons that are twenty or more years behind those of the Russian divisions occupying their countries.

Hot Problem

Although little remarked upon, should a major war break out in Europe, a nuclear disaster could result even if not a single nuclear weapon was to be used. There are about forty nuclear reactors in Central Europe. Even if both sides made strenuous efforts to safeguard such installations, it would be unreasonable to assume that none would be significantly damaged in the event of major conventional operations occurring in the vicinity. And given the destructive proclivities of armies and air forces, it would be more likely that nuclear reactors would become prime targets. The results would be almost as disastrous as a "limited" nuclear exchange.

The Expanding Nuclear Club

The "Nuclear Club," those powers possessing nuclear weapons, officially consists of the United States, Russia, Britain, France, and China. Unofficially, Israel and South Africa are both generally regarded as members, while India is a probable member, and Pakistan a threshold member. Current prospective members are rather numerous: Argentina, Brazil, Iraq, Libya, South Korea, and Taiwan all appear to have nuclear-weapons programs. Potential members are even more numerous, for virtually every industrialized country possessing a nuclear industry could readily jump on the bandwagon in relatively short order: One major European country with a reputation for pacifism and neutrality is generally believed to have tested the mechanical side of a nuclear device in recent years.

The Information Bureaucracy

As a result of U.S. hostages' being taken in the Middle East in the late 1970s, the Department of Defense put together an American hostage-rescue organization. Recognizing that a key element of this undertaking would be information gathering, the ISA (Intelligence Support Activity) was set up in direct competition with the CIA, with whom the ISA immediately ran into problems. The CIA insisted that ISA go through the CIA before any ISA agents were deployed outside the United States, which caused a lot of ill will and bureaucratic obstruction. Congress also took a dim view of yet another undercover overseas intelligence operation. Sure enough, the ISA was soon accused of involvement in illegal Central American operations and other irregularities. And then several ISA officers were caught padding their expense accounts and otherwise bending the rules for personal benefit. Like most similar operations, ISA successes could not be revealed without endangering the lives of agents and foreign operatives.

Eye Injuries in Modern War

Changing conditions and weapons have resulted in changes in the nature of the wounds to which troops in combat are subject. Of particular importance has been an enormous increase in eye injuries as a percentage of total combat-related injuries over the last 130-odd years. British and American experience during the Crimean War (1854–56) and the American Civil War (1861–65) showed that less than 0.6% percent of wounds were to the eyes. By World War I (1914–18), this figure had risen to 2.1 percent, and it climbed to about 4.1 percent in World War II (1939–40), and reached a remarkable 9.0 percent in Vietnam (1964–72). Though this last figure may be anomalous, examination of Israeli casualties in the Six-Day War (1967) and the October War (1973) yields eye-injury rates of 5.6 percent and 6.7 percent respectively.

Several factors have contributed to this increase. The critical issue is the degree to which the eyes are exposed to danger. The eyes represent only a very small portion of the human target, and theoretically are less likely to be injured than some other part of the anatomy. As most engagements prior to about a century ago were essentially open-field, stand-up actions, wounds to the eyes were relatively rare. However, wars fought under cover expose the body relatively less, while increasing the exposure of the head, thereby resulting in a higher rate of injury to the eyes. Technology plays a role as well, since the eyes are more sensitive than most other parts of the body and far more exposed. Thus, minor fragments of metal, glass, gravel, and whatnot that might fail to penetrate bare skin—which requires some 75 psi—might still cause serious injury to the eyes. The development of armored warfare and high-tech weaponry have not helped, since the vision slits on armored vehicles and various optical instruments also greatly increase the danger to the eyes. Finally, environment plays a role. Troops fighting in rocky areas or urban settings are more likely to have eye injuries than those in fields, since hard fragments are generated in greater profusion in such environments, so much so that on the Jerusalem front in 1967 eye injuries amounted to 10 percent of total injuries suffered by Israeli troops. Nor is the trend toward increasing injury to the eyes likely to level off, with the development of certain laser weapons, the sole purpose of which is precisely to damage the eyes. Several U.S. airmen have been temporarily blinded in recent years by Soviet laser devices, and a number of Iranian troops were reportedly blinded by Iraqi use of such a weapon. As a result, most armies are experimenting with the use of laser-proof goggles, which will degrade the combat performance of troops but preserve their eyesight.

A Realistic Attitude

"So come along and die, it shall be great fun."—Rupert Brooke, British poet, dead of blood poisoning during the Gallipoli campaign, 1915

What Russian Threat?

One tangible result of the Russian "peace campaign" in the late 1980s was a West German opinion poll showing that 75 percent of the population no longer considers Russia a "problem." These sentiments are also expressed through increasing public opposition to the thousands of ground and air exercises the nearly 1 million NATO troops undertake in West Germany each year. In the United States, the percentage of people believing a nuclear war with Russia was very possible fell from over 40 percent to under 10 percent through the 1980s.

The Posse Comitatus Act

In many countries, the armed forces are involved in civic-action programs, such as providing medical care for the impoverished or engaging in improvements to the local infrastructure. Of late, many proposals have been made to get the U.S. armed forces involved in similar activities. Some of these are quite innovative, such as having the Corps of Engineers assist in clearing the enormous backlog of structures requiring demolition in many older cities, or having military medical personnel lend a hand at hospital emergency rooms. Others would have the troops help out in the war on drugs, by using military aircraft and personnel to assist regular police forces. There are several obstacles to such endeavors. The most important one is an obscure law, the Posse Comitatus Act of 1888, which essentially prevents armed-forces personnel from being used in situations where civilian personnel are at least theoretically available.

This law was passed because, a century ago, local law-enforcement authorities in the Old West were wont to commandeer military personnel for police duties rather than disturb the local civilians to whom they owed their jobs. Even if the law were to be repealed or amended, however, the armed forces themselves are likely to resist a civic-action role, on the reasonable grounds that such duties would interfere in preparations for the primary role of the military, war. This is a compelling and largely valid argument. Nevertheless, it overlooks the training possibilities of such civic-action programs: Thus, medical corps personnel serving in a hospital emergency room would be gaining experience in the treatment of trauma on a scale that nothing short of war could possibly duplicate. Moreover, the armed forces have expressed a willingness to permit the National Guard, as a state force not restricted by the terms of the Posse Comitatus Act, to become involved in antidrug and border-patrol activities. The 1989 budget request from the National Guard Bureau included an allocation of $40 million toward the training and development of National Guard military police and helicopter units for such civil police duties. Interestingly, the armed forces have no difficulty employing regular medical and engineer personnel in a variety of civic-action duties outside the United States, so that American troops on maneuvers in several areas of the world regularly run clinics, build roads, and drill wells, none of which are barred by the Posse Comitatus Act, since it does not apply to personnel stationed abroad.

Tail to Teeth

Roughly speaking, for every two uniformed men and women on active duty with the American armed forces, there is one civilian employee of the defense establishment.

Russian Riot Police Take Their Lumps.

During 1987–88, over a thousand Russian internal-security troops were seriously injured by rioting citizens. These losses included 6 dead and over 300 whose wounds required long-term hospital care. In 1989 and into 1990, the casualty list grew, with more deaths among troops and rioters. These troops are the MVD, and consist of over 300,000 soldiers organized into thirty divisions. Their primary function is the maintenance of order in rear areas during wartime. During peacetime they are called out to put down major disturbances that local authorities cannot handle. Normally, this includes labor disputes, which are rarely reported in the press, and crowd control for rowdy spectators at sporting events and the like. The MVD troops are always under the control of the central government, never the local authorities. A large number of these injuries occurred in Armenia, Georgia, and Azerbaijan. Large numbers of MVD troops are also presently concentrated in the Baltic States and the Ukraine.

Peacetime Military Innovation

Military innovation during peacetime has always been a worrisome exercise. Unable to test innovations in combat without actually having combat, military leaders are reluctant to bet the farm on something that might go terribly wrong in practice. Historical experience demonstrates that the perils are not as great as one would imagine. There have been several major military innovations in this century that began during peacetime and were then successfully put to the test in wartime. The most famous was the German development of mechanized warfare in the twenties and thirties. What was remarkable was that several nations worked up their own version of what mechanized warfare should be, and all were fairly effective. The Germans were just a bit better, and had the better hardware to make it work. In the air, most nations worked on new equipment and techniques for using aircraft. The British developed radar and centralized control of interceptors. This 1930s development stopped the Germans during the aerial Battle of Britain, and those techniques are basically still in use today.

At sea, there were two innovations. The aircraft carrier came from nowhere in the 1920s to become the principal warship type twenty years later. Ironically, the aircraft carrier got a big boost from a 1920s arms-limitation treaty that cut back the use of more traditional battleships. Effective amphibious-warfare techniques were also nonexistent in the 1920s. Seeing a need to rapidly establish bases on enemy-held islands in the Pacific, the U.S. Marine Corps developed the tactics and equipment. By 1943 the techniques and means were largely complete and were used frequently and successfully until their last large-scale application under fire in 1950 at Inchon, Korea. Another innovation has gone largely unnoticed outside the armed forces. During the 1930s, the U.S. Army developed techniques and equipment allowing artillery observers to call in the fire of hundreds of guns. This was a very ambitious application of electronic communications and indirect artillery fire. It worked and played a large part in keeping U.S. casualties down and enemy losses up during World War II and subsequent conflicts.

Some innovations didn't work. The strategic bomber was a failure, at least in terms of the optimistic claims made by its pre-1939 proponents. Fixed fortifications also proved an expensive failure, despite all of the up-to-date technology lavished on them. In the last forty years, several new weapons systems have appeared, with mixed success. Air-to-air missiles were oversold at first, and took several decades before they became reliable enough to supplement, but not replace, cannon. Antitank missiles finally made the grade after a decade of trial and error. Nuclear attack submarines have not yet had a real workout in combat, so it's hard to tell how successful they will be. Fairly realistic peacetime exercises indicate that they will have a profound effect, but to what extent is unknown. Electronic warfare has not been used on a large scale as yet, particularly in ground combat; what use there has been indicates that jamming will probably cause much confusion, at least initially. Much more complex and extensive communications systems are now in use, but few of them have as yet been used extensively in combat. These systems are liable to come off second best during initial encounters with electronic warfare. Computer-controlled and robotic missiles, mines, and other weapons will be increasingly prevalent in the 1990s. Though equally untried, if past experience is a guide, robots will eventually take over many battlefield missions.

NATO's Weak Link

For over ten years, a coalition of pacifist political parties has gradually reduced Danish defense spending to the point where Denmark's armed forces are the most outdated and least combat-ready in NATO. Most of their weapons are at least a generation behind other NATO forces', and their ammunition stocks are not expected to last more than a week or two in combat. Warsaw Pact forces no doubt plan their wartime activities accordingly. The Danes would probably get hit by an exceptionally large attack in wartime in the expectation that their armed forces would quickly succumb.

Junior Achievement

Negotiations for an international Convention on the Rights of Children, which began under United Nations auspices in 1979, generated rather more controversy than anticipated at an eighty-nation conference in late 1988, because of a proposal to raise the internationally recognized minimum age at which soldiers may be sent into combat from fifteen to eighteen. Under the 1977 "First Protocol to the Geneva Conventions on International Humanitarian Law," children who have not reached their fifteenth birthday may not take part in direct hostilities. However, there is a loophole that permits countries having an age of majority lower than fifteen to send such personnel into combat. The eighteen-year-old proposal was sparked by the spectacle of an estimated 95,000 boys as young as eleven who were killed during the Iran-Iraq War and by the extensive use of child soldiers in a number of other recent conflicts, such as in Cambodia, Burma, the Philippines, and Uganda. The principal objections to the revised standard were raised by the United States on two grounds. The first is that the United States permits enlistment at seventeen with parental consent, making it very difficult to "guarantee that the 17 year-olds would be separated out" in the event of hostilities. The second objection is a technical one, concerning the appropriateness of including the provision in the Convention on the Rights of Children, rather than in a further revision to the Geneva Conventions. Although the United States proposed a compromise that would require nations to "take all feasible measures" to keep those under eighteen out of combat, only Russia supported the suggestion. As a result, the conference broke up without passing the desired resolution.

Hard Times in the PLA

The Chinese People's Liberation Army has fallen on hard times. In 1980, some 20 percent of the national budget went to defense; now, it is only 1 percent. Troop strength has been cut by over a million in that time. Moreover, many units must pay their way by operating farms and factories, in addition to their military duties. Frequently, officer promotions are based more on factory performance than military readiness. If this weren't bad enough, military pay is so bad that teenage factory workers make more than regimental commanders. Concern over how to handle disputes with Vietnam have caused the army to halt its program for modernizing the entire army and instead to concentrate on creating several well-prepared airborne divisions. The army's extensive network of factories has not been idle, but they are expected to earn their keep by exporting weapons for hard currency. This they have been doing at the rate of several billion dollars a year. Troop morale is quite low. Even the military hospitals, long the envy of civilians, are now open to civilians willing to pay, and fee-paying civilians often displace military patients. The possibility of a military coup, however, is low. The military in China is kept on a short leash by the Communist party and thousands of party functionaries serve in the armed forces.

Action/Reaction

One adverse result of the outbreak of "peace" in the world could be a serious shortage of civil-aviation pilots, since most commercial pilots worldwide received their flight training while in military service. Fortunately, it's much cheaper to train people for commercial aircraft. While combat pilots cost millions to train, commercial-pilot candidates cost several hundred thousand dollars to qualify for a position in a twin-engine jet. The commercial-aviation trainee can dispense with all that business about weapons and combat maneuvers. Flying time is also much cheaper for commercial aircraft, although the simulators are nearly as expensive as the military ones. As a bonus, airlines won't find themselves stripped of many of their pilots if the reserves are called up. Many former military pilots join the air-force reserve so they can continue to fly their first love, combat aircraft, on weekends. From the commercial air travelers' point of view, the additional cost will be hardly noticeable, less than a dollar a ticket. The flight crew accounts for less than 15 percent of aircraft-operating expense, and the additional training expense of nonmilitary pilots would be spread over the twenty-to-thirty-plus-year career of the pilot.

" 'Ere Now, Mind the Bats, Guv'nor."

Troubled by an infestation of bats at an underground ammunition dump in Wiltshire, England, Britain's Ministry of Defense decided to consult various authorities on wildlife in the hope of finding a solution to the problem. Unfortunately, it turned out that the winged creatures were of an unusual species, and the installation was promptly designated "the most important bat sanctuary in Britain." As a result, the ammunition and the bats will have to live in peaceful coexistence for the future, with management of the site being shared by the defense and environmental authorities.

Deadly Forgetfulness

"Though all under heaven be at peace, if the arts of war be forgotten there is peril."—Chinese proverb

The Frugal Dutch

Although strongly committed to NATO, the Netherlands, confronted by the twin problems of the enormous expense of maintaining large-scale military forces and the universal disinclination to spend time in the ranks, has developed a unique military system. Draftees serve their entire tours of duty with the same company, which is good for morale and unit cohesion. When new conscripts are absorbed, they are formed into a training company that counts as one of the three active companies of each battalion. After about four months of training, the company is considered combat-ready. By this time, the senior company of the battalion has seen twelve months' service, four months in training and eight in ready status, so the troops are sent on "short leave" for about four months before their discharge, to be replaced on active duty by a new training company just raised from conscripts. In the event of mobilization, the companies on short leave will be recalled to duty within hours, giving each battalion three active and one training company, thus raising infantry combat strength by about a third. Moreover, recently discharged companies are liable to recall as reservists for up to two years, providing each battalion with a pool of reservists equal to six full companies. This makes everyone happy, for the taxpayers save a good deal of money, while the conscripts get out of four months' active duty. Everyone, that is, except the battalion commanders, who always have to conduct battalion exercises with two trained companies, but who will have to fight with three.

Anatomy of a Civil War

The civil war in Lebanon has been raging since 1975. The principal factions consist of various Christian sects, Shiite Moslems, Druze Moslems, Sunni Moslems, and the Syrian Army. For a short while in the early 1980s, the Lebanese Army was rebuilt. But over the next five years it fell apart due to religious differences. The army's eleven brigades ended joining their sectarian brothers.

> 1st Brigade went over to pro-Syrian Shiites
> 2nd, 3rd, and 4th Brigades disintegrated
> 5th Brigade went over to the Christians
> 6th Brigade went over to the Shiite Amal Militia
> 7th Brigade went over to pro-Syrian Christians

8th, 9th, and 10th Brigades went over to anti-Syrian Christians

11th Brigade went over to the Druze

12th Brigade went over to the Sunni Moslems

Less than 15,000 troops remain in all these brigades. The real military power is in the sectarian militias, who number well over 100,000. The strongest is the Christian militia, with 6,000 regulars and 30,000 reservists and backing from two odd bedfellows, Israel and Iraq. For this reason, the more numerous Moslem troops and the Syrian Army do not want to attempt a military solution against the Christians. To further complicate matters, there are pro- and anti-Syrian factions among both Moslems and Christians. The Moslems have twice the population of the Christians.

Even Professional Football?

"Compared to war, all other forms of human endeavor shrink to insignificance."—George S. Patton, American general, World War II

The Sturdy, and Frugal, Swiss

Switzerland's military system imposes a heavy burden on her citizens. Although some provision exists for alternative service for religious reasons, military service is obligatory for all able-bodied male citizens. Twice each year, 17,000 twenty-year-olds, most of whom have already received some premilitary training in high school, are inducted for seventeen weeks of training by the national cadre, which comprises 1,500 regulars. Upon discharge, each man passes into the Elite, the first-line reserves, and undergoes eight 3-week refresher training periods until age thirty-two. At thirty-two, a man passes into the Landwehr or militia, and undergoes three 2-week refresher training periods until age forty-two, whereupon he passes into the Landsturm or home guard, and will undergo two 1-week refresher courses until his service obligation expires at age fifty. Thus, about a half-million Swiss undergo an average of about thirty days' military training each year. This is the equivalent of over 40,000 full-time troops. As a result, in the normal course of events, and assuming he is not called out for mobilization, security duty, or disaster work, the average Swiss man undergoes a bit less than a year of active military service over a period of thirty years, rather less than what most European powers require of their conscripts, who must serve it all at once, and who don't get to keep their weapons at home.

Officer candidates, officers, noncommissioned officers, and certain specialists must take additional training during their period of liability, and some accumulate as many as 700 days on duty as a result. Swiss social customs stipulate that an executive cannot advance in his company unless he maintains his position as an officer in the national armed forces. The net result of all of this is that the Swiss can field an army of over 585,000 heavily equipped men, comprising twelve divisions and seventeen independent brigades, plus an air force of 45,000 men and women, with nearly 400 combat aircraft, supported by about 600,000 militia organized into territorial defense forces, and supplemented by over 500,000 civil-defense workers, with the result that, upon mobilization, some 1 million Swiss would be involved in the defense of their country, nearly 26 percent of the population. Nor does all of this cost a lot of money. In an average year, Switzerland, which has a very high per capita income, about $15,400, devotes just about 2 percent of its GNP, or about $300 per Swiss.

Addicts?

"Men grow tired of sleep, love, singing, and dancing, sooner than of war."—Homer, ancient Greek poet and military press agent

The Gang of Five

The United States, Russia, Europe, China, and Japan. We usually think of the "superpowers" only in terms of the United States and Russia. In terms of military resources, the title certainly is accurate. But there is more to superpower status than the quantity of armaments one has piled up. Economy and population also count for quite a lot, as it is from these that the wherewithal to build armaments comes. In economic terms, the European Economic community (EEC) has the world's second-largest economy (nearly $4 trillion). In 1992, the EEC drops nearly all national trade barriers and becomes one "national" market. Most EEC members also belong to NATO, so their 2.5 million troops are also somewhat united. The EEC's 330 million population is also larger than America's or Russia's.

The other two superpowers are more problematic. Japan has one-eighth China's 1.1 billion people, while China has one-seventh Japan's $2.4 trillion GNP. Japan also has one tenth of China's 2.5 million armed forces. But there are also the technology and quality aspects. Japan is one of the world's leading developers and manufacturers of high-tech equipment. Its nonagricultural workforce is 56 million compared to 200 million in China. Japan exports over $200 billion in goods and services each year, China only about $50 billion. China is a formidable military power as long as it doesn't have to move far beyond its borders. But between the Chinese quantity and Japanese quality, these two nations define "superpower" for Asia and the Pacific in particular and the rest of the world in general. These five nations, the Gang of Five, dominate world affairs, and will continue to for the foreseeable future.

When Discussion Fails

"There can be no peace but that which is forced by the sword."— Henry Halleck, nineteenth-century American military writer and inept Civil War general

The Blue Berets

Winners of the 1988 Nobel Prize for Peace, the "Blue Berets" of the United Nations peacekeeping forces, number over 16,000 men from over two dozen countries, serving on a variety of missions in several different parts of the world. UN peacekeeping missions have ranged from the Korean War, of 1950–53, which involved hundreds of thousands of men, down to small contingents of as few as three men. The most confused and remarkable UN operation, however, was that in the former Belgian Congo (now Zaire), in the early 1960s, when over 20,000 men were engaged from twenty-nine separate countries. The services of the "Blue Berets" have been in particular demand in 1988–90. At the beginning of 1988, there were five contingents of UN troops on duty totaling a bit less than 10,000 men: 1,279 on the Golan Heights since 1974; 2,340 men on Cyprus since in 1964; about 5,800 troops in southern Lebanon since 1978; 36 soldiers on the Indo-Pakistani truce line in Kashmir since 1949; and 298 other troops in the Middle East supervising various agreements dating back to 1948.

By the middle of 1988, a year that saw an unusual number of wars coming to an end, two more contingents of UN troops were established, including 50 men to monitor the Soviet-Afghan peace agreement and 400 others who are supervising the Iran-Iraq truce. Soon, several more UN contingents took to the field, as a result of agreements concluded in the course of 1988, a 2,000-man force to supervise a plebiscite in Western Sahara, which may mark the end of the Polisario-Moroccan war, a 90-man force to oversee the Cuban withdrawal from Angola, a contingent of 4,800 troops plus 2,000 civilians and 360 civil police that is to supervise the truce in Namibia and oversee free elections, and a 160-man contingent to help implement the terms of the Central American peace accords concluded in 1988. The cost of UN peacekeeping operations is considerable, running about $30,000 to $40,000 per soldier: One perennial problem is providing suitable rations for the men, who frequently have exotic culinary tastes. One result of the recent expansion of UN peacekeeping operations is that expenses, which have been running at some $200 million to $300 million a year, are expected to rise to as much as $1.5 billion with the new contingents for Western Sahara, Angola, and Namibia.

Since most of the money for UN peacekeeping operations is borne by the Security Council "Big Five," the United States (which frequently handles transportation and logistical arrangements for UN contingents), Russia, France, Britain, and China, in a rare instance of unanimity, managed to secure a reduction in the proposed Namibian peacekeeping force by about 35 percent, for a savings of some $300 million, with a proviso that about 3,000 additional troops would be available in the event that the situation in Namibia deteriorated further. A small military staff drawn from several countries sits in New York and supervises the activities of the UN contingents. The Korean experience aside, most UN troops are drawn for smaller Western bloc or neutral countries, with Scandinavians, Austrians, and Canadians predominating. Among Communist countries, only Yugoslavia, Poland, and Russia have been involved on a regular basis. Sweden has probably participated in more UN military missions than any other power, and even has units organized and trained for UN duty. However, it is likely that more Norwegians have served than any other nationality: Over 32,000 have worn UN colors since 1947, about 8 percent of the 400,000 who have served, the Korean War aside. Despite this, it is Fiji that has had the greatest commitment to such operations, approximately two thirds of its proficient if small armed forces have been engaged in UN or other international peacekeeping efforts for many years. The Fijians are also probably the best troops the UN has, for many of the other contingents are ill-trained conscripts led by officers and noncoms with no combat experience. As a result, when they find themselves in an exposed position, with conflicting directives from UN headquarters, and confronted by determinedly hostile forces, some have been known to duck and pretend nothing was happening. After all, who wants to die for peace?

Nevertheless, UN troops, although of varying quality and effectiveness, have frequently proved useful in helping to calm tense situations. In addition to the tens of thousands of casualties in the Korean conflict, 733 UN troops have lost their lives in the performance of their duties. Footnote: The Sinai. The international peacekeeping force in the Sinai since 1979, as a result of the Camp David Accords between Egypt and Israel, is not directly affiliated with the United Nations, and consists of about 2,800 men.

Inevitability

"A war postponed may be a war averted."—Winston L. S. Churchill, British soldier, politician, historian, and bricklayer

Swedish Smorgasbord

It is widely known that Switzerland does not have an army, but rather a large reserve force that can put most of the adult males under arms and ready to fight in twenty-four hours. Sweden is the only other country with a similar system. Although currently undergoing reorganization, Swedish combat forces consist of 270,000 troops with 32 weeks' training organized into 21 brigades and 100 independent battalions. This is the equivalent of about 18 divisions. For local defense, there are 165,000 troops with 22 weeks' training organized into territorial battalions. This is the equivalent of another eight divisions. To guard over 4,000 "sensitive positions," there are 110,000 troops with ten weeks' training. Locally based Home Guards comprise another 125,000 troops. The navy has as its core a dozen coastal submarines. The air force has 500 combat aircraft and helicopters. Active forces comprise only 40,000 professional troops, plus conscripts undergoing training.

Hard Times on Russia's Eastern Front

Russia gained its Pacific territories in the last century when it seized lands claimed, but lightly held, by China. Since then, this "Far Eastern Province" has gained a population of only 8 million, but a military garrison of over 500,000 troops, 1,000 aircraft, and over 200 warships. Despite enormous natural resources, the lack of population and capital gives the province a GNP of under $100 billion. Next door is Japan, with 250,000 well-armed troops and a GNP of over $2 trillion. Over 55,000 U.S. troops, plus the Seventh Fleet, assist in the defense of Japan, whose exports to the United States and Europe have grown from $46 billion to $208 billion between 1967 and 1987. Imports from these areas have grown from $46 billion to $119 billion in the same period. China has nearly 300 million people in the provinces adjacent to Russia's Far Eastern province and more, although less well-equipped, troops. China's economic and political ties to Japan, the United States, and Europe grow each year. China wants its lost province back. Russia will never have an easy time holding on to it.

Lessons from the Ancient Greeks for Modern Soldiers

Thousands of years ago, Greek soldiers discovered, by trial and error, that it was prudent to fast the night before a battle and not to eat until the combat was over. Modern medical research has discovered that assault-rifle bullets, particularly the AK-47, do much less damage to internal organs if the bladder and intestines are empty. In other words, if you expect to be shot at by AK-47s, try not to eat for twenty-four hours beforehand and don't drink anything for several hours before the encounter. If you should be so unfortunate as to get hit in the belly, this advice could save your life.

What Am I Offered for a Panzer Division?

West Germany is shipping several hundred Leopard I tanks to Turkey, enough to equip an armored division. The deal is worth nearly $2 billion. But Turkey is giving the West Germans something more in return. In 1992 the Common Market, to which both West Germany and Turkey belong, drops practically all economic barriers between countries. In theory, millions of Turks could then head for West Germany looking for work. In return for the tanks, Turkey will see to it that such a mass exodus does not take place.

Just Whistle.

"Diplomacy without armaments is like music without instruments."—Frederick the Great, eighteenth-century Prussian soldier-king, philosopher, musician, social reformer, and petty bureaucrat

How Much Is Enough?

Although it is common to regard the size of contemporary armed forces as unusually large, it is worth recalling that on a population base of about 246 million, the United States has armed forces that, including both active (2,125,000) and reserve components (1,150,000), presently total about 3,275,000 men and women, not quite 1.4 percent of the population, while in 1914, France, with fewer than 40 million people, maintained active (605,000) and reserve forces (3,300,000) totaling nearly 4 million men, roughly 10 percent of the population. On this basis, U.S. active forces would total some 3,650,000, some 10 percent more than the mobilization figure, and reservists would total nearly 22 million men. And in 1914 there were no women in anyone's armed forces.

Targets, We Got Targets.

The United States and Russia each have about 6,000 targets for strategic nuclear weapons. In the United States, there are 1,100 ICBM silos and control centers, 870-odd other military bases, including airfields and naval bases, 700 government and communications centers, 1,000 defense plants, and 2,000 electric power and fuel plants. In Russia there are 1,500 ICBM silos and related facilities, 1,900 other military facilities, 1,100 government command posts and communications centers, 1,000 major defense plants, and 500 electric power and fuel plants. Each side has over 10,000 warheads in service, but can't expect to be able to use all of them. Civilian losses from a nuclear exchange on military targets would be "only" 80 million immediately in the United States and over 100 million in Russia. These losses would more than double in a year's time from the aftereffects of radiation, breakdowns in food supply, and the spread of disease.

Ends and Means

"The end of war is not battle, but the defeat of the adversary."— Basil Henry Liddell Hart, British military theorist and inventor of the blitzkrieg

European Maneuvers and Notification Requirements

Since the 1976 Helsinki Accords, any of the signatories planning to hold maneuvers or major unit rotations in Europe involving 13,000 men, or 300 tanks, or 200 aircraft, or the amphibious or airborne landing of 3,000 troops, must give prior notice of such events to the other signatories. Depending upon the size of the maneuvers—17,000 men or more—the other contracting powers may exercise a right to send observers. In the first ten years of this agreement, 161 maneuvers were held in Europe that fell under the terms of the Helsinki agreement, for an average of 16.1 per year. Of these, 87 were conducted by NATO powers, 8.7 a year, 49 by Warsaw Pact powers, 4.9 a year, and 25 by nonaligned powers, 2.5 per year. The busiest year was 1987, with 39 maneuvers requiring notification, of which NATO and the Warsaw Pact each accounted for 17, and the Neutrals for 5. The "slowest" years were 1980 (6, 3, and 0) and 1984 (7, 2, and 0), with 9 each. It should be noted that while the largest NATO maneuvers have involved no more than about 100,000 troops, the Warsaw Pact has occasionally conducted exercises of as many as 300,000.

If You're Lucky

"War, if reason prevails, is waged to obtain a better peace than that which existed prior to the hostilities."—Bela K. Kiraly, Hungarian general and American military historian

War in the World

Depending upon how one counts these things, at the end of 1989 there were from 40 to 100 wars going on in the world, virtually all internal, involving armed forces that totaled over 5 million people, including about 700,000 people operating as insurgents against their own governments. There is no way to arrive at more precise figures since several countries were engaged in multiple internal conflicts, which makes counting difficult: One could argue that there are twenty wars going on in Lebanon and as many as a dozen in Burma. Then, too, some of these affairs are quite modest in scale, the "body count" for the West Irian War running to "only" a few score a year. In contrast, during 1988, 153 police officers were killed in the line of duty in the United States, where there were over 20,000 murders, raising questions as to definition. A number of long-running conflicts that only occasionally erupt into violence, such as the U.S.-Libyan and Sino-Vietnamese wars, have been excluded from the total, as have the literally dozens of extremely low-intensity internal wars plaguing many countries, such as the Puerto Rican National Liberation Front's war against the United States or the Corsican NLF's war against France.

Altogether, about forty separate countries are directly involved in these wars to the extent of having troops in combat. Several of these wars have been going on for decades: At present, the record is a tie among the Israeli-Palestinian, Colombian, and Burmese wars, all essentially internal conflicts that began shortly after World War II. Vietnam presently holds the record for the greatest number of wars, being involved in internal wars in both Kampuchea (Cambodia) and Laos, and in the Lao-Thai border war, while trying to deal with two insurgencies of its own as well, one smallish affair involving dissident Meo tribesmen and the other a rather larger one involving remnants of the ARVN, a tally that does not include the intermittent border war with China. Cuba comes in second in this dubious sweepstakes, being directly involved in the essentially internal wars in Angola, Ethiopia, and Mozambique. By far the largest and most intense war currently going on is that in Afghanistan, where perhaps 100,000 government troops are holding on in the face of perhaps twice as many Mujahedin, which, including the 1979–89 Russian phase, has been going on for about a dozen years and has cost 1.3–1.5 million lives and generated 5–6 million refugees. Second place would be difficult to determine, but is likely to be the three-in-one Ethiopian war, with about 230,000 government troops facing some 65,000 to 75,000 insurgents in two separatist and one internal movements, which have been fighting for over twenty years at a cost of some 750,000 dead and 3–4 million refugees. The Lebanese civil war is probably third, involving 120,000 troops, all sides considered, which has produced perhaps 100,000 to 200,000 dead and a half-million refugees over the past fifteen or so years. The distinction of being the most obscure war probably belongs to that in West Irian, involving Indonesia against New Guinean separatists. Interestingly, virtually all of these wars are essentially internal, although, in many, foreign troops are involved in support of one of the factions, the record being the RENAMO insurgency in Mozambique, which involves Zimbabwean, Malawian, and Cuban troops, as well as Soviet and East German military and security advisers, and American economic advisers, all in support of the central government.

International war seems to be very much on the wane: With the end of the Iran-Iraq War in 1988—a good year for peace—the only primarily international conflict is the Lao-Thai border war. The human cost of these ongoing wars has been enormous, for they have created an estimated 25 million refugees, and a body count of about 5.5 million people, of whom about 1–2 million died in Kampuchea and 1.3–1.5 million in Afghanistan, leaving "only" 2–3 million corpses to the account of the other thirty-eight wars.

The Last Word

"The nuclear tornado will sweep away socialists and capitalists alike."—Mikhail Gorbachev, Russian politician

Conclusion

As noted earlier in this chapter, the advent of nuclear weapons appears to have produced the longest peace between the major military powers in many centuries. Mr. Gorbachev has stated a grim fact about nuclear weapons (see above) that is widely accepted by citizens and leaders alike in most nations. But we still live in a warlike world, with upward of a million people a year dying from the direct and indirect effects of numerous "little wars." The ultimate Dirty Little Secret is that wars have not stopped. The pattern has shifted from a large war every generation or so to numerous small wars all the time. Meanwhile, the so-called "minor powers" are gaining access to ever-more-sophisticated arms. As a result, the intensity and frequency of little wars are likely to increase even as the major powers demonstrate a growing willingness to lay down their arms. And it may well be that a hardware-happy minor power embarking on a little war could spark a larger conflict that could easily find the superpowers being dragged in almost against their will. It happened in 1914, and many times previous to that. It could as easily happen again.

Another Dirty Little Secret that is getting a lot more play in the press is the proliferation of intermediate-range ballistic missiles and chemical weapons among nonsuperpower nations. Iraq used both ballistic missiles and chemical weapons during its recent war with Iran. Iraq did not use chemical warheads on its missiles, but this might have changed if Iran had been more successful on the battlefield. Iran had already declared a holy war, so Iraq had little to lose from going the chemical-missile route against a more successful Iranian invasion. What probably held the Iraqis back more than anything else was technical problems. Using chemicals in a missile warhead is a tricky business, but not insurmountable if you are determined, or desperate, enough.

Desperation brings out the worst in nations. Israel has nearly a hundred nuclear weapons, and aircraft and missiles that can deliver them. Faced with national destruction, do you really believe Israel would allow itself to be overrun without at least threatening nuclear retaliation? Many other, less stable nations either have, or can obtain, long-range missiles and chemical warheads. There will be more Iraqs in the future.

We may see the superpowers joining together to restrain smaller powers from getting carried away with weapons of mass destruction. Until these missiles and chemical/nuclear warheads became widely available, the superpowers were content to let the lesser nations blast away at each other with conventional weapons. The smaller nations once were unable to reach superpower targets, even with long-range aircraft, because the superpowers had superior defense weapons. But now Israel has unstoppable nuclear missiles that can hit targets in southern Russia. And next time Iran declares a jihad, the Iranians may back it up with long-range missiles and chemical warheads. Russia is the superpower within range of many of these unstable, but well-armed, nations. In 1989 the KGB offered to cooperate with the FBI and CIA to combat international terrorism. There *are* some changes afoot.

If nothing else, we have demonstrated in this book that war is often a less-than-rational process. Actual or potential combat gets the juices flowing, and reason often goes out the window. Peace is unlikely to break out in the near future, and one of those ever-more-common "nasty little wars" may end up moving into your own backyard.

Index

(Authors' Note: Here's one last Dirty Little Secret. The length of a book index is not determined by how long it should be but by how many pages are left over when the book is manufactured to various "standard" book sizes (etc.). Thus this index is not as long as it should be. But then, with a book like this, a complete index could easily be a third the size of the book itself. So we were not able to index a lot of items we wanted to. Not to worry. In most cases, you will find other references to an item on adjacent pages to items that are indexed. Moreover, the organization of the book itself allows you to find information on a topic by going to the appropriate section. Good hunting.)